STANDARDS OF INVEST

Standards of Investment Protection

Edited by
AUGUST REINISCH

OXFORD
UNIVERSITY PRESS

OXFORD
UNIVERSITY PRESS

Great Clarendon Street, Oxford OX2 6DP

Oxford University Press is a department of the University of Oxford.
It furthers the University's objective of excellence in research, scholarship,
and education by publishing worldwide in

Oxford New York

Auckland Cape Town Dar es Salaam Hong Kong Karachi
Kuala Lumpur Madrid Melbourne Mexico City Nairobi
New Delhi Shanghai Taipei Toronto

With offices in

Argentina Austria Brazil Chile Czech Republic France Greece
Guatemala Hungary Italy Japan Poland Portugal Singapore
South Korea Switzerland Thailand Turkey Ukraine Vietnam

Oxford is a registered trade mark of Oxford University Press
in the UK and in certain other countries

Published in the United States
by Oxford University Press Inc., New York

© August Reinisch, 2008

The moral rights of the author have been asserted

Crown copyright material is reproduced under Class Licence
Number C01P0000148 with the permission of OPSI
and the Queen's Printer for Scotland

Database right Oxford University Press (maker)

First published 2008

All rights reserved. No part of this publication may be reproduced,
stored in a retrieval system, or transmitted, in any form or by any means,
without the prior permission in writing of Oxford University Press,
or as expressly permitted by law, or under terms agreed with the appropriate
reprographics rights organization. Enquiries concerning reproduction
outside the scope of the above should be sent to the Rights Department,
Oxford University Press, at the address above

You must not circulate this book in any other binding or cover
and you must impose the same condition on any acquirer

British Library Cataloguing in Publication Data

Data available

Library of Congress Cataloging in Publication Data

Data available

Typeset by Newgen Imaging Systems (P) Ltd., Chennai, India
Printed in Great Britain
by
Biddles Ltd., King's Lynn, Norfolk

ISBN 978–0–19–954743–2 (Hbk.)
ISBN 978–0–19–954744–9 (Pbk.)

1 3 5 7 9 10 8 6 4 2

Preface

As a result of the increased use of dispute settlement, primarily in the form of mixed investor-State arbitration, international investment law is developing rapidly. The protection afforded to foreign investors is based on treaties, on customary international law standards, largely derived from the classical law on the 'treatment of aliens', as well as on the national law of host States.

The growing number of investment arbitration awards has helped to provide more specific meaning to the general standards of investment protection found in the majority of international investment instruments, in particular in the currently more than 2500 bilateral investment treaties (BITs). Such standards are regularly contained and fairly similarly formulated in these numerous international agreements. Almost all of them include certain rules on the admission of investments, the two non-discrimination standards of most-favoured-nation as well as national treatment, absolute treaty standards, such as fair and equitable treatment, full protection and security, as well as protection against arbitrary and unreasonable measures, guarantees against uncompensated expropriations, and provisions on the transfer of funds.

In the currently prevailing treaty-arbitration, ie direct investor-State arbitration mostly based upon BITs or other investment treaties and dealing with alleged violations of these investment standards, it is crucial to give more precise significance to the rather vague and generally worded standards of treatment. Such deeper understanding of the present law on the treatment of foreign investment may be derived from a close analysis of the developing jurisprudence of investment tribunals.

The contributors to this book have agreed to focus on the identification of a possibly emerging consensus on how these substantive treatment standards are to be interpreted. They closely examine the origin and variations of the wording used in investment agreements and their analysis focuses on the actual application of the treatment standards in the practice of investment tribunals. The resulting book is intended to provide a first-hand road-map to substantive investment law.

The authors, renowned experts in the field of investment law from academia and practice, are all members of the International Law Association's Committee on International Law of Foreign Investment. Their contributions to this book are based on papers they have presented at the Conference on Standards of Investment Protection at the Law School of the University of Vienna on 21 September 2007.

This conference was made possible through the support of the Austrian Science Fund (FWF) which is funding a research project of the editor of this book on international investment law in the practice of arbitral tribunals. Of course, people made all this happen. I am particularly grateful to Christina Knahr, Claudia Luxon, Scarlett Ortner, Christoph Schreuer, Johanna Willmann, Jakob Wurm, and Anton Geist for their fantastic support in planning, preparing and organizing this conference. I am equally indebted to the authors who did not only submit their contributions of outstanding quality on time but also made the editor's life easier by complying with the manuscript style prerequisites of Oxford University Press. In this regard, my special thanks go to Johanna Willmann for her meticulous editorial assistance in the final preparation of this volume.

Last but not least, I would like to thank John Louth and Rebecca Smith of Oxford University Press for their enduring support during the production stage of this book.

August Reinisch
Vienna, 29 January 2008

Contents—Summary

Notes on Contributors   xv
Table of Cases   xvii
Table of Treaties   xxvii

1. Introduction: Interrelationship of Standards   1
   Christoph Schreuer
2. Admission and Establishment in the Context of Investment Protection   9
   Anna Joubin-Bret
3. National Treatment   29
   Andrea K. Bjorklund
4. Most-Favoured-Nation (MFN) Treatment   59
   Andreas R. Ziegler
5. Arbitrary and Unreasonable Measures   87
   Veijo Heiskanen
6. Fair and Equitable Treatment Standard: Recent Developments   111
   Katia Yannaca-Small
7. Full Protection and Security   131
   Giuditta Cordero Moss
8. Indirect Expropriation   151
   Anne K. Hoffmann
9. Legality of Expropriations   171
   August Reinisch
10. Capital Transfer Restrictions under Modern Investment Treaties   205
    Abba Kolo and Thomas Wälde

Bibliography   245
Index   257

Table of Contents

Notes on Contributors	xv
Table of Cases	xvii
Table of Treaties	xxvii

1. Introduction: Interrelationship of Standards   1
Christoph Schreuer

2. Admission and Establishment in the Context of Investment Protection   9
Anna Joubin-Bret

A. Introduction	9
B. Approaches to Admission in IIAs	10
Entry of Foreign Investment	10
Admission Model	11
MFN Treatment Only	12
Pre-establishment Model	13
C. Admitting Investment in Accordance with the Laws and Regulations of the Host State: Case Studies	16
Salini v Morocco	20
Tokios Tokelės v Ukraine	21
Bayindir v Pakistan	22
Aguas del Tunari v Bolivia	22
Inceysa v El Salvador	24
Fraport v Philippines	25
Ioannis Kardassopoulos v Georgia	26
D. Conclusions	26

3. National Treatment   29
Andrea K. Bjorklund

A. Introduction	29
B. Background and Treaty Practice	30
C. Investment Case Law	37
Like Circumstances	38
Less Favourable Treatment	48
Treatment 'No Less Favourable' v 'Best' or 'Most Favourable' Treatment	54
Burden of Proof	56
D. Conclusions	58

4. Most-Favoured-Nation (MFN) Treatment 59
Andreas R. Ziegler
  A. Introduction 59
  B. Historical Developments and Theoretical Foundations
     of the MFN Clause 60
     Typical Examples 60
     Historical Developments 61
  C. Main Types and Economic Foundation of MFN Treatment 64
  D. Important Investment Arbitration Awards relating to MFN 67
     Asian Agricultural Products Ltd (AAPL) v Sri Lanka 67
     Pope and Talbot v Canada 67
     Maffezini v Spain 68
     ADF v USA 68
     *The Loewen Group, Inc, Raymond L. Loewen v
        The United States of America* 68
     Yaung Chi Oo (YCO) Trading Pte Ltd v Myanmar 69
     Tecmed v Mexico 69
     MTD v Chile 69
     Siemens v Argentina 70
     Salini v Jordan 70
     Lucchetti v Peru 70
     Plama v Bulgaria 71
     CMS v Argentina 71
     Impregilo S.p.A. v Pakistan 71
     Camuzzi v Argentina 72
     Gas Natural v Argentina 72
     Bayindir v Pakistan 72
     Continental Casualty v Argentina 73
     National Grid Transco plc v Argentina 73
     Telenor v Hungary 73
     *Suez, Sociedad General de Aguas de Barcelona S.A., and
        Vivendi Universal S.A. v Argentina* and *AWG
        Group Ltd v Argentina* 73
     Berschader v Russia 74
  E. Specific Issues Addressed in Investor-State Arbitration 74
     The *Ejusdem Generis* Principle 74
     Explicit Descriptions of the Scope 75
     General and Explicit Exceptions from MFN Treatment 79
     Specifically Negotiated Provisions 83
     Relevance for Procedural Provision 84
  F. Outlook 86

Table of Contents

5.	**Arbitrary and Unreasonable Measures**	87
	Veijo Heiskanen	
	A. Introduction	87
	B. Non-impairment Standard: Three Perspectives	89
	The Perspective of 'Judicial Economy'	91
	'Methodological' Perspective	93
	'Substantive' Perspective	101
	'I know it when I see it'	101
	Due process approach	103
	The non-impairment standard and customary international law	106
	C. Conclusion	109
6.	**Fair and Equitable Treatment Standard: Recent Developments**	111
	Katia Yannaca-Small	
	A. Introduction	111
	B. Does the Standard belong to a Specific Legal Order or is it an Autonomous Standard?	113
	C. What is the Normative Content of the Fair and Equitable Treatment Standard as it has been Formulated by Arbitral Tribunals?	118
	Obligation of Vigilance and Protection	118
	Denial of Justice, Due Process	119
	Lack of Arbitrariness and Non-discrimination	120
	Transparency and Stability	121
	Legitimate Expectations	124
	Proportionality	126
	D. Conclusion	129
7.	**Full Protection and Security**	131
	Giuditta Cordero Moss	
	A. Introduction	131
	B. The Sources	132
	Overview of the Different Formulations	133
	Importance of the Formulations	134
	C. International Standard	136
	International Law as a Ceiling	136
	International Law as a Floor	136
	International Law as Equivalent	137

	D.	Physical Safety	138
		Causality	138
		Forms of Behaviour	139
		Due diligence	139
		Subjective or objective standard?	140
		Sovereign appreciation	141
	E.	Application beyond Physical Safety	142
		Scope of Application Restricted to Physical Safety	143
		Scope of Application beyond Physical Safety	144
		Availability of the legal system	144
		Legal security as an independent standard	144
		Overlap with other Standards	146
		Fair and equitable treatment	146
		Action in combat	149
	F.	Conclusion	150

8. Indirect Expropriation — 151
Anne K. Hoffmann

A.	Introduction	151
B.	The Current State of Affairs Regarding the Doctrine of Indirect Expropriation	152
	The Criteria Used to Define Indirect Expropriations	156
	The substantiality of the interference: the 'sole effect doctrine'	156
	The Durational Aspect	159
	Interference by Actions and Omissions	160
	The Enrichment of the Host State	160
	The intentions of the State	161
	Investment-backed expectations of the investor	162
	The requirement of proportionality	163
C.	Indirect Expropriation and the State's Right to Regulate	165
D.	Recent Developments	166
E.	Concluding Considerations	167

9. Legality of Expropriations — 171
August Reinisch

A.	Introduction	171
	Legality Requirements under General International Law	173
	Legality Requirements in International Investment Agreements	176
B.	The Interpretation Given to the Legality Requirements in the Practice of Investment Arbitration	178
	Public Purpose	178

	Non-discrimination	186
	Due Process	191
	Compensation	194
	Implications of the Legality/Illegality of an Expropriation for Remedies	199
C.	Conclusions	204

10. Capital Transfer Restrictions under Modern Investment Treaties 205
Abba Kolo and Thomas Wälde

A.	Introduction	205
B.	The Development of International Law on Foreign Exchange Regulation	206
C.	Treatment of Capital Transfer Restrictions under Modern Investment Treaties	213
D.	Application of the Doctrine of Necessity under International Law to Exchange Restriction Measures	217
E.	Exchange Restrictions and Indirect Expropriation	227
F.	Other Investment Obligations, in Particular, Fair and Equitable Treatment	233
	Transparency and the Protection of Legitimate Expectations	235
	Freedom from Coercion or Harassment	236
	Procedural Propriety	237
	Protection against Arbitrariness; Discrimination and 'National Treatment'	238
	Good Faith	239
G.	Remedies and Compensation	240
H.	Conclusion	242

Bibliography   245
Index   257

Notes on Contributors

Andrea K. Bjorklund is Professor at the University of California, Davis, School of Law. Before joining UC Davis, she spent two years as a Bigelow Fellow and Lecturer in Law at the University of Chicago Law School. From 1999 to 2001, she was an attorney-adviser in the Office of the Legal Adviser at the US Department of State, where she defended the United States in investor-State arbitrations brought under Chapter Eleven of the NAFTA.

Giuditta Cordero Moss is Professor at the Department of Private Law, University of Oslo, in charge of International Commercial Law, Comparative Law, and Private International Law. She is also honorary lecturer and principal research fellow at the Dundee University Centre for Energy, Petroleum and Mineral Law & Policy. Before becoming a full professor, she practised international business law, primarily as a corporate lawyer at FIAT S.p.A., Italy (1985–1989) and Norsk Hydro ASA, Norway (1989–1999).

Veijo Heiskanen is Partner with Lalive, Geneva, Switzerland. He specializes in international commercial arbitration, international investment disputes, and international law, including international claims. He has acted as counsel or arbitrator in numerous international arbitration proceedings under the arbitration rules of the ICC, ICSID, WIP., UNCITRAL, Swiss Rules of International Arbitration and the Cairo Regional Centre for International Commercial Aribitration. Dr. Heiskanen is a member of the panel of arbitrators at ICSID.

Anne K. Hoffmann is Senior Associate in the International Arbitration Group of Python & Peter, Geneva. She has a wide range of experience in international arbitration proceedings where she acts as counsel (for example ICC, ICSID, UNCITRAL, LCIA, *ad hoc*) in disputes arising, inter alia, out of general contractual matters, foreign investment and expropriation, construction, telecommunications, and licensing.

Anna Joubin-Bret is Senior Legal Advisor, Work Programme on International Investment Agreements, Division on Investment, UNCTAD. She is the technical assistance and training coordinator of the Work Programme on International Investment Agreements (IIAs) and oversees the research of the programme, including the publication of the UNCTAD Series on Issues in International Investment Agreements.

Abba Kolo is Lecturer in Energy and Investment Law at the Dundee University Centre for Energy, Petroleum and Mineral Law & Policy.

August Reinisch is Professor of International and European Law at the University of Vienna, Austria, and Professorial Lecturer at the Bologna Center of SAIS/Johns Hopkins University in Bologna, Italy.

Christoph Schreuer is Professor of International Law at the University of Vienna. From 1992 to 2000 he was the Edward B. Burling Professor of International Law and

Organization at the Paul H. Nitze School of Advanced International Studies (SAIS) of the Johns Hopkins University in Washington, DC.

Thomas Wälde is a specialist in international investment, economic, oil, gas, energy and mineral law, with a particular focus on arbitration in these fields. He is Professor (and Jean-Monnet Chair) of International Economic, Natural Resources & Energy Law at the University of Dundee, Rechtsanwalt (Frankfurt) and barrister (Lincoln's Inn—Essex Court Chambers, London), former Interregional Adviser on Petroleum, Mineral & Investment Law with the United Nations.

Katia Yannaca-Small is the Legal Advisor to the OECD Investment Division, Directorate for Financial and Enterprise Affairs. She is responsible for analytical work on all legal issues related to international investment agreements and in particular developments in investor-State dispute settlement. She is currently a Visiting Fellow at the Institute of International Economic Law at Georgetown Law Center.

Andreas R. Ziegler is Professor at the Université de Lausanne and Visiting Professor at the Swiss Federal Institute of Technology in Zurich and the University of New South Wales in Sydney teaching Economic Law, European Union Law, Public International Law, International Trade Law, and International Investment Law. For several years he has worked for the Swiss administration, the European Commission, and the Secretariat of the European Free Trade Association (EFTA).

Table of Cases

ADC Affiliate Limited and ADC & ADMC Management Limited v Republic of Hungary (Case No. ARB/03/16), Award, 2 October 2006, available at http://ita.law.uvic.ca. 1, 173, 184–5, 189, 190, 193, 199, 202, 203
ADF Group Inc. v United States (Case No. ARB (AF)/00/1), Award, 9 January 2003, 18 ICSID Review—Foreign Investment Law Journal 195 (2003); 6 ICSID Reports 470 . . . . 5, 6, 44–5, 50, 68, 84, 107–8, 115, 125
Adriano Gardella S.p.A. v Côte d'Ivoire (Case No. ARB/74/1), Award, 29 August 1977, 1 ICSID Reports 287 (excerpts). 172
AGIP S.p.A. v People's Republic of the Congo (Case No. ARB/77/1), Award, 30 November 1979, 1 ICSID Reports 309; 64 Rivista di diritto internazionale 863 (1981); 71 Revue critique de droit international privé 92 (1982); 21 ILM 726 (1982); 67 ILR 318 (1984). 172
Aguas del Tunari S.A. v Republic of Bolivia (Case No. ARB/02/3), Decision on Jurisdiction, 21 October 2005, available at http://ita.law.uvic.ca, http://icsid.worldbank.org/ICSID . . . 22, 23
Ambatielos Case (Greece v United Kingdom), Award, 6 March 1956, XII UNRIAA 83 (1963) 78
Amco Asia Corporation and Others v Republic of Indonesia (Case No. ARB/81/1), Award, 20 November 1984, 1 ICSID Reports 413; 1 Int'l Arb. Rep. 601 (1986); 89 ILR 405 (1992). 172, 182, 197
American International Group Inc., et al. v Islamic Republic of Iran, et al., Award No. 93-2-3, 19 December 1983, 4 *Iran-US CTR* (1983) 96 . . . . 181, 196
American Manufacturing & Trading, Inc v Republic of Zaire (Case No. ARB/93/1), Award, 21 February 1997, 36 ILM 1534 (1997); 12 Int'l Arb. Rep., No. 4, at Sect. A (Apr. 1997); 5 ICSID Reports 14; 125 Journal du droit international 243 (1998); Individual Opinions, 21 February 1997, 5 ICSID Reports 14 . . . . 119, 134, 137, 140, 149
Amoco International Finance Corporation v The Government of the Islamic Republic of Iran, Award No. 310-45-3, 14 July 1987, 15 *Iran-US CTR* (1987) 189 . . . . 181–2, 188, 198, 201
Anglo-Iranian Oil Company (Jurisdiction) Case (United Kingdom v Iran), Judgment, 22 July 1952, ICJ Reports (1952) 93. 74
Application of the Convention of 1902 Governing the Guardianship of Infant (Netherlands v Sweden), Judgment, 28 November 1958, ICJ Reports (1958) 55 97
Asian Agricultural Products Limited v Democratic Socialist Republic of Sri Lanka (Case No. ARB/87/3), Award, 27 June 1990, 6 ICSID Review—Foreign Investment Law Journal 526 (1991); 30 ILM 577 (1991); 6 Int'l Arb. Rep., No. 5, at Sect. A (May 1991); 4 ICSID Reports 250 . . . . 67, 119, 133, 137, 139, 140, 141, 150
Atlantic Triton Company Limited v People's Revolutionary Republic of Guinea (Case No. ARB/84/1), Award, 21 April 1986, 115 Journal du droit international 181 (1988) (excerpts); [English translation of French original] 3 ICSID Reports 13 172
Attorney-General of Canada v S.D. Myers, Inc. and United Mexican States (Intervener), Canada, Federal Court, 13 January 2004, 8 ICSID Reports 194 39
Azurix v Argentine Republic (Case No. ARB/01/12), Decision on Jurisdiction, 8 December 2003, 43 ILM 262 (2004); 10 ICSID Reports 416; Award, 14 July 2006, 10 ICSID Reports 412 . . . . 4, 5, 96, 100, 102, 108, 116, 117, 119, 134, 135, 136–7, 146–7, 162, 164, 171, 228
Banco Nacional de Cuba v Farr, 243 F.Supp. 957 (SDNY 1965) 187

xviii *Table of Cases*

Banco Nacional de Cuba v Sabbatino, 307 F.2d 845 (SDNY 1961) 187
Batson v Kentucky, 476 US 79, 106 S. Ct. 1712 (1986) 44
Bayindir Insaat Turizm Ticaret Ve Sanayi A.S. v Islamic Republic of Pakistan
  (Case No. ARB/03/29), Decision on Jurisdiction, 14 November 2005, available at
  http://ita.law.uvic.ca, http://icsid.worldbank.org/ICSID 6, 22, 72–3
Biloune and Marine Drive Complex Ltd v Ghana Investments Centre and the
  Government of Ghana, UNCITRAL *ad hoc* Tribunal, Award on Jurisdiction and
  Liability, 27 October 1989, 95 ILR 183 (1989) 156, 161
BP Exploration Co (Libya) Ltd v The Government of the Libyan Arab Republic,
  The BP/Libya Concession Tribunal, Award (Merits), 10 October 1973,
  53 ILR 297 . . . . 172, 181, 187, 198
BV v Argentina, Final Award, 24 December 2007.
Brumărescu v Romania, Appl. No. 28342/95, ECtHR, 28 October 1999;
  (2001) 35 ECHR 35 182
Camuzzi International S.A. v The Argentine Republic (Case No. ARB/03/2),
  Decision on Jurisdiction, 11 May 2005, available at http://ita.law.uvic.ca 72, 85
Canada—Certain Measures Affecting the Automotive Industry, Panel Report,
  11 February 2000, and Appellate Body Report, 31 May 2000, WT/DS139/AB/R
  and WT/DS142/AB/R. 78
Case-503/99 *Commission v Belgium (Golden Shares)* [2002] ECR I-4809 211
Case C-483/99 *Commission v French Republic (Golden Shares)* [2002] ECR I-4781 211
Case C-398/98 *Commission v Greece* (*Emergency Stocks of Petroleum Products*)
  [2001] ECR I-7915, 3 CMLR (2001) 62 224
Case C-367/98 *Commission v Portuguese Republic (Golden Shares)* [2002]
  ECR I-4731 211
Case C-367/89 *Criminal proceedings against Richardt* [1991] ECR I-4621 224
Case C-302/97 *Klaus Konle v Republik Oesterreich* [1999] ECR I-3099 211
Case C-222/97 *Manfred Trummer and Peter Mayer* [1999] ECR I-1661 211
Case C-452/01 *Margarethe Ospelt v Schlössle Weissenberg Familienstiftung*
  [2003] ECR I-9473 211
Case C-331/88 *R v Minister for Agriculture, Fisheries and Food, ex parte Fedesa* [1990]
  ECR I-4023. 235
Case Concerning Certain German Interests in Polish Upper Silesia
  (*Germany v Poland*), Judgment (Merits), 25 May 1926,
  PCIJ Ser. A, No. 7 (1926) 180
Case Concerning the Payment in Gold of Brazilian Federal Loans Contracted in France
  (*France v Brazil*), Judgment, 12 July 1929, *PCIJ Ser. A*, No. 21 (1929) 208
Case Concerning the Payment of Various Serbian Loans Issued in France, Judgment,
  12 July 1929, *PCIJ Ser. A*, No. 20 (1929) 208, 218
Case Concerning Rights of Nationals of the United States of America in Morocco
  (*France v United States of America*), Judgment, 27 August 1952,
  ICJ Reports (1952) 176. . . . . 62, 232
Case of the Former King of Greece v Greece, Appl. No. 25701/94, ECtHR, 23 November
  2000, 2000-XII ECHR 228
Case of the Former King of Greece v Greece, Appl. No. 25701/94, ECHR (2000-XII),
  28 November 2002; (2001) 33 ECHR 21. 231
CCL v Republic of Kazakhstan, Final Award, 2004,
  1 *SIAR* 123 (2005) 162
Certain Norwegian Loans (*France v Norway*), Judgment, 6 July 1957,
  ICJ Reports (1957) 9 226
Champion Trading Company, Ameritrade International, Inc, James T. Wahba,
  John B. Wahba, Timothy T. Wahba v Egypt (Case No. ARB/02/9), Award,
  27 October 2006, available at http://ita.law.uvic.ca 97

Table of Cases xix

*Channel Tunnel Group Limited, France-Manche S.A. v United Kingdom and the
Republic of France (Eurotunnel)*, Partial Award, 30 January 2007, available at
http://ita.law.uvic.ca 137, 138, 139, 142
Chassagnou & Others v France, Appl. Nos 25088/94, 28331/95 and 28443/95,
ECtHR, 29 April 1999, ECHR 1999-III; (1999) 29 EHRR 615. 228
Chobady Claim, US Foreign Claims Settlement Commission, 5 February 1958,
26 *ILR* 292 (1958-II) 229
CME Czech Republic B.V. (The Netherlands) v The Czech Republic, Partial Award,
13 September 2001, 9 ICSID Reports 121; Final Award, 14 March 2003,
9 ICSID Reports 264. . . . . 54, 92–3, 133, 145, 146, 148,
149, 158, 160, 171
CMS Gas Transmission Company v Argentina (Case No. ARB/01/8), Decision on Jurisdiction,
17 July 2003, 42 ILM 788 (2003); 7 ICSID Reports 494; Award, 12 May 2005,
44 ILM 1205 (2005); Decision of the *Ad Hoc* Committee on the Application
for Annulment of the Argentine Republic, 25 September 2007, available at
http://ita.law.uvic.ca 5, 32, 71, 94, 121, 123, 124, 126, 164,
171, 202, 205, 217, 218, 219,
220, 222, 227, 230, 232
Compañiá de Aguas del Aconquija S.A. and Vivendi Universal v Argentine Republic
(Case No. ARB/97/3), Resubmitted Case: Award, 20 August 2007, available at
http://ita.law.uvic.ca, http://www.investmentclaims.com 1, 116, 133, 135, 145–6,
149, 153, 159, 161, 171,
232, 236, 239
Compañia del Desarrollo de Santa Elena S.A. v Republic of Costa Rica (Case No. ARB/96/1),
Award, 17 February 2000, 15 ICSID Review—Foreign Investment Law Journal 169
(2000); 5 ICSID Reports 157; 39 ILM 1317 (2000). 165, 182, 198
Consortium R.F.C.C. v Kingdom of Morocco (Case No. ARB/00/6),
see *RFCC v Kingdom of Morocco*. 38, 51, 71, 159, 162
Continental Casualty Company v Argentina (Case No. ARB/03/9), Decision on Jurisdiction,
22 February 2006, available at http://ita.law.uvic.ca 73
de Sabla Claim (US v Panama), Award, 29 June 1933, VI UNRIAA 358 . . . . 172, 194
Delagoa Bay and East African Railway Co (US and Great Britain v Portugal), in
Whiteman (ed.), 3 *Damages in International Law* (1943) 1694. 194
Dolan v City of Tigard, 512 US 374, 114 S. Ct. 2309 (1994) 231
Duke Energy International Peru Investments No. 1, Ltd v Peru (Case No. ARB/03/28),
Decision on Jurisdiction, 1 February 2006, available at http://ita.law.uvic.ca 205, 233
Eastern Enterprises v Apfel, 524 US 498, 118 S. Ct. 2131 (1998) 231
Elettronica Sicula S.p.A. (ELSI) (United States of America v Italy), Judgment,
20 July 1989, ICJ Reports (1989) 15. . . . . 34–5, 88, 101, 102, 105, 134,
137, 139, 141, 144, 238
Empresas Lucchetti, S.A. and Lucchetti Perú, S.A. v Peru (Case No. ARB/03/4),
see *Industria Nacional de Alimentos v Peru* 70–1
EnCana Corporation v Republic of Ecuador (LCIA Case No. UN3481), Award,
3 February 2006, 45 ILM 901 (2006) 171, 241
Enron Corporation and Ponderosa Assets, L.P. v Argentine Republic
(Case No. ARB/01/3), Decision on Jurisdiction, 14 January 2004, 11 ICSID
Reports 273; Award, 22 May 2007, available at http://ita.law.uvic.ca,
http://www.investmentclaims.com 3, 53, 102, 116, 123, 127, 159,
171, 218, 219, 220, 222–3
Eudoro A. Olguín v Republic of Paraguay (Case No. ARB/98/5), Award, 26 July 2001,
6 ICSID Reports 164. . . . . 160, 161, 230
Eureko B.V. v Republic of Poland, Partial Award, 19 August 2005,
12 ICSID Reports 335 . . . . 133, 143, 162, 172, 188–9, 190, 238

xx   *Table of Cases*

European Communities—Measures Affecting Asbestos and Asbestos-Containing Products,
  Appellate Body Report, 5 April 2001, WT/DS135/AB/R (2001) 36
Evanoff Claim, US Foreign Claims Settlement Commission, 13 August 1958,
  26 *ILR* 301 (1958-II) 229
Factory at Chorzów (Claim for Indemnity) (Germany v Poland), Judgment (Merits),
  13 September 1928, *PCIJ Series A*, No. 17 (1928) 200–1, 202–3
Feldman v Mexico (Case No. ARB(AF)/99/1), Award, 16 December 2002, 18 ICSID
  Review—Foreign Investment Law Journal 488 (2003); 42 ILM 625 (2003);
  7 ICSID Reports 341; Dissenting Opinion, 16 December 2002, 18 ICSID
  Review—Foreign Investment Law Journal 580 (2003) 42–3, 49, 52, 55, 57, 166, 172, 183
Fraport AG Frankfurt Airport Services Worldwide v Philippines (Case No. ARB/03/25),
  Award, 16 August 2007, available at http://ita.law.uvic.ca,
  http://www.investmentclaims.com 25
French v Banco Nacional de Cuba, 23 NY2d. 46, 242 NE2d 704,
  295 NYS2d 433 (1968) 231
Fireman's Fund v Mexico, Award, 17 July 2006, available at
  http://www.naftalaw.org 228, 229, 232
Gabcikovo-Nagymaros Project (Hungary v Slovakia), Judgment, 25 September 1997,
  ICJ Reports (1997) 7 .... 217, 218, 219
GAMI Investments, Inc v The Government of the United Mexican States, Award,
  15 November 2004, 44 ILM 545 (2005) 44, 49, 172
Gas Natural SDG, S.A. v The Argentine Republic (Case No. ARB/03/10),
  Decision on Jurisdiction, 17 June 2005, available at http://ita.law.uvic.ca 72, 85
Generation Ukraine, Inc. v Ukraine (Case No. ARB/00/9), Award,
  16 September 2003, 44 ILM 404 (2005); 10 ICSID Reports 240 .... 158, 230
Genin, Eastern Credit Limited, Inc and A.S. Baltoil v Estonia (Case No. ARB/99/2),
  Award, 25 June 2001, 17 ICSID Review—Foreign Investment Law Journal 395
  (2002); 6 ICSID Reports 241 .... 5, 102, 107, 109, 120, 122
Goetz and Others v Burundi (Case No. ARB/95/3), Award (Embodying the Parties'
  Settlement Agreement), 10 February 1999, [French original] 15 ICSID
  Review—Foreign Investment Law Journal 457 (2000); [English translation of French
  original] 6 ICSID Reports 5. .... 152, 162, 183, 192–3, 199
Gruslin v Malaysia (Case No. ARB/99/3), Award, 27 November 2000,
  5 ICSID Reports 484 205
Handyside v UK, Appl. No. 5493/72, ECtHR, 7 December 1976,
  (1976) 1 EHRR 737 224
Helbert Wagg & Co Ltd, In re [1956] 1 All ER 129, HL 222
Himpurna v Indonesia, 14 *Mealey's International Arbitration Report* No. 12 (1999) 208
Hood Corporation v The Islamic Republic of Iran, Award No. 142-100-3, 13 July 1984,
  7 *Iran-US CTR* (1984) 36. .... 229, 231
Impregilo S.p.A. v Islamic Republic of Pakistan (Case No. ARB/03/3), Decision on
  Jurisdiction, 22 April 2005, 12 ICSID Reports 245 .... 5, 71
INA Corp. v The Government of the Islamic Republic of Iran, Award No. 184-161-1,
  13 August 1985, 8 *Iran-US CTR* (1985) 373. 181
Inceysa Vallisoletana S.L. v Republic of El Salvador (Case No. ARB/03/26), Award, 2 August
  2006, available at http://ita.law.uvic.ca; http://icsid.worldbank.org/ICSID/Index.jsp 24–5
India—Quantitative Restrictions on Imports of Agricultural, Textile and Industrial Products,
  6 April 1999, WT/DS90/R, as modified by Appellate Body Report, 23 August 1999,
  WT/DS90/AB/R 212
Industria Nacional de Alimentos, S.A. and Indalsa Perú, S.A. v Peru (Case No. ARB/03/4),
  Award, 7 February 2005, [English original] 19 ICSID Review—Foreign Investment Law

Table of Cases xxi

Journal 359 (2004); [Spanish original] 19 ICSID Review—Foreign Investment Law
  Journal 389 (2004); 12 ICSID Reports 219 .... 70, 71
International Thunderbird Gaming Corporation v Mexico, Award, 26 January 2006,
  available at http://ita.law.uvic.ca 52, 120, 124, 125, 126, 128,
  129, 162, 163, 172, 233, 235
Iurii Bogdanov, Agurdino-Invest Ltd and Agurdino-Chimia JSC v Republic of Moldova,
  Award, 22 September 2005, available at http://ita.law.uvic.ca 159
Jacobellis v Ohio, 378 US 184, 84 S. Ct. 1676 (1964) 103
Japan—Alcoholic Beverages, Appellate Body Report, 4 October 1996, WT/DS8/AB/R 39
Kaiser Bauxite v Jamaica, Award, 6 July 1975, 1 ICSID Reports 296 172
Kardassopoulos v Georgia (Case No. ARB/05/18), Decision on Jurisdiction, 6 July 2007,
  available at http://www.investmentclaims.com 26
*Klöckner Industrie-Anlagen GmbH and Others v United Republic of Cameroon and Société
  Camerounaise des Engrais* (Case No. ARB/81/2), Award, 21 October 1983, 1984 Revue
  de l'arbitrage 19 (excerpts); 111 Journal du droit international 409 (1984) (excerpts); English
  translations of French original in 1 J. Int'l Arb. 145 (1984) (excerpts); 10 Y.B. Com. Arb. 71
  (1985) (excerpts); 2 ICSID Reports 9 (excerpts); 114 ILR 157 (1999) (excerpts); Dissenting
  Opinion of October 21, 1983, 111 Journal du droit international 441 (1984) (excerpts);
  English translations of French original in 1 J. Int'l Arb. 332 (1984) (excerpts), 2 ICSID
  Reports 77 (excerpts) 172
Kuwait v American Independent Oil Company (Aminoil), Award, 24 March 1982,
  21 ILM 976 (1982). 162, 188, 196
LAFICO v Burundi, 4 March 1991, 96 ILR 279 (1996) 219
Legal Consequences of the Construction of a Wall in the Occupied Palestinian Territory,
  Advisory Opinion, 9 July 2004, ICJ Reports (2004) 136........................ 218, 219
Liberian Eastern Timber Corporation v Republic of Liberia (Case No. ARB/83/2),
  Award, 31 March 1986, rectified 10 June 1986, 2 ICSID Reports 346;
  26 ILM 647 (1987) 172, 183, 184, 189, 198, 199
Libyan American Oil Company (Liamco) v Libya, Award, 12 April 1977, 20 ILM 1
  (1981); 62 ILR 140.. 172, 181, 187, 188
*LG&E Energy Corp, LG&E Capital Corp. and LG&E International Inc v Argentine
  Republic* (Case No. ARB/02/1), Decision on Liability, 3 October 2006,
  46 ILM 40 (2007) 5, 34, 35, 52–3, 105, 121, 123, 127, 164, 172, 218, 219, 222, 228
Link-Trading Joint Stock Company v Moldova, Award, 18 April 2002, available at
  http://ita.law.uvic.ca 3
Loewen Group, Inc and Raymond L. Loewen v United States of America
  (Case No. ARB(AF)/98/3), Award, 26 June 2003, 42 ILM 811 (2003), 7 ICSID
  Reports 442; Decision on Request for Reconsideration, 13 September 2004,
  44 ILM 836 (2005); 10 ICSID Reports 444.............. 5, 43, 44, 51, 68–9, 107, 120, 237
Lustig-Prean & Beckett v UK, Appl. Nos 31417/96 and 32377/96, ECtHR,
  27 September 1999, 29 EHRR (2000) 548; (2000) 29 EHRR 548 224
Maffezini v Kingdom of Spain (Case No. ARB/97/7), Decision on Objections to
  Jurisdiction, 25 January 2000, 16 ICSID Review—Foreign Investment
  Law Journal 212 (2001); 5 ICSID Reports 396; 124 ILR 9 (2003);
  40 ILM 1129 (2001)..................................... 62, 67, 68, 72, 75, 77–8,
  81–2, 83, 84–5, 249
M.C.I. Power Group L.C. and New Turbine, Inc v Ecuador
  (Case No. ARB/03/6), Award, 31 July 2007, available
  at http://ita.law.uvic.ca, http://www.investmentclaims.com 102, 117, 127, 172
Metalclad Corporation v Mexico (Case No. ARB(AF)/97/1),
  Award, 30 August 2000, 16 ICSID Review—Foreign Investment

Law Journal 168 (2001); 40 ILM 36 (2001); 26 Y.B. Com. Arb. 99 (2001)
(excerpts); 119 ILR 618 (2002); 5 ICSID Reports 212 .... 7, 37, 112, 114, 121, 122,
157–8, 159, 160, 162,
172, 202, 237

Methanex Corporation v United States of America, Award,
3 August 2005, 44 ILM 1345 (2005) 2, 36, 45–6, 48, 162, 165, 172, 183, 224, 230, 232

Middle East Cement Shipping and Handling Co S.A. v Arab Republic of Egypt
(Case No. ARB/99/6), Award, 12 April 2002, 18 ICSID Review—Foreign
Investment Law Journal 602 (2003); 7 ICSID Reports 178 .... 152–3, 159, 172, 237

Mihaly International Corporation v Sri Lanka (Case No. ARB/00/2), Award,
15 March 2002, 17 ICSID Review—Foreign Investment Law Journal 142 (2002); 41 ILM
867 (2002); 6 ICSID Reports 310; Concurring Opinion, 15 March 2002, 17 ICSID
Review—Foreign Investment Law Journal 161 (2002); 6 ICSID Reports 323 6

*Military and Paramilitary Activities in and against Nicaragua (Nicaragua v United States of
America)*, Judgment (Merits), 27 June 1986, ICJ Reports (1986) 14 .... 218, 223, 225

Mobil Oil Corporation and Others v New Zealand (Case No. ARB/87/2), Findings on
Liability, Interpretation and Allied Issues, 4 May 1989, 4 ICSID Reports 140 172

Mondev International Ltd v United States of America (Case No. ARB(AF)/99/2),
Award, 11 October 2002, 42 ILM 85 (2003); 6 ICSID Reports 192;
125 ILR 110 (2004) 5, 37, 114–15, 118, 120, 136

MTD Equity Sdn. Bhd. and MTD Chile S.A. v Republic of Chile
(Case No. ARB/01/7), Award, 25 May 2004, 44 ILM 91 (2005);
12 ICSID Reports 6 .... 5, 6, 7, 69–70, 84, 96–7,
121, 128, 172, 234

Muresan Claim, US Foreign Claims Settlement Commission, 5 February 1958,
26 ILR 294 (1958-II) 229

National Grid plc v The Argentine Republic, Decision on Jurisdiction, 20 June 2006,
available at http://ita.law.uvic.ca 73, 85

Neer v Mexico, Award, 15 October 1926, IV UNRIAA 60 115

Noble Ventures, Inc v Romania (Case No. ARB/01/11), Award, 12 October 2005,
available at http://ita.law.uvic.ca 5, 6, 34, 53, 88, 95, 96, 99, 101,
102, 134, 137, 139, 142

Nollan v California Coastal Commission, 483 US 825, 107 S. Ct. 3141 (1987).............. 231

Norman v Baltimore & Ohio Railroad Co, 294 US 240, 55 S. Ct. 407 (1935) 207

Nortz v United States, 294 US 317, 55 S. Ct. 428 (1935) 207

Norwegian Shipowners' Claims (Norway v US), Special Agreement, 30 June 1921;
Award 13 October 1922, I UNRIAA 307 .... 155, 179–80, 194, 201

Nykomb Synergetics Technology Holding AB v Latvia, Stockholm Rules
(Energy Charter Treaty), Award, 16 December 2003,
11 ICSID Reports 158 ....38, 57, 92, 98, 100

Occidental Exploration and Production Company v Republic of Ecuador
(LCIA Case No. UN 3467), Award, 1 July 2004,
12 ICSID Reports 59................................4, 5, 38, 39, 40, 92, 96, 119, 123,
134, 135, 140, 147, 172, 234

Oil Platforms (Islamic Republic of Iran v United States of America), Preliminary
Objection, Judgment, 12 December 1996, ICJ Reports (1996) 803; Judgment,
6 November 2003, ICJ Reports (2003) 161 .... 218, 223

Oppenheimer v Cattermole (Inspector of Taxes) [1975] 1 All ER 538, HL 187

Pan American Energy LLC and BP Argentina Exploration Company v Argentine Republic
(Case No. ARB/03/13) and *BP America Production Co and Others v Argentine Republic*
(Case No. ARB/04/8), Decision on Preliminary Objections, 27 July 2006, available at
http://ita.law.uvic.ca 3

Table of Cases   xxiii

Parkerings-Compagniet AS v Lithuania (Case No. ARB/05/8), Award, 11 September 2007, available at http://ita.law.uvic.ca, http://www.investmentclaims.com 88, 126, 128
Penn Central Transportation Co v New York City, 438 US 104, 98 S. Ct. 2646 (1978) 167
Perry v United States, 294 US 330, 55 S. Ct. 432 (1935) 207
Petrobart Limited v Kyrgyz Republic, SCC No. 126/2003 (Energy Charter Treaty Arbitration), Final Award, 29 March 2005, 3 Stockholm Int'l Arbitration Rev. 45 (2005) 6, 98, 100
Plama Consortium Limited v Bulgaria (Case No. ARB/03/24), Decision on Jurisdiction, 8 February 2005, 20 ICSID Review—Foreign Investment Law Journal 262 (2005); 44 ILM 721 (2005) 71, 75, 78, 85
Pope & Talbot Inc v The Government of Canada, Interim Award, 26 June 2000, 7 ICSID Reports 69; Procedural Order No. 2, 28 October 1999; Award in Respect of Damages, 31 May 2002, 7 ICSID Reports 148; Award on Merits Phase 2, 10 April 2001, 7 ICSID Reports 102 .... 5, 39, 41, 42, 51, 52, 54, 55, 56, 57, 67–8, 157, 166, 172, 236
Pressos Compania Naviera S.A. v Belgium, Appl. No. 17849/91, ECtHR, 20 November 1995; (1995) 21 EHRR 301 228
PSEG Global Inc, The North American Coal Corporation, and Konya Ilgin Elektrik Üretim ve Ticaret Limited Sirketi v Republic of Turkey (Case No. ARB/02/5), Award, 19 January 2007, available at http://ita.law.uvic.ca, http://icsid.worldbank.org/ICSID, http://www.investmentclaims.com 2, 4, 5, 119, 121, 129, 134, 138, 143, 148, 159, 172
Republic of Ecuador v Occidental Exploration and Production Company, 9 September 2005 [2005] EWCA Civ. 1116, 12 ICSID Reports 129 41
Republic of Ecuador v Occidental Exploration & Production Co, 2 March 2006 [2006] EWHC 345 (Comm.), available at http://ita.law.uvic.ca 41
Republic of Ecuador v Occidental Exploration & Production Co, 4 July 2007 [2007] EWCA Civ. 656, available at http://ita.law.uvic.ca................................ 41
Revere Copper and Brass Inc v Overseas Private Investment Corporation, Award, 24 August 1978, 56 ILR 258 .... 162, 232
R.F.C.C. v Kingdom of Morocco (Case No. ARB/00/6), Award, 22 December 2003, available at http://ita.law.uvic.ca, http://icsid.worldbank.org/ICSID................................. 38, 57, 71, 159, 162
Robert Azinian and Others v United Mexican States (Case No. ARB(AF)/97/2), Award, 1 November 1999, 14 ICSID Review—Foreign Investment Law Journal 538 (1999), 39 ILM 537 (2000); 121 ILR 2 (2002); 5 ICSID Reports 272 .... 37, 237
Ronald S. Lauder v Czech Republic, Award, 3 September 2001, 9 ICSID Reports 66 .... 5, 53–4, 87, 90, 92, 100, 102, 105, 134, 140, 144, 145, 161, 172
Russian Indemnity Case (Russia v Turkey), Award, 11 November 1912, XI UNRIAA 431 .... 218, 219
Salini Construttori S.p.A. and Italstrade S.p.A. v The Hashemite Kingdom of Jordan (Case No. ARB/02/13), Decision on Jurisdiction, 29 November 2004, 20 ICSID Review—Foreign Investment Law Journal 148 (2005); 44 ILM 573 (2005) 70, 85
Salini Construttori S.p.A. and Italstrade S.p.A. v Morocco (Case No. ARB/00/4), Decision on Jurisdiction, 23 July 2001, [English original] 16 ICSID Review—Foreign Investment Law Journal 469 (2001); 6 ICSID Reports 400; 42 ILM 609 (2003); [Spanish original] 16 ICSID Review—Foreign Investment Law Journal 515 (2001) 20, 21, 22, 25

Table of Cases

Saluka Investments BV (The Netherlands) v The Czech Republic,
  Partial Award, 17 March 2006, available at
  http://ita.law.uvic.ca 2, 5, 89, 92, 94, 96, 104–5, 117, 121, 124, 127,
  133, 138, 139, 141, 142, 143, 144,
  172, 183, 213, 221, 234, 235
S.A.R.L. Benvenuti & Bonfant v People's Republic of the Congo (Case No. ARB/77/2),
  Award, 15 August 1980, [English translations of French original] 21 ILM 740 (1982),
  with correction at 21 ILM 1478 (1982); 8 Y.B. Com. Arb. 144 (1983); 67 ILR 345
  (1984); 1 ICSID Reports 335 .... 172, 197
Schering v Iran, Award No. 122-38-35, 16 April 1984, 5 *Iran-US CTR* (1984) 361 228
S.D. Myers, Inc v Canada, Award (Merits), 13 November 2000,
  8 ICSID Reports 18 .... 5, 38–9, 40, 49, 50, 66, 79, 114, 121,
  127, 152, 158, 159, 165, 172, 221, 230
Sea-Land Services, Inc v The Islamic Republic of Iran, Award No. 135-33-1, 20 June 1984,
  6 *Iran-US CTR* (1984) 149 .... 160, 229
Sempra Energy International v The Argentine Republic (Case No. ARB/02/16), Award and
  Partial Dissenting Opinion, 28 September 2007, available at http://ita.law.uvic.ca,
  http://icsid.worldbank.org/ICSID 53, 111–12, 116–18, 123, 213, 217,
  218–19, 220, 222, 223,
  225, 227, 233, 234
Shahin Shaine Ebrahimi v The Government of the Islamic Republic of Iran,
  Award No. 569-44/46/47-3, 12 October 1994, 30 *Iran-US CTR* (1994) 170 196–7
Shufeldt Claim (US v Guatemala), Award, 24 July 1930, II UNRIAA 1079 179
Siemens A.G. v Argentine Republic (Case No. ARB/02/08), Decision on
  Jurisdiction, 3 August 2004, 44 ILM 138 (2005), 12 ICSID Reports 174;
  Award, 6 February 2007, available at http://ita.law.uvic.ca,
  http://www.investmentclaims.com 1, 5, 70, 78, 84, 102, 116, 125, 133,
  134, 135, 136, 145, 146, 148, 172,
  185–6, 199, 203, 236
Smith & Grady v UK, Appl. Nos 33985/96 and 33986/96, ECtHR, 27 September
  1999, 29 EHR (2000) 493; (1999) 29 EHRR 493 224
Société Commerciale de Belgique, Judgment, 15 June 1939, *PCIJ Series A/B*,
  No. 78 (1939) 218
Société Ouest Africaine des Bétons Industriels v Senegal (Case No. ARB/82/1), Award,
  25 February 1988, 2 ICSID Reports 190; 117 Journal du droit international 192 (1990)
  (excerpts); 6 ICSID Review—Foreign Investment Law Journal 125 (1991) 172
Southern Pacific Properties (Middle East) Limited v Arab Republic of Egypt
  (Case No. ARB/84/3), Award, 20 May 1992, 3 ICSID Reports 189............... 182, 202
Starrett Housing Corporation v The Government of the Islamic Republic of Iran,
  Award No. ITL 32-24-1, 19 December 1983, 4 *Iran-US CTR* (1983) 122 157
*Suez, Sociedad General de Aguas de Barcelona S.A., and Vivendi Universal S.A. v
  The Argentine Republic* (Case No. ARB/03/19) and *AWG Group Ltd v The Argentine
  Republic* UNCITRAL, Decision on Jurisdiction, 3 August 2006, available at
  http://ita.law.uvic.ca 73, 74–5, 85
Tabar Claim (No. 3), US International Claims Commission, 20 ILR 242 (1953) 231
Técnicas Medioambientales Tecmed, S.A. v United Mexican States
  (Case No. ARB(AF)/00/2), Award, 29 May 2003, [Spanish original]
  19 ICSID Review—Foreign Investment Law Journal 158 (2004);
  43 ILM 133 (2004); 10 ICSID Reports 134............. 69, 83, 84, 115–16, 121–3, 133, 138,
  139, 142, 143, 144, 153, 154, 158, 159, 161,
  162, 163, 164, 165, 172, 206, 221,
  222, 228, 234–5, 236, 239

Table of Cases xxv

Telenor Mobile Communications A.S. v Republic of Hungary (Case No. ARB/04/15), Award,
13 September 2006, available at http://ita.law.uvic.ca, http://icsid.worldbank.org/ICSID,
http://www.investmentclaims.com 73, 85, 172
*Texaco Overseas Petroleum Company (Topco)/California Asiatic (Calasiatic) Oil
Company v Libya*, Award, 19 January 1977, 17 ILM 1 (1978) 172, 201
Tippetts, Abbett, McCarthy, Stratton v TAMS-AFFA Consulting Engineers of Iran,
Award No. 141–7-2, 22 June 1984, 6 *Iran-US CTR* (1984) 219 .... 157, 159, 161
Tokios Tokelés v Ukraine (Case No. ARB/02/18), Decision on Jurisdiction, 29 April
2004, 20 ICSID Review—Foreign Investment Law Journal 205 (2005); 11 ICSID
Reports 313; Dissenting Opinion, 29 April 2004, 20 ICSID Review—Foreign
Investment Law Journal 245 (2005); 11 ICSID Reports 341 .... 21, 22
United Parcel Service of America, Inc v Canada, Award, 24 May 2007;
Separate Statement of Dean Cass, 24 May 2007, available at
http://ita.law.uvic.ca 37, 46, 47, 48, 50, 55
United States—Measures Affecting the Cross-border Supply of Gambling & Betting Services,
Appellate Body Report, 7 April 2005, WT/DS285/AB/R 212
United States—Measures Affecting Imports of Woven Wool Shirts and Blouses from India,
Appellate Body Report, 6 January 1997, WT/DS33/AB/R.......................... 57
United States—Section No. 337 of the Tariff Act of 1930, GATT Panel Report,
7 November 1989, reprinted in 36 *GATT Basic Instruments and Selected Documents*
(1990) 345 .... 78, 84
Vacuum Salt Products Ltd v Republic of Ghana (Case No. ARB/92/1), Award, 16 February
1994, 4 ICSID Reports 329; 9 ICSID Review—Foreign Investment Law Journal 72
(1994); International Arbitration Report, No. 4, at Sec. B (April 1994) 172
Walter Fletcher Smith Claim (US v Cuba), Award, 2 May 1929, II UNRIAA 913 .... 180, 200
Waste Management, Inc v United Mexican States (Case No. ARB(AF)/98/2),
Award, 2 June 2000, 15 ICSID Review—Foreign Investment Law Journal 214 (2000);
40 ILM 56 (2001); 121 ILR 30 (2002); 5 ICSID Reports 445; Dissenting Opinion,
2 June 2000, 15 ICSID Review—Foreign Investment Law Journal 241 (2000);
5 ICSID Reports 462... 153
Waste Management, Inc v United Mexican States (Case No. ARB(AF)/00/3),
Award, 30 April 2004, 43 ILM 967 (2004); 11 ICSID
Reports 361 ....5, 120, 121, 172, 230, 234, 238–9
Wena Hotels Limited v Arab Republic of Egypt (Case No. ARB/98/4), Award,
8 December 2000, 41 ILM 896 (2002); 6 ICSID Reports 89.............. 4, 119, 133, 138,
139, 144, 147, 159
West v Multibanco Comermex, 807 F.2d 820 (1987) 220
Yaung Chi Oo Trading Pte Ltd v Myanmar (ASEAN I.D. Case No. ARB/01/1),
Award, 31 March 2003, 8 ICSID Reports 463.................................. 69

Table of Treaties

BILATERAL INVESTMENT TREATIES AND FREE TRADE AGREEMENTS (ALPHABETICAL)

Model Agreements

Canadian Model BIT, Agreement between Canada and...for the Promotion
and Protection of Investments (2004) 32, 76, 79, 81, 113, 177, 178, 187,
191, 192, 195, 196, 228
France Model BIT, Accord entre le Gouvernement de la République Française et le
Gouvernement de...sur l'Encouragement et la Protection Réciproques des
Incestissements (2005), reprinted in: R. Dolzer/C. Schreuer, *Principles
of International Investment Law* (2008), 360. 113
German Model BIT, Treaty between the Federal Republic of Germany
and...Concerning the Encouragement and Reciprocal Protection
of Investments (2004), reprinted in: R. Dolzer/C. Schreuer, *Principles
of International Investment Law* (2008), 368. .... 61, 113, 178, 195
India Model BIT, Agreement between the Government of the Republic of India
and the Government of the Republic of...for the Promotion and Protection
of Investments (2003) 61, 214
Netherlands Model BIT, Agreement on Encouragement and Reciprocal Protection
of Investments between...and the Kingdom of the Netherlands (1994) 23, 60–1
United Kingdom Model BIT, Agreement between the Government of the United Kingdom
of Great Britain and Northern Ireland and the Government of...for the Promotion and
Protection of Investments (1991), reprinted in: R. Dolzer/M. Stevens, *Bilateral Investment
Treaties* (1995) 32, 33, 191
United States Model BIT, Treaty between the Government of the United States
of America and the Government of...concerning the Encouragement and
Reciprocal Protection of Investment (2004), reprinted in: R. Dolzer/C. Schreuer,
Principles of International Investment Law (2008), 360 .... 7, 32, 39, 56, 76, 113, 119, 167,
176, 178, 187, 191, 195,
196, 224, 225, 228

Concluded Agreements

Afghanistan/Germany BIT, Vertrag zwischen der Bundesrepublik Deutschland und der
Islamischen Republik Afghanistan über die Förderung und den gegenseitigen
Schutz von Kapitalanlagen, 20 April 2005, *Law Gazette* Bundesblatt (2007) 101 192
Argentina/Belgo-Luxembourg Economic Union BIT, Convenio entre la República
Argentina y la Union Belgo-Luxemburgesa para la Promocion y la Proteccion
Reciproca de las Inversiones y Notas Reversales, 28 June 1990. 72
Argentina/France BIT, Accord entre le gouvernement de la république française et la
république argentine sur l'encouragement rt la protection réciproques des
investissements, 3 July 1991 .... 73, 116, 133
Argentina/Germany BIT, Vertrag zwischen der Bundesrepublik Deutschland und der
Argentinischen Republik über die Förderung und den gegenseitigen Schutz von
Kapitalanlagen, 9 April 1991, 1910 UNTS 198 .... 133, 70, 146, 185

Table of Treaties

Argentina/Spain BIT, Acuerdo para la Promocion y la Proteccion Reciproca de
  Inversions entre el Reino de Espana y la Republica Argentina, 3 October 1991 ... 68, 72, 73, 75
Australia/Egypt BIT, Agreement between the Government of Australia and the
  Government of the Arab Republic of Egypt on the Promotion and Protection
  of Investments, 3 May 2001, 2208 UNTS 362. 12
Australia/Singapore FTA, Singapore–Australia Free Trade Agreement (SAFTA),
  17 February 2003, 2257 UNTS 104 10
Australia/Thailand FTA, Thailand–Australia Free Trade Agreement, 5 July 2004 ....10, 14
Austria/Georgia BIT, Abkommen zwischen der Republik Österreich und Georgien über die
  Förderung und den Schutz von Investitionen, 1 October 2001, *Law Gazette*
  Bundesgesetzblatt No. III, 45/2004. 191
Austria/Saudi Arabia BIT, Agreement between the Republic of Austria and the Kingdom
  of Saudi-Arabia concerning the Encouragement and Reciprocal Protection
  of Investments, 30 June 2001. ....17, 18
Bahrain/Thailand BIT, Agreement between the Government of the Kingdom
  of Thailand and The Government of the Kingdom of Bahrain for the Promotion
  and Protection of Investments, 21 May 2002. 17
Bangladesh/Japan BIT, Agreement between Japan and the People's Republic
  of Bangladesh concerning the Promotion and Protection of Investment,
  10 November 1998. .... 12, 13, 228
Belgium/Burundi BIT, Convention entre l'Union Economique Belog-Luxembourgeoise
  et la Republique du Burundi concernant l'Encouragement et la Protection reciproques
  des Investissements, 13 April 1989, 1957 UNTS 450. 192
Bolivia/Netherlands BIT, Agreement on encouragement and reciprocal protection
  of investments between the Kingdom of the Netherlands and the Republic
  of Bolivia, 10 March 1992 .... 22, 23, 33, 34
Bolivia/Peru BIT, Convenio entre la República del Perú y el Gobierno de la República
  de Bolivia sobre Promocion y Proteccion de Inversiones, 30 July 1993 .... 61, 77
Bosnia and Herzegovina/Germany BIT, Treaty between the Federal Republic
  of Germany and Bosnia and Herzegovina concerning the Encouragement
  and Reciprocal Protection of Investments, 18 October 2001 11
Canada/Egypt BIT, Agreement between the Government of Canada and the
  Government of the Arab Republic of Egypt for the Promotion and Protection
  of Investments, 13 November 1996, 2025 UNTS 314 76
Canada/Latvia BIT, Agreement between the Government of Canada and the
  Government of Latvia for the Promotion and Protection of Investments, 26 April 1995 76
Canada/Panama BIT, Treaty between the Government of Canada and the Government
  of the Republic of Panama for the Promotion and Protection of Investments,
  12 September 1996 76
Canada/Peru BIT, Agreement between Canada and the Republic of Peru for the
  Promotion and Protection of Investments, 13 November 1996 10
Canada/South Africa BIT, Agreement between the Government of Canada and the
  Republic of South Africa for the Promotion and Protection of Investments,
  27 November 1995. .... 76, 235
Canada/Thailand BIT, Agreement between the Government of Canada and the Kingdom
  of Thailand for the Promotion and Protection of Investments, 17 January 1997. 76
Canada/Ukraine BIT, Agreement between the Government of Canada and the
  Government of Ukraine for the Promotion and Protection of Investments,
  24 October 1994, 2025 UNTS 388 235
Canada/Venezuela BIT, Agreement between the Government of Canada and the Republic of
  Venezuela for the Promotion and Protection of Investments, 1 July 1996, 2221 UNTS 8 ... 76

Table of Treaties

Central America–Dominican Republic/United States FTA, The Central
America–Dominican Republic–United States Free Trade Agreement
(CAFTA), 5 August 2004 ....82, 113, 167, 225,
Chile/Argentina BIT, Tratado entre la Republica Argentina y la Republica de
Chile sobre Promocion y Proteccion reciproca de Inversiones,
2 August 1991 ....61, 68
Chile/Croatia BIT, Agreement between the Government of the Republic of Chile and
the Government of the Republic of Croatia on the reciprocal Promotion and
Protection of Investments, 28 November 1994 97
Chile/Korea FTA, Free Trade Agreement between the Republic of Korea and the
Republic of Chile, 15 February 2003 10
Chile/Malaysia BIT, Convenio entre el Gobierno de Malasia y el Gobierno de la
Republica de Chile sobre la Promocion y Proteccion de las Inversiones,
11 November 1992...69, 70, 96, 97
Chile/Peru BIT, Convenio entre el Gobierno de la Republica del Peru y el
Gobierno de la Republica de Chile para la Promocion y Proteccion Reciproca
de las Inversiones, 2 February 2000 .... 10, 71
Chile/Peru FTA, Acuerdo de Libre Comercio entre el Gobierno de la República del
Perú y el Gobierno de la República de Chile, 22 August 2006 10
China/Argentina BIT, Agreement between the Government of the People's Republic
of China and the Government of the Argentine Republic on the Promotion and
Reciprocal Protection of Investments, 5 November 1992........................... 61
China/Botswana BIT, Agreement between the Government of the Republic of Botswana
and the Government of the People's Republic of China on Promotion and Protection
of Investments, 12 June 2000.. 215
China/Kuwait BIT, Agreement Between the Government of the People's Republic
of China and the Government of the State of Kuwait for the Promotion and
Protection of Investments, 23 November 1985...........................215, 221, 228
China/Poland BIT, Agreement between the Government of the People's Republic of
China and the Government of the Polish People's Republic on the Reciprocal
Encouragement and Protection of Investments, 7 June 1988 .... 177, 187, 192
China/Thailand BIT, Agreement between the Government of the Kingdom
of Thailand and the Government of the People's Republic of China for the
Promotion and Protection of Investments, 12 March 1985 215
Cyprus/Hungary BIT, Agreement between the Government of the Republic
of Cyprus and the Government of the Hungarian People's Republic on Mutual
Promotion and Protection of Investments, 24 May 1989 .... 184, 193, 195, 202
Czechoslovakia/Netherlands BIT, Agreement on Encouragement and Reciprocal
Protection of Investments between the Kingdom of the Netherlands and the
Czech and Slovak Federal Republic, 29 April 1991 .... 54, 89, 92, 133, 135, 177, 178
Czech Republic/Slovak Republic BIT, Agreement between the Government of the
Slovak Republic and the Government of the Czech Republic Regarding the
Promotion and Reciprocal Protection of Investments, 23 November 1992 ....133, 135
EFTA/Singapore FTA, Agreement between the EFTA States and Singapore,
26 June 2002 ....76, 77, 79, 80
Egypt/Pakistan BIT, Agreement on the Promotion and Protection of Investments
between the Government of the Islamic Republic of Pakistan and the Government
of the Arab Republic of Egypt, 16 April 2000 17
Ethiopia/Russian Federation BIT, Agreement between the Government of the Federal
Democratic Republic of Ethiopia and the Government of the Russian Federation on the
Promotion and Reciprocal Protection of Investments, 10 February 2000 11

Finland/Brazil BIT, Agreement between the Government of the Republic of Finland and the Government of the Federative Republic of Brazil on the Promotion and Protection of Investments, 24 May 1995 214
France/Hong Kong BIT, Agreement between the Government of Hong Kong and the Government of the Republic of France for the Reciprocal Promotion and Protection of Investments, 30 November 1995 .... 179, 187, 195
France/Uganda BIT, Agreement between the Government of the Republic of France and the Government of the Republic of Uganda on the Reciprocal Promotion and Protection of Investments, 1 January 2002 ....215, 221
Germany/Barbados BIT, Agreement between Barbados and Germany, 2 December 1994..... 77
Germany/China BIT, Agreement between the People's Republic of China and the Federal Republic of Germany on the Encouragement and Reciprocal Protection of Investments, 1 December 2003. 152
Germany/Guyana BIT, Treaty between the Federal Republic of Germany and the Co-operative Republic of Guyana concerning the Encouragement and Reciprocal Protection of Investment, 6 December 1989 .... 77, 80
Germany/Pakistan BIT, Pakistan and Federal Republic of Germany Treaty for the Promotion and Protection of Investments, 25 November 1959 177
Germany/Russia BIT, Federal Republic of Germany and Union of Soviet Socialist Republics, Agreement concerning the Promotion and Reciprocal Protection of Investments, 13 June 1989.. 230
Hungary/Czech Republic BIT, Agreement between the Czech Republic and the Republic of Hungary for the Promotion and Reciprocal Protection of Investments, 14 January 1993.. 61
India/Singapore CECA, Comprehensive Economic Cooperation Agreement between the Republic of India and the Republic of Singapore, 29 June 2005............... 216, 225
Iran/Kazakhstan BIT, Agreement on Reciprocal Promotion and Protection of Investments between the Government of the Republic of Kazakhstan and the Government of the Islamic Republic of Iran, 16 January 1996... 61
Italy/Morocco BIT, Tra il Governo della Repubblica Italiana e il Governo del Regno del Marocco sulla Promozione e Protezione degli Investimenti, 18 July 1990............. 20
Italy/Pakistan BIT, Agreement between the Government of the Islamic Republic of Pakistan and the Government of the Italian Republic on the Promotion and Protection of Investments, 10 July 1997... 71
Japan/Korea BIT, Agreement between the Government of the Republic of Korea and the Government of Japan for the Liberalisation, Promotion and Protection of Investment, 22 March 2002.. 10, 235
Japan/Mexico Economic Partnership Agreement, Agreement between Japan and the United Mexican States for the Strengthening of the Economic Partnership, 17 September 2004 .... 10, 113, 215
Japan/Singapore FTA, Agreement between the Republic of Singapore and Japan for a New-Age Economic Partnership, 13 January 2002 10
Japan/Thailand FTA, Agreement between Japan and the Kingdom of Thailand for an Economic Partnership, 3 April 2007 10
Japan/Vietnam BIT, Agreement between Japan and the Socialist Republic of Vietnam for the Liberalization, Promotion and Protection of Investment, 14 November 2003 10
Jordan/Italy BIT, Agreement between the Government of the Hashemite Kingdom of Jordan and the Government of the Italian Republic on the Promotion and Protection of Investments, 21 July 1996... 70
Korea/Malaysia BIT, Agreement between the Government of the Republic of Korea and the Government of Malaysia for the Promotion and Protection of Investments, 11 April 1988... 215

Lithuania/Kuwait BIT, Agreement between the Republic of Lithuania and the State
of Kuwait for the Encouragement and Reciprocal Protection of Investments,
5 January 2001.. 235
Mexico/Austria BIT, Agreement between the United Mexican States and the Republic
of Austria on the Promotion and Protection of Investments, 18 February 1998 69
Netherlands/Argentina BIT, Agreement on Encouragement and Reciprocal Protection
of Investments between the Kingdom of the Netherlands and the Argentine Republic,
20 October 1992, 2233 UNTS 178 12
Netherlands/Lithuania BIT, Agreement on Encouragement and Reciprocal Protection
of Investments between the Government of the Kingdom of the Netherlands and the
Government of the Republic of Lithuania, 26 January 1994, 2010 UNTS 330 61
Netherlands/Poland BIT, Agreement between the Kingdom of the Netherlands and the
Republic of Poland on Encouragement and Reciprocal Protection of Investments
(with protocol), 7 September 1992..133, 135
Netherlands/Russia BIT, Agreement on Encouragement and Reciprocal Protection
of Investments between the Kingdom of the Netherlands and the Union of Soviet
Socialist Republics, 5 October 1989... 230
Netherlands/Sudan BIT, Agreement on Economic and Technical Co-operation between the
Government of the Kingdom of the Netherlands and the Government of the Democratic
Republic of the Sudan, 22 August 1970 178
Norway/Chile BIT, Convenio entre el Gobierno de la Republica de Chile y el Gobierno
del Reino de Noruega sobre la Promocion y Proteccion reciproca de las Inversiones,
1 June 1993 61
Norway/Hungary BIT, Agreement between the Kingdom of the Netherlands and the
Hungarian People's Republic for the Encouragement and Reciprocal Protection
of Investments, 8 April 1991 73
Peru/United States Trade Promotion Agreement, The United States–Peru Trade Promotion
Agreement, 12 April 2006 13
Philippines/Myanmar BIT, Agreement between the Government of the Republic of the
Philippines and the Government of the Union of Myanmar for the Promotion and
Reciprocal Protection of Investments, 17 February 1998 69
Russia/France BIT, Accord entre le gouvernement de la république française et le
gouvernement de l´union des républiques socialistes soviétiques sur l'encouragement
et la protection réciproques des investissements, 4 July 1989 230
Russian Federation/Thailand BIT, Agreement between the Government of the Kingdom
of Thailand and the Government of the Russian Federation on the Promotion and
Reciprocal Protection of Investments, 17 October 2002 192
Spain/Mexico BIT, Acuerdo para la promocion y proteccion reciproca
de inversiones entre el reino de españa y los Estados Unidos Mexicanos,
10 October 2006 163
Switzerland/Colombia BIT, Agreement on the Promotion and Protection of Investments
with Colombia, 17 May 2006 83
Switzerland/El Salvador BIT, Accord entre la Confédération Suisse et la République
d'El Salvador concernant la promotion et la protection réciproque des investissements,
8 December 1994.. 61
Switzerland/Iran BIT, Agreement between the Swiss Confederation and the Islamic
Republic of Iran on the Promotion and Reciprocal Protection of Investments,
8 March 1998.. 61
Switzerland/Sri Lanka BIT, Accord entre le Gouvernement de la Confédération Suisse
et le Gouvernement de la République démocratique socialiste de Sri Lanka
concernant l'encouragement et la protection réciproque des investissements,
23 September 1981... 67

Table of Treaties

Switzerland/Pakistan 1955 BIT, Accord entre la Confédération suisset la République islamique du Pakistan concernant la promotion et la protection réciproque des investissements, 11 July 1995 71
Turkey/Pakistan BIT, Agreement between the Islamic Republic of Pakistan and the Republic of Turkey concerning the Reciprocal Promotion and Protection of Investments, 16 March 1995 .... 71, 72, 73
United Kingdom/Argentina BIT, Agreement between the Government of the United Kingdom of Great Britain and Northern Ireland and the Government of the Republic of Argentina for the Promotion and Reciprocal Protection of Investments, 11 December 1990, 1765 UNTS 33 .... 73, 228
United Kingdom/Azerbaijan BIT, Agreement between the Government of the United Kingdom of Great Britain and Northern Ireland and the Government of the Azerbaijan Republic for the Promotion and Protection of Investments, 4 January 1996, 1972 UNTS 50 214
United Kingdom/Bolivia BIT, Agreement between the Government of the United Kingdom of Great Britain and Northern Ireland and the Government of the Republic of Bolivia for the Promotion and Protection of Investments, 24 May 1988, 1640 UNTS 4 .... 221, 228
United Kingdom/Chile BIT, Agreement between the Government of the United Kingdom of Great Britain and Northern Ireland and the Government of the Republic of Chile for the Promotion and Protection of Investments, 8 January 1996, 1986 UNTS 107 214
United Kingdom/Costa Rica BIT, Convenio entre el Gobierno de Costa Rica y el Reino Unido de Gran Bretaña e Irlanda del Norte sobre Promoción y Protección de Inversiones, 7 September 1982 179
United Kingdom/Czech Republic BIT, Agreement between the Government of the United Kingdom of Great Britain and Northern Ireland and the Government of the Czech and Slovak Federal Republic for the Promotion and Protection of Investments, 10 July 1990, 1765 UNTS 4 214
United Kingdom/Ecuador BIT, Agreement between the Government of the United Kingdom of Great Britain and Northern Ireland and the Government of the Republic of Ecuador for the Promotion and Protection of Investments, 19 May 1994 214
United Kingdom/Egypt BIT, Agreement between the Government of the United Kingdom of Great Britain and Northern Ireland and the Government of the Arab Republic of Egypt for the Promotion and Protection of Investments, 11 June 1975 .... 133, 135
United Kingdom/Kazakhstan BIT, Agreement between the Government of the United Kingdom of Great Britain and Northern Ireland and the Government of the Republic of Kazakhstan for the Promotion and Protection of Investments, 23 November 1995 214
United Kingdom/Nigeria BIT, Agreement between the Federal Republic of Nigeria and the Government of the United Kingdom of Great Britain and Northern Ireland for the Promotion and Protection of Investments, 11 December 1990, 1658 UNTS 523 214
United Kingdom/Pakistan BIT, Agreement between the Government of the United Kingdom of Great Britain and Northern Ireland and the Government of the Islamic Republic of Pakistan for the Promotion and Protection of Investments, 30 November 1994 214
United Kingdom/Russia BIT, Agreement between the Government of the United Kingdom of Great Britain and Northern Ireland and the Government of the Union of Soviet Socialist Republics for the Promotion and Reciprocal Protection of Investments, 6 April 1989 230
United Kingdom/South Africa BIT, Agreement between the Government of the United Kingdom of Great Britain and Northern Ireland and the Government of the Republic of South Africa for the Promotion and Protection of Investments, 20 September 1998 214

United Kingdom/Sri Lanka BIT, Agreement between the Government of the
United Kingdom of Great Britain and Northern Ireland and the Government
of the Democratic Socialist Republic of Sri Lanka for the Promotion and Protection
of Investments, 13 February 1980 133

United Kingdom/Venezuela BIT, Agreement between the Government of the
United Kingdom of Great Britain and Northern Ireland and the Government
of the Republic of Venezuela for the Promotion and Protection of Investments,
15 March 1995, 1957 UNTS 75... 214

United Kingdom/Zimbabwe BIT, Agreement between the Government of the
United Kingdom of Great Britain and Northern Ireland and the Government
of the Republic of Zimbabwe for the Promotion and Protection of Investments,
1 March 1995.. 214

United States/Albania BIT, The Treaty between the Government of the United States
of America and the Government of the Republic of Albania concerning the Encouragement
and Reciprocal Protection of Investment, 11 January 1995 68

United States/Argentina BIT, Treaty between United States of America and
the Argentine Republic concerning the Reciprocal Encouragement and
Protection of Investment, 14 November 1991 .... 3, 34, 52, 61, 71, 72, 73, 108,
123, 134, 135, 219, 221, 222

United States/Australia FTA, Free Trade Agreement between the United States
of America and Australia, 3 March 2004 .... 113, 167

United States/Azerbaijan BIT, Treaty between the Government of the United States
of America and the Government of the Republic of Azerbaijan concerning the
Encouragement and Reciprocal Protection of Investment, 1 August 1997,
together with an Amendment to the Treaty set forth in an exchange of Diplomatic
Notes, 8 August 2000, and 25 August 2000.................................... 10, 67

United States/Bahrain BIT, Treaty between the Government of the United States
of America and the Government of the State of Bahrain concerning the
Encouragement and Reciprocal Protection of Investment, 29 September 1999 222

United States/Chile FTA, United States–Chile Free Trade Agreement,
6 June 2003 .... 113, 167, 216

United States/Czech Republic BIT, Treaty with the Czech and Slovak Federal
Republic concerning the Reciprocal Encouragement and Protection
of Investment, 22 October 1991 .... 53, 88, 100, 133, 134

United States/Ecuador BIT, Treaty between the United States of America and the
Republic of Ecuador concerning the Encouragement and Reciprocal Protection
of Investment, 27 August 1993 .... 96, 123, 134

United States/Egypt BIT, Treaty between the United States of America and the Arab
Republic of Egypt concerning the Reciprocal Encouragement and Protection
of Investments, June 27 1992.. 10

United States/El Salvador BIT, Treaty between the Government of the United States
of America and the Government of the Republic of El Salvador concerning the
Encouragement and Reciprocal Protection of Investment, 10 March 1999........ 24, 25, 76

United States/Estonia BIT, Treaty between the Government of the United States
of America and the Government of the Republic of Estonia for the Encouragement
and Reciprocal Protection of Investment, 19 March 1994, 1987 UNTS 145 68

United States/Georgia BIT, Treaty between the Government of the United States
of America and the Government of the Republic of Georgia concerning the
Encouragement and Reciprocal Protection of Investment, 7 March 1994 10

United States/Jordan BIT, Treaty between the Government of the United States
of America and the Government of the Hashemite Kingdom of Jordan concerning
the Encouragement and Reciprocal Protection of Investment, 2 July 1997 .... 61, 76

United States/Morocco FTA, United States–Morocco Free Trade Agreement,
  15 June 2004 .... 10, 113, 167, 225
United States/Nicaragua BIT, Treaty between the Government of the United States
  of America and the Government of the Republic of Nicaragua concerning the
  Encouragement and Reciprocal Protection of Investment, 1 July 1995 76
United States/Panama TPA, United States–Panama Trade Promotion Agreement,
  28 June 2007 216
United States/Peru TPA, United States–Peru Trade Promotion Agreement,
  12 April 2006. .... 10, 113, 216
United States/Republic of Korea FTA, Free Trade Agreement between the United States
  of America and the Republic of Korea, 1 April 2007 10
United States/Romania BIT, Treaty between the Government of the United States
  of America and the Government of Romania concerning the Reciprocal
  Encouragement and Protection of Investment, 28 May 1992 .... 88, 95, 134, 137
United States/Russia BIT, Treaty between the United States of America and the
  Russian Federation Concerning the Encouragement and Reciprocal Protection
  of Investment, 17 June 1992. .... 80, 228
United States/Singapore FTA, United States–Singapore Free Trade Agreement,
  15 January 2003. .... 113, 167, 216
United States/Turkey BIT, Treaty between the United States of America and the
  Republic of Turkey concerning the Reciprocal Encouragement and Protection
  of Investments, 3 December 1985 134
United States/Uruguay BIT, Treaty between the United States of America and the
  Oriental Republic of Uruguay concerning the Encouragement and Reciprocal
  Protection of Investment, 4 November 2005 .... 10, 167
United States/Zaire BIT, Bilateral Agreement concerning the Reciprocal Encouragement
  and Protection of Investment, 3 August 1984 134
USSR/Belgium BIT, Accord entre les Gouvernments du Royaume de Belgique et du
  Grand-Duche de Luxembourg, et le Gouvernement de l'Union des Republiques
  Socialistes Sovietiques, concernant l'Encouragement et la Protection Reciproques
  des Investissements, 9 February 1989. 74

GENERAL (CHRONOLOGICAL)

Treaty of Peace and Amity between President and Citizens of the United States
  of North America and Hassan Bashaw Dey of Algiers, 5 September 1795,
  available at http://www.yale.edu/lawweb/avalon/diplomacy/barbary/bar1795t.htm 62
Treaty of Peace, Friendship, Navigation and Commerce between the United States and
  Venezuela, 31 May 1836, available at http://www.yale.edu/lawweb/avalon/diplomacy/
  venezuela/venez_001.htm 62
Belgian-American Diplomacy Treaty of Commerce and Navigation, 10 November 1845,
  available at http://www.yale.edu/lawweb/avalon/diplomacy/belgium/bel001.htm 62–3
Treaty of Friendship, Commerce and Navigation between Argentina and the
  United States, 27 July 1853, available at http://www.yale.edu/lawweb/avalon/
  diplomacy/argentina/argen02.htm 62
Treaty of Friendship, Commerce, and Reciprocal Establishment between Great Britain and
  Switzerland, 6 September 1855, available at http://www.treatyaccord.gc.ca/ViewTreaty.
  asp?Treaty_ID=100707 62–3
Convention between Greece and Switzerland regarding conditions of Residence and
  Legal Protection (Convention d'établissement et de protection juridique que la
  Suisse et la Grèce), 1 December 1927, (1929) LNTS 273 75

Table of Treaties

Articles of Agreement of the International Monetary Fund, 22 July 1944,
    2 UNTS 39 .... 215, 217, 233
General Agreement on Tariffs and Trade (GATT), 30 October 1947,
    55 UNTS 194 .... 59, 63, 78, 79, 84
Treaties of Friendship, Commerce and Navigation between the United States and Italy,
    2 February 1948, Supplementary Agreement, 26 September 1951, 79 UNTS 172,
    404 UNTS 326. .... 34, 35, 88, 134
Universal Declaration of Human Rights, 10 December 1948, UN Doc A/810 (1948) 29
European Convention for the Protection of Human Rights and Fundamental Freedoms,
    4 November 1950, ETS No. 5 .... 29, 155, 163, 224
Treaty of Amity, Economic Relations, and Consular Rights between the Unites States
    of America and Iran, 15 August 1955, 284 UNTS 110....................... 197, 201, 223
Treaty establishing the European Economic Community, 25 March 1957 209
Convention establishing the European Free Trade Association, 4 January 1960,
    379 UNTS 5 14
Convention on the Organisation for Economic Co-operation and Development,
    14 December 1960, 888 UNTS 179. 209
Convention on the Settlement of Investment Disputes between States and Nationals
    of Other States, 18 March 1965, 575 UNTS 159 .... 19, 20, 23, 86, 197
OECD Draft Convention on Protection of Foreign Property, 12 October 1967,
    7 ILM 117 .... 112, 154–5, 209, 227
Vienna Convention on the Law of Treaties, 23 May 1969, 8 ILM 679 .... 65, 108, 115, 227
American Convention on Human Rights, 22 November 1969, OASTS No. 36, 1144
    UNTS 128 .... 29, 155
Charter of Economic Rights and Duties of States, 12 December 1974, 14 ILM 251 (1975),
    69 AJIL 484 (1975) 178
Convention establishing the Multilateral Investment Guarantee Agency
    (MIGA Convention), 11 October 1985, 1508 UNTS 99 227
ASEAN Agreement: Agreement among the Government of Brunei Darussalam,
    the Republic of Indonesia, Malaysia, the Republic of the Philippines, the Republic
    of Singapore and the Kingdom of Thailand for the Promotion and Protection
    of Investments Manila, 15 December 1987, 27 ILM 596 69
Convention on Jurisdiction and the Enforcement of Judgments in Civil and Commercial
    Matters (Lugano Convention), 16 September 1988, 28 ILM 620. 75
Treaty on European Union (Maastricht Treaty), 7 February 1992, 32 ILM 1693. 211
North American Free Trade Agreement between the Government of Canada, the
    Government of the United Mexican States, and the Government of the
    United States of America (NAFTA), 17 December 1992, 32 ILM 289. .... 177, 241
Marrakesh Agreement Establishing the World Trade Organization, 15 April 1994,
    33 ILM 1144 29
General Agreement on Tariffs and Trade (GATT), 15 April 1994,
    33 ILM 1153 .... 36, 59, 80, 81, 86, 106, 114, 206,
                                                  212, 222, 224, 225, 226
General Agreement on Trade in Services (GATS), 15 April 1994,
    33 ILM 1167 .... 59, 79, 80, 86, 212, 217
Agreement on Trade-Related Aspects of Intellectual Property Rights (TRIPS),
    15 April 1994, 33 ILM 1212. .... 59, 63
Treaty establishing a Common Market (Asunción Treaty) between the Argentine
    Republic, the Federative Republic of Brazil, the Republic of Paraguay and the
    Eastern Republic of Uruguay, 26 March 1991. Protocol on educative integration
    and recognition of certificates, titles and studies at primary and secondary
    non-technical level (with annex), 5 August 1994, 2140 UNTS 319, 2145 UNTS 387 12

Table of Treaties

Energy Charter Treaty, 17 December 1994, 34 ILM 381 . . . . 89, 100, 106, 107, 177, 192, 214, 227, 240, 241

Euro-Mediterranean Agreement establishing an association between the European Communities and their Member States, of the one part, and the Kingdom of Morocco, of the other part, 26 February 1996, 2126 UNTS 346 15–16

OECD Draft Multilateral Agreement on Investment (Draft MAI), 12 February 1998, DAFFE/MAI/NM(98)2 210

Framework Agreement on the ASEAN Investment Area, 8 October 1998, available at http://www.aseansec.org/2280.htm 15, 16, 69, 215

1
Introduction: Interrelationship of Standards

Christoph Schreuer

The upsurge of investment arbitration in the last 10 years or so has made a strong impact on the substantive standards provided by investment treaties. Practice has shifted remarkably. Some standards have gained importance while others have waned. Some have proved their autonomy while others often appear in tandem with other standards. Some appear fairly straightforward while the meaning of others is multifaceted and had to evolve through practice. Some are central to practically every case while others are rarely invoked.

By way of introduction, it is worth considering the interrelationship of some of the standards that are discussed in this book. Traditionally, the most important standard was expropriation. In fact, there was a time when investor protection was virtually synonymous with protection against uncompensated expropriation. Recently, the practical relevance of expropriation in investment disputes has receded. Direct expropriations have become rare. Cases involving claims for indirect expropriations through regulatory measures are much more prevalent. But practice indicates that it is an uphill struggle for an investor to convince a tribunal that a regulatory expropriation has occurred. I have found 15 awards since the beginning of 2006 in which the claimant argued that it had been expropriated. Of these, the tribunals only found in three cases that there had, in fact, been an expropriation, one involving the rare situation of a direct expropriation.[1] That leaves only two instances of a successful invocation of indirect expropriation in the last two years.[2]

I believe that there are two reasons for this development. One is the requirement that for an indirect expropriation the investor must be deprived of the economic benefits of its investment entirely or in substantial part. If any commercial value remains it becomes extremely difficult to argue expropriation. The other

---

[1] *ADC v Hungary*, Award, 2 October 2006.
[2] *Siemens v Argentina*, Award, 6 February 2007; *Compañía de Aguas del Aconquija, S.A. & Vivendi Universal v Argentina*, Award, 20 August 2007.

reason is a growing sympathy on the part of tribunals for regulatory measures in the public interest. In order to avoid the undesirable consequence of a finding of expropriation, which entails full compensation, some tribunals have declared that if only the public interest is clear and due process is followed there is no expropriation.[3] The consequence is that the investor gets nothing. This unsatisfactory state of affairs has led to calls for a more balanced approach that would abandon the current 'all or nothing' situation between full compensation and zero compensation. The two are divided by a thin line that is increasingly difficult to make out in the shifting sands of arbitral practice. A suggestion on how to remedy this situation was made by Ursula Kriebaum.[4]

It is no exaggeration to say that the current law on expropriation is in a state of crisis. The fact that two contributors to this book address the topic, Anne Hoffmann at Chapter 8 and August Reinisch at Chapter 9, attests to its complexity.

The pivotal position, once occupied by protection from expropriation, has been taken over by fair and equitable treatment (FET). For the period since the beginning of 2006 I have been able to make out 13 awards dealing with FET. In eight of these the claimants have successfully convinced the tribunals that there had indeed been violations of that standard. We get a fuller exposition of this standard and its many facets by Katia Yannaca-Small at Chapter 6.

It is clear that FET is currently the most promising standard of protection from the investor's perspective. In an investment dispute the burden of proof for an investor to demonstrate a violation of FET is lighter than to establish an expropriation. Not to invoke FET where it is available under an applicable treaty would probably have to be considered as amounting to malpractice.

The tribunal in *PSEG v Turkey*[5] described this relationship in the following terms:

238. The standard of fair and equitable treatment has acquired prominence in investment arbitration as a consequence of the fact that other standards traditionally provided by international law might not in the circumstances of each case be entirely appropriate. This is particularly the case when the facts of the dispute do not clearly support the claim for direct expropriation, but when there are notwithstanding events that need to be assessed under a different standard to provide redress in the event that the rights of the investor have been breached.[6]

A look at decisions rendered over the last couple of years shows that tribunals frequently find a violation of the FET standard but simultaneously deny that there has been an expropriation. At the same time, it is difficult to envisage an

---

[3] *Methanex v United States*, Award, 3 August 2005, Part IV, D, paras 7, 15; *Saluka v Czech Republic*, Partial Award, 17 March 2006, para. 255.
[4] U. Kriebaum, 'Regulatory Takings, Balancing the Interests of the Investor and the State', 8 *The Journal of World Investment and Trade* (2007) 717.
[5] *PSEG v Turkey*, Award, 19 January 2007.
[6] Ibid., para. 238.

uncompensated expropriation that would not also involve a violation of the FET standard.

Does this mean that we can happily accept that the central role once played by protection against expropriation has simply been taken over by the FET standard? I believe this would be a mistake. Protection against expropriation has by no means become superfluous through the introduction of FET. At times, reliance on FET may not be possible. Most but not all treaties provide protection against unfair and inequitable treatment. Investment insurance typically covers expropriation but not the violation of FET. Under some treaties, jurisdiction for investor-State arbitration exists only with respect to expropriation, sometimes only for the amount of compensation due, but not for violations of FET. In order to establish the tribunal's jurisdiction the claimant will have to base its claim on expropriation.

Other treaties contain carve-outs for tax matters. This means that the treaty is inapplicable, in principle, to matters of taxation. However, the carve-out does not apply if an expropriation is involved.[7] Therefore, in order to obtain protection the claimant would have to prove expropriation by way of a tax measure.

Just to make things even more complicated, some treaties, including NAFTA, in their provisions on expropriation, contain references to FET.[8] For instance the Argentina/US BIT not only provides that any expropriation must be for a public purpose, non-discriminatory, and against prompt, adequate and effective compensation, it also requires that any expropriation must be in accordance with due process of law and FET as well as other principles of treatment.[9] In this way the FET standard gets imported into the provision on expropriation.[10]

Therefore, FET and protection against expropriation, while clearly separate standards, are still connected. FET may be part of the requirements for a legal

---

[7] Article XII Argentina/US BIT provides in relevant part: '1. With respect to its tax policies, each Party should strive to accord fairness and equity in the treatment of investments of nationals and companies of the other Party. 2. Nevertheless, the provisions of this Treaty, and in particular Article VII and VIII, shall apply to matters of taxation only with respect to the following: (a) expropriation, pursuant to Article IV; (b) transfers, pursuant to Article V; (c) the observance and enforcement of terms of an investment agreement or authorization as referred to in Article VII(1)(a) or (b), [...].'

[8] Article 1110(1) NAFTA.

[9] Article IV(1) Argentina/US BIT provides in relevant part: 'Investments shall not be expropriated or nationalized either directly or indirectly through measures tantamount to expropriation or nationalization ("expropriation") except for a public purpose; in a non-discriminatory manner; upon payment of prompt, adequate and effective compensation; and in accordance with due process of law and the general principles of treatment provided for in Article II(2).' The principles of treatment in Article II(2) of the BIT are: fair and equitable treatment, full protection and security, treatment no less than required by international law, no arbitrary or discriminatory measures, and observance of obligations entered into with regard to investments.

[10] For cases on provisions of this type see *Link-Trading v Moldova*, Award, 18 April 2002, para. 64; *Enron v Argentina*, Decision on Jurisdiction, 14 January 2004, para. 66; *Pan American v Argentina*, Decision on Preliminary Objections, 27 July 2006, para. 136.

expropriation. Even where jurisdiction extends only to claims based on expropriation, the tribunal may have to look at the FET standard to establish whether the expropriation was legal.

The practical difference between a successful claim based on expropriation and one based on a violation of FET, or for that matter of any of the other standards, manifests itself in the calculation of compensation and damages. Anyone who still believes that there is no relevant distinction at the *quantum* stage between compensation for an otherwise legal expropriation and damages for an illegal act should read Irmgard Marboe's article on this topic.[11]

The interrelationship of other standards of treatment is less clear. As Giuditta Cordero Moss explains in Chapter 7, tribunals are at odds as to whether full protection and security is an autonomous standard or a subspecies of fair and equitable treatment. Some tribunals regard the two standards as more or less equivalent,[12] while others emphasize their distinction.[13] One would think that the texts of the relevant treaties would give some indication of that relationship. Some of these treaties do indeed treat the two standards in conjunction while others offer them separately. But rather surprisingly, arbitral practice on this question, while diverse, does not seem to be determined by the wording and context of the respective provisions.

The view that the two standards, FET and protection and security, are to be seen as different obligations strikes me as the better one. As a matter of interpretation, it appears unconvincing to assume that two standards, listed separately in the same document, have the same meaning. An interpretation that deprives a treaty provision of its independent meaning is implausible to say the least. As a matter of substance, I believe that the content of the two standards is distinguishable. The FET standard consists mainly of an obligation on the host State's part to desist from a certain course of action. By contrast, by promising full protection and security the host State assumes an obligation to actively create a framework that grants security.

Clauses protecting investors from arbitrary and unreasonable measures are common in investment treaties. Veijo Heiskanen tells us all about them in Chapter 5. These clauses vary in their wording. Sometimes 'arbitrary' or 'unjustified' is coupled with 'discriminatory'. The relationship of this standard to other standards, especially FET, is also far from clear.

In a number of cases the tribunals dealt with the prohibition of unreasonable or arbitrary measures in close conjunction with the FET standard. This tendency is particularly pronounced with tribunals applying the NAFTA.

---

[11] I. Marboe, 'Compensation and Damages in International Law, The Limits of "Fair Market Value"', 7 *The Journal of World Investment and Trade* (2006) 723.

[12] *Wena Hotels Ltd v Arab Republic of Egypt*, Award, 8 December 2000, paras 84–95; *Occidental Exploration and Production Co v Ecuador*, Award, 1 July 2004, para. 187; *PSEG v Turkey*, Award, 19 January 2007, paras 257–259.

[13] *Azurix Corp v The Argentine Republic*, Award, 14 July 2006, paras 407, 408.

Introduction: Interrelationship of Standards

It may be explained, at least in part, by the fact that the NAFTA does not contain a separate provision on arbitrary treatment.[14] But a number of cases concerned BITs that contained specific references to a prohibition of arbitrary and unreasonable or discriminatory treatment in addition to the FET standard. Nevertheless, the tribunals applied these two standards in close conjunction.[15]

Despite this tendency of some tribunals to amalgamate the prohibition of arbitrary or discriminatory measures with FET, there are good reasons for treating the two standards as conceptually different. Again, it is unclear why treaty drafters would use two different terms when they mean one and the same thing. Equally, it is difficult to see why one standard should be part of the other when the text of the treaties lists them side by side as two standards without indicating that one is merely an emanation of the other. Of course, this does not deny that there may be considerable overlap and that one particular set of facts may violate both the FET standard and the rule against arbitrary or discriminatory treatment.

A number of tribunals have, in fact, examined compliance with the standards of FET and unreasonable or arbitrary treatment separately.[16] Although there is often no explicit discussion of the relationship of the two concepts,[17] their sequential and separate treatment in awards indicates that the tribunals regarded them as distinct standards.

The tendency to fuse the prohibition of arbitrariness with FET is probably more a consequence of the insecurity of tribunals confronted with two relatively novel and unspecific standards. As the case law evolves, it may be expected that tribunals develop a clearer perception of the precise implications of each of these principles.

---

[14] For the use of the concept of arbitrariness in the context of interpreting the fair and equitable treatment standard under Article 1105(1) NAFTA, see *S.D. Myers v Canada*, Award on Liability, 13 November 2000, para. 263; *Mondev Int'l Ltd v United States of America*, Award, 11 October 2002, para. 127; *Waste Management, Inc. v United Mexican States*, Award, 30 April 2004, para. 98; *Pope & Talbot v Canada*, Award in Respect of Damages, 31 May 2002, paras 63, 64; *ADF Group Inc v United States of America*, Award, 9 January 2003, paras 188, 191; *Loewen Group Inc. and Raymond L. Loewen v United States of America*, Award, 26 June 2003, paras 131–133.

[15] *CMS Gas Transmission Co. v Argentina*, Award, 12 May 2005, para. 290; *Impregilo v Pakistan*, Decision on Jurisdiction, 22 April 2005, paras 264–270; *MTD Equity Sdn Bhd and MTD Chile S.A. v Republic of Chile*, Award, 25 May 2004, para. 196; *Saluka Investments BV (The Netherlands) v The Czech Republic*, Partial Award, 17 March 2006, para. 460; *PSEG v Turkey*, Award, 19 January 2007, para. 261.

[16] See *Occidental Exploration and Production Co v Ecuador*, Award, 1 July 2004, paras 159–166; *Ronald S. Lauder v The Czech Republic*, Award, 3 September 2001, paras 214–288; *Genin, Eastern Credit Ltd Inc and AS Baltoil v Republic of Estonia*, Award, 25 June 2001, paras 368–371; *Noble Ventures v Romania*, Award, 11 October 2005, paras 175–180; *Azurix Corp v The Argentine Republic*, Award, 14 July 2006, paras 385–393; *Siemens v Argentina*, Award, 6 February 2007, paras 310–321.

[17] But see explicit treatment of this question in *LG&E v Argentina*, Decision on Liability, 3 October 2006, paras 162, 163.

Some tribunals have found that FET was an overarching principle that embraces the other standards.[18] The tribunal in *Noble Ventures v Romania*,[19] a case decided on the basis of the Romania/US BIT, seemed to think that the FET standard was just a more general label for a number of standards:

Considering the place of the fair and equitable standard at the very beginning of Art. II(2), one can consider this to be a more general standard which finds its specific application in *inter alia* the duty to provide full protection and security, the prohibition of arbitrary and discriminatory measures and the obligation to observe contractual obligations towards the investor.[20]

National treatment has a long pedigree and is older than FET. Andrea Bjorklund provides the details at Chapter 3. National treatment is clearly an independent standard. Yet, it also has its connections to FET and other standards. It is difficult to imagine that a tribunal would not regard a case of clear discrimination on grounds of nationality as a violation of FET. In addition, it would most probably regard discrimination of foreign investors as arbitrary. After all, arbitrary treatment is often coupled with discriminatory treatment in BITs. Of course, when it comes to expropriation, discrimination on grounds of nationality would make the expropriation illegal.

Most-favoured-nation clauses (MFN clauses) are also designed to avoid discrimination. Their potential for interaction with other standards of treatment is undeniable. Here we are talking not about the relationship of two or several standards all appearing in one treaty. Rather, the issue is to what extent standards not provided for in a treaty may be imported by way of an MFN clause in that treaty. For instance, where an applicable treaty lacks reference to the FET standard it is possible to import that standard from another treaty of the respondent by way of an MFN clause.[21] Andreas Ziegler enlightens the reader in this respect in Chapter 4.

Surprisingly, the most contentious issues with respect to MFN clauses have not arisen in relation to the substantive standards of treatment. Rather, the action and excitement is on a different front. It concerns the question to what extent MFN clauses also cover dispute settlement, in particular jurisdictional provisions in investment treaties.

Anna Joubin-Bret's contribution at Chapter 2 deals with admission. In a way admission is the threshold that investors must cross before they begin to enjoy the substantive standards that are the subject matter of this volume.[22] But admission

---

[18] *Petrobart v The Kyrgyz Republic*, Award, 29 March 2005, 2005: 3 *Stockholm Int'l Arbitration Rev.* 45, at 82.
[19] *Noble Ventures Inc v Romania*, Award, 12 October 2005.
[20] Ibid., para. 182.
[21] See *ADF v United States*, Award, 9 January 2003, paras 193–198; *MTD v Chile*, Award, 25 May 2004, paras 100–104, 197–206; *Bayindir v Pakistan*, Decision on Jurisdiction, 14 November 2005, paras 227–232.
[22] *Mihaly v Sri Lanka*, Award, 15 March 2002, 6 *ICSID Reports* 310.

is not always a simple one-step process. As the investment gets under way, the investor often needs a number of permits. Several cases show that this process can be hazardous if not fatal to the investment. Failure to grant the necessary permits may amount to a violation of FET or even an expropriation.[23]

Some treaties actually link admission to other standards. For instance, many BITs of the United States and Canada, as well as the US Model BIT of 2004, extend national treatment as well as MFN treatment to admission and establishment, at least in principle.

The last topic of this book is transfers. Guarantees of money transfers in and out of the host State appear in many if not most BITs. These guarantees have attracted little attention in recent years and may be regarded as the stepchild of investment arbitration practice. The editor of this book has acted wisely in inviting Thomas Wälde to write on this topic. His ability to speak and write incisively and extensively on any topic of investment law is legendary.

---

[23] *Metalclad v Mexico*, Award, 30 August 2000, 5 *ICSID Reports* 212; *MTD v Chile*, Award, 25 May 2004.

2

Admission and Establishment in the Context of Investment Protection

*Anna Joubin-Bret**

A. Introduction

Provisions relating to entry of investments by foreign investors in a host country are usually found at the very outset of international investment agreements (IIAs) on the promotion and protection of investment. In traditional bilateral investment treaties (BITs), these provisions are combined with the promotion of investment whereby the parties to the agreement undertake to promote and admit investments by investors of the other party. Protection is then granted to these investments and it is this protection that constitutes in traditional BITs the indirect promotion of investment flows from the capital exporting country. Once the issue of promotion and admission has been dealt with, the rest of the treaty is devoted to the protection afforded to foreign investments.

IIAs have traditionally taken two main approaches: admission of investments in accordance with the laws and regulations of the host country, or a right of establishment granted to the foreign investor under the treaty through the granting of national treatment at the pre-establishment phase. These two approaches, their rationale, content and consequences have been analysed in great detail in a number of studies, papers, and articles.[1]

This chapter will look at the issue of admission and establishment in the context of investment protection and, more particularly, explore the link between the admission and the entry of investors and the protection they will receive under

---

* This chapter is based on research and publications of the UNCTAD work programme on International Investment Agreements and has received inputs from Suzy Nikiema as well as comments from Joerg Weber. The views of the author do not express the views of the UNCTAD Secretariat. The author also acknowledges with thanks Dr. Christina Knahr and her article of September 2007 on 'Investments "in accordance with host state law"', 4(5) *Transnational Dispute Management* (2007), 24.

[1] Cf. UNCTAD, *International Investment Agreements: Key Issues*, Volume I, UNCTAD/ITE/IIT/2004/10, 81–85; UNCTAD, *Key Terms and Concepts in IIAs: A Glossary*, UNCTAD Series on Issues in International Investment Agreements, UNCTAD/ITE/IIT/2004/2, 3–12.

BITs and other IIAs. Given the two different approaches taken by traditional BITs on the one hand, and by more recent BITs concluded by the United States, Canada, Japan, and Australia[2] to admission and entry on the other, this chapter will also briefly look into issues arising from these different approaches.

It will consider the issue arising in traditional BITs that investors are admitted and their investments must be made in compliance with the laws and regulations of the host State. This requirement will raise the question of the role of admission of an investor in the protection afforded under the BIT.

This chapter will also identify the different approaches taken to admission and establishment, look into the admission model in BITs and regional trade agreements and at the pre-establishment model in BITs and Free Trade Agreements (FTAs). It will then look into recent awards dealing with admission in accordance with the laws and regulations of the host State and seek to draw some conclusions.

B. Approaches to Admission in IIAs

Entry of Foreign Investment

It is a principle of international law that States hold the sovereign right to regulate the admission of foreign investors into their economy, to refuse entry, or set conditions to the entry and operation of foreigners. Sovereign States can also enter into international agreements with other States in order to define the rules that will apply to the entry and protection of foreign investors from the other party into their territory.

Broadly, IIAs have dealt with the entry of foreign investment from a home to a host country using one of two models. The 'Admission' model[3]—also sometimes referred to as the 'Investment-Control' model—is generally found in traditional BITs concluded initially by European countries (but also by Western Hemisphere countries in their early BITs) and followed by a vast majority of developing countries. Over 90 per cent of the BITs concluded to date follow this admission model approach. Under this model, the host country does not grant positive rights of

---

[2] A number of BITs signed by Canada, Japan, and the United States grant foreign investors national treatment and MFN treatment at the pre-establishment stage. See, among others, Article 2(a) United States/Egypt BIT (1992); Article 2 United States/Georgia BIT (1994); Article 2 United States/Azerbaijan BIT (2000); Article 2 United States/Uruguay BIT (2005); as well as Article 3 Canada/Peru BIT (2006); Article 2 Japan/Vietnam BIT (2003); Article 2 Japan/Republic of Korea BIT (2002). However, this clause is more common in recent FTAs signed by the United States, Canada, Japan, Australia, Chile, or Mexico. See, for example, Article 10.3 United States/Morocco FTA (2004); Article 11.3 United States/Republic of Korea FTA (2007); Article 10.3 United States/Peru FTA (2006); Article 11.3 United States/Australia FTA (2004); see also Article 904 Australia/Thailand FTA (2004); Ch. 8, Article 3 Australia/Singapore FTA (2003); Article 73 Japan/Singapore FTA (2002); Article 93 Japan/Thailand FTA (2007); Article 58 Japan/Mexico FTA (2004); Article 10.3 Chile/Republic of Korea FTA (2003); Article 11.2 Chile/Peru FTA (2006).

[3] See below at n. 7.

entry and establishment to investors from the other contracting party, and may apply any admission and screening procedures for foreign investment that it may have or wish to apply and determine the conditions under which foreign investment will be allowed to enter and operate in the country.

The other approach that has been used consistently by countries seeking to liberalize conditions to entry and operation for their investors in addition to ensuring their protection is the 'Pre-establishment' or 'Combined National Treatment and Most-Favoured nation Treatment' model.[4] Under this model, foreign investors are granted national treatment ('treatment no less favourable than that accorded to nationals engaged in the same line of business as the foreign investor')[5] and most-favoured-nation (MFN) treatment ('treatment no less favourable than that accorded to other foreign investors in the same line of business')[6] with respect to the very entry and establishment of the investment. This approach may be found in BITs concluded by Canada, the United States, Japan, and a vast majority of FTAs concluded by Asian and Latin American countries.

As a result of this, more and more developing countries now apply two different model BITs, depending on the treaty partner, with the 'admission clause' model used mostly in BITs with European countries and developing countries, and the 'pre-establishment' model used in BITs concluded by Canada, Japan, and the United States, and more generally in FTAs. Both models are described in more detail below.

Admission Model

Treaties following the admission model encourage the parties to promote favourable investment conditions between them, but leave the conditions of entry and establishment up to the discretion of each country, ie to the laws and regulations of each country. For example, Article 2.1 of the BIT between Ethiopia and the Russian Federation (2000) reads:

Each Contracting Party shall encourage and create favourable conditions for Investors of the other Contracting Party to invest in its territory and *admit such investments in accordance with its laws and regulations.*[7]

BITs concluded by most European countries follow this approach consistently. For example, the BIT between Bosnia and Herzegovina and Germany provides:

Each Contracting State shall in its territory promote as far as possible investments by investors of the other Contracting State and admit such investments *in accordance with its legislation.*[8]

---

[4] See below at n. 13.
[5] See A. Bjorklund at Chapter 3 below.
[6] See A. Ziegler at Chapter 4 below.
[7] Article 2.1 Ethiopia/Russian Federation BIT (2000) (emphasis added).
[8] Article 2(1) Bosnia and Herzegovina/Germany BIT (2001) (emphasis added).

The same point is also made in the BIT concluded by the Netherlands with Argentina, although in a more elaborate fashion:

Either Contracting Party shall, within the framework of its laws and regulations, promote economic cooperation through the protection in its territory of investment of investors of the other Contracting Party. *Subject to its right to exercise powers conferred by its laws or regulations, each Contracting Party shall admit such investments.*[9]

This approach also means that the laws and regulations relating to entry of foreign investment may change over time and there is no commitment as to a level of liberalization of entry conditions or to remove any restriction or eliminate discriminatory legislation affecting the establishment of foreign investment (unless the BIT states otherwise).

The BIT between Australia and Egypt, for instance, expressly allows for:

Each Party shall encourage and promote investments in its territory by investors of the other Party and shall, in accordance with its laws and investment policies *applicable from time to time*, admit investments.[10]

The admission model is also used in several regional agreements. In the framework of the Southern Common Market (MERCOSUR), for instance, each Member State agrees to promote investments from non-Member States according to its laws and regulations.[11]

However, once admitted, foreign investment is granted full national treatment, MFN treatment, and protection. Treaties using the admission model do not contain country specific exceptions (closed sectors, operational conditions, entry requirements, etc) to MFN and national treatment—since the entry and establishment of foreign investment is within the complete discretion of the host country, there is no need for such exceptions.

MFN Treatment Only

Some BITs, despite containing an admission clause, also provide some rights, namely MFN treatment, to investors at the pre-establishment stage. For example, the BIT between Bangladesh and Japan grants no right of entry beyond rights included in domestic legislation of the parties (para. 1), but grants MFN in the pre-establishment phase (para. 2):

1. Each Contracting Party shall, subject to its rights to exercise powers *in accordance with the applicable laws and regulations*, encourage and create favorable conditions

---

[9] Article 2 The Netherlands/Argentina BIT (1992) (emphasis added).
[10] Article 3 Australia/Egypt BIT (2001) (emphasis added).
[11] See specifically, Article 2.A.1 (Definiciones) and 2.B.1 (Promociòn de Inversiones) of the Protocol on Promotion and Protection of Investments Coming from States not Parties to MERCOSUR, signed on 5 August 1994.

for investors of the other Contracting Party to make investment in its territory, and, subject to the same rights, shall admit such investment.
2. Investors of either Contracting Party shall within the territory of the other Contracting Party be accorded treatment no less favorable than that accorded to *investors of any third country* in respect of matters relating to the admission of investment.[12]

Pre-establishment Model

Treaties using the pre-establishment model grant foreign investors a positive right to national treatment and MFN treatment not only once the investment has been established, but also with respect to the actual entry and establishment of the investment. In other words, national treatment and MFN treatment are granted at all stages of the life-span of an investment: establishment, acquisition and expansion, management, use, conduct, operation, sale, and other disposition of the investment. The pre-establishment phase, where the investor is still seeking to make or in the process of making his investment, is defined by 'establishment' and 'acquisition', and in some cases where expansion requires special approval procedures, also 'expansion'.

Essentially, under this model each host State accepts, to a certain extent, a limit on its sovereignty to regulate foreign investment. However, this is subject to the right of host States to adopt or maintain exceptions to this general commitment. Thus, in contrast to the admission model, BITs using the pre-establishment model include lists of exceptions ('negative lists') to national treatment and MFN treatment. A variation of this is the 'positive list' approach, whereby national treatment and MFN is only granted for certain enumerated sectors or activities—however, the negative list approach is more common. An example of MFN and national treatment granted at pre-establishment may be found in the Peru/United States Trade Promotion Agreement:[13]

Article 10.3: National Treatment
1. Each Party shall accord to investors of another Party treatment no less favorable than that it accords, in like circumstances, to its own investors with respect to the establishment, acquisition, expansion, management, conduct, operation, and sale or other disposition of investments in its territory.

Article 10.4: Most-Favored-Nation Treatment
1. Each Party shall accord to investors of another Party treatment no less favorable than that it accords, in like circumstances, to investors of any non-Party with respect to the establishment, acquisition, expansion, management, conduct, operation, and sale or other disposition of investments in its territory.

---

[12] Article 2 Bangladesh/Japan BIT (1998) (emphasis added).
[13] Articles 10.3, 10.4 Peru/United States Trade Promotion Agreement (2006).

The Thailand–Australia Free Trade Agreement (TAFTA 2004) uses a positive list approach to commitments of national treatment in the pre-establishment phase:

Part. II—Liberalization of investments
[…]
Article 904—Pre-establishment National Treatment
In the sectors inscribed in Annex 8, and subject to any conditions and qualifications set out therein, each Party shall accord to investors of the other Party treatment no less favorable than it accords, in like circumstances, to its own investors, with respect to the establishment and acquisition of investments in its territory.

For countries used to the traditional BIT approach submitting the admission of an investor to the laws and regulations of the host State, the granting of a positive right of establishment (pre-establishment national treatment (NT) and MFN) raises not only sensitive sovereignty issues but also questions concerning the content of this positive right of establishment through NT and MFN, the commitment made to protect this right, and the compensation that could arise from a violation or infringement of this right granted by the treaty to foreign investors. Although the level of protection afforded to investors in the 'pre-establishment' phase and the extent to which the violation of the right of establishment can give rise to compensation has been discussed at the Vienna Conference and is particularly interesting and relevant in relation to protection of investments, the chapter will not concentrate on it. Jurisprudence on compensation for pre-establishment costs is scarce and not based on pre-establishment rights stemming from treaties but rather from pre-contractual rights. It is therefore difficult to draw conclusions.

Economic Integration Agreements (EIAs) often include commitments regarding the entry and establishment of investment that have significant liberalization effects for the parties. There are three basic approaches to the right of establishment within EIAs, corresponding somewhat to the admission models outlined above.

Under one approach, investors in member countries have the right to establish investments in other member countries, subject to exceptions. The European Free Trade Association (EFTA) Agreement, for example, reads:

[w]ithin the framework of, and subject to, the provisions of this Convention, there shall be no restrictions on the right of establishment of companies, or firms, formed in accordance with the law of a Member State and having their registered office, central administration or principal place of business in the territory of the Member States. This shall also apply to the setting up of agencies, branches or subsidiaries by companies or firms of any Member State established in the territory of any other Member State.

The rights of establishment shall include the right to set up, acquire and manage undertakings, in particular companies or firms… under the conditions laid down for its own undertakings by the law of the Member State where such establishment is effected.[14]

---

[14] Article 23 The European Free Trade Association Agreement.

B. Approaches to Admission in IIAs

Article 23(3) of the EFTA Agreement allows parties to set out exceptions to the right of establishment in an annex, provided that parties endeavour gradually to remove discriminatory measures, while Article 23(4) prohibits any restrictions to the right of establishment.[15]

Similarly, the Framework Agreement on the ASEAN Investment Area provides, that

[s]ubject to the provisions of this Article, each Member State shall [...] open immediately all its industries for investments by ASEAN investors.[16]

Article 7 then continues to list temporary exceptions to the right of establishment, to be gradually phased out by 2010. Article 14 of the Agreement allows for an emergency safeguard measure whereby a member may take provisional, non-discriminatory, safeguard measures to remedy a threat or serious injury caused by the implementation of a liberalization programme.

Under the second approach, MFN and national treatment is granted for the right of establishment, with a negative list of exceptions. This approach is employed in the North American Free Trade Agreement (NAFTA), granting national treatment to foreign investment at the pre-establishment stage:

1. Each Party shall accord to investors of another Party treatment no less favorable than that it accords, in like circumstances, to its own investors with respect to the establishment, acquisition, expansion, management, conduct, operation, and sale or other disposition of investments.
2. Each Party shall accord to investments of investors of another Party treatment no less favorable than that it accords, in like circumstances, to investments of its own investors with respect to the establishment, acquisition, expansion, management, conduct, operation, and sale or other disposition of investments.[17]

Article 1103 grants MFN treatment in the same manner and, lastly, Article 1108 provides for an annex of exceptions to MFN and national treatment.

Finally, a third approach is simply to provide for future liberalization in the regional agreement. For example, the Euro-Mediterranean Association Agreement with Morocco provides:

1. The Parties agree to widen the scope of this Agreement to cover the right of establishment of one Party's firms on the territory of the other and liberalisation of the provision of services by one Party's firms to consumers of services in the other.
2. The Association Council will make recommendations for achieving the objective described in paragraph 1.

   In making such recommendations, the Association Council will take account of past experience of implementation of reciprocal most-favoured-nation treatment and of the respective obligations of each Party under the General Agreement on Trade in

---

[15] UNCTAD, Investment Provisions in Economic Integration Agreements (2006) 76–77.
[16] Article 7(1) Framework Agreement on the ASEAN Investment Area.
[17] Article 1102 NAFTA.

Services annexed to the Agreement establishing the WTO, hereinafter referred to as the 'GATS', particularly those in Article V of the latter.
3. The Association Council will make a first assessment of the achievement of this objective no later than five years after this Agreement enters into force.[18]

This method does not, of course, result in any liberalization upon the entry into force of the agreement, and its impact depends on the future actions of the parties.

A related issue is the question of the admission of foreign investment by non-members of an EIA. There are some EIAs that explicitly address this question. These provisions tend to be more restrictive than those provisions granting rights to members, using, for example, the investment-control model. The MERCOSUR Protocol on Protection and Promotion of Investments from Third Parties, for instance, sets out that investments from non-members are to be admitted according to members' national laws. Other agreements, such as the European Community Treaty, have more open-door policies with respect to cross-border movement of capital from third countries, and yet others, such as the Framework Agreement on the ASEAN Investment Area, grant rights of establishment for investments from non-member countries at a future date.

C. Admitting Investment in Accordance with the Laws and Regulations of the Host State: Case Studies

The question here is whether the protection afforded by the BIT is subject to the admission in accordance with the laws and regulations of the host country and whether an investment that has not been admitted in accordance with the laws and regulations of the host country, or that has been made in violation of the admission rules or that violates rules of the general legal framework of the host country can benefit from the protection of the BIT.

In order to answer this question, we will look into recent arbitral awards and the way they have dealt with the role of laws and regulations of the host State in affording treaty protection. Before doing so, two remarks are important.

First, reference to the laws and regulations of the host country is found in some treaties also in the articles on 'Definitions' and on 'Scope of application'. The article on definition in some treaties will subject the definition of investment to the laws and regulations of the host country by referring to an investment made in accordance with the laws and regulations of the host country and then make specific reference to the laws on nationality or on companies to define who qualifies as an investor.

---

[18] Article 31 Euro-Mediterranean Association Agreement with Morocco (2000).

C. Investment in Accordance with the Laws & Regulations of the Host State

For example, the BIT between Egypt and Pakistan states that:

[t]he term investment means every kind of assets [...] invested by investors of a Contracting Party in the territory of the other Contracting party *in accordance with the laws and regulations* of that Party.[19]

In some treaties, a reference to the laws and regulations of the host country can also be found in a separate article defining the scope of application of the treaty. For example, the BIT between Bahrain and Thailand states:

The benefits of this Agreement shall apply to the investments by the investors of one Contracting Party in the territory of the other Contracting Party which is *specifically approved in writing* by the competent authority in accordance with the laws and regulations of the latter Contracting Party.[20]

Some treaties, albeit not many, will then consistently repeat the reference to the host country's laws and regulations throughout the substantive protection provisions of the treaty, underlining that each specific standard of treatment or protection is subject to the legislation of the country granting it. An example is the case of the BIT between Austria and Saudi Arabia, which consistently refers to the domestic laws of the contracting parties:

Article 2
1. Each Contracting Party shall in its territory promote as far as possible investments by investors of the other Contracting Party and admit such investments in accordance *with its legislation*.

Article 3
2. *In accordance with its laws and regulations*, each Contracting Party shall grant investments once admitted and investment returns of the investors of the other Contracting Party a treatment not less favourable than that accorded to investments and investment returns of its investors.

Article 4
2. Investments by investors of either Contracting Party shall not be expropriated, nationalized, or subjected to any other measure, the effects of which would be tantamount to expropriation or nationalization by the other Contracting Party except for the public interest of that Contracting Party and against prompt, adequate and effective compensation, provided that these measures are not discriminatory and *in accordance with domestic laws of general application*.
   [...]
Article 11
[...]
6. Issues in dispute under Article 8, paragraph 2 of this Agreement shall be decided, absent other agreement, *in accordance with the law of the Contracting Party*, party to the

---

[19] Article 1(1) Egypt/Pakistan BIT (2000) (emphasis added).
[20] Article 2 Bahrain/Thailand BIT (2002) (emphasis added).

dispute, including its rules on the conflict of laws, the law governing the authorisation or agreement and such rules of international law as may be applicable.[21]

7. The award shall be binding and shall not be subject to any appeal or remedy other than those provided for in the said Convention. The award shall be enforced promptly *in accordance with domestic law*.[22]

Most treaties, however, do not have a separate clause dealing with the scope of application of the treaty. They will define investment, investors and the other key terms of the treaty, with the admission clause being the only substantive provision of the treaties that introduces the laws and regulations of the host country and gives it a determining role in the admission of the investment.

It can be argued that the definitions article in the treaty will only deal with actually defining terms and concepts and that the reference to laws and regulations in this article does not play a role in defining the investment and the investor but in ensuring that no unlawful and/or illegal activities are covered by the BIT. In accordance with principles of international law and in the absence of any reference to laws and regulations in the definitions article, the admission clause will be the only reference to the active role played by the host State in affording actual protection, since it is the promotion and admission of the investor that will make him eligible for the protection under the BIT and ensure that no investment made in violation of the laws and regulations of the host State can benefit from the treaty protection. North American treaty practice uses the denial of benefits clause to precisely deny the benefits of the treaty to certain categories of investments, it could then be argued that the same is achieved by the reference to laws and regulations of the host State in the classical admission model BITs, where the protection does not need to be denied because it needs to be granted positively. It is only after the admission of the investment that the investor will enjoy the full benefits of the BIT in the classical admission approach.[23]

The second preliminary question is to identify the laws and regulations that are referred to in the treaties, relating to admission of investments by foreign investors. Almost all countries have legislation specifically addressing investments by foreign investors, in the form of investment codes, investment laws, exchange control regulations, specific procedural requirements such as permits, licences, authorizations, and registrations. The conditions and procedures may vary from a very liberal approach with very light procedures such as ex-post registration with the investment authorities or even simply incorporation of a company with the company registry ranging through to screening procedures,

---

[21] Article 8(2) Austria/Saudi Arabia BIT (2001) provides: 'Each Contracting Party shall observe any other obligation it has assumed with regard to investments in its territory by investors of the other Contracting Party.'

[22] Austria/Saudi Arabia BIT (2001) (emphasis added).

[23] Even though these admission clauses are stated in some treaties in the form of obligations 'each Contracting Party shall', they are not creating a right of entry for investors and could not be invoked by the investor to challenge a decision by the State not to admit.

C. Investment in Accordance with the Laws & Regulations of the Host State 19

specific authorizations, and approval procedures by the competent authorities. In addition to specific substantive and procedural rules and conditions to the quality, the entry, the form, and the operation of the foreign investor and his investment, all the laws and regulations of the host country will apply to the investor, as to any other economic actor in the host country. The foreign investor will be subjected to the general legal framework consisting of tax laws, labour laws, environmental laws, corporate laws, competition laws, and intellectual property laws and will have to abide by these laws and regulations just like any other national economic operator.

But from the BIT or any other IIA aiming at protection, the investor derives rights that are granted to him because of his alien character. This gives him extraordinary rights to protection such as access to international dispute settlement, rights to repatriation of capital and profits and other rights of protection. The very purpose of entering into such investment protection agreements is precisely to grant foreign investors these special rights to protection and to derogate, for foreign investors, from the general legal framework in some areas. The enjoyment of these rights is subject to the laws and regulations on foreign investment that will range from the simple recognition that it is an entity that qualifies as a foreign investor to an actual approval/authorization process. It could therefore be argued that these laws and regulations on admission play a role in the investment protection stemming from the BIT.

Coming back to the first remark, it can be further argued that the more liberal the entry and operation conditions, the more easily investments will benefit from the full protection of the investment treaty; and, the more restrictive or procedural the conditions, the more conditional the protection. This holds true regardless of whether the parties to the treaty have expressed it clearly—as for example in treaties concluded by Thailand—or whether the reference to laws and regulations is only found in the admission clause. But this interpretation would also mean that investments that have not gone through the admission process and have been made without express authorization, licence, permit, or other relevant procedure would not benefit from the treaty protection. And this conclusion would then be incorrect as far as countries that have taken a very liberal attitude towards entry of investment are concerned.

Let us turn now to the way recent awards have looked into the role of laws and regulations of the host country and seek to identify some elements of an answer as to the admission in accordance with the laws and regulations of the host country.

Relatively few awards have looked into the link between the laws and regulations of the host country and the protection afforded under a BIT. Those who have looked at it from the point of view of competence or jurisdiction under Article 25 of the ICSID Convention have examined the possibility for the investor to revert to the use of the dispute settlement provisions of the BIT. In most cases, tribunals have had to deal with jurisdictional issues raised by the defendant State and have looked into the definitions given by host States' laws and regulations of given activities or given economic actors in order to apply the criteria of Article 25 ICSID Convention.

A first set of three recent awards are interesting in so far as they remove the reference to the laws and regulations of the host State from the area of definitions of investment and confine them to a test of validity of the investment. In so doing, they also confirm that the BITs are not meant to give protection to investments that would not respect the laws and regulations of the host country or, in particular, that would be illegal.

Salini v Morocco

The *Salini* case[24] is one of the first awards to deal with the meaning of the terms 'in accordance with laws and regulations'. In response to the Kingdom of Morocco's objection on jurisdiction,[25] the tribunal had to decide on the existence of an investment within the meaning of the Italy/Morocco BIT which refers to the laws and regulations of the host State.[26]

The tribunal asked if the term 'in accordance with the laws and regulations' of the host State refers to the definition or to the validity of investment. The tribunal decided that it concerned the validity in those terms:

The Tribunal cannot follow the Kingdom of Morocco in its view that paragraph 1 of Article 1 refers to the law of the host State for the definition of 'investment'. In focusing on *'the categories of invested assets (...) in accordance with the laws and regulations of the aforementioned party,'* this provision refers to the validity of the investment and not to its definition. More specifically, it seeks to prevent the Bilateral Treaty from protecting investments that should not be protected, particularly because they would be illegal.[27]

Interestingly, the tribunal also sought to identify these laws and regulations of the host State, although it did not use this reasoning in reaching its decision on jurisdiction.

The tribunal also considered in the Award that

[...] to be considered as investments, the rights enumerated under letters (c) and (e) *'must be the object of contracts approved by the competent authority'* under the terms of Article 1(g)

---

[24] *Salini Costruttori S.p.A and Italstrade S.p.A v Kingdom of Morocco*, ICSID Case No. ARB/00/4, Decision on Jurisdiction, 23 July 2001.

[25] In this case, the Kingdom of Morocco alleged that the jurisdiction of the Tribunal is dependent on the existence of an investment. It considered that because of Article 1(1) of the Italy/Morocco BIT (1990) which refers to the laws and regulations of the host State, the laws and regulations of Morocco must be looked at to define the notion of investment. And according to the national law, the transaction in question is not an investment contract.

[26] Article 1 of the Italy/Morocco BIT (1990) provides that 'the term "investment" designates all categories of assets invested, [...], *in accordance with the laws and regulations of the aforementioned party.* In particular, but in no way exclusively, the term "investment" includes: [...] (g) *the elements mentioned in (c), (d), and (e) above must be the object of contracts approved by the competent authority*' (emphasis added).

[27] *Salini v Morocco*, above n. 24, para. 46.

C. Investment in Accordance with the Laws & Regulations of the Host State 21

and that

the Bilateral Treaty does not indicate who the competent authority is, *this being likely to vary according to the contract. The competent authority is determined according to the laws and regulations of the State on the territory of which the investments are made (cf.* Article 1, paragraph 1).[28]

Tokios Tokelės v Ukraine

In the *Tokios Tokelės* case,[29] the tribunal had to look into an objection to jurisdiction raised by the Government of the Ukraine according to which the investment in question had not been made 'in accordance with laws and regulations' of Ukraine as required by Article 1(1) of the applicable BIT. The respondent also alleged that it had identified errors in the documents provided by the claimant, including, in some cases, the absence of a necessary signature or notarization.

On this issue, the tribunal refers to the *Salini* case:

The requirement in Article 1(1) of the Ukraine-Lithuania BIT that investments be made in compliance with the laws and regulations of the host state is a common requirement in modern BITs. The purpose of such provisions, as explained by the tribunal in *Salini Costruttori S.p.A and Italstrade S.p.A v Morocco*, is 'to prevent the Bilateral Treaty from protecting investments that should not be protected, particularly because they would be illegal'.[30]

Having said that, the tribunal focused on the question of whether the investment of Tokios Tokelės was made according to Ukraine laws and regulations. It responded that the claimant's investment activity—advertising, printing, and publishing—was not illegal *per se*, and that in fact governmental authorities of the respondent had registered the claimant's subsidiary as a valid enterprise.[31]

In its decision on jurisdiction, the tribunal looked at the absence of a denial of benefits clause and explained that if the contracting parties had wanted to deny benefits of the treaty protection to certain investors they could have done so by using a denial of benefits clause.[32] This argument, although interesting for our discussion, is however questionable, as traditional admission model BITs do not use denial of benefits clauses because they are based on active admission by the host State and all the rights of the investor are granted after the admission has taken place.

---

[28] Ibid., para. 47 (emphasis added).
[29] *Tokios Tokelės v Ukraine*, ICSID Case No. ARB/02/18, Decision on Jurisdiction, 29 April 2004.
[30] Ibid., para. 84.
[31] Ibid., para. 86.
[32] Ibid., para. 36.

Bayindir v Pakistan

The *Bayindir* case[33] indeed confirms the approach which determines that an 'in accordance with the state laws and regulation' clause refers to the legality (validity) and not to the definition of an investment.

With regard to the criteria to determine if an investment was made in accordance with the host State law, the tribunal decided that

[...] since Pakistan does not contend that Bayindir's purported investment actually violates Pakistani laws and regulations, the Tribunal considers that the reference to the 'hosting Party's laws and regulations' in Article I(2) of the Treaty could not in any case oust the Tribunal's jurisdiction in the present case.[34]

Much more relevant for our discussion is the *Aguas del Tunari v Bolivia* case and the arguments raised by Bolivia based on the admission clause contained in its BIT with the Netherlands. The reference to the laws and regulations was not in the Article on definitions but in the admission clause. The tribunal therefore looked into the scope of application of the Admission clause.

Aguas del Tunari v Bolivia

This case arose out of the termination of a concession contract.[35] *Aguas del Tunari*, a company organized under the laws of Bolivia, concluded in September 1999 a concession contract to supply and process drinking water for the city of Cochabamba, Bolivia. Bolivia raised a series of objections to the tribunal's jurisdiction and argued among others that '[...] Article 2 of the BIT contains references to Bolivian law which in this case preclude ICSID jurisdiction'. Bolivia argued that Article 2 of the BIT addressed the Bolivian law as the framework under which foreign investments would be admitted and protected and that this in turn entailed that the dispute in question must be subject to Bolivian laws and courts.[36]

This Bolivia/Netherlands BIT provided:

[...] Subject to its right to exercise powers conferred by its laws and regulations, each contracting Party shall admit such investment.[37]

The wording of the admission clause here is slightly different from the admission clauses found in other BITs, like the BITs involved in the *Salini*, *Bayindir*, or *Tokios Tokelės* cases. In the Bolivia/Netherlands BIT, admission is not directly

---

[33] *Bayindir Insaat Turizm Ticaret Ve Sanayi A.Ş. v Islamic Republic of Pakistan*, ICSID Case No. ARB/03/29, Decision on Jurisdiction, 14 November 2005.
[34] Ibid., para. 110.
[35] *Aguas del Tunari S.A. v Republic of Bolivia*, ICSID Case No. ARB/02/3, Decision on Jurisdiction, 21 October 2005.
[36] See ibid., paras 139–140.
[37] Article 2 Bolivia/Netherlands BIT (emphasis added).

C. Investment in Accordance with the Laws & Regulations of the Host State 23

submitted to the accordance of host State laws and regulations, but to the State's right to exercise powers conferred by those laws and regulations, in fact to the positive right to admit investments.

Does this difference in terminology matter? In *Aguas del Tunari* the tribunal did not ponder this question but it interpreted the meaning of Article 2 in the Award:

> The obligation to admit is 'subject to' the decision of Bolivia ('its right') to 'exercise powers conferred by its laws or regulations'. The Tribunal concludes that the inclusion of the term 'subject to' indicates that the duty to admit investments is limited by 'the right to exercise powers conferred by its laws or regulations'. The Tribunal notes that the reference specifically subjects the State's duty to admit investments not to the laws and regulations of Bolivia, but rather to the 'right to exercise powers' conferred by such laws or regulations. *The Tribunal finds this language significant as it implies an act at the time of admittance in accordance with the laws or regulations in force at that time.*[38]

Some may consider this to be a very narrow reading of the Bolivia–Netherlands treaty and more specifically of the admission clause. In addition, this approach is used in the Netherlands model treaty and in most of the treaties concluded by the Netherlands that are using a classical admission model.

The tribunal then goes on and looks into the consequences of the admission clause on the operation of the ICSID Convention:

> [...] The scope of the [...] reference in Article 2 must be understood in terms of their context and purpose. In this regard, it needs to be recalled that a primary objective of the BIT, measured both in terms of the motivation for its conclusion and in terms of its substantive provisions, is agreement upon ICSID as an independent and neutral forum for the resolution of investment disputes in accordance with a substantive applicable law specified in the BIT. *In this light, the Tribunal concludes that the State Parties cannot have intended the references to national law in Article 2 to be so encompassing as to defeat the object and purpose of the Treaty.*[39]

In conclusion, the narrow interpretation of the tribunal on the meaning of Article 2 of the BIT partially answers our question because it denies the admission clause a role in treaty protection, particularly in the access to investor-State dispute settlement procedures under the treaty. This answer by the tribunal is, however, triggered by the arguments used by the defendant when reading into the laws and regulations of Bolivia a jurisdiction for the local courts of Bolivia.

Interestingly, the tribunal also interpreted the meaning or the scope of the laws and regulations of Bolivia and interpreted them to be

> [...] limited to the details of how each contracting party undertakes in its national laws and regulations to promote economic cooperation through the protection of investments.

---

[38] *Aguas del Tunari S.A. v Republic of Bolivia*, above n. 35, para. 147 (emphasis added).
[39] Ibid., para. 153 (emphasis added).

Unfortunately for our analysis the tribunal does not go further and simply concludes that

> [...] the Respondent's interpretation would permit a host State to take its affirmative responsibility to 'promote economic cooperation through the protection in its territory of investments of nationals of the other Contracting Party' and transform it into an opportunity to introduce exclusive local jurisdiction for investment disputes.[40]

But this is precisely what BITs do in a positive way. The essential *quid pro quo* of BITs is to promote investments by protecting them and to protect them by granting among other protections access to international arbitration to settle investor-State disputes.

Three further cases are also of interest to see the interpretation given by arbitral tribunals to the admission of investments in accordance with the laws and regulations of the host country.

Inceysa v El Salvador

The *Inceysa* case[41] is related to a contract on establishment of motor vehicle inspection facilities in El Salvador. The claimant went to arbitration and argued, among others, that the denial of the exclusivity granted to it in the contract amounted to an unjust unilateral termination of the contract.

El Salvador raised an objection to the tribunal's jurisdiction based on the assertion that the BIT extended protection only to investments made in El Salvador in accordance with its laws, and that it never consented to treaty protection of investments that were procured by fraud, forgery, or corruption. Thus, because the investment has been done illegally, it could not be arbitrated pursuant to the BIT.

For the tribunal, the respondent's objection concerned the 'so-called jurisdiction *rationae* [sic] *voluntatis*'.[42] It proceeded with a step-by-step analysis. The tribunal examined the BIT and the *travaux préparatoires* to find out whether the contracting parties intended to limit their consent to investments made in accordance with law and regulations. It concluded that

> Without any doubt, [...] the will of the parties to the BIT was to exclude from the scope of application and protection of the Agreement disputes originating from investments which were not made in accordance with laws of the Host State.[43]

The tribunal took the view that any investment made against the laws of El Salvador was outside the protection of the BIT and therefore outside of the competence of the tribunal.

---

[40] Ibid., para. 153.
[41] *Inceysa Vallisoletana S.L. v Republic of El Salvador*, ICSID Case No. ARB/03/26, Decision on Jurisdiction, 2 August 2006.
[42] Ibid., para. 144.
[43] Ibid., para. 195.

C. Investment in Accordance with the Laws & Regulations of the Host State

The tribunal, to identify those laws and regulations, looked at the BIT itself, which was considered part of El Salvador's domestic law (according to El Salvador's constitution). However, the treaty itself was silent as to what would or would not constitute an investment made in accordance with the law. The tribunal then turned to the generally recognized rules and principles of international law, which had been referred to in the Spain–El Salvador treaty.

It permeates from the tribunal's analysis that, first, it must consider the BIT provisions and, in case of silence, the general principles of law. The national laws and regulations themselves are not examined; this is contrary to the *Salini v Morroco* case where the tribunal referred to national law in order to determine the competent authority for authorizing the investment.[44]

The tribunal identified some of the general principles of law, including good faith, international public policy, the prohibition of unlawful enrichment, and guidelines setting out that no one should profit from their own fraud.

In fact, the tribunal found that Inceysa had submitted false financial statements, forged documents, and misrepresented its experience in the field. It held that these misrepresentations were sufficient to render the investment illegal, and that it therefore could not benefit from the BIT. The tribunal held that Inceysa's actions clearly were against all of these general principles and therefore that it did not have jurisdiction.

Fraport v Philippines

In the recent *Fraport v Philippines* case,[45] the tribunal had also to look into the actual violation by the foreign investor of the laws and regulations of the Philippines.

In the *Fraport* case, the Philippines alleged a violation by the claimant of the Anti-Dummy Law of the Philippines that specifically sets conditions for foreign ownership, therefore a typical Foreign Direct Investment (FDI) law. In the treaty between Germany and the Philippines, the laws and regulations of the host country are referred to both in the definitions and in the article on admission. The tribunal found that the violation by the claimant of the Anti-Dummy Law was a violation of the laws and regulations of the Philippines that are explicitly mentioned in the treaty as a requirement for the investment. Further, in order to assess this violation, the tribunal looked into the laws of the Philippines itself. Interestingly, the tribunal also established in paragraph 394 of the award on jurisdiction that 'a failure to comply with the national law to which a treaty refers will have an international legal effect'. The tribunal concluded that it did not have jurisdiction over this case as the investor was not covered under this BIT.

---

[44] *Salini v Morocco*, above n. 24, para. 47.
[45] *Fraport AG Frankfurt Airport Services Worldwide v Republic of the Philippines*, ICSID Case No. ARB/03/25, Award, 16 August 2007.

It is important to note that the dissenting opinion by one of the arbitrators of the tribunal argued that this issue should not have prevented the tribunal from establishing jurisdiction but should have been examined at the stage of the merits.

Ioannis Kardassopoulos v Georgia

In the *Ioannis Kardassopoulos* case, the tribunal looked into the issue from the point of view of the action of the State. In that case, the tribunal noted:

'Protection of investments' under a BIT is obviously not without some limits. It does not extend, for instance, to an investor making an investment in breach of the local laws of the host State. A State thus retains a degree of control over foreign investments by denying BIT protection to those investments that do not comply with its laws. As noted by one scholar, 'no State has taken its fervour for foreign investment to the extent of removing any controls on the flow of foreign investment into the host State'. This control, however, relates to the *investor's actions* in making the investment. It does not allow a State to preclude an investor from seeking protection under the BIT on the ground that its *own actions* are illegal under its own laws. In other words, a host State cannot avoid jurisdiction under the BIT by invoking its own failure to comply with its domestic law.[46]

The tribunal went on to hold that, since it was Georgia itself that was arguing the agreement was void due to its State-owned enterprises having violated Georgian law by exceeding their authority, the provision in the BIT relating to investments in accordance with Georgian law could not be invoked to exclude the claimant's investment from protection. The analysis made by the tribunal of the degree of control a State can keep over the admission of an investment through its laws and regulations is most interesting for our discussion.

D. Conclusions

In treaty practice, the admission model submits the admission of investments by foreign investors to the laws and regulations of the host State. What are the concrete implications of this positive right of the sovereign State to set the rules for admission of a foreign investment in relation to the BIT? Especially when the BIT does not refer to the laws and regulations of the host State in other articles than the admission clause or when it does not expressly provide for a limitation of the scope of application of the treaty to approved investments. Is this limitation part of the admission model or does it not play any role as far as the protection under the BIT is concerned?

---

[46] *Ioannis Kardassopoulos v Georgia*, ICSID Case No. ARB/05/18, Decision on Jurisdiction, 6 July 2007, para. 182.

D. Conclusions

It could be argued that the admission clause plays the important role of the filter to the protection under the BIT to ensure that no investment made in violation of the laws and regulations of the host State can benefit from the treaty protection. But also it is the positive act of admitting investment in accordance with the laws and regulations that will be the basis for the protection granted (another positive action by the host State) to the foreign investor. The consequences are important for countries with restrictive admission conditions but also for those that have liberalized their admission procedures. The current trend of national FDI laws is to become more and more liberal[47] and used merely to spell out the policy priorities of the country vis-à-vis investments that will impact on the local economy. This would clearly leave out some foreign investments from the scope of application of these laws and the question of BIT protection would arise.

The jurisprudence on admission in accordance with law and regulation is scarce but we could retain three points of interest for our discussion:

– BITs are not meant to protect investments that are unlawful or illegal. The protection under the BIT does not extend to investors making an investment in breach of the local laws of the host State.

– The reference to the laws and regulations in the definitions article does not have the same role as in the article on admission. In the article on definitions, it does not refer to the definitions given by the laws and regulations of the host State but to the validity of the investment.

– Few tribunals have looked into the content of the laws and regulations used to deny the protection of the BIT to investments made in violation of the same.

Some issues fall into a grey area and give rise to more questions than actual conclusions. In particular, what are those laws and regulations? Is it the set of national regulations that apply only to foreign investors and their investments or laws and regulations of general application? Is the answer to be found in principles of international law or in the laws of the host State if the treaty itself is silent? Which criteria should tribunals look for to determine whether the claimant's investment is made in accordance with host regulations? Is the tribunal entitled to assess objectively or subjectively the degree of the violation and draw consequences on jurisdiction of minor as opposed to severe violations? What are the consequences of unlawful or illegal investments with regard to the access of the investor to international dispute settlement and other protection standards under the BITs? Are the consequences to be drawn at the stage of jurisdiction or at the stage of merits of the case?

---

[47] In 2006, a total of 184 national regulatory changes were identified by UNCTAD, 80% of which were in the direction of making the host country environment more favourable to FDI. For more details on this issue, see *World Investment Report* (2007) 14–16.

From looking at recent jurisprudence, one could draw the conclusion that tribunals are looking more carefully into the laws and regulations of the host country and are reading them into the object and purpose of a BIT, that is not meant to protect investments that do not meet the conditions set by those laws and regulations. This would seem to be the logical purpose of admission model treaties where the State maintains its sovereign right to decide on the admission of the investment. But one would need more decisions to see whether this is an actual trend. It will be interesting to monitor how this particular aspect of international investment agreements develops in the future.

3
National Treatment

Andrea K. Bjorklund

A. Introduction

The principle of according national treatment—avoiding discrimination based on nationality—underpins many types of international agreement. It is, of course, a core obligation in the General Agreement on Tariffs and Trade (GATT) and its related treaties.[1] Human rights treaties also require countries to extend equal treatment to all similarly situated persons within their jurisdictions.[2] In addition, nearly all investment treaties contain national treatment obligations.[3] At bottom, all of these treaties recognize that foreign entities, whether goods, corporations, or people, might be subject to less favourable treatment due to their status as outsiders. The national treatment obligation attempts to neutralize the protectionist tendency of governments to protect domestic investors and producers from foreign competition. It has been called

[...] perhaps the single most important standard of treatment enshrined in international investment agreements (IIAs). At the same time, it is perhaps the most difficult to achieve, as it touches upon economically (and politically) sensitive issues.[4]

National treatment is a relative, or contingent, obligation. It requires that a host State treat foreign investments or investors as well as similarly situated national investors. A national treatment analysis thus usually requires identifying the appropriate comparator against which to measure the allegedly less favourable

---

[1] See, eg, Article III General Agreement on Tariffs and Trade (GATT); Article XV General Agreement on Trade in Services (GATS); Marrakesh Agreement Establishing the World Trade Organization (1994), Annex IB, Annex IC; Article 3 Agreement on Trade-Related Aspects of Intellectual Property Rights (1994).

[2] See, eg, Article 1 European Convention for the Protection of Human Rights and Fundamental Freedoms (1950); Article 1(1) Organization of American States, American Convention on Human Rights; see also Article 2 Universal Declaration of Human Rights (1948).

[3] UNCTAD, *National Treatment*, Volume IV, UNCTAD/ITE/IIT/11 (1999) 15–24, noting the importance of the national treatment obligation in investment codes and international investment agreements.

[4] Ibid., 1.

treatment. If the claimant is not 'in like circumstances' with the more favourably treated entity, the national treatment claim will fail. If the claimant is in fact in like circumstances with the more favourably treated entity, an arbitral tribunal seized with the dispute will determine whether the host State had legitimate, non-nationality-based reasons for the difference in treatment.

The national treatment obligation protects against discrimination, whether *de jure* or *de facto*, on the basis of nationality. In practice there are few cases of *de jure* discrimination; most of the cases centre on the differential effect of a facially neutral measure. Prevailing on a national treatment claim does not require demonstrating discriminatory intent; such a hurdle would be too great for most claimants to overcome. Rather,

[...] in the absence of a legitimate rationale for the discrimination between investors in like circumstances, the tribunal will presume—or at least infer—that the differential treatment was a result of the claimant's nationality.[5]

There are still unresolved questions, however, as to whether or when the burden of proof to demonstrate the legitimacy, or lack of legitimacy, of the rationale may rest on the claimant. An additional source of dispute is whether according treatment 'no less favourable' than that afforded to domestic investors requires the best treatment accorded any domestic investor, or whether the purpose of the provision is to provide only equality of opportunity to foreign and domestic investors.[6]

This chapter addresses first the historical background of the national treatment obligation and sets forth exemplars of relevant investment treaty provisions, in addition to introducing some of the controversial issues surrounding the national treatment obligation. It then analyses the case law in which the contours of the national treatment obligation have evolved.

B. Background and Treaty Practice

National treatment obligations date back to Hanseatic League treaties of the 12th and 13th centuries.[7] They were part of a group of protections (which also included most-favoured-nation treatment and the minimum standard of

---

[5] A. Newcombe, L. Paradell, and D. Krishan, 'National Treatment', *The Law and Practice of Investment Treaties* (forthcoming 2008) 36.
[6] C. McLachlan, L. Shore, and M. Weiniger, *International Investment Arbitration: Substantive Principles* (2007) 251: '[...] the requirement of national treatment [...] aims to provide a level playing-field for foreign investors (at least post establishment)'; cf. Newcombe, Paradell, and Krishan, above n. 5, 41: 'References to "no less favourable" treatment in [international investment agreements] do not clarify whether the investor is entitled to the best treatment afforded to any other investor, national or foreign, or the average treatment afforded to a group of like investors.'
[7] P. Verlooren van Themaat, *The Changing Structure of International Economic Law* (1981) 19–21; G. Schwarzenberger, 'The Principles and Standards of International Economic Law', 117 *Recueil des Cours* (1966) 1, 18–26.

treatment) accorded foreign merchants during what might roughly be termed the Middle Ages.[8] National treatment obligations were also part of the trading treaties prevalent in the 19th century, and are now a familiar part of the 20th and 21st century international economic law landscape. They are perhaps most familiar in the context of trade in goods, but national treatment obligations are also included in most investment treaties.

Professor Schwarzenberger traced the evolution of international economic law standards in his course at The Hague Academy, and noted that of the seven he identified, six were concerned in some measure with equality of treatment.[9] Just what constitutes equal treatment is often a matter of debate, and in some instances equal treatment might not be sufficient to protect the interests of foreigners. National treatment is a relative standard; it requires only that the foreign investor or investment be given the same treatment as that given to nationals. The Argentine jurist Carlos Calvo argued vigorously that national treatment was the most foreign investors had any right to demand; the 'Calvo' clause found in the laws of several developing countries and in many state contracts recognizes that philosophical position.[10]

Theoretically, at least, national treatment obligations could provide no protection to foreigners should nationals be treated badly. This potential drawback illustrates the weakness of national treatment provisions. While in many circumstances a national treatment provision will benefit foreign investors by ensuring that they gain market access on an equal footing with nationals, it can also act to limit the rights of foreign investors in circumstances where nationals have limited rights.[11] In order to remedy this shortcoming, the international minimum standard of treatment provides a floor below which treatment cannot fall, regardless of any relevant relative comparison.[12]

Despite its long pedigree, national treatment remains a conventional obligation.[13] 'A degree of discrimination in the treatment of aliens as compared with nationals is, generally, permissible as a matter of customary international law'.[14]

---

[8] See A. Ziegler, 'Most-Favoured-Nation (MFN) Treatment' at Chapter 4 below; C. Yannaca-Small, 'Fair and Equitable Treatment', at Chapter 6 below.
[9] Schwarzenberger, above n. 7, 67. Those he identified were: (1) the minimum standard; (2) the standard of preferential treatment; (3) the most-favoured-nation standard; (4) the national standard; (5) the standard of identical treatment; (6) the standard of the 'open door'; and (7) the standard of equitable treatment.
[10] D. Shea, *The Calvo Clause* (1955) 35–36.
[11] M. Kinnear, A. Bjorklund, and J. Hannaford, *Investment Disputes Under NAFTA: An Annotated Guide to NAFTA Chapter 11* (2007) 1102.12, noting that national treatment obligations have been used both to limit and to expand the rights of foreign traders and investors.
[12] R.B. Lillich, *The Human Rights of Aliens in Contemporary International Law* (1984) 17; A. Bjorklund, 'Reconciling State Sovereignty and Investor Protection in Denial of Justice Claims', 45 *Virginia Journal of International Law* (2005) 809, 836–837.
[13] McLachlan, Shore, and Weiniger, above n. 6, 212–213.
[14] R. Jennings and A. Watts (eds), *Oppenheim's International Law* (9th edn, 1996) 932.

In contrast, the international minimum standard is a part of customary international law.[15] There are specific areas in which one could view the international minimum standard and the national treatment obligation as having coalesced—when discriminating on the basis of nationality violates the international minimum standard. The best example of this is in the provision of justice.[16] Another area of potential overlap is in a State's obligation to provide 'fair and equitable' treatment,[17] which encompasses a non-discrimination obligation in some instances.[18] In addition, as discussed more fully below, some treaties specifically prohibit States from according 'arbitrary and discriminatory' treatment, a formulation that to some degree conflates the minimum standard and national treatment obligations.[19]

The scope of the national treatment obligation varies by treaty. Some treaties accord protection only post-establishment—eg only after the investment is permitted to enter the country—while others extend rights of establishment as well. Some treaties extend protection only to investments, others protect both investments and investors. This distinction tends to accord with the pre- and post-entry coverage.[20] If a treaty accords rights of establishment, it likely extends protection to investors who have not yet made an investment, as well as to the investment itself. NAFTA Chapter 11, the 2004 US Model BIT, and the 2004 Canadian Model FIPA (Foreign Investment Promotion and Protection Agreement) contain broad pre-entry protections.[21] The UK Prototype, on the other hand, provides that a State is only required to permit the investment of capital '[...] subject to its right to exercise powers conferred by its laws'.[22] If a

---

[15] Schwarzenberger, above n. 7, 78.

[16] See, eg, Bjorklund, above n. 12, 837–838; E. Root, 'The Basis of Protection to Citizens Residing Abroad', 4 *American Society of International Law Proceedings* (1910) 16, 20: 'Each country is bound to give to the nationals of another country in its territory the benefit of the same laws, the same administration, the same protection, and the same redress for injury which it gives to its own citizens, and neither more nor less: provided the protection which the country gives to its own citizens conforms to the established standard of civilization.'

[17] There has been a vigorous debate about whether the fair and equitable treatment standard is a subset of the international minimum standard or whether it operates as a discrete obligation that confers more rigorous obligations onto State Parties to the treaty incorporating such an obligation. See generally McLachlan, Shore, and Weiniger, above n. 6, 218–221, Kinnear, Bjorklund, and Hannaford, above n. 11, 1105.17–1105.43. These questions need not be resolved here.

[18] McLachlan, Shore, and Weiniger, above n. 6, 239–240, noting that international law does not preclude all distinctions between foreigners and nationals in the absence of a specific treaty obligation or customary international law principle.

[19] See, eg, the award in *CMS v Argentina*, in which the tribunal noted that it could not 'hold that arbitrariness and discrimination are present in the context of the crisis noted, and to the extent that some effects become evident they will relate rather to the breach of fair and equitable treatment than to the breach of separate standards under the Treaty'. *CMS Gas Transmission Co v Argentina*, ICSID Case No ARB/01/8, Award, 12 May 2005, para. 295.

[20] Newcombe, Paradell, and Krishan, above n. 5, 16.

[21] Articles 1102(1), 1102(2) North American Free Trade Agreement (NAFTA) (1992); Article 3(1), (2) US Model BIT (2004); Article 3(1), (2) Canadian Model FIPA (2003).

[22] Article 2(1) UK Model BIT (2005), available in McLachlan, Shore, and Weiniger, above n. 6, Appendix 4, 380.

treaty accords only rights post-establishment, its obligation likely extends only to the investment itself, rather than to the investor.

Another area of difference between treaties is the extent of the protection offered, whether pre- or post-establishment. Some treaties offer an open-ended list of the activities to which the standard applies, while others have closed lists. An example of the former is the Energy Charter Treaty, which states that national treatment applies to '[...] investments [...] of Investors of other Contracting Parties, and their related activities including management, maintenance, use, enjoyment or disposal, [...]'.[23]

An example of the latter is the UK Model BIT, which extends national (and MFN) treatment to the '[...] management, maintenance, use, enjoyment, or disposal of [investors'] investments'.[24] Some treaties contain more extensive lists; NAFTA Chapter 11 is an example of a broad, but closed, pre-establishment obligation:

Each Party shall accord to investors of another Party treatment no less favorable than that it accords, in like circumstances, to its own investors with respect to the establishment, acquisition, expansion, management, conduct, operation, and sale or other disposition of investments.[25]

The NAFTA Parties have undertaken the same obligations with respect to investments of investors.[26]

In some treaties the national treatment obligation appears as a stand-alone obligation. In others it is coupled with a most-favoured-nation obligation:

Neither Contracting Party shall in its territory subject investments or returns of nationals or companies of the other Contracting Party to treatment less favourable than that which it accords to investments or returns of its own nationals or companies or to investments or returns of nationals or companies of any third State.[27]

In nearly all cases the treaty makes clear that the investor or investment is entitled to the better of national or MFN treatment.[28]

Yet another treaty formulation juxtaposes discriminatory and arbitrary treatment. The Dutch treaties generally conflate the two.[29] For example, the Bolivia/Netherlands BIT provides:

Each Contracting Party shall ensure fair and equitable treatment to the investments of nationals of the other Contracting Party and shall not impair, by unreasonable or

---

[23] Article 10(7) Energy Charter Treaty (1995).
[24] Article 3(2) UK Model BIT.
[25] Article 1102(1) NAFTA.
[26] Article 1102(2) NAFTA.
[27] Article 3(1) UK Model BIT.
[28] See, eg, Article 1104 NAFTA; Newcombe, Paradell, and Krishan, above n. 5, 41.
[29] Ibid., 15.

discriminatory measures, the operation, management, maintenance, use, enjoyment, or disposal thereof by those nationals.[30]

Most tribunals, and most commentators, have treated 'discriminatory' in that context as precluding nationality-based discrimination.[31] It likely prohibits discrimination on other grounds as well—Dolzer and Stevens suggest that a measure is discriminatory if it results in actual injury to the alien and if it is implemented with the intention of harming the aggrieved alien.[32] Such a conclusion is supported by the fact that many treaties, including the Argentina/United States BIT, contain both obligations to accord national treatment[33] and to refrain from according discriminatory and arbitrary treatment.[34] The principle of effective interpretation suggests that the latter be interpreted so as to be sure that each provision be read to have meaning.[35]

Tribunals considering whether a State has accorded an investment, or an investor, arbitrary and/or discriminatory treatment also have had to grapple with nationality-based discrimination. Much of the focus in those cases is on arbitrariness,[36] but several cases have addressed the discrimination component. The starting point for that analysis has sometimes been the test set forth by the International Court of Justice in *ELSI*, a case in which a chamber of the Court considered whether Italy had violated the Italy/United States Treaty of Friendship,

---

[30] Article 3(1) Bolivia/Netherlands BIT. The BIT's full protection and security provision also contains a national treatment obligation: 'More particularly, each Contracting Party shall accord to such investments full security and protection which in any case shall not be less than that accorded either to investments of its own nationals or to investments of nationals of any third States, whichever is more favourable to the investor.'

[31] See, eg, *Noble Ventures, Inc v Romania*, ICSID Case No. ARB/01/11, Award, 12 October 2005, para. 180; *LG&E Energy Corp v Argentine Republic*, ICSID Case No. ARB/02/1, Decision on Liability, 3 October 2006, para. 146; Newcombe, Paradell, and Krishan, above n. 5, 15, referring to the OECD model treaty, which made clear that nationality-based discrimination is included in the reference to discrimination; see also McLachlan, Shore, and Weiniger, above n. 6, 239–240, noting cases in which the tribunal had considered whether fair and equitable treatment requirements encompassed a non-discrimination obligation.

[32] R. Dolzer and M. Stevens, *Bilateral Investment Treaties* (1995) 61–63; see also A. Maniruzzaman, 'Expropriation of Alien Property and the Principle of Non-Discrimination in International Law of Foreign Investment: An Overview', 8 *Journal of Transnational Law & Policy* (1998) 57, 69–70, describing different types of discrimination.

[33] Article II(1) Argentina/US BIT: 'Each Party shall permit and treat investment, and activities associated therewith, on a basis no less favorable than that accorded in like situations to investment or associated activities of its own nationals or companies [...].'

[34] Ibid., Article II(2)(b): 'Neither Party shall in any way impair by arbitrary or discriminatory measures the management, operation, maintenance, use, enjoyment, acquisition, expansion, or disposal of investments.'

[35] See I. Sinclair, *The Vienna Convention on the Law of Treaties* (2nd edn, 1984) 118–119, noting principle of effective interpretation, but cautioning that it must be read in conjunction with the teleological approach to treaty interpretation; A. McNair, *The Law of Treaties* (1961) 385, quoting *Cayuga Indians Claims* case: 'Nothing is better settled, as a canon of interpretation in all systems of law, than that a clause must be so interpreted as to give it a meaning rather than so as to deprive it of meaning.'

[36] See V. Heiskanen, 'Arbitrary and Unreasonable Measures', at Chapter 5 below.

Commerce and Navigation.[37] Those criteria are: (i) intentional treatment, (ii) in favour of a national, (iii) against a foreign investor, (iv) that is not taken under similar circumstances against another national.[38] The relevant portions of these cases are also addressed below.[39]

Most parties to investment treaties have taken exceptions or reservations from their national treatment obligations. Many treaties contain general exceptions for measures taken for diverse reasons, such as protecting public health, public morality, and national security.[40] In some instances, the exceptions are certain business or economic sectors.[41] For example, all three NAFTA countries have taken exceptions with respect to air transportation and social services.[42] Canada has famously taken an exception to protect its cultural industries.[43] Some treaties have exceptions for measures seeking to enhance the status of historically disadvantaged minorities. Thus, under the NAFTA (and its other investment treaties) the United States '[...] reserves the right to adopt or maintain any measure according rights or preferences to socially or economically disadvantaged minorities [...]'.[44] A few treaties have exceptions to permit States to address 'development considerations'.[45]

Reservations and exceptions come in different temporal guises. Some, particularly those regarding economic or business sectors, are prospective, while others protect existing laws, but provide that any change in the law must not result in less favourable treatment for foreign investors.[46] This provision essentially acts as a ratchet; while countries protect their ability to discriminate in accordance with their current regulatory structure, they undertake to ensure that any change is more favourable for foreign investors.

For federal States, a difficult matter will sometimes be the status of provincial or local government measures. As a matter of customary international law, federal governments are responsible for the acts of their constituent States. Thus,

---

[37] *Elettronica Sicula SpA (ELSI) (US v Italy)*, 20 July 1989, 1989 *ICJ Rep.* 15, 56, 61–62.
[38] *LG&E v Argentine Republic*, above n. 31, para. 146.
[39] Discriminatory treatment is also a feature of illegal expropriation cases. It is addressed in this volume in A. Reinisch, 'Legality of Expropriation', at Chapter 9 below; see also Maniruzzaman, above n. 32.
[40] UNCTAD, above n. 3, 44–45.
[41] Ibid., 45–46.
[42] See respectively NAFTA, Annex I, at I-C-10, I-M-55, I-U-13; NAFTA, Annex II, at II-C-9, II-M-11, II-U-5.
[43] Article 2106 NAFTA; NAFTA, Annex 2106. See generally Kinnear, Bjorklund, and Hannaford, above n. 11, Article 1108 commentary; O.R. Goodenough, 'Defending the Imaginary to the Death? Free Trade, National Identity, and Canada's Cultural Preoccupation', 15 *Arizona Journal of International & Comparative Law* (1998) 203.
[44] NAFTA, Annex II-U-6.
[45] UNCTAD, above n. 3, 47–50.
[46] See, eg, D. Price, 'An Overview of the NAFTA Investment Chapter: Substantive Rules and Investor-State Dispute Settlement', 27 *International Lawyer* (1993) 727, 731; Kinnear, Bjorklund, and Hannaford, above n. 11, 1108.13.

absent an exception or reservation, State or local government measures could give rise to national treatment violations in the event an investment treaty contained a national treatment obligation. Because local government entities will sometimes attempt to give preferential treatment to local industries, those obligations can be problematic for the federal government. Therefore, some investment treaties have special provisions pertaining to State and local governments both with respect to exceptions and reservations and with respect to the national treatment obligation itself.[47] The import of these provisions has not always been clear, as discussed more fully below.

The need to interpret national treatment obligations in investment agreements has arisen relatively recently with the rapid rise in investor-State dispute settlements since the mid-1990s. Yet, national treatment has long been an issue in GATT practice with respect to trade in goods. In that context the issue has been whether the goods that are discriminated against are 'like products' to the goods allegedly receiving more favourable treatment.[48] National treatment is also an obligation in the General Agreement on Trade in Services (GATS), though as yet GATS cases are few in number.[49] Thus, the question arises to what extent GATT 'like products' analyses provide fruitful analogies for 'like circumstances', or 'like situations', analyses. In practice, especially as investment treaties themselves generate case law, the answer seems to be that GATT jurisprudence will be at best a subsidiary source of guidance for tribunals. The general approach to GATT/WTO case law is well captured by the *Methanex* tribunal's approach, which was that it '[...] would be open to persuasion based on legal reasoning developed in GATT and WTO jurisprudence, if relevant, [...]'[50] but that it considered GATT like-products analysis inappropriate guidance in the context of an investment treaty's 'like circumstances' analysis.[51] Thus, investor-State tribunals may consult GATT/WTO practice in some instances, but it is unlikely to be the primary source of guidance for them. This is especially true as they develop an investment-specific approach in the increasing number of investment treaty cases.[52]

---

[47] See, eg, Article 1108 NAFTA, excluding from national treatment obligations existing non-conforming federal government measures set out in a Schedule to Annex I; existing state or provincial government measures listed within two years of NAFTA's entry into force; and existing local government measures. As the deadline for the state and provincial governments to list their existing non-conforming measures became imminent, the Parties agreed simply to a short general reservation excluding all existing State or provincial government measures. NAFTA Trilateral Agreement on Listing State and Provincial Reservations; Kinnear, Bjorklund, and Hannaford, above n. 11, 1108.13.

[48] See, eg, WTO Appellate Body Report, *European Communities—Measures Affecting Asbestos and Asbestos-Containing Products*, WT/DS135/AB/R (2001), para. 99.

[49] Kinnear, Bjorklund, and Hannaford, above n. 11, 1102.16.

[50] *Methanex Corp v United States of America* (NAFTA), Award, 3 August 2005, Part II, Ch. B, para. 6.

[51] Ibid.

[52] Many have recently written on the use of investment arbitration decisions as a kind of *de facto* precedent. See, eg, C. Schreuer, 'Diversity and Harmonization of Treaty Interpretation in Investment Arbitration', 3 *Transnational Dispute Management* (2006); J. Commission, 'Precedent

C. Investment Case Law

The cases decided by arbitral tribunals in the last several years are the best source for studying the application of the national treatment obligation in practice. They illustrate the key legal issues in nearly every national treatment case, such as the identification of the appropriate comparator and an analysis of the treatment allegedly accorded. In addition, some cases address the question of best in-province versus best out-of-province treatment, while others explain their approach to procedural questions, such as the burden of proof.

NAFTA Chapter 11 has been the most fertile source of decisions regarding national treatment obligations. All but two NAFTA Chapter 11 cases that have proceeded to arbitration have contained allegations of national treatment violations.[53] Despite these initial allegations, national treatment has not necessarily played a leading role in every one of the awards rendered. In some cases the focus shifts during the case's development to other grounds.[54] Notwithstanding this qualification, however, NAFTA Chapter 11 awards have played a leading role in developing the national treatment jurisprudence.

Tribunals have not been uniform in their approach to national treatment cases, yet there is a discernible general practice isolating essential elements in the cases. An essential step in a national treatment case involves identifying the appropriate domestic comparator against which to measure the treatment accorded the allegedly injured investment (or investor). A second step requires identification of treatment that was less favourable than that given the domestic comparator. Finally, tribunals have considered whether the host government had legitimate reasons that justified the difference in treatment.[55]

The analysis is not always undertaken in separate steps or in the order suggested above. Indeed, tribunals and commentators have recognized that the type of treatment at issue is not necessarily severable from the like circumstances inquiry.[56] For example, a State might apply different pollution control regimes

---

in Investment Treaty Arbitration: A Citation Analysis of a Developing Jurisprudence', 24 *Journal of International Arbitration* (2007) 129; A. Bjorklund, 'Investment Treaty Arbitral Decisions as Jurisprudence Constante', in C. Picker, I. Bunn, and D. Arner (eds), *International Economic Law: The State and Future of the Discipline* (2008).

[53] Kinnear, Bjorklund, and Hannaford, above n. 11, 1102.20.

[54] Ibid., noting that in *Azinian v Mexico*, *Mondev v United States*, and *Metalclad v Mexico* the national treatment allegations played virtually no role in the conduct of the case.

[55] Newcombe, Paradell, and Krishan, above n. 5, 19; McLachlan, Shore, and Weiniger, above n. 6, 253–254.

[56] *United Parcel Service of America Inc v Canada* (NAFTA), Separate Statement of Dean Cass, 24 May 2007, paras 49–50. Dean Cass noted the inappropriateness of segregating completely the determination of whether circumstances are the same, and whether there is less favorable treatment. He was concerned that one might determine that two entities are not in like circumstances *because of* the different treatment they receive, rather than because there were legitimate reasons for structuring the differential treatment.

to high pollution areas of the country such that different companies in the same economic sector could be affected differently. In such a situation the treatment accorded—a stricter regulatory regime—might affect the like circumstances determination such that only factories in the affected areas are deemed to be in like circumstances with respect to the implementation of pollution control measures.

Like Circumstances

Identification of the appropriate comparator is probably the most important part of the national treatment analysis, as the outcome in most cases hinges on whether the more favourable treatment was accorded to an entity in like circumstances.[57] If the allegedly favoured entity is not in like circumstances, the inquiry ends. While some treaties do not specify the basis for comparison, tribunals to date have declined to address any arguments that the absence of any reference to such a comparator suggests a less rigorous approach to a national treatment claim and have assumed that the inquiry requires that the comparator be similarly situated.[58] In some cases there will be only one comparator, but that is sufficient to establish a violation if that entity receives more favourable treatment.

In rare circumstances there may be no actual comparator. In cases of *de facto* national treatment violations, such a lack will nearly always be fatal. A claimant must demonstrate that an ostensibly neutral measure has discriminatory effect in order to prevail in its national treatment claim, and it is hard to show discriminatory effect if no other entity receives any treatment whatsoever. In the case of a *de jure* measure, however, one need not show that a domestic entity has actually received any treatment if such is inherent in the terms of the measure. For example, the existence of an investment incentive available only to domestic-owned entities could establish a national treatment violation, even if no domestic entities had availed themselves of the opportunity.[59]

The manner in which tribunals have approached identifying the comparator has varied. It is fair to say that the approach is flexible, and varies according to the circumstances of the investment or investor and according to the treatment at issue. One formulation was borrowed by the *S.D. Myers v Canada* tribunal from

---

[57] Kinnear, Bjorklund, and Hannaford, above n. 11, 22.1102; McLachlan, Shore, and Weiniger, above n. 6, 251–254, 263. Some treaties refer to those 'similarly situated' or 'in like situations'. Newcombe, Paradell, and Krishan, above n. 5, 17. It is unlikely that any difference in outcome hinges on the use of 'same' or 'like' or 'similar'. Ibid., 18 and note 98.
[58] See, eg, *Occidental Exploration and Production Company v Ecuador*, LCIA Case No UN 3467, Final Award, 1 July 2004, para. 170; *Nykomb Synergetics Technology Holding AB v Latvia* (Energy Charter Treaty), Award, 16 December 2003, 34; *Consortium RFCC v Morocco*, ICSID Case No. ARB/00/6, Award, 22 December 2003, para. 53.
[59] See, eg, Newcombe, Paradell, and Krishan, above n. 5, 35, discussing possible breach if preferential tax treatment is given only to qualified domestic investments.

WTO practice: 'The accordion of "likeness" stretches and squeezes in different places as different provisions of the WTO Agreement are applied'.[60]

According to the *Pope & Talbot v Canada* tribunal:

[…] [b]y their very nature, 'circumstances' are context dependent and have no unalterable meaning across the spectrum of fact situations […] the concept of 'like' can have a range of meanings, from 'similar' all the way to 'identical'.[61]

One subtlety that can help guide the like-circumstances analysis involves considering whether the appropriate comparison is between the like-circumstanced investments (or investors), or the like-circumstanced treatment. This is in fact what many tribunals are doing when determining the appropriate comparators. It is also consistent with the placement of the modifier in many treaties. The US Model BIT, for example, provides: 'Each Party shall accord to investors of the other Party treatment no less favorable than that it accords, *in like circumstances*, to its own investors […]'.[62]

The placement of the phrase 'in like circumstances' suggests modification of 'treatment', rather than 'investor'. In practice, given the flexibility with which tribunals have approached the matter, this distinction might not matter. But it is useful to remember that the comparison can and should take into account the regulatory context in addition to the relationship between the investments (or investors).

In a related vein, the existence of a competitive relationship between the comparator and the claimant is not essential to a finding of like circumstances, but it helps. The notion of competition is in part a legacy of GATT/WTO jurisprudence. Products are 'like' if they compete with each other, even if they are not identical. This distinction is necessary in order to avoid protectionist measures designed to limit competition from products that are substitutable for the local product. In an investment case the protection a measure apparently gives a competing entity may give rise to an inference of nationality-based preference. Competitiveness was a feature of the finding in *S.D. Myers v Canada*; lack of competitiveness characterized the decision in *Occidental Petroleum v Ecuador*.

In *S.D. Myers v Canada*, the issue was whether Canada's closing of the border to the export of polychlorinated biphenyls (PCB) waste violated Canada's obligations by unduly affecting S.D. Myers, a US company that wished to compete in Canada for contracts to process PCB waste at its Ohio remediation facility. To determine whether S.D. Myers was in like circumstances with Canadian PCB remediation companies, the tribunal determined that generally comparisons should be made

---

[60] *S.D. Myers Inc v Canada* (NAFTA), Partial Award, 13 November 2000, para. 244, citing *Japan—Alcoholic Beverages*, WT/DS38/AB/R, paras 8.5 and 9; *Attorney General of Canada v Myers*, 2004 FC 38, 13 January 2004, at 32 (Trial Division).

[61] *Pope & Talbot Inc v Canada* (NAFTA), Award on the Merits of Phase 2, 10 April 2001, para. 75.

[62] Article 3(1) US Model BIT (2004) (emphasis added).

between firms operating in the same sector (which included both business and economic sectors), and that general policy considerations, such as environmental concerns, should also play a role in the analysis.[63] The tribunal considered not only environmental concerns justifying treating companies differently to protect the public interest, but also obligations to avoid trade distortions not justified by environmental concerns.[64] It concluded that S.D. Myers and its Canadian investment were in like circumstances with the Canadian PCB waste-disposal industry, and pointed to the importance of their competitive relationship:

> It was precisely because SDMI [S.D. Myers International, the Canadian corporation deemed to be an investment] was in a position to take business away from its Canadian competitors that [they] lobbied the Minister of the Environment to ban exports when the US authorities opened the border.[65]

Occidental Exploration and Production Co v Ecuador provides the best example of a tribunal finding two entities to be in like circumstances notwithstanding the lack of any competitive relationship between them. Ecuador permitted certain exporters, including those dealing in flowers, mining, and seafood products, to claim the refund of VAT on all exports, but did not permit Occidental to claim a VAT refund on exports of oil. Occidental claimed a violation of the national treatment obligation in the Ecuador/United States BIT. Ecuador argued that the VAT refund was not available to any exporters of oil, including Petroecuador, the State-owned oil company, and that there was thus no evidence of any attempt to discriminate against foreign companies.

The tribunal was not persuaded by Ecuador's arguments. It held that the purpose of the national treatment obligation is to protect foreign investors, and that it would be inappropriate to address '[...] exclusively the sector in which that particular activity is undertaken'.[66] Further, the tribunal concluded that exporters should not be placed at a disadvantage in foreign markets because they had to pay more taxes in the country of origin.[67]

The *Occidental* tribunal's conclusion was unusual. While the like circumstances determination is indeed flexible and must depend on the circumstances of any particular case, the lack of any competitive relationship between the comparators would ordinarily be a difficult hurdle to overcome with respect to the like-circumstances determination. On the other hand, to the extent the tribunal's decision reflected an assessment that VAT refunds were denied to the oil exploration sector because it was dominated by foreign competitors, the decision is less surprising.[68]

[63] *S.D. Myers v Canada*, above n. 60, para. 250.
[64] Ibid., paras 247, 250.
[65] Ibid., para. 251.
[66] *Occidental v Ecuador*, above n. 58, para. 60.
[67] Ibid., para. 175.
[68] Ecuador moved to set aside the award, but its petition was denied. Because the award was subject to challenge on only limited grounds, the English courts did not address the proper application

As noted above, the issue of like circumstances is inter-related with that of the treatment alleged to cause injury. Thus, the policy considerations underlying the treatment have a significant effect on the outcome. In *Pope & Talbot v Canada*, another NAFTA Chapter 11 case, Pope & Talbot, a US investor that owned three lumber mills in British Columbia, challenged Canada's implementation of the US/Canada Softwood Lumber Agreement, one of the many treaties over the years that have temporarily suspended the long-running trade dispute between the neighbouring countries over exports of Canadian softwood lumber to the United States. Under the Softwood Lumber Agreement, Canada agreed to limit the exports of softwood lumber from the four 'covered' provinces—Alberta, British Columbia, Quebec, and Ontario—that had historically been the largest exporters of softwood lumber to the United States. In return the United States would not institute any unfair trade remedies cases against Canadian softwood lumber exporters for the five years the Agreement remained in effect.

Under the Agreement up to 14.7 billion board feet of lumber could be exported free of charge; exports between 14.7 and 15.35 billion board feet would be charged a duty at the rate of US$50 per board foot; and exports in excess of 15.35 billion board feet would be charged a duty at the rate of US$100 per board foot.[69] Lumber exports from the non-covered provinces were not limited. In each of the covered provinces Canada allocated a quota among Canadian lumber producers based on their historic levels of export to the United States.

Pope & Talbot did not challenge the Softwood Lumber Agreement itself, but only the manner in which Canada implemented it. It claimed a violation of Article 1102, NAFTA's national treatment provision, because lumber producers in the non-covered provinces were not subject to the quota and were thus accorded more favourable treatment than lumber producers in the covered provinces. Pope & Talbot also claimed that it was treated less favourably than certain other producers in the covered provinces, including producers in Quebec and in British Columbia.

Thus, the first question for the *Pope & Talbot* tribunal was whether Pope & Talbot was in like circumstances with lumber producers in the non-covered provinces. The *Pope & Talbot* tribunal approached this question slightly differently from some other tribunals. In effect, the *Pope & Talbot* tribunal conflated the question of like circumstances and whether the government offered a rationale for the difference in treatment. It concluded that the first order of business was to determine whether the foreign investor was in like circumstances with

---

of the non-discrimination principle. See *Occidental Exploration Production Co. v Republic of Ecuador* [2005] EWCA Civ. 1116, 9 September 2005; *Republic of Ecuador v Occidental Exploration & Production Co* [2006] EWHC 345 (Comm), 2 March 2006; *Republic of Ecuador v Occidental Exploration & Production Co* [2007] EWCA Civ. 656, 4 July 2007. See generally S.D. Franck, 'International Decision: Occidental Exploration & Production Co. v. Republic of Ecuador', 99 *American Journal of International Law* (2005) 675, 679–680.

[69] *Pope & Talbot v Canada*, above n. 61, para. 18.

the allegedly more favourably treated domestic investor, which required merely that the two entities operating in the same economic sector received differential treatment.[70] If the foreign investor could make such a showing, the burden then shifted to the respondent to show that some legitimate government objective justified the differential treatment and thereby demonstrate that the two were not really in like circumstances: '[...] once a difference in treatment between a domestic and a foreign-owned investment is discerned, the question becomes, are they in like circumstances?'[71]

The *Pope & Talbot* tribunal determined that Pope & Talbot's investments in British Columbia were not in like circumstances with any of the allegedly more favourably treated investments. It came to this conclusion because of the policy reasons Canada was able to offer to explain the differences in treatment. First, the tribunal concluded that the manner in which Canada implemented the Softwood Lumber Agreement—limiting exports only from the four covered provinces—was rational given the historical background of the case. The United States had never imposed duties on producers in the non-covered provinces. Thus, limiting exports from only the covered provinces was '[...] reasonably related to the rational policy of removing the threat of CVD [countervailing duty] actions'.[72] Secondly, the tribunal concluded that the allegedly more favourable treatment given to producers in Quebec than to producers in British Columbia was also justified. The federal government of Canada set aside some quota to allocate to new entrants into the lumber industry, but most of those new entrants were in Quebec. The tribunal determined that British Columbian producers were not in like circumstances with Quebecois new entrants; in any event, Pope & Talbot was not a new entrant.[73] Finally, within British Columbia interior producers of lumber were required to pay an extra fee to settle a dispute about British Columbian stumpage fees (the amount British Columbia charges producers for the privilege of cutting timber on Crown land). Again, the *Pope & Talbot* tribunal determined that Pope & Talbot was not in like circumstances with the more favourably treated coastal producers.[74]

Some tribunals have been faced with cases in which the question is discriminatory effect, but there are few comparators against which to compare the treatment accorded. *Feldman v Mexico* involved a challenge to a Mexican tax rebate law by the investor in a Mexican enterprise, CEMSA, that resold and exported cigarettes from Mexico. Feldman claimed that Mexican laws, though neutral on their face, discriminated against his company because the rebates were available only to exporters who were also producers of cigarettes, rather than to resellers of cigarettes. He also claimed that, notwithstanding the law, in practice Mexican

[70] Ibid., para. 78. [71] Ibid., para. 79.
[72] Ibid., para. 87. [73] Ibid., para. 93.
[74] Ibid., para. 103.

resellers/exporters of cigarettes were able to claim rebates. There were very few potential entities in like circumstances.

The *Feldman* tribunal determined that CEMSA was not in like circumstances with the producers/exporters. It noted that Mexico had rational bases for treating producers differently from resellers, including '[...] better control over tax revenues, discourag[ing] smuggling, protect[ing] intellectual property rights, and prohibit[ing] gray market sales'.[75] The decision does not clarify whether the tribunal was determining that CEMSA was not in like circumstances with the producer/exporters, or whether, notwithstanding the like circumstances, Mexico had good reason for treating the two differently.[76]

The *Feldman* tribunal did hold that CEMSA was in like circumstances with the one Mexican reseller/exporter which the tribunal identified based on the rather sparse evidence presented to it, and that it was given less favourable treatment.[77] The dissenting arbitrator argued that a tribunal could not find *de facto* discrimination based on facts involving a single domestic investor, but only if there were '[...] composite acts involving a set of conducts of a State evincing a systemic practice'.[78] In support he cited the International Law Commission's State Responsibility Article on composite acts.[79]

While it may perhaps be unusual to have a situation in which there is a single domestic entity that allegedly received the more favourable treatment, nothing in treaty language or practice suggests that only systemic discrimination can qualify as a violation of a State's national treatment obligation. The crux of ILC State Responsibility Article 15 is that certain breaches consist of composite acts, and that such a breach can extend over an extended time period; it is not that only composite acts can be a breach of a State's obligations.[80]

Though it is known primarily as a denial of justice case, *The Loewen Group Inc. v United States* involved a national treatment claim as well. The claimants (The Loewen Group Inc and its US subsidiary, collectively 'Loewen') challenged the acts of the Mississippi judiciary as violations of NAFTA's national treatment Article 1102, on the grounds that they were permeated with bias because of Loewen's Canadian origin. The *Loewen* tribunal held that it could not address the 1102 claim because there was no appropriate comparator; in the circumstances of a trial, the comparator could not be the other litigant, and there were no other comparators in like circumstances.[81] The *Loewen* tribunal thus seemed to suggest

---

[75] *Feldman v United Mexican States*, ICSID Case No ARB(AF)/99/1, Award, 16 December 2002, para. 170.
[76] Ibid.
[77] Ibid., paras 177–180.
[78] *Feldman v United Mexican States*, ICSID Case No ARB(AF)/99/1, Dissenting Opinion of Arbitrator Covarrubias Bravo, 3 December 2002, para. 15.
[79] Ibid.
[80] J. Crawford, *The International Law Commission's Articles on State Responsibility: Introduction, Text and Commentaries* (2002) 141–144.
[81] *The Loewen Group Inc. & Raymond L. Loewen v United States*, ICSID Case No. ARB(AF)/98/3, Award, 26 June 2003, para. 149.

that there had to be a comparator to sustain a national treatment claim, even where such a claim was arguably based on *de jure* discriminatory treatment. One should probably not read too much into the *Loewen* tribunal's decision on the point. The case involved the intersection of national treatment and the international minimum standard in the context of a denial of justice claim, and the parties concentrated their efforts on that aspect of the case. Certainly, the mere fact that the domestic party wins and the foreign party loses should not be a differential effect sufficient to sustain a national treatment claim. Nonetheless, other differences in treatment accorded the litigants during a trial could, if sufficiently egregious and evidently based on nationality-based discrimination, form the basis for a national treatment violation.[82]

In several cases the initial like-circumstances analysis was outcome-determinative. *GAMI v Mexico* involved a straightforward programme of nationalization of certain sugar mills by the Government of Mexico. Only some mills were expropriated under the programme, and the question was whether GAMI's Mexican subsidiary, GAM, which owned five mills, all of which were expropriated, was in like circumstances with owners of non-expropriated mills. Although GAMI presented evidence that suggested one domestic-owned mill with very similar characteristics to GAM's mills was not expropriated, the tribunal concluded that the circumstances were not so alike as to make the difference in treatment wrong.[83] Part of the tribunal's analysis was that GAM's mills fell within the category of insolvent sugar mills that Mexico had determined to nationalize in the public interest. While Mexico's drawing of the line between mills to expropriate and not to expropriate might have been clumsy, there was no evidence that it was discriminatory.[84]

ADF Corporation v United States involved the application of the Buy America Act, a statute that requires contractors using funds provided by the US government to purchase US-origin products. On its face the statute appears discriminatory; an initial question for the tribunal was whether the purchase of steel by the State of Virginia for use in a highway construction project was covered by the exceptions in Article 1108 (the tribunal held that it was).[85] The tribunal also considered whether the application of the law resulted in a violation of the national treatment provision. It first had to identify the appropriate comparators.

---

[82] A domestic law analogy is the case of race-based peremptory challenges to potential jurors, which are prohibited in the United States. *Batson v Kentucky*, 476 US (1986) 79. It is difficult, but not impossible, to demonstrate that an attorney's pattern of striking jurors is based on their race. See, eg, S. Benson, 'Reviving the Disparate Impact Doctrine to Combat Unconscious Discrimination', 31 *Thurgood Marshall Law Review* (2005) 43, 51 and note 55; A. Raphael, 'Discriminatory Jury Selection: Lower Court Implementation of Batson v. Kentucky', 25 *Willamette Law Review* (1989) 293, 298–299 and note 36.

[83] *GAMI Investments Inc v Mexico* (NAFTA), Final Award, 15 November 2004, para. 113.

[84] Ibid., para. 114.

[85] *ADF Group Inc v United States*, ICSID Case No ARB(AF)/00/1, Award, 9 January 2003, paras 162–168.

ADF, a Canadian-owned company, proposed to purchase steel manufactured in the United States, transport it to Canada for fabrication in ADF's factory there, and then convey it to the contractor. The amount of processing done to the steel in Canada would make it 'Canadian' for purposes of the Buy America Act and ineligible for purchase. The tribunal concluded that the appropriate comparison was between the investment of the investor, which it identified as its steel in the United States, and the investments of US investors, which it defined as US-origin steel.[86] Given that either investment, if subject to sufficient fabrication in Canada, would lose its US-origin designation, the tribunal concluded for the investments in like circumstances there was no difference in treatment.[87] The tribunal thus rejected ADF's argument that the appropriate comparison be made between Canadian steel fabricators, whose facilities would tend to be in Canada, and US steel fabricators, whose facilities would tend to be in the United States.[88]

Methanex Corp v United States involved the challenge by a Canadian producer of methanol to California's ban on methyl tertiary-butyl ether (MTBE), a gasoline additive for which methanol is a feedstock. MTBE is an oxygenate added to gasoline to help it burn more cleanly; high-pollution areas in the United States are required to sell only oxygenated gasoline in order to improve air quality. The only effective competitor of MTBE is ethanol, because other oxygenates are not yet commercially viable. Methanex argued, inter alia, that California banned MTBE in order to assist the US-dominated ethanol industry. In order to prevail on its national treatment claim, Methanex had to show that it was in like circumstances with producers of ethanol, who received the more favourable treatment, rather than with producers of methanol, or producers of MTBE. For the *Methanex* tribunal, this was a difficult hurdle to overcome because

[...] it would be as perverse to ignore identical comparators if they were available and to use comparators that were less 'like', as it would be perverse to refuse to find and to apply less 'like' comparators when no identical comparators existed.[89]

Thus, because Methanex was in like circumstances with other producers of methanol, all of whom were affected in the same manner by the ban on MTBE, it could not prevail on its national treatment claim.[90]

One of the interesting contributions made by the *Methanex* tribunal was its scepticism about the use of GATT/WTO jurisprudence about 'like products' to

---

[86] Ibid., para. 155.
[87] Ibid., para. 156.
[88] This decision has been criticized. 'The tribunal appeared to ignore the de facto results of the decision to refuse [ADF's need] to use steel fabricated in its Canadian facility [...] Given that the business model of ADF's investment was naturally predicated on the use of its parent company's facilities when necessary, it seems absurd to arrive at this conclusion.' T. Weiler, 'Prohibitions Against Discrimination in NAFTA Chapter 11', in T. Weiler (ed.), *NAFTA Investment Law and Arbitration: Past Issues, Current Practice, Future Prospects* (2004) 27, 36.
[89] *Methanex v United States of America*, above n. 50, Part IV, Ch. B, para. 17.
[90] Ibid., para. 28.

illuminate a like-circumstances analysis. For the *Methanex* tribunal, the NAFTA negotiators were '[...] fluent in GATT law and incorporated, in very precise ways, the term "like goods" and the GATT provisions relating to it when they wished to do so'.[91]

The *Methanex* tribunal thus rejected the claim that ethanol and methanol (or MTBE) were like products because they competed in the gasoline oxygenate market, and rejected any suggestion that Article 1102 of NAFTA, the national treatment provision be read to contain the words '[...] any like, directly competitive or substitutable goods'.[92]

United Parcel Service Inc v Canada is the most recent NAFTA case to address national treatment. At issue was whether Canada accorded more favourable treatment to Canada Post in the non-monopoly postal services market than it accorded to the US company United Parcel Service (UPS) or its Canadian subsidiary UPS Canada. UPS also alleged that Canada Post was treated more favourably because it had better access to Canada Post's monopoly network. Three programmes were primarily at issue: the Courier Low Value Shipment Program, the Customs international mail processing system, and the Postal Imports Agreement. Courier shipments by companies such as UPS and UPS Canada are processed under the Courier Low Value Shipment Program, whereas regular mail shipments are processed under the Customs international mail processing system. Courier companies pay a fee to Customs Canada for processing, whereas Canada Post pays no such fee. In addition, under the Postal Imports Agreement, Canada Post performs certain functions that would ordinarily be performed by Customs Canada, including the collection of duties, for which Customs Canada pays it a fee.

The majority of the *UPS* tribunal found that UPS had failed to establish that either UPS or UPS Canada was in like circumstances with Canada Post. It distinguished between the importation of goods by post and the importation of goods by courier, and held that the different characteristics of each required different customs treatment.[93] Such characteristics included: (1) couriers' provision of detailed advance information on shipments to permit Customs to perform risk assessments and other checks; (2) the self-assessment permitted via the Courier Low Value Shipment Program as opposed to officer-made determinations in the postal process; (3) the greater security of courier shipments because they are made through secure shipping routes and trade chain controls; (4) the need for expedited clearance by couriers to meet their time-sensitive delivery standards; (5) the existence of contractual relationships between couriers and their clients; and (6) the different roles, such as warehousing and brokerage, performed by couriers.[94] Thus, UPS's claim failed.

---

[91] Ibid., Part IV, Ch. B, para. 30.
[92] Ibid., para. 37.
[93] *United Parcel Service of America, Inc v Canada* (NAFTA), Award, 24 May 2007, para. 99.
[94] Ibid., para. 102.

C. Investment Case Law

The dissenting arbitrator disagreed with this determination. He found that the appropriate comparison was between the investor and the entity with which it was in a competitive relationship with respect to the matters at issue.[95] Once the investor had established such a relationship, the burden would shift to the respondent to demonstrate why the two competing enterprises were not in like circumstances.[96] The dissenting arbitrator thus focused on two primary complaints by UPS: one was that Canada Customs pays handling fees to Canada Post for services that UPS must perform without compensation, and the second was that Canada Customs does not levy the same fines against Canada Post for failure to comply with Customs regulations as it does against UPS, nor does it collect the same duties and taxes from Canada Post. He concluded that UPS was indeed in like circumstances with Canada Post and was accorded different treatment, and that Canada had not discharged its burden of showing that the difference in treatment was justified.[97] In fact, he suggested that the different characteristics advanced by Canada to explain why mail services were different from courier services did not justify less favourable treatment of the latter; on the contrary, the differences suggested that even providing equal treatment to the courier services would not be enough to equalize the effect of the differences in treatment, although he stopped short of asserting that the national treatment obligation in Article 1102 would actually require such action.[98] He suggested in particular that express mail services were very similar to courier services, and that appropriate lines might be drawn between regular post and express mail/courier services.[99]

The *UPS* tribunal also had to address the Publications Assistance Program (PAP)—Canada's programme of subsidizing postal rates for eligible Canadian publications '[...] to connect Canadians to each other through the provision of accessible Canadian cultural products' and to 'sustain and develop the Canadian publishing industry'.[100]

These subsidies are available only to Canada Post. The majority found first that the PAP was covered by the cultural industries exception to NAFTA.[101] It went on to consider, however, whether UPS would have been in like circumstances with Canada Post had it gone on to consider the merits of the case, and concluded it was not. Only Canada Post had the capacity to deliver to every postal address in Canada. Given this ability, the tribunal found that Canada Post was not in like circumstances with UPS, which had somewhat more limited delivery capabilities.[102] Given the objectives of the PAP,

---

[95] *UPS v Canada*, above n. 56, para. 17.
[96] Ibid., paras 23–26.
[97] Ibid., paras 33, 39.
[98] Ibid., paras 47–48.
[99] Ibid., paras 43–45.
[100] *UPS v Canada*, above n. 93, para. 146.
[101] Ibid., para. 137.
[102] Ibid., paras 173–174.

Canada was justified in limiting the availability of the subsidy to Canada Post.[103]

Again the dissenting arbitrator took issue with this conclusion. He concluded that both UPS and Canada Post deliver materials of the sort for which delivery payments are made under the PAP, both do so as a routine part of their business, and both make money for so doing.[104] Given this *prima facie* showing that the two were in like circumstances, the burden shifted to Canada to explain the difference in treatment. While he would have found Canada's reasoning persuasive had it been the only consideration, he was persuaded by UPS's argument that Canada's justification that only Canada Post could deliver to all addresses was merely a post-hoc rationalization designed to protect the programme from attack during dispute resolution proceedings.[105]

Depending on the analytical approach of the tribunal, the like-circumstances determination is a fact-specific inquiry that often dictates the outcome of the case. An entity not like the allegedly more favourably treated entity can sustain no claim. Identifying the entity in like circumstances requires a flexible analysis that takes into account the type of treatment accorded. In most cases the differently treated entities will have a competitive relationship, and the measure in question will give the domestic entity some kind of competitive advantage. Yet the existence of a competitive relationship is not necessary if it appears the State is taking advantage of sectoral dominance by foreign entities to impose a burden on them. Moreover, a competitive relationship is not sufficient if similarly situated domestic entities bear the same burden placed on the allegedly less-favourably-treated foreign entity.

Less Favourable Treatment

In addition to identifying the appropriate comparator, a claimant alleging a national treatment obligation must demonstrate that the allegedly violative treatment is less favourable than that accorded to the domestic comparator. In most instances this will not be difficult as the alleged difference in treatment will be relatively clear. Again, it is important to note the interplay of this aspect of the obligation with the like-circumstances determination; determining that the investor is not in like circumstances with the more favourably treated entity will negate any claim, notwithstanding a clear difference in treatment. Thus, in *Methanex* the conclusion that Methanex was not in like circumstances with the

---

[103] Given its conclusion with respect to the cultural industries exception, the majority did not consider whether the programme also fell within the purview of the subsidies exception. The dissenting arbitrator concluded that it did not.
[104] *UPS v Canada*, above n. 56, para. 94.
[105] Ibid., paras 124–125.

more favourably treated producers of ethanol eliminated any possible national treatment violation.

National treatment obligations preclude *de jure* or *de facto* discrimination on the basis of nationality. Some claimants have argued that any treatment that differentially affects a foreign investor, even if the difference is not attributable to considerations of nationality, can be sufficient to sustain a national treatment claim. The effect of this argument is to import the whole of the discrimination element in the 'arbitrary or discriminatory' treatment standard into the national treatment obligation. It has not generally been successful. First, it is inconsistent with the understanding that most have formed of the national treatment obligation over the years. Secondly, such an interpretation is also inconsistent with the existence in most treaties of non-contingent obligations. Unreasonable treatment accorded a foreign-owned investment is likely a violation of the fair and equitable treatment standard; there is no need to import such an obligation into the national treatment obligation, and doing so would render one of the two provisions redundant.

One of the strongest statements of the nationality-based discrimination approach can be found in the *GAMI* decision. The *GAMI* tribunal disposed of any suggestion that mere differential treatment could result in a successful national treatment claim. There was no question in *GAMI* that some sugar mills had not been expropriated, but that the US investor's mills had been. They thus received less favourable treatment than had some Mexican-owned mills. According to the tribunal, however,

[...] [i]t is not conceivable that a Mexican corporation becomes entitled to the anti-discrimination protections of international law by virtue of the sole fact that a foreigner buys a share of it.[106]

Prevailing on a nationality-based discrimination claim does not require actual proof of protectionist intent. As the tribunal in *S.D. Myers* said, 'Intent is important, but protectionist intent is not necessarily decisive on its own'.[107] There must also be some negative impact on the claimant.[108] One reason not to impose an intent requirement is the difficulty of demonstrating that a government entity, which might comprise many different actors with different motivations, actually had an 'intent' to discriminate. The *Feldman* tribunal said that requiring proof of intent would effectively limit a national treatment claim to *de jure* violations, and would severely limit the effectiveness of the obligation.[109]

The majority of the case law accords with the suggestion that the less favourable treatment must have been predicated on nationality considerations. For the

---

[106] *GAMI v Mexico*, above n. 83, para. 115.
[107] *S.D. Myers v Canada*, above n. 60, para. 254.
[108] Ibid.
[109] *Feldman v United Mexican States*, above n. 75, para. 183.

S.D. Myers tribunal, in assessing the compliance of a measure with a national treatment norm, the appropriate factors to be taken into account are:

[...] whether the practical effect of the measure is to create a disproportionate benefit for nationals over non-nationals; whether the measure, on its face, appears to favour its nationals over non-nationals who are protected by the relevant treaty.[110]

Although Canada's ban on the export of PCB waste was ostensibly neutral, S.D. Myers claimed that the practical effect of the ban was to put the claimant at a disadvantage compared with the Canadian PCB waste disposal industry.[111] This effect, coupled with evidence that the ban was motivated at least in part by protectionist motives, led the tribunal to reject Canada's argument that the ban was simply part of a uniform regulatory regime.[112]

The *UPS* tribunal considered the matter of according treatment to be distinct from the question of discrimination. Thus, the first question was whether Canada had accorded any treatment whatsoever to either the investor or its investment. The tribunal determined that Canada had indeed accorded treatment to UPS and UPS Canada. In so doing it rejected Canada's arguments that the only treatment alleged to have been given was the processing of goods shipped by UPS into Canada,[113] and that the processing did not encompass treatment accorded to UPS or UPS Canada. Such an argument, said the tribunal, '[...] would essentially open an enormous hole in the protection of investments and investors'.[114] Given the *UPS* tribunal's decision with respect to like circumstances, it did not need to consider whether the treatment allegedly given was less favourable or was based on nationality. It did suggest in *obiter dicta*, however, that the appropriate question would be whether the disparate treatment suggested some nationality-based motivation: '[...] the rationale for providing distribution assistance through Canada Post does not comprise any nationality-based discrimination'.[115]

The tribunal in *ADF* addressed the question of discrimination only briefly and in *obiter dicta* due to its conclusion that the alleged treatment fell within the government procurement exception to NAFTA Article 1102. The tribunal acknowledged that the ostensibly equal treatment it had identified—that all steel was treated the same, regardless of ownership—could hide *de facto* discrimination. In order to make such a determination, however, the tribunal suggested it would need information, such as evidence that steel fabrication costs were much lower in Canada, suggesting that the measure had actual discriminatory effect and had been adopted as a result of a protectionist impulse.[116]

---

[110] *S.D. Myers v Canada*, above n. 60, para. 252.
[111] Ibid., para. 209.
[112] Ibid., para. 242.
[113] *UPS v Canada*, above n. 93, para. 85.
[114] Ibid.
[115] Ibid., para. 177.
[116] *ADF v United States*, above n. 85, para. 157.

The *Loewen* tribunal's treatment of the national treatment claims was cursory, but the tribunal confirmed that mere differential effect would be insufficient to sustain a national treatment claim. According to the *Loewen* tribunal, NAFTA's national treatment obligation relates only to

[...] nationality-based discrimination and [...] it proscribes only demonstrable and significant indications of bias and prejudice on the basis of national origin, of a nature and consequence likely to have affected the outcome of the trial.[117]

In *Consortium RFCC v Morocco*, the tribunal suggested that a national treatment claim should be predicated on distinctions made because of nationality. It held that the offers made by the Italian and Moroccan companies, respectively, were objectively different, and the choice between them was made on the basis of objective criteria, thus suggesting no way in which the non-discrimination provision of the BIT was violated.[118]

A few tribunals have been less straightforward in their analysis of whether a successful national treatment claim must involve anything more than differential impact on a foreign investor. Like the majority of cases, *Pope & Talbot* involved a case of *de facto*, rather than *de jure*, discrimination. Given that the focus was the allegedly differential effect of the implementation of the Softwood Lumber Agreement, Canada argued that Pope & Talbot needed to show that Canadian-owned mills received a disproportionate disadvantage, a test similar to that employed in some WTO cases, when compared to US-owned mills. The *Pope & Talbot* tribunal rejected this approach, concluding that while it might be relevant in certain cases, the circumstances of the case before it did not require that approach, or demand such a conclusion.[119] Because NAFTA plainly contemplated a case brought by one investor to vindicate its rights, the question was whether that investor was at a disadvantage because of the ostensibly neutral government measure.[120] It would place too large a burden on the investor, and that burden would be inconsistent with the investment-liberalizing principles of the NAFTA, to require it to gather evidence to permit comparisons between all of the US-owned lumber producing companies and all of the Canadian-owned lumber producing companies.

Simply to state this approach is to show how unwieldy it would be and how it would hamstring foreign owned investments seeking to vindicate their Article 1102 rights.[121]

The *Pope & Talbot* tribunal's position was that the important focus was the like-circumstances determination, which it described as requiring a tribunal to address

[...] any difference in treatment, demanding that it be justified by showing that it bears a reasonable relationship to rational policies not motivated by preference of domestic over foreign owned investments.[122]

---

[117] *Loewen v United States*, above n. 81, para. 139.
[118] *Consortium RFCC v Morocco*, above n. 58, para. 75.
[119] *Pope & Talbot v Canada*, above n. 61, paras. 43–69.
[120] Ibid., paras 56, 71.
[121] Ibid., para. 72.
[122] Ibid., para. 79.

It thus appeared to adopt, albeit cautiously, a requirement that claimants demonstrate some nationality-based impetus for the difference in treatment, rather than merely demonstrating a differential impact.

The *Feldman* tribunal's decision does not make altogether clear whether, in its view, differential treatment alone is enough to sustain a national treatment claim, or whether some presumption of national-origin discrimination must be found to underlie that differential treatment. The tribunal cited the US Statement of Administrative Action's discussion of the national treatment obligation's preventing discrimination 'by reason of nationality'.[123] On the other hand, it noted that the plain language of Article 1102, '[...] by its terms suggests that it is sufficient to show less favourable treatment for the foreign investor than for domestic investors in like circumstances'.[124]

The tribunal's concern, which it found reflected in the *Pope & Talbot* tribunal's decision, was that requiring *proof* of discrimination based on nationality would forestall most *de facto* national treatment claims; on the other hand, establishing a presumption that differential treatment between similarly situated foreign and domestic investors was a result of nationality-based discrimination would be more consistent with the investment-liberalizing goals of NAFTA.[125] In the end, the tribunal found that there was a connection between the discrimination and the claimant's US nationality.[126] Mexico had failed to offer any rational evidence for the treatment given to CEMSA

[...] other than the obvious fact that CEMSA was owned by a very outspoken foreigner who had, prior to the initiation of the audit, filed a NAFTA Chapter 11 claim against the Government of Mexico.[127]

In *International Thunderbird Gaming Corporation v Mexico*, the tribunal emphasized that Thunderbird need not show that any less favourable treatment accorded it was 'motivated because of nationality'.[128] Yet the tribunal suggested that Thunderbird, in addition to proving the existence of less favourable treatment, also needed to show 'the reason why there was a less favourable treatment',[129] although it did not explain what it meant by that statement.

National treatment claims can also arise in the context of the provision found in several investment agreements that prohibits 'arbitrary and discriminatory' treatment. The Argentina/US BIT contains such a provision, so the issue has arisen in several of the cases arising from the Argentine financial crisis. In *LG&E v Argentina*, the tribunal considered whether the less favourable treatment

---

[123] *Feldman v United Mexican States*, above n. 75, para. 181.
[124] Ibid.
[125] Ibid., paras 183–184.
[126] Ibid., para. 182.
[127] Ibid.
[128] *International Thunderbird Gaming Corp. v Mexico* (NAFTA), Award, 26 January 2006, paras. 175–176.
[129] Ibid., para. 177.

accorded to gas distribution companies than to other public utility companies violated the prohibition against arbitrary and discriminatory treatment. The tribunal concluded that claimants had not proved that the measures targeted their investments specifically as *foreign* investments, although the measures discriminated against gas distribution companies as compared to others.[130] The *Enron v Argentina* tribunal approached the matter somewhat differently. It did not specify that there would need to be discrimination on the basis of nationality with respect to measures affecting different sectors of the economy. The only issue was whether Argentina had good reason to treat different sectors differently.

The Tribunal does not find that there has been any capricious, irrational or absurd differentiation in the treatment accorded to the Claimants as compared to other entities or sectors.[131]

Noble Ventures v Romania involved an allegation that judicial measures initiated against a US-owned steel mill were 'unreasonable or discriminatory' under the Romania/US BIT. The tribunal assumed, without discussion, that to prevail the US investor would have to show the measures were '[. . .] directed specifically against a certain investor by reason of his, her or its nationality'.[132] The US investor could not do so; the proceedings were well founded, and there was no suggestion that Romanian-owned ventures with equally grave debt problems were not also the subject of proceedings initiated by the Romanian government.[133]

The *Lauder v Czech Republic* tribunal, which was deciding a case under the Czech Republic/US BIT, also concluded that the prohibition on according 'arbitrary and discriminatory' treatment addressed discrimination on the basis of nationality.[134] In that case, the tribunal could refer to Clause 3 of the Treaty Annex, which provides that

[c]onsistent with Article II, paragraph 1, the Czech and Slovak Federal Republic reserves the right to make or maintain limited exceptions to national treatment in the sectors or matters it has indicated below.[135]

There was thus textual evidence that, at least in view of one of the treaty parties, discrimination included nationality-based discrimination. The *Lauder* tribunal found that the Czech Republic's refusal to permit the award of a licence to operate a television station in the Czech Republic to a German company controlled by Mr Lauder amounted to arbitrary and discriminatory treatment because it resulted from fear of the political outcry that would ensue should a foreign-owned

---

[130] *LG&E v Argentine Republic*, above n. 31, para. 147.
[131] *Enron Corp. & Ponderosa Assets LP v Argentina*, ICSID Case No ARB/01/3, Award, 22 May 2007, para. 282. The award in *Sempra Energy International v Argentina*, ICSID Case No. ARB/02/16, Award, 28 September 2007, para. 319 was similar.
[132] *Noble Ventures v Romania*, above n. 31, para. 180.
[133] Ibid.
[134] *Ronald S. Lauder v Czech Republic* (UNCITRAL), Award, 3 September 2001, paras 219–220.
[135] Ibid., para. 218.

entity be awarded a licence.[136] However, the bottom line was that there was no evidence that this act injured Mr Lauder's companies, as they were able to structure their holdings to get around the requirements, and any actual damage later inflicted on the claimant was done by a private individual, not by the Czech Republic.[137] Mr Lauder thus did not prevail in his case.

CME v Czech Republic was brought against the Czech Republic by Mr Lauder's Czech subsidiary. It was based on the Czech Republic/Netherlands BIT, which also contained a provision precluding arbitrary or discriminatory measures. That tribunal's conclusion famously differed from that of the *Lauder* tribunal, and its decision rested primarily on the expropriation provision of the BIT. Nonetheless, in its brief consideration of whether the treatment of CME's investment was arbitrary or discriminatory, it held that the intention of the Czech Media Council's actions was to deprive the foreign investor of its investment, and concluded that '[t]he behaviour of the Media Council also smacks of discrimination against the foreign investor'.[138]

Treatment 'No Less Favourable' v 'Best' or 'Most Favourable' Treatment

Treaty provisions requiring States to accord national treatment contain some variation in language. The most commonly used provision requires that the treatment accorded be 'no less favourable' than that accorded to domestic investors in like circumstances.[139] Yet some treaty provisions refer to 'the same' or 'as favourable' treatment. The 'no less favourable' formulation implies more readily that foreign investors may be treated better than nationals, but 'as favourable' does not necessarily preclude such a result.[140] Neither formulation addresses whether a foreign investor must be given the most favourable treatment given to any national, or only the average level of treatment. In practice these differences in formulation have not yet made a great deal of difference, but they have been addressed in a few cases.

In *Pope & Talbot v Canada*, the tribunal relied in part on GATT jurisprudence to conclude that the national treatment guarantee in NAFTA Article 1102 required a State to give the foreign investor the best treatment accorded any one domestic investor.[141] The *Pope & Talbot* tribunal rejected the contentions of all three NAFTA parties (two of whom had filed submissions under Article 1128 of the NAFTA, which permits non-participating Parties to file *amicus curiae*-type

---

[136] Ibid., paras 229–231.
[137] Ibid., paras 232–235.
[138] *CME Czech Republic B.V. v Czech Republic* (UNCITRAL), Partial Award, 13 September 2001, para. 612.
[139] UNCTAD, above n. 3, 37.
[140] Ibid., 35–37.
[141] *Pope & Talbot v Canada*, above n. 61, para. 41.

briefs on interpretive matters) that treatment 'no less favourable' did not mean the best treatment.[142]

The decision of the tribunal in *Feldman* was slightly different. The *Feldman* tribunal suggested that the provision was

[...] on its face unclear as to whether the foreign investor must be treated in the most favorable manner provided for any domestic investor, or only with regard to the treatment generally accorded to domestic investors, or even the least favorably treated domestic investor.[143]

Yet the *Feldman* tribunal also acknowledged that the formulation of the national treatment provision differed from that of the MFN provision, which clearly provided for a covered investor to receive the same treatment afforded the 'most-favoured' nation.[144] Because there was only one other entity in like circumstances with Feldman's investment, however, the *Feldman* tribunal did not need to decide which approach was more accurate.[145]

The *UPS* tribunal did not address the issue as it disposed of the case on like-circumstances grounds. The dissenting arbitrator, however, noted his view that the national treatment obligation required 'an effective parity' between foreign and domestic investors and investments.[146] He amplified on this statement by suggesting that parity could not exist if a host State favours a national entity over foreign entities, and also suggested that such favouritism could not be mitigated by showing that some domestic entities also received less favourable treatment.[147]

The issue is also presented in some cases involving provincial measures. In NAFTA and several US and Canadian investment treaties the States parties have included special provision for state and local governments with respect to the scope of the national treatment obligation. NAFTA Article 1102(3) provides:

The treatment accorded by a Party under paragraphs 1 and 2 means, with respect to a state or province, treatment no less favorable than the most favorable treatment accorded, in like circumstances, by that state or province to investors, and to investments of investors, of the Party of which it forms a part.

This formulation raises several interesting issues because of the ambiguity of the text.

One question is whether the formulation 'treatment no less favorable than the *most* favorable treatment accorded' articulates a different, and higher, standard than the simpler 'no less favourable' formulation in the other paragraphs of Article 1102. Does this mean that subnational governments actually have a higher obligation than do the federal governments? The *Pope & Talbot* tribunal rejected this

---

[142] Ibid., para. 39. See also Kinnear, Bjorklund, and Hannaford, above n. 11, 1102.53.
[143] *Feldman v United Mexican States*, above n. 75, para. 185.
[144] Ibid.
[145] Ibid., para. 186.
[146] *UPS v Canada*, above n. 56, para. 59.
[147] Ibid., para. 60.

interpretation; indeed, it was one of the bases for the *Pope & Talbot* tribunal's decision that the NAFTA requires host States to afford the best treatment.[148]

The second question is precisely what obligations the constituent provinces have undertaken vis-à-vis foreign investors. The obligation requires a province to treat foreign investors (and investments) as it treats investors (and investments) 'of the Party of which it forms a part'. Is an 'investor of the Party of which it forms a part' an investor from outside the province? Or is an 'investor of the Party of which it forms a part' any investor of that party, whether located within or without the province?[149] A straightforward textual interpretation would suggest the latter. There is no qualification in the language, since an investor of the party of which it forms a part does not on its face exclude an in-province party-based investor. Yet, as discussed below, the new US Model BIT includes a modification adopting the former interpretation.

A third question is whether the purpose of the provision is to make clear that a province need only apply its own laws, rather than the possibly more favourable laws of another province, with respect to investment. If, for example, Alberta offers incentives to lure foreign investment, the provision makes clear that British Columbia is not obliged to offer those incentives as well. Mexico has stated that it favours this latter interpretation. In a submission filed under Article 1128, Mexico made clear that Article 1102(3) means that the treatment given by one province is not the standard by which to judge treatment given by another province.[150]

The provision changed slightly in the US Model BIT.

The treatment to be accorded [...] means, with respect to a regional level of government, treatment no less favorable than the treatment accorded, in like circumstances, by that regional level of government to natural persons resident in and enterprises constituted under the laws of other regional levels of government of the Party of which it forms a part, and to their respective investments.[151]

It now appears clear that States parties to treaties with this modified provision are required to accord only the treatment given to out-of-State nationals.

Burden of Proof

In general, the claimant bears the burden of proof to sustain her claims under international law.[152] However, the tribunals deciding cases involving national treatment violations have not taken a uniform approach to the burden-of-proof question, in part because they have not taken a uniform approach to analysing the existence of a violation.

---

[148] *Pope & Talbot* v *Canada*, above n. 61, para. 40.
[149] For a more thorough discussion of this issue, see Kinnear, Bjorklund, and Hannaford, above n. 11, 1102.55–1102.57; Newcombe, Paradell, and Krishan, above n. 5, 43–44.
[150] *Pope & Talbot Inc. v Canada* (NAFTA), Mexican 1128 Submission, 3 April 2000, para. 65.
[151] Article 3(3) US Model BIT (2004).
[152] S. Rosenne, *The Law and Practice of the International Court, 1920–1996* (1997), Volume II, 1083.

Many tribunals have not paid explicit attention to burden-of-proof issues. Others, however, have explicitly addressed it. The *Pope & Talbot* tribunal stated:

> Differences in treatment will presumptively violate Article 1102(2), unless they have a reasonable nexus to rational government policies that (1) do not distinguish, on their face or *de facto*, between foreign-owned and domestic companies, and (2) do not otherwise unduly undermine the investment liberalizing objectives of NAFTA.[153]

This appears to set a low hurdle for a claimant to establish a *prima facie* case. The *Feldman* tribunal explicitly embraced a burden-shifting approach, and quoted the WTO Appellate Body in support:

> If [the party asserting a claim or defense] adduces evidence sufficient to raise a presumption that what is claimed is true, the burden then shifts to the other party, who will fail unless it adduces sufficient evidence to rebut the presumption.[154]

The dissenting arbitrator in the *Feldman* case took issue with the burden-shifting approach, stating: '[N]either the NAFTA nor international law provides any grounds to account for the fact that, as in this case, the burden of proof should shift to the Respondent [...]', when the claimant has made a *prima facie* case.[155] Rather, the burden remained with the claimant at all times.[156]

The tribunal in *Nykomb v Latvia*, an Energy Charter Treaty case, also endorsed a burden-shifting approach. According to the *Nykomb* tribunal, the claimant had established that Nykomb's investment, an electricity co-generating plant, was in like circumstances with two (and particularly with one) other such facilities, and that it had received less favourable treatment. In such circumstances,

> [...] and in accordance with established international law, the burden of proof lies with the Respondent to prove that no discrimination has taken or is taking place. The Arbitral Tribunal finds that such burden of proof has not been satisfied, and therefore *concludes* that Windau has been subject to a discriminatory measure in violation of Article 10(1).[157]

Professor Newcombe suggests that the appropriate approach to a claim of *de facto* national treatment discrimination is to require a claimant to identify the relevant subjects for comparison, demonstrate that it is in like circumstances with the domestic entity with respect to the treatment at issue, and demonstrate that it has received less favourable treatment.[158] At that stage the burden would shift to the State to justify the measure based on legitimate public policy considerations.[159] This approach is generally consistent with the requirement that the claimant

---

[153] *Pope & Talbot v Canada*, above n. 61, para. 78.
[154] *Feldman v United Mexican States*, above n. 75, para. 177, quoting *United States—Measures Affecting Imports of Woven Wool Shirts and Blouses from India*, WT/DS33/AB/R (1997), 14.
[155] *Feldman v United Mexican States*, above n. 78, 9–10.
[156] Ibid.
[157] *Nykomb v Latvia*, Award, above n. 58, 34.
[158] Newcombe, Paradell, and Krishan, above n. 5, 20.
[159] Ibid.

bears the burden of proof to present a *prima facie* case. Because the respondent would ordinarily have control of the evidence that would rebut the presumption established by the investor, shifting the burden of proof to the respondent makes sense from the standpoint of ensuring procedural fairness. It is important, however, that the burden not shift too early; in other words, the case established by the claimant should give rise to an inference that the difference in treatment was attributable to nationality considerations. The respondent would then have the opportunity to rebut that presumption by demonstrating a neutral rationale for the measure at issue.

D. Conclusions

National treatment is a viable and important cause of action in investment treaty cases. Notwithstanding the apparent simplicity of the concept, however, it can be difficult to apply. The majority of tribunals agree that the national treatment obligation is directed at measures that distinguish on the basis of nationality, rather than on neutral criteria. Moreover, it is well established that a claimant need not establish discriminatory intent, but that discriminatory effect will suffice to sustain a claim. Determining whether a State has actually violated its national treatment obligation in any given case, however, requires an often difficult assessment about whether it is appropriate to treat the allegedly less favoured entity like the more favoured entity. That assessment usually requires consideration of the kind of treatment accorded in addition to analysing the competitive relationship between the two entities. While the existence of a competitive relationship is neither necessary nor sufficient to undergird a national treatment claim, most of the time the aggrieved entity will be in competition with the more favourably treated entity, and the treatment in question will redound to its benefit.

In recent years national treatment has been eclipsed by other investment agreement claims, including those based on alleged violations of 'fair and equitable' treatment or 'arbitrary and discriminatory' treatment. There are several likely explanations for this. First, establishing a fair and equitable treatment violation does not require a cumbersome like-circumstances analysis, nor does it require demonstrating nationality-based discrimination, whether *sub rosa* or overt. Secondly, as noted above, a claimed violation of arbitrary and discriminatory treatment is often read to encompass a national treatment violation, but a violation on the basis of arbitrary treatment will suffice to sustain a claim in most cases. Thirdly, discriminatory treatment is one of the factors involved in assessing whether a State has expropriated a foreign investment. Nationality-based discrimination may be said to play a supporting role, rather than a starring role, in cases involving expropriation claims. Notwithstanding these observations, national treatment remains one of the key investment treaty obligations.

4
Most-Favoured-Nation (MFN) Treatment

Andreas R. Ziegler

A. Introduction

For many years the clauses relating to Most-Favoured-Nation (MFN) treatment in bilateral investment treaties (BITs) did not raise any particular questions.[1] They were normally considered as a relic of the traditional way to negotiate establishment and treatment rights for foreign investors in the 19th century. Only very recently, the scope of the MFN treatment clauses has become of interest to arbitrators and legal writers.[2] It is especially the question whether the clause applies also to procedural rights (in particular dispute settlement) and definitions (eg the definition of a foreign direct investment or a foreign investor) that remains controversial. This discussion is very different from the more substantive discussion in other areas of international economic law, eg in relation to trade under the General Agreement on Tariffs and Trade (GATT), the General Agreement on Trade in Services (GATS) or to trade-related intellectual property rights (TRIPs) under the respective Agreement of the World Trade Organization (WTO).

---

[1] See on the MFN clause in the area of Foreign Direct Investment (FDI) in general: UNCTAD, *Most-Favoured Nation Treatment*, Series on Issues on International Investment Agreement Series, Volume III, UNCTAD/ITE/IIT/10 (1999), based on a manuscript prepared by J. Karl, available at http://www.unctad.org/Templates/webflyer.asp?docid=186&intItemID=2322&lang=1 (last visited 9 November 2007).

[2] For very recent examples see G. Egli, 'Don't Get Bit: Addressing ICSID's Inconsistent Application of Most-Favoured-Nation Clauses to Dispute Resolution Provisions', 34 *Pepperdine Law Review* (2007) 1045; S. Vesel, 'Clearing a Path Through a Tangled Jurisprudence: Most-Favored-Nation Clauses and Dispute Settlement Provisions in Bilateral Investment Treaties', 32 *The Yale Journal of International Law* (2007) 125; O. Chukwumerije, 'Interpreting Most-Favoured-Nations Clauses in Investment Treaty Arbitrations', 8 *The Journal of World Investment and Trade* (2007) 597. See also earlier D.H. Freyer and D. Herlihy, 'Most-Favored-Nation Treatment and Dispute Settlement in Investment Arbitration: Just How "Favored" is "Most-Favored"?', 20 *ICSID Review—Foreign Investment Law Journal* (2005) 58; L. Hsu, 'MFN and Dispute Settlement—When the Twain Meet', 7 *The Journal of World Investment and Trade* (2006) 25; F. Orrego Vicuña, 'Bilateral Investment Treaties and the Most-Favored-Nation Clause: Implications for Arbitration in the Light of a Recent ICSID Case', in G. Kaufmann-Kohler (ed.), *Investment Treaties and Arbitration: ASA Swiss Arbitration Association Conference in Zurich of January 25 2002* (2002) 133.

This chapter looks first at the historical developments and underpinnings of the MFN clause (Part B) before it analyses a number of varieties of the clause as currently found in BITs of major players in this field (Part C). In a third part, the topical arbitration awards will be presented and analysed (Part D). The following section (Part E) will try to classify the existing awards and opinions relating to the proper application of MFN clauses in investment agreements. An outlook on the open issues and questions taking into account the most recent developments in academia and international negotiations will conclude the chapter (Part F).

B. Historical Developments and Theoretical Foundations of the MFN Clause

Typical Examples

When we speak of an MFN clause, we normally refer to a provision in a treaty under which a State agrees to accord to the other contracting party treatment that is no less favourable than that which it accords to other or third States. MFN treatment is a particular form of non-discrimination and often combined with or compared to the national treatment (NT).[3] They are both relative standards as they do not specify the exact treatment to be accorded but rather create a non-discrimination obligation to nationals or individuals of other nations.[4] In view of the potential divergences between relative standards and absolute standards (such as fair and equitable treatment, full protection and security, etc), negotiators often tend to combine them all in the text of BITs (or even in one provision) in order to obtain absolutely the most favourable treatment possible in absolute and relative terms.[5]

A typical example of this combination can be found in the Netherlands Model BIT:

[...] each Contracting Party shall ensure fair and equitable treatment of the investments of nationals of the other Contracting Party and shall not impair, by unreasonable or discriminatory measures, the operation, management, maintenance, use, enjoyment or disposal thereof by those nationals. Each Contracting Party shall accord to such investments full physical security and protection.

More particularly, each Contracting Party shall accord to such investments treatment which in any case shall not be less favourable than that accorded either to the investments

---

[3] See A. Bjorklund at Chapter 3 above.
[4] See also P. Acconci, 'Most-Favoured Nation Treatment and International Law on Foreign Investment', in P. Muchlinski, F. Ortino, and C. Schreuer (eds), *The Oxford Handbook of International Investment Law* (forthcoming 2008), Section 1.
[5] See ibid.; F. Horchani, 'Le droit international des investissements à l'heure de la mondialisation', *Journal de droit international* (2004) 368, 388.

of its own nationals or to investments of any third State, whichever is more favourable to the national concerned.[6]

In their attempt to agree upon a Multilateral Agreement on Investment (MAI), the OECD Member States agreed until the suspension of the negotiations in 1998[7] to include the most-favoured-nation and national treatment standards in the Draft Agreement as follows:

[...] each Contracting Party shall accord to investors of another Contracting Party and to their investments, treatment no less favourable than the treatment it accords [in like circumstances] to investors of any other Contracting Party or of a non-Contracting Party, and to the investments of investors of any other Contracting Party or of a non-Contracting Party, with respect to the establishment, acquisition, expansion, operation, management, maintenance, use, enjoyment, and sale or other disposition of investments.[8]

Historical Developments

Hudec shows that the City of Mantova (Italy) obtained from the Holy Roman Emperor the promise that it would always benefit from any privilege granted by the Emperor to 'whatsoever other town'.[9] Jackson holds that the term MFN as such appears for the first time at the end of the 17th century.[10] For example, a 1654 treaty between Great Britain and Sweden[11] provided:

The people, subjects and inhabitants of both confederates shall have, and enjoy in each other's kingdoms, countries, lands, and dominions, as large and ample privileges, relations, liberties and immunities, as any other foreigner at present doth and hereafter shall enjoy.

---

[6] Netherlands Model BIT (1994), this example is provided by Acconci, above n. 4. She refers also to similar examples in Articles 2 and 3 German Model BIT (2004); Article II US/Argentina BIT (1991); Article 3(2) China/Argentina BIT (1992); Article 3 Hungary/Czech Republic BIT (1993); Article 3 Bolivia/Peru BIT (1993); Article 4(1) Norway/Chile BIT (1993); Article 3 Netherlands/Lithuania BIT (1994); Article 3(2) Switzerland/El Salvador BIT (1994); Article 4 Iran/Kazakhstan BIT (1996); Article II US/Jordan BIT (1997); Article 4 Switzerland/Iran BIT (1998). See in general on treatment the relevant chapters of this book and M.I. Khalil, 'Treatment of Foreign Investment in Bilateral Investment Treaties', in The World Bank Group (ed.), *Legal Framework for the Treatment of Foreign Investment* (1992), Volume I, 13, 25.

[7] See, eg, R. Dattu, 'Essay: A Journey from Havana to Paris: The Fifty-Year Quest for the Elusive Multilateral Agreement on Investment', 24 *Fordham International Law Journal* (2000) 275.

[8] See the Consolidated Text of the MAI, DAFFE/MAI/NM(98)2 (1998), 13.

[9] R.E. Hudec, 'Tiger, tiger in the house: a critical evaluation of the case against discriminatory trade measures', in E.-U. Petersmann and M. Hilf, *The New GATT Round of Multilateral Trade Negotiations: Legal and Economic Problems* (1988) 165–212, 177 and note 11.

[10] J. Jackson, *The World Trading System—Law and Policy of International Economic Relations* (1997) 158.

[11] Treaty of Peace and Commerce between Great Britain and Sweden (1654), as referred to in International Law Commission, *Most-Favoured-Nation Clause—Report of the Working Group*, Doc. A/CN.4/L.719 (2007), para. 4.

The more recent models for today's MFN treatment clauses, as we find them in modern BITs,[12] can be traced back to the early times of treaty negotiations between sea-faring nations regarding the access right of foreign merchants and ships to port and market facilities in the late 18th[13] and early 19th centuries.[14] These treaties were often called 'Treaties of Friendship, Commerce and Navigation' (FCN Treaties)[15] or if they involved landlocked countries—like Switzerland— 'Treaties of Friendship, Commerce and (Reciprocal) Establishment'.[16]

The 1836 Treaty of Peace, Friendship, Navigation and Commerce between the United States and Venezuela[17] constitutes an early example:

It is likewise agreed that it shall be wholly free for all merchants, commanders of ships and other citizens of both countries to manage themselves their own business in all the ports and places subject to the jurisdiction of each other, as well with respect to the consignment and sale of their goods and merchandize by wholesale or retail, as with respect to the loading, unloading, and sending off their ships, *they being in all these cases to be treated as citizens of the country in which they reside or at least to be placed on a footing with the subjects or citizens of the most favoured nation.*[18]

Another example (referring to the tax and customs treatment of imported goods) we find in the 1845 Treaty of Commerce and Navigation between the United States and Belgium:[19]

Articles of every description, imported into the United States from other countries than Belgium, under the Belgian flag, shall pay no other or higher duties whatsoever than if

---

[12] See also M. Herdegen, *Internationales Wirtschaftsrecht* (5th edn, 2005) 221.

[13] For late 18th-century examples see Articles 2 and 14 Treaty of Peace and Amity between President and Citizens of the United States of North America and Hassan Bashaw Dey of Algiers (1795).

[14] See for a detailed analysis Ch. Hyde, 'Concerning the Interpretation of Treaties', 3 *American Journal of International Law* (1909) 46; S.K. Hornbeck, 'The Most-Favored-Nation Clause', 3 *American Journal of International Law* (1909) 395; S.B. Crandall, 'The American Construction of the Most-Favored-Nation Clause', 7 *American Journal of International Law* (1913) 708; F. Hepp, *Théorie générale de la clause de la nation la plus favorisée en droit international privé* [A general theory of the MFN clause in private international law] (1914); S. Basdevant, *La clause de la nation la plus favorisée* [The Most-Favoured-Nation Clause] (1929); B. Baron Nolde, 'La clause de la nation la plus favorisée et les tariffs préférentiels' [The Most-Favoured-Nations Clause and Preferential Tariffs], 35 *Recueil des Cours of the Hague Academy of International Law* (1932); and R.C. Snyder, *The Most-Favored-Nation Clause: Analysis with Particular Reference to the Recent Treaty Practice and Tariffs* (1948); all also referred to by P. Mavroidis, *The General Agreement on Tariffs and Trade—A Commentary* (2005), 112. With regard to the practice after 1945 see also J. Kurtz, 'The Delicate Extension of Most-Favoured-Nation Treatment to Foreign Investors: Maffezini v. Kingdom of Spain', in T. Weiler (ed.), *International Investment Law and Arbitration—Leading Cases from the ICSID, NAFTA, Bilateral Treaties and Customary International Law* (2005) 523–555.

[15] Treaty of Friendship, Commerce and Navigation between Argentina and the United States (1853).

[16] Such as the Treaty of Friendship, Commerce, and Reciprocal Establishment between Great Britain and Switzerland (1855).

[17] United States/Venezuela Treaty of Peace, Friendship, Navigation and Commerce (1836).

[18] Ibid., Article 7 (emphasis added).

[19] United States/Belgium Treaty of Commerce and Navigation (1845).

B. Historical Developments & Theoretical Foundations of the MFN Clause

they had been imported under *the flag of the most favored foreign nation*, other than the flag of the country from which the importation is made. And reciprocally, articles of every description imported under the flag of the United States into Belgium, from other countries than the United States, shall pay no other or higher duties whatsoever than if they had been imported under the flag of *the foreign nation most favored, other than that of the country from which the importation is made.*[20]

The 1855 Treaty of Friendship, Commerce, and Reciprocal Establishment between Great Britain and Switzerland constitutes an older example of the European Treaty practice:

No other or higher duty, tax, impost, or charge, either in time of peace or in time of war, shall, under any circumstances, be imposed or levied upon, or in respect of, any property held by a subject or citizen of one of the two Contracting Parties in the territories of the other, than is, or may be, imposed or levied upon, or in respect of, *the like property belonging to a subject or citizen of the country, or to a subject or citizen of the most favoured nation.*[21]

Despite the very common practice throughout the 19th and early 20th centuries to include MFN treatment[22] in treaties relating to bilateral economic relations, there is no customary obligation of States to grant MFN treatment according to the predominant position.[23] This led to the inclusion of MFN treaties in most BITs concluded after World War II,[24] but also in the GATT of 1947 and other regional free trade agreements as well as, for example, treaties on intellectual property.[25]

At its sixteenth session in 1964, the International Law Commission (ILC) considered a proposal by one of its members, Mr Jimenez de Arechaga, to include a provision on the most-favoured-nation clause in its draft articles on the law of treaties. As a result, the ILC worked on the topic until 1978 as it was felt to be an important topic in relation to the growing tensions in the area of foreign direct investment between developed States and developing countries.[26] The Special Rapporteur appointed was Mr Endre Ustor from Hungary. In 1978, the Commission adopted draft articles on the topic of the Most-Favoured-Nation (MFN) clause.[27] No action was taken on them by the General Assembly.

---

[20] Ibid., Article VIII (emphasis added).
[21] See above n. 16, Article VI.
[22] See for an example concerning the interpretation of these treaties *The Case Concerning Rights of Nationals of the United States of America in Morocco (France v United States of America)*, Judgment, 27 August 1952.
[23] See, eg, Herdegen, above n. 12, 11.
[24] See also A.H. Qureshi and A.R. Ziegler, *International Economic Law* (2nd edn, 2007) para. 14–014 and Part II.
[25] See below, Part E with relation to Article I GATT, Article II GATS and Article 4 TRIPS.
[26] For a summary of the work undertaken during this time see Report of the International Law Commission on the work of its 30th session, UN GAOR, 33rd Sess., Supplement (1978) available at http://www.un.org/law/ilc/index.htm (last visited 9 November 2007).
[27] Draft Articles on Most-Favoured-Nation Clauses (1978) as available at http://untreaty.un.org/ilc/texts/instruments/english/draft%20articles/1_3_1978.pdf (last visited 9 November 2007).

Only at the 58th session of the ILC in 2006—following the debate on the topic related to recent arbitral awards in the investment area[28]—the long-term Working Group discussed whether the MFN clause should be re-considered and if the topic ought to be included in its long-term programme of work, but the Commission did not make any decision on the matter. The Commission then invited the views of governments. At the 61st session of the Sixth Committee, one State supported the idea but two States expressed doubts about the wisdom of taking on the topic. At its 29th meeting on 1 June 2007, the ILC established an open-ended Working Group, chaired by Mr Donald M. McRae, to examine the possibility of the inclusion of the topic 'Most-favoured-nation clause' in its long-term programme of work. The Working Group held two meetings on 16 and 17 July 2007 and recommended in its Report of 20 July 2007 that the topic of the most-favoured-nation clause be included in the long-term programme of work of the Commission as it was felt that

[...] the Working Group concluded that the Commission could play a useful role in providing clarification on the meaning and effect of the most-favoured-nation clause in the field of investment agreements. Such work was seen as building on the past work of the Commission on the most-favoured-nation clause.[29]

C. Main Types and Economic Foundation of MFN Treatment

Most-favoured-nation treatment is treatment accorded by the granting State to the beneficiary State, or to persons or things in a determined relationship with that State, not less favourable than treatment extended by the granting State to a third State or to persons or things in the same relationship with that third State.[30]

A most-favoured-nation treatment clause *per se* entails international obligations and rights not only among the Contracting States of the international treaty incorporating it (often referred to as 'the basic treaty'), but also among these Contracting States and other States (often referred to as 'the third-party treaty') by virtue of different international treaties. Therefore, a most-favoured-nation treatment clause is not only a normal treaty clause, but also a source of international obligations other than those explicitly included in the basic treaty. It allows 'borrowing' treaty provisions from other treaties or possibly State practice regarding third States. The material scope of the MFN is thus open, as the contents of future treaties and State practice cannot be totally foreseen and identified

---

[28] See below, Part C.
[29] ILC, Most-Favoured-Nation Clause—Report of the Working Group, UN Doc. A/CN.4/L.719 (2007), para. 4, available at http://www.un.org/law/ilc/index.htm.
[30] See Article 5 Draft Articles on Most-Favoured-Nation Clauses (1978), above n. 27.

C. Main Types and Economic Foundation of MFN Treatment 65

when the basic treaty is concluded. Even with regard to existing treaty obligations in relation to third States, it may be that negotiators are not always completely aware of them.[31]

By its very nature the MFN clause is different from other international obligations that are usually agreed upon as it seems at first view contrary that the general principle of treaty negotiations that normally a treaty does not create either obligations or rights for a third State without its consent as enshrined also in Article 34 of the Vienna Convention on the Law of Treaties.[32] However, a closer analysis shows that MFN is in conformity with the principle that the consent of a State can lead to the creation of new rights as a consequence of a treaty between third States,[33] although it is not a requirement that the contracting States of the later treaty intended the provision also to accord that right to the third State. More importantly, one can say that with regard to MFN treatment the new right is not created by the new treaty but was already encompassed under the basic treaty and thus is not a case of the application of the rules covered by Part III Section 4 of the Vienna Convention on the Law of Treaties. As a matter of fact, the 1969 Vienna Convention left this issue basically untouched, thereby justifying the ongoing work of the ILC in this context.[34]

In the case of the MFN clause, the basic treaty becomes a dynamic source of law in so far as the practice of either party, in particular with regard to later treaties, to the basic treaty becomes of relevance to existing rights and duties under the basic treaty. The MFN clause thus constitutes a prior consent to extend favours extended to third States to the contracting parties of the basic treaty.

It is important to note that the MFN principle does not require identical treatment but 'treatment at least as favourable'. Often this will mean identical treatment, as any other treatment would lead to new problems in relation to third States, but it may also lead to a better treatment or different treatment that is considered to be qualitatively identical to or at least as favourable as the treatment of third parties. This distinction may be of lesser importance in the area of investment but can be important when it comes to tariff concessions in the area of trade.

This very nature of the MFN principle is contrary to a strict application of the reciprocity principle so cherished by States in their traditional diplomatic relations.[35] While, normally, States will mutually grant each other MFN treatment, the material content of this provision may differ from the beginning or,

---

[31] See International Law Association, *Report of the Committee on Foreign Direct Investment*, presented at the Biennial Meeting 2008 (forthcoming), Section B4.
[32] Vienna Convention on the Law of Treaties (1969).
[33] Ibid., Article 36.
[34] See above n. 26; and Acconci, above n. 4, with reference to para. 59 of the *Rapport de la Commission à l'Assemblée générale sur les travaux de sa trentième session*, 16.
[35] See, eg, C. Lo, *The Reciprocity Principle in the International Regulation of Economic Relations*, Thesis Typescript (S.J.D.) Harvard Law School (1989), available at http://de.scientificcommons.org/4449832 (last visited 9 November 2007).

especially, change over time. This is the main reason why some politicians and even lawyers have always been critical of the MFN clause. They consider it to be a disincentive to negotiate mutually acceptable improvements of their relations, eg investment or trade, as one party may benefit from improvement only made by the other party without having to improve its own standards. It thus can lead to so-called free rider effects. MFN clauses are only reciprocal in the sense that they are reciprocally granted, but their content is open to divergences and dynamic developments and thus not subject to the reciprocal granting of identical treatment and market access rights.

One way to limit these effects of the MFN principle is to make it not automatic or unconditional but conditional (conditional MFN treatment). An alternative is to provide explicit (temporary) exceptions. This has been discussed[36] in particular with regard to tariff concessions before World War II, but also with regard to more recent negotiations such as under GATS.[37] Conditional MFN treatment normally means that the application of new more favourable rules or preferences is only granted to existing treaty partners if they agree to apply the same rules; conditional MFN treatment therefore is basically a right to obtain the more favourable treatment upon condition to do the same (reciprocity) while unconditional MFN treatment requires no renewed commitment by the beneficiary. Economic theory, especially in the field of trade, has shown that liberalization, even unilateral, is more likely to lead to increased welfare and hence often recommends unconditional MFN treatment.[38] Generally, MFN clauses found in modern BITs are unconditional[39] but they may be limited in scope and/or subject to exceptions. The basic problem to develop a coherent theory in view of the existing case law stems from the fact that the clauses at stake were often very differently phrased. While they all fall into the same category, their wording allows (at least) technically for a differentiation with regard to their scope.[40]

---

[36] See, eg, J. Wolf, 'Vorwort', in L. Glier (ed.), *Die Meistbegünstigungsklausel* (1905) v.
[37] Article II:2 GATS; see in this respect A. Lowenfeld, *International Economic Law* (2002) 117.
[38] See for an overview on recent economic studies in this field C.E.J.M. Zarazaga, 'Measuring the Benefits of Unilateral Trade Liberalization', *Economic and Financial Policy Review* (2000), Part 2: dynamic models, 29–39.
[39] See also Acconci, above n. 4, Section 3.
[40] See the diverging case law as reported in the next section and, for details, Acconci, above n. 4, Section 3.1, who rightly refers to D. Anzilotti, *Cours de droit international* (1929) 438, pointing out that '[...] juridiquement parlant, il n'existe pas *une clause* de la nation la plus favorisée; il existe autant de stipulations distinctes qu'il y a de traités qui la contiennent, de sorte que toute question relative à la nature et aux effets de la clause est avant tout une question d'interprétation d'une clause donnée dans un traité déterminé'. See also R. Dolzer and T. Myers, 'After Tecmed: Most-Favored-Nation Clauses in Investment Protection Agreements', 19 *ICSID Review—Foreign Investment Law Journal* (2004) 50; E. Gaillard, 'Establishing Jurisdiction through a Most-Favored-Nation Clause', *New York Law Journal* (2005) 8. For an overview over existing examples see UNCTAD, *Recent Developments in International Investment Agreements*, UNCTAD/WEB/ITE/IIT/2005/1; UNCTAD, *International Investment Rule-Setting: Trends, Emerging Issues and Implications*, TD/B/COM.2/68 (2006).

D. Important Investment Arbitration Awards relating to MFN

The MFN clause has been rediscovered in the context of international investment arbitration following the decision of an arbitral tribunal in the case of *Maffezini v Spain*[41] in 2000. Since then a number of tribunals have had to address the issue of the correct application and interpretation of the MFN clause.[42]

The following provides a very short overview of the most relevant cases with respect to their contribution to the discussion of MFN treatment in order to facilitate the later discussion of the specific issues addressed.

Asian Agricultural Products Ltd (AAPL) v Sri Lanka

In this first ICSID case relating to an arbitration clause contained in a BIT,[43] Article 3 of the agreement provided for most-favoured-nation treatment which, according to the investor, allowed for the incorporation of the liability standards (no 'war clause' and no 'civil disturbance exemption') contained in the 1981 BIT between Switzerland and Sri Lanka, as they were more favourable than those contained in the UK/Sri Lanka BIT. The tribunal rejected this claim, by establishing that it was not clear that the Sri Lanka/Switzerland Treaty contained more favourable provisions.[44]

Pope and Talbot v Canada

A US investor had originally invoked the MFN treatment clause of NAFTA[45] against Canada in order to be given the 'fair and equitable treatment' as contained in various BITs concluded by Canada with third States which might go beyond what is contained in Article 1105 NAFTA (Minimum Standard of

---

[41] *Maffezini v Spain*, ICSID Case No. ARB/97/7, Decision on Jurisdiction, 25 January 2000, paras 53 *et seq*. See below for details. For comments see St. Fietta, 'Most Favoured Nation Treatment and Dispute Resolution under Bilateral Investment Treaties: a Turning Point?', 8 *International Arbitration Law Review* (2005) 131–138; L. Liberti, 'Arbitrato ICSID, clausola della nazione più favorita e problemi di attribuzione', *Rivista dell'arbitrato* (2004) 580.

[42] For an overview on the case law see M.-F. Houde and F. Pagani, 'Most Favoured Nation Treatment in International Investment Law', in OECD (ed.), *International Investment Law: A Changing Landscape—A Companion Volume to International Investment Perspectives* (2005), Chapter 4; R. Teitelbaum, 'Who's Afraid of Maffezini? Recent Developments in the Interpretation of Most Favored Nation Clauses', 22 *Journal of International Arbitration* (2005) 225–238; Acconci, above n. 4; A. Reinisch, 'Maffezini v. Spain Case', in *Encyclopedia of Public International Law* (forthcoming).

[43] UK/Sri Lanka BIT (1980).

[44] *Asian Agricultural Products Ltd (AAPL) v Republic of Sri Lanka*, ICSID Case No. ARB/87/3, Award, 27 June 1990, para. 54. On this award see Acconci, above n. 4, Section 4.1; and S. Manciaux, *Investissements étrangers et arbitrage entre États et ressortissants d'autres États* (2004) 582–585.

[45] Article 1103 NAFTA.

Treatment). The claim was later dropped and therefore not assessed substantively by the tribunal.[46]

Maffezini v Spain

An Argentinean investor in Spain requested the application of the MFN clause contained in Article IV(2) of the Spain/Argentina BIT to benefit from the allegedly more favourable provision in the Chile/Argentina BIT (no waiting period of 18 months until an arbitral tribunal can be seized). The tribunal rejected Spain's argument that the application of the MFN clause was limited to substantive matters or material aspects of the treatment granted to investors and did not cover procedural or jurisdictional questions.[47]

ADF v USA

A Canadian investor invoked the MFN clause contained in Article 1103 NAFTA in order to benefit from the allegedly further-reaching protection in the US/Estonia and US/Albania BITs (fair and equitable treatment), similar to the original claims presented in *Pope & Talbot v Canada* (2001/2002). The tribunal concluded that even if the United States had granted a better protection under the respective BITs (which seemed doubtful to the tribunal) the United States was not in breach of this standard.[48]

The Loewen Group, Inc, Raymond L. Loewen v The United States of America

NAFTA's most-favoured-nation treatment clause (Article 1103) was invoked to avoid the requirement of maintaining ' "continuous nationality" during investment disputes' which allegedly was not necessary under other BITs concluded by the United States. The ICSID did not address this claim and upheld the US objection to its jurisdiction due to the lack of the claimant's continuous nationality.[49]

---

[46] *Pope & Talbot Inc. v The Government of Canada*, UNCITRAL (NAFTA), Procedural Order No. 2, 28 October 1999, as referred to in M. Kinnear, A.K. Bjorklund, and J.F.G. Hannaford, *Investment Disputes under NAFTA—An Annotated Guide to NAFTA Chapter 11* (2006) 1103–1109. See also Acconci, above n. 4, Section 4.2.

[47] See above n. 41 and on this award, among others, Acconci, above n. 4, Sections 4.2, 5.1. For a critical assessment of the *Maffezini* decision, above n. 41, see St. Fietta, 'Most Favoured Nation Treatment and Dispute Settlement Resolution Under Bilateral Investment Treaties: A Turning Point', 8 *International Arbitration Law Review* (2005) 131; for a more favourable assessment see J. Boscariol and O. Silva, 'The Widening Application of the MFN Obligation and its Impact on Investor Protection', 11 *International Trade Law and Regulation* (2005) 61.

[48] *ADF Group Inc. v United States* (NAFTA), ICSID Case No. ARB (AF)/00/1, Award, 9 January 2003, paras 193 *et seq*. See also Acconci, above n. 4, Section 4.2.

[49] *The Loewen Group, Inc., Raymond L. Loewen v The United States of America*, ICSID Case No. ARB(AF)/98/3, Award, 26 June 2003, in particular para. 225. See also *Raymond L. Loewen v The*

Yaung Chi Oo (YCO) Trading Pte Ltd v Myanmar

Myanmar was not a member of ASEAN at the time YCO (an investor from Singapore) had entered a joint venture with Myanmar Foodstuff Industries and the State Industrial Organization of Myanmar. Myanmar acceded to the ASEAN Agreement (1987) only in July 1997 and became a party to the Framework Agreement for ASEAN Investment (1998). YCO, inter alia, claimed that the ASEAN Arbitral Tribunal had jurisdiction under the 1998 Framework Agreement (to which both Singapore and Myanmar were parties) relating to measures taken before 1998 by invoking the most-favoured-nation provision of Article 8, citing more favourable treatment to investors under the Philippines/Myanmar BIT (1998) (consent to international arbitration). The tribunal declined jurisdiction on this ground, noting that the claimant had failed to invoke the MFN clause at the initiation of arbitration proceedings. It further observed that, in any event, there was no indication that there would be arbitral jurisdiction under any BIT entered into by Myanmar under the present facts. The tribunal therefore concluded that it was unnecessary for it to consider jurisdiction under the Framework Agreement (1998).[50]

Tecmed v Mexico

A Spanish investor tried to overcome jurisdictional limitations *ratione temporis* by invoking an MFN clause in the Mexico/Spain BIT (1995) and thereby borrowing the more generous clause on temporal scope in the BIT between Mexico and Austria (1998). The ICSID tribunal did not allow the retroactive application of substantive standards as contained in this treaty with a third party

> [...] because it deem[ed] that matters relating to the application over time of the Agreement [...] due to their significance and importance, go to the core of matters that must be deemed to be specifically negotiated by the Contracting Parties.[51]

MTD v Chile

The Malaysian company MTD Equity Sdn Bhd had invoked the MFN clause contained in the Chile/Malaysia BIT in order to benefit from two other BITs concluded by Chile with Denmark and Croatia which contained more detailed treaty language on fair and equitable treatment, including obligations to award

---

United States of America, Petition to Vacate, 13 December 2004, note 2. On 31 October 2005, the US District Court for the District of Columbia denied this petition.

[50] *Yaung Chi Oo Trading Pte Ltd v Myanmar*, ASEAN I.D. Case No. ARB/01/1, Award, 31 March 2003; see also Acconci, above, n. 4, Section 5.3.

[51] *Técnicas Medioambientales Tecmed, S.A. v United Mexican States*, ICSID Case No. ARB(AF)/00/2, Award, 29 May 2003, para. 69.

permits subsequent to the approval of an investment and to fulfil contractual obligations, respectively. The tribunal agreed to incorporating the provisions of the Croatian and Danish treaties into the Treaty between Malaysia and Chile by virtue of the 'wide scope' of the latter treaty's MFN clause—and deeming this importation to be 'in consonance with' the purpose of the Chile/Malaysia BIT.[52]

Siemens v Argentina

The investor, the German company Siemens, invoked the more favourable terms of a bilateral investment treaty (absence of a waiting period of 18 months before an arbitral tribunal can be seized) between Argentina and Chile—by virtue of the MFN clause contained in the Argentina/Germany BIT. Argentina objected to Siemens' failure to exhaust an 18-month time period set out in the Argentina/Germany BIT for recourse to local courts, prior to turning to international arbitration. The arbitral tribunal determined that the relevant MFN clause allowed the investor to choose more favourable dispute settlement provisions from various other agreements.[53]

Salini v Jordan

The Italian investor invoked the MFN clause in the BIT between Jordan and Italy in order to benefit from more favourable dispute settlement provisions in the BITs with the United States and the UK. In the view of the claimants, the United States and UK treaties contained a dispute settlement clause 'which is more favourable than that contained in Article 9 of the Jordan-Italy BIT', by virtue of its supposed inclusion of contractual breaches. The relevant MFN clause was silent on the question of the application of MFN to the dispute settlement process; accordingly, the tribunal rejected the claimants' contention that the MFN clause should be interpreted so as to apply to procedural matters.[54]

Lucchetti v Peru

The claim concerned how the respondent State, Peru, had applied the fair and equitable treatment standard, national treatment and most-favoured-nation

---

[52] *MTD Equity Sdn. Bhd and MTD Chile S.A. v Republic of Chile*, ICSID Case No. ARB/01/7, Award, 25 May 2004, para. 103. See the comments by L. Peterson, 'Malaysian firm wins BIT case against Chile; "wide scope" of MFN clause looms large', International Institute for Sustainable Development (ed.), *INVEST-SD: Investment Law and Policy Weekly News Bulletin* (23 August 2004), available at www.iisd.org/investment.

[53] *Siemens A.G. v The Argentine Republic,* ICSID Case No. ARB/02/8, Decision on Jurisdiction, 3 August 2004, para. 120.

[54] *Salini Costruttori S.p.A and Italstrade S.p.A v The Hashemite Kingdom of Jordan*, ICSID Case No. ARB/02/13, Decision on Jurisdiction, 29 November 2004.

treatment. According to the claimant, Peru had breached all of its treaty obligations provided in the BIT between Chile and Peru (2000).[55] The ICSID tribunal did not address the issue as it declined jurisdiction.

Plama v Bulgaria

The tribunal refused to permit the Cypriot investor to invoke the MFN clause contained in the BIT between Bulgaria and Cyprus in order to borrow the arbitration clause found in another investment treaty by Bulgaria, which would have paved the way for arbitration under a different set of rules and over a much broader range of claims.[56]

CMS v Argentina

The investor relied on the most-favoured-nation treatment clause included in the 1991 BIT between the United States and Argentina to maintain that the liability standards (no exceptions) incorporated in other BITs concluded by Argentina should apply. The tribunal rejected this assertion since it was 'not convinced that the clause [had] any role to play in this case'. The tribunal established that such an assertion would in any event fail under the *ejusdem generis* rule.[57]

Impregilo S.p.A. v Pakistan

The Italian investor claimed that by applying the MFN clause in the 1997 Italy/Pakistan BIT, it was entitled to request ICSID arbitration in relation to contractual claims covered under the so-called 'umbrella clauses', such as contained in the 1995 Switzerland/Pakistan BIT. The Italy/Pakistan BIT did not provide for the coverage of purely contractual claims as investment claims. Although the tribunal ultimately held that the claims were not claims against Pakistan as a party to the agreement but against a separate entity, it did not exclude the possibility of invoking the umbrella clause on the basis of the MFN clause:

even assuming *arguendo* that Pakistan through the MFN clause and the Swiss/Pakistan BIT, has guaranteed the observance of the contractual commitments into which it has entered together with Italian investors, such a guarantee would not cover the present Contracts—since they are agreements into which it has not entered.[58]

---

[55] *Empresas Lucchetti, S.A. and Lucchetti Peru, S.A. v Republic of Peru*, ICSID Case No. ARB/03/4, Decision on Jurisdiction, 7 February 2005, para. 23.
[56] *Plama Consortium Ltd v Bulgaria*, ICSID Case No. ARB/03/24, Decision on Jurisdiction, 8 February 2005. See also Acconci, above n. 4, Section 5.3.
[57] *CMS Gas Transmission Co v Argentina*, ICSID Case No. ARB/01/8, Award, 12 May, 2005, para. 377. On the *ejusdem generis* principle see next section.
[58] *Impregilo S.p.A. v Pakistan*, ICSID Case No. ARB/03/3, Decision on Jurisdiction, 22 April 2005, para. 223. See D. Foster, 'Internationalisation—Contractual Claims in BIT Arbitrations', *Global Arbitration Review*, available at http://www.globalarbitrationreview.com/

Camuzzi v Argentina

In this case, Argentina did not object at all to the claimant's attempt to refer to the MFN clause included in the BIT between Argentina and the Belgo-Luxembourg Economic Union (1990) (the basic treaty) in order to borrow a more favourable dispute settlement clause (no waiting period) provided by the US/Argentina BIT (1991). In view of Argentina's missing objection, the ICSID tribunal did not 'decide on the relevance of that clause' in the case. However, for the sake of clarity, the tribunal specified that Argentina had probably considered the 'eighteen months in domestic courts' requirement met, since Camuzzi had 'submitted the dispute to [its] national courts' which had left it unresolved.[59]

Gas Natural v Argentina

An investor invoked the MFN clause contained in the 1991 Agreement between Argentina and Spain in order to borrow the allegedly more favourable dispute settlement provisions in several BITs concluded by Argentina with third states. The *Gas Natural* tribunal followed the *Maffezini* approach stating that there was 'no "public policy" reason not to give effect to the most-favored-nation provision with respect to the right to proceed directly to international arbitration'[60] because the applicable MFN clause related to 'all matters' and thus covered dispute settlement. In the tribunal's view '[...] assurance of independent international arbitration is an important—perhaps the most important—element in investor protection'.[61]

Bayindir v Pakistan

The BIT between Turkey and Pakistan (1995) did not expressly include a fair and equitable treatment clause. The investor asserted that he was entitled to such a treatment as provided in other treaties entered into by Pakistan through the MFN clause. The ICSID tribunal accepted jurisdiction with regard to this request as other BITs concluded by Pakistan contained '[...] an explicit fair and equitable treatment clause'.[62] The claimant had also contended a direct violation of the most-favoured-nation clause included in the Turkey/Pakistan BIT as Pakistan had engaged in a selective tendering process allegedly intended

---

handbooks/3/sections/5/chapters/32/internationalisation-contractual-claims-bit-arbitrations (last visited 19 November 2007).

[59] *Camuzzi International S.A. v Argentina*, ICSID Case No. ARB/03/2, Decision on Objections to Jurisdiction, 11 May 2005, para. 121. See for details Acconci, above n. 4, Section 5.1.

[60] *Gas Natural SDG, S.A. v Argentina*, ICSID Case No. ARB/03/10, Decision on Preliminary Questions on Jurisdiction, 17 June 2005, para. 28. See on this case, among others, Reinisch, above n. 42.

[61] *Gas Natural*, above n. 60, para. 49.

[62] *Bayindir Insaat Turizm Ticaret Ve Sanayi A.Ş. v Islamic Republic of Pakistan*, ICSID Case No. ARB/03/29, Decision on Jurisdiction, 14 November 2005, para. 231.

D. Important Investment Arbitration Awards relating to MFN

to squeeze Bayindir out of the market. In this respect the tribunal equally confirmed its jurisdiction.[63]

Continental Casualty v Argentina

Argentina objected to ICSID jurisdiction based on the MFN clause in the BIT between Argentina and the United States (1991). The claimant used this provision in order to obtain better substantive treatment and not merely procedural improvements. The ICSID tribunal therefore accepted jurisdiction.[64]

National Grid Transco plc v Argentina

In this case, again the 18-month-waiting period before an arbitral tribunal can be seized (as contained in the 1990 United Kingdom/Argentina BIT) was removed by an UNCITRAL tribunal by allowing the investor from the UK to rely on the more favourable provision in the Argentina/US BIT.[65]

Telenor v Hungary

The investor referred to the MFN clause included in the Norway/Hungary BIT (1991) and asked for the incorporation of more favourable dispute settlement provisions in other agreements concluded by Hungary which allowed for a more generous jurisdiction of an ICSID tribunal (not limited to expropriation claims as in the 1991 Norway/Hungary BIT) to be permitted. The tribunal refused such incorporation.[66]

Suez, Sociedad General de Aguas de Barcelona S.A., and Vivendi Universal S.A. v Argentina and AWG Group Ltd v Argentina

In this case immediate access to an ICSID arbitral tribunal for British and Spanish investors was achieved through the most-favoured-nation clauses included in the basic treaties (the 1990 Argentina/UK BIT and the 1991 Argentina/Spain BIT). The dispute settlement clause of the Argentina/France BIT (1991) according to

---

[63] Ibid., para. 223; para. 206 reads: 'The mere fact that Bayindir had always been subject to exactly the same legal and regulatory framework as everybody else in Pakistan does not necessarily mean that it was actually treated in the same way as local (or third countries) investors. In other words, as is evident from the broad wording of Article II (2) of the Turkey/Pakistan BIT, the treatment the investor is offered under the MFN clause is not limited to "regulatory treatment"'; para. 223 reads: 'The fact remains that, taken together, Bayindir's allegations in respect of the selective tender, and that the expulsion was due to Pakistan's decision to favor a local contractor, and that the local contractor was awarded longer completion time-limits, if proven, are clearly capable of founding a MFN claim.'

[64] *Continental Casualty Co. v Argentina*, ICSID Case No. ARB/03/9, Decision on Jurisdiction, 22 February 2006.

[65] *National Grid plc v The Argentine Republic* (UNCITRAL), Decision on Jurisdiction, 20 June 2006, paras 53 *et seq*.

[66] *Telenor Mobile Communications A.S. v Hungary*, ICSID Case No. ARB/04/15, Award, 13 September 2006.

which no prior litigation in local courts was necessary was borrowed again as being a more favourable treatment.[67]

Berschader v Russia

An arbitral tribunal at the Stockholm Arbitration Institute declined jurisdiction to hear a claim by two Belgian businessmen brought pursuant to the USSR/Belgium BIT. The tribunal noted that the relevant dispute settlement provision in the BIT originally concluded between the USSR and Belgium was rather narrow and permitted investor-state arbitration only in case of disputes over the amount of compensation owing in the event of an expropriation or nationalization. By a majority of two-to-one the tribunal refused to allow the Belgian investors to invoke the MFN clause in this agreement in an effort to 'borrow' more favourable dispute settlement rules found in more recent bilateral investment treaties signed by Russia.[68]

E. Specific Issues Addressed in Investor-State Arbitration

The *Ejusdem Generis* Principle

The dynamic nature of the MFN clause is intended to operate only in situations where a treatment occurs in 'like situations' or 'like circumstances'. One can see it as a normal limitation of any non-discrimination rule as it exists in most if not all legal systems. When it comes to the application of the MFN clause in the basic treaty to invoke the applicability of a specific treatment provision in a third party treaty this principle is normally referred to as the '*ejusdem* (or *eiusdem*) *generis* principle'. It is normally understood to mean that the third party treaty must, in principle, regulate the same subject-matter as the basic treaty, otherwise the specific treatment standard would be taken out of its context and thus not be accorded in 'like circumstances' or in 'like situations'. No other rights can be claimed under an MFN clause than those falling within the limits of the subject-matter of the clause. Furthermore, one can extend this principle to the 'persons and things' covered by the standard which must be of the same category.[69]

---

[67] *Suez, Sociedad General de Aguas de Barcelona S.A., and Vivendi Universal S.A. v The Argentine Republic*, ICSID Case No. ARB/03/19; and *AWG Group Ltd v The Argentine Republic* (UNCITRAL), Decision on Jurisdiction, 3 August 2006.

[68] According to L. Peterson, *Investment Treaty News (ITN)* (23 August 2006), available at www.iisd.org/pdf/2006/itn_aug23_2006.pdf (last visited 19 November 2007), the reasons, along with the fuller arbitral award, have not been published. The names of the presiding arbitrators have not been released; however the website of one well-known Canadian attorney, Todd Grierson Weiler, who acts on behalf of various foreign investors in such disputes, discloses that he was a member of the three person arbitral tribunal, see http://www.toddweiler.com/3_arbitration.html (last visited 19 November 2007).

[69] E. Ustor, 'Most Favoured Nation Clause', 3 *Encyclopaedia of Public International Law* (1997) 472, as referred to also by Acconci, above n. 4. See also *The Anglo-Iranian Oil Company (Jurisdiction)*

E. *Specific Issues Addressed in Investor-State Arbitration* 75

So far, ascertaining the application of this principle has not given rise to controversial issues within investment cases. In reality, the *ejusdem generis* principle has been extensively discussed only by the ICSID tribunals of the *Maffezini* and *Suez* cases.[70] This can be explained by the fact that investors have normally invoked rules contained in third party BITs under the MFN clause of a BIT (basic treaty). Even where the treaty does not specify that the MFN principle applies only to 'like circumstances' or in 'like situations', it can be considered as an inherent principle underlying the MFN principle.[71]

An interesting example for a different situation from a domestic context where this question was discussed is a legal opinion by the Swiss Directorate of Public International Law, a unit of the Swiss Department of Foreign Affairs of 1994.[72] In this case, a plaintiff invoked under the MFN clause contained in Article 4 of the Convention on Establishment and Legal Protection of 1927[73] the procedural rights contained in the Convention of 16 September 1988 on Jurisdiction and the Enforcement of Judgments in Civil and Commercial Matters (so-called Lugano Convention).[74] The authority denied such a right invoking the *ejusdem generis* principle as the two treaties did not have 'the same objective'.

Explicit Descriptions of the Scope

Some MFN clauses are very general in scope. A typical example is the clause in the Agreement between Spain and Argentina, as it was at stake in the *Maffezini* decision. Article IV(2) of the Argentina/Spain BIT[75] is relatively open or unspecific with regard to the exact scope of the MFN clause:

In *all matters subject to this Agreement*, this *treatment* shall not be less favourable than that extended by each Party to the investments made in its territory by investors of a third country.[76]

Case (*United Kingdom v Iran*), 22 July 1952; and Articles 9 and 10 of the Draft Articles on Most-Favoured-Nation Clauses (1978), above n. 27.

[70] See Acconci, above n. 4. See on the application of this principle with regard to the *Maffezini* and *Plama* cases also C. McLachlan, L. Shore, and M. Weiniger, *International Investment Arbitration—Substantive Principles* (2007) 254–257.

[71] See also with regard to the specific case of Swiss BITs, M. Schmid, *Swiss Investment Protection Agreements: Most-Favoured-Nation Treatment and Umbrella Clauses* (2007) 43.

[72] Direction du droit international public, Avis, 11 mars 1994; reprinted in French in *Revue suisse de droit international et de droit européen* (1995) 25 *et seq.*; equally reprinted in *Jurisprudence des autorités administratives de la Confédération (JAAC)* (No. 59), 155; available at http://www.vpb.admin.ch/deutsch/doc/59/59.155.html (last visited 9 November 2007).

[73] Convention d'établissement et de protection juridique que la Suisse et la Grèce (1927).

[74] At the time of the dispute Greece was not yet a Party to this Convention.

[75] Argentina/Spain BIT (1991).

[76] English translation of the Spanish original, 'En todas las material regidas por el presente Acuerdo, este tratamiento no será menos favorable que el otorgado por cada Parte a los inversiones realizadas en su territorio por inversores de un tercer país.'

Certain MFN clauses go further in their explicitness and define the types of situations in which the treatment is subject to the MFN standard. Article 1103 (Most-Favoured-Nation Treatment) of the North American Free Trade Agreement (NAFTA) (which resembles very much Article 4 of the 2004 US Model BIT) reads:

1. Each Party shall accord to investors of another Party treatment no less favorable than that it accords, in like circumstances, to investors of any other Party or of a non-Party *with respect to the establishment, acquisition, expansion, management, conduct, operation, and sale or other disposition of investments.*
2. Each Party shall accord to investments of investors of another Party treatment no less favorable than that it accords, in like circumstances, to investments of investors of any other Party or of a non-Party *with respect to the establishment, acquisition, expansion, management, conduct, operation, and sale or other disposition of investments.*[77]

This MFN treatment clause is specific—in comparison to those clauses concluded especially by most European States (at least until recently)—in so far as it includes besides the 'management, conduct, operation, and sale or other disposition of investments' also the 'establishment, acquisition, expansion' and thus extends MFN treatment to market access or establishment, ie rights normally related to the pre-establishment phase of foreign direct investment. While traditionally only the United States and Canada regularly included such market access rights, it is now very common for many States to include them in the general scope of the treatment standards of an agreement.[78]

Similarly, Article 40(1) (National Treatment and Most-Favoured-Nation Treatment) of the Investment Chapter in the EFTA/Singapore Free Trade Agreement reads:

Each Party shall accord to investors and investments of investors of another Party, *in relation to the establishment, acquisition, expansion, management, conduct, operation and disposal of investments*, treatment that is no less favourable than that which it accords *in like situations* to its own investors and their investments or to investors and their investments of any other State, whichever is more favourable.[79]

Here again, we see that the extension of the MFN clause is limited to certain operations (including pre-establishment rights) and only applies in 'like situations'.

---

[77] Article 1103 NAFTA (emphasis added).
[78] See for many examples from the Canadian and US practice, Acconci, above n. 4, Section 3.1, with reference, eg, to Article II(3) Canada/Latvia BIT (1995); Article II(3) Canada/South Africa BIT (1995); Article II(1) US/Nicaragua BIT (1995); Article II(3) Canada/Egypt BIT (1996); Article II(3) Canada/Panama BIT (1996); Article II(3) Canada/Venezuela BIT (1996); Article II(3) Canada/Thailand BIT (1997); Article II(1) US/Azerbaijan BIT (1997); Article II(1) US/Jordan BIT (1997); Article 2(1) US/Bahrain BIT (1999); Article II(1) US/El Salvador BIT (1999). See also Article 4 Canadian Model BIT (2004); and Article 4 US Model BIT (2004). See also J.W. Salacuse, 'Do BITs Really Work? An Evaluation of Bilateral Investment Treaties and Their Grand Bargain', 46 *Harvard International Law Journal* (2005) 67, 93–94.
[79] Article 40(1) EFTA/Singapore FTA (emphasis added).

E. Specific Issues Addressed in Investor-State Arbitration

Similarly, NAFTA speaks of 'like circumstances'. Other variations of the MFN clause may not specify at all what kinds of treatment they apply, ie specific standards, treatment in general, or any provision of the treaty. Article 3 (first part) of the Treaty between the Federal Republic of Germany and the Co-operative Republic of Guyana concerning the Encouragement and Reciprocal Protection of Investments of 6 December 1989 reads:

Neither Contracting Party shall subject investments in its territory owned or controlled by nationals or companies of the other Contracting Party to *treatment* less favourable than it accords to investments of its own nationals or companies of any third State.

Neither Contracting Party shall subject nationals or companies of the other Contracting Party, as regards their *activity in connection with investments in its territory, to treatment less favourable* than it accords to its own nationals or companies of any third State.[80]

More specifically when it comes to the treatment of investors, Article 4 of the 1995 Swiss Model BIT provides:

(2) Each Contracting Party shall in its territory accord investments or returns of investors of the other Contracting Party *treatment not less favourable* than that which it accords to investments or returns of its own investors or to investments or returns of investors of any third State, whichever is more favourable to the investor concerned.

(3) Each Contracting Party shall in its territory accord investors of the other Contracting Party, as regards the *management, maintenance, use, enjoyment or disposal of their investments, treatment* not less favourable than that which it accords to its own investors or investors of any third State, whichever is more favourable to the investor concerned.[81]

Here the scope of the protection of investors is limited to specific situations when it comes to the protection of investors but not when it comes to the treatment of investments as such although the term 'treatment' appears in both instances.[82]

Finally, it is possible to include an additional MFN standard in a specific treaty provision thereby limiting the scope of this particular provision to the specific standard.[83]

Some BITs, such as certain treaties negotiated by the UK, clearly specify that their MFN treatment clauses are to be applied also to dispute settlement. The ICSID tribunal in *Maffezini v Spain* noted, however, that such clear intention explicitly mentioned in the text was not very common, as far as investment treaties

---

[80] Article 3 Germany/Guyana BIT (1989) (emphasis added).
[81] Article 4 Swiss Model BIT (1995) (emphasis added).
[82] It should be noted that this MFN clause applies only to the post-establishment phase, contrary to the solution negotiated by Switzerland with its EFTA partners in the Agreement with Singapore as shown above.
[83] See Acconci, above n. 4, Section 3.1, with reference to Article 4(4) Germany/Barbados BIT (1994). See also Article 7 Bolivia/Peru BIT (1993).

were concerned.[84] Yet, in 1978, the Commentaries by the ILC included the administration of justice in general among the possible subject-matters of MFN clauses.[85] Whether this means that all aspects relating to investor-State dispute settlement are considered to be part of the treatment to be accorded is an open question.[86]

The specific question as to whether a non-discrimination obligation applied also to procedural standards besides substantive treatment provisions has also arisen in the framework of trade, more specifically in relation to the GATT of 1947, in the case *United States—Section No 337 of the Tariff Act of 1930*.[87] The case concerned an allegation by the European Community that the United States accorded to imported products challenged as infringing US patents treatment less favourable than the treatment accorded to products of US origin similarly challenged. This application of different procedural requirements regarding the administration of justice was considered an infringement of Article III(4) (National Treatment) of the GATT of 1947. Furthermore, the jurisprudence of GATT/WTO panels and more recently the WTO Appellate Body has developed a very comprehensive case law not only applying to *de jure* discrimination but also to *de facto* violations of the MFN clause.[88]

While some arbitral tribunals in investment disputes have tried to distinguish the application of MFN clauses in investment cases that do not specify in detail their applicability to specific areas from the application of more open-worded provisions, it seems overall that the resulting theory is rather weak and makes the outcome of a specific arbitration unpredictable.[89] Of course, one may try to elaborate a coherent theory regarding the fundamental differences in the text of various treaties in question and the circumstances in which the MFN question arose,[90] but such an approach has clear limits and may be difficult to maintain

---

[84] *Maffezini v Spain*, above n. 41, paras 42 *et seq.*, and in this respect also Acconci, above n. 4, Section 5.1, with reference to *The Ambatielos Case (Greece v United Kingdom)*, Award, 6 March 1956, XII UNRIAA (1963), 107. She confirms that the Draft Articles prepared by the UN International Law Commission, above n. 27, para. 24, included also the 'administration of justice' among the possible subject-matters of a most-favoured-nation clause.

[85] Draft Articles on most-favoured-nation clauses (1978), above n. 27, paras 16 *et seq.*

[86] See, eg, R. Dolzer and M. Stevens, *Bilateral Investment Treaties* (1995) 58; or J.-P. Laviec, *Protection et Promotion des Investissements: Etude de Droit International Economique* (1985) 98; and the arbitral awards of *Plama Consortium v Bulgaria*, above n. 56, para. 189; or *Siemens A.G. v Argentina*, Decision on Jurisdiction, above n. 53, para. 106.

[87] GATT Panel Report of 7 November 1989, reprinted in 36 *GATT Basic Instruments and Selected Documents* (1990) 345. See also on this issue Acconci, above n. 4, Section 1.

[88] See, eg, *Canada—Autos (Japan v Canada)*, Panel Report, 11 February 2000, and Appellate Body Report, 31 May 2000.

[89] See also Egli, above n. 2, 1075, who states correctly: 'It is important to note, however, that the Maffezini Tribunal did not base its decision on the breadth of the MFN clause in the Argentina-Spain BIT. Instead, it asserted that "there are good reasons to conclude that today dispute settlement arrangements are inextricably related to the protection of foreign investors."'; *Maffezini v Kingdom of Spain*, above n. 41, para. 54.

[90] Such as attempted by S. Vesel, 'Clearing a Path Through a Tangled Jurisprudence: Most-Favored-Nation Clauses and Dispute Settlement Provisions in Bilateral Investment Treaties', 32 *Yale Journal of International Law* (2007) 125, 127.

over time. As a consequence, several States have started to prefer to clearly state in the negotiating history or in the agreement itself what should be exempted from the application of an MFN clause.[91]

General and Explicit Exceptions from MFN Treatment

Like any treaty provision, the guarantee of the MFN clause can be subject to general exceptions contained in the Treaty. While this is well known in respect of the GATT (Article XX) or the GATS (Article XIV), it is a more recent tendency in BITs. The 2004 Canadian Model BIT

[...] includes a modified GATT Article XX-like general exceptions provision that applies to all obligations in the model treaty. The general exceptions cover measures to protect human, animal or plant life or health, to ensure compliance with law and for conservation purposes. This type of general exceptions provision, while common in trade treaties, has not been used extensively in BITs.[92]

Hence, the meaning of these exceptions with regard to investments is less tested; as a consequence, some agreements provide for the application *mutatis mutandis* of the exceptions known from trade in goods and trade in services. For example, the Free Trade Agreement between the EFTA States and Singapore[93] contains a chapter on investment and in this chapter Article 49 provides:

The following provisions shall apply, *mutatis mutandis*, to this Chapter: Articles 33 [General Exceptions in the area of trade in services], 34 [Security exceptions in the area of trade in services] and 35 [Restrictions to Safeguard the Balance-of-Payments], as well as Article 19 (e) [General exceptions relating to the trade in goods and prison labour], (f) [General exceptions relating to the trade in goods and the protection of national treasures of artistic, historic or archaeological value] and (g) [General exceptions relating to the trade in goods and measures relating to the conservation of exhaustible natural resources if such measures are made effective in conjunction with restrictions on domestic production or consumption].

It is also possible that the applicability of the MFN clause is explicitly excluded in relation to specific treaties concluded with third States that go further in their scope and nature than the treaty including the MFN clause.[94] Another possibility is to exclude certain regulatory areas in general, such as taxation.[95]

---

[91] See below, next section.
[92] See also A. Newcombe, 'Canada's New Model Foreign Investment Protection Agreement', 14 *Canadian Council on International Law Bulletin* (2004), 30, available at http://www.ccil-ccdi.ca (last visited 19 November 2007).
[93] EFTA/Singapore FTA (2002).
[94] See also Dolzer and Myers, above n. 40, 49 *et seq.*; and Herdegen, above n. 12, 221.
[95] See Acconci, above n. 4, Section 3, with reference to K.J. Vandevelde, 'The Political Economy of a Bilateral Investment Treaty', 92 *American Journal of International Law* (1998) 621; and A.A. Fatouros, 'Towards an International Agreement on Foreign Direct Investment?', 10 *ICSID Review—Foreign Investment Law Journal* (1995) 188, 195–196.

The exclusion of specific treaties is particularly common in relation to so-called economic integration agreements in relation to mere investment protection agreements or chapters. Often the respective exception is referred to as the REIO (Regional Economic Integration Organisation) exception.[96] This practice parallels the exception of Article XXIV GATT, later applied also under Article V GATS.[97]

Article 3 (second part) of the Treaty between Guyana and Germany of 1989 reads:

[...] Such treatment shall not relate, to privileges which either Contracting Party accords to nationals or companies of third States on account of its membership of or association with: customs or economic union, a common market or free trade area; or other regional economic cooperation Agreements which have similar objections.

The treatment granted under this Article shall not relate to advantages which either Contracting Party accords to nationals or companies of third States by virtue of a *double taxation agreement or other agreements regarding matters of taxation*.[98]

Similarly Article 40(2) of the EFTA/Singapore Agreement provides:

2. If a Party accords more favourable treatment to investors of any other State or their investments by virtue of a *free trade agreement, customs union or similar agreement that also provides for substantial liberalisation of investments*, it shall not be obliged to accord such treatment to investors of another Party or their investments. However, upon request from another Party, it shall afford adequate opportunity to negotiate the benefits granted therein.[99]

This last example is particularly interesting as it excludes even '*any agreement that also provides for substantial liberalisation of investments*' but confers a right to negotiate the same benefits. Such negotiations shall be initiated only upon request and they are obviously without any guarantee of a positive outcome. The general good faith principle remains, however, applicable to such negotiations.

A particular problem may relate to the fact that one party to a BIT or an investment chapter in an FTA is not a party to the GATT or the GATS or has opted for very limited commitments (possibly including reservations) in the framework of the GATT. Such constellations may require exemptions from the scope of an MFN clause with regard to these commitments in order to avoid unwanted modifications of the respective commitments under the WTO.[100] The EFTA/Singapore FTA contains a rule to separate the scope of application

---

[96] UNCTAD, *The REIO exception in MFN treatment clauses*, UNCTAD Series on Issues in International Investment Agreements (2004).
[97] See below, Part F.
[98] Article 3 Germany/Guyana BIT (1989) (emphasis added).
[99] Article 40 EFTA/Singapore FTA (2002) (emphasis added).
[100] See Acconci, above n. 4, Section 3.1 *in fine*; with regard to the GATT she refers to the fact that the US/Russia BIT (1992) provides for a specific exception which reads as follows: '[...] the exclusion from the most-favored-nation treatment obligations shall apply also to advantages accorded by the United States by virtue of its binding obligations under any multilateral

E. Specific Issues Addressed in Investor-State Arbitration

of the guarantees contained in the investment chapter from those in the chapter on trade in services under mode 3 (commercial presence) to avoid undesirable consequences:

Article 40 (1) [*National Treatment and Most-Favoured-Nation Treatment*] shall not apply to measures affecting trade in services whether or not a sector concerned is scheduled in Chapter III [Trade in Services] [...] Article 40 (1) shall also not apply to investors of a Party in services sectors and their investments in such sectors. This provision is subject to review after a period of ten years from the date of entry into force of this Agreement, with a view to examining its continued need.

More recently, in view of the uncertainty relating to the scope of MFN clauses following *Maffezini*[101] several States have started to explicitly address the issue of the scope in their Model agreements or in actually concluded agreements. The Canadian Model BIT (2004) (Foreign Investment Protection Agreement), inter alia, includes a specific provision eliminating the possibility to borrow treaty provisions from treaties with third parties.[102] According to Annex III to the Canadian Model BIT, its Article 4 (MFN clause):

[...] shall not apply to treatment accorded under all bilateral and multilateral international agreements in force or signed prior to the date of entry into of this Agreement.

Under this mechanism MFN treatment does not extend to treatment accorded under existing treaties.

The MFN guarantee is therefore prospective. This ensures that foreign investors under the new model cannot reach back and try to obtain the protection afforded by previous treaties. This provision seeks to avoid investment treaty shopping—the argument that MFN applies not only to the actual treatment of other foreign investors but also to the protection guaranteed to other foreign investors in other FIPAs.[103]

The 2003 Draft FTAA Agreement includes a footnote (no. 13) whose text is to be deemed 'as a reflection of the Parties' shared understanding of the most-favoured-nation Article and the *Maffezini* case'. It reads currently:

One delegation proposes the following footnote to be included in the negotiating history as a reflection of the Parties' shared understanding of the Most-Favoured-Nation Article and the *Maffezini* case. This footnote would be deleted in the final text of the Agreement:
The Parties note the recent decision of the arbitral tribunal in Maffezini (Arg.) v. Kingdom of Spain, which found an unusually broad most favored nation clause in an Argentina-Spain agreement to encompass international dispute resolution procedures.

---

international agreement concluded under the framework of the GATT after the signature of this Treaty [...].' With regard to the GATS see also Acconci, above n. 4, Section 3.2.

[101] See above n. 41.
[102] See Acconci, above n. 4, Section 6; and Newcombe, above n. 92.
[103] Ibid.

See Decision on Jurisdiction §§ 38–64 (January 25, 2000), reprinted in 16 ICSID Rev.—F.I.L.J. 212 (2002). By contrast, the Most-Favoured-Nation Article of this Agreement is expressly limited in its scope to matters 'with respect to the establishment, acquisition, expansion, management, conduct, operation, and sale or other disposition of investments.' The Parties share the understanding and intent that this clause does not encompass international dispute resolution mechanisms such as those contained in Section C.2.b. (Dispute Settlement between a Party and an Investor of Another Party) of this Chapter, and therefore could not reasonably lead to a conclusion similar to that of the Maffezini case.[104]

Similarly, during the negotiations for a Central America–Dominican Republic– United States Free Trade Agreement (CAFTA) in 2004 the parties had included at some point a footnote in the draft text with the following text:

The Most-Favored-Nation Treatment Article of this Agreement is expressly limited in its scope to matters 'with respect to the establishment, acquisition, expansion, management, conduct operation and sale or other dispositions of investments.' The Parties share the understanding and intent that this clause does not encompass international dispute resolution mechanisms such as those contained in Section C of this chapter, and therefore could not reasonably lead to a conclusion similar to that of the *Maffezini* case.

The footnote was to be eliminated before the conclusion of the negotiations but its insertion in 2004 was specifically intended to make it part of the negotiating history. To the United States this approach obviously seems to be a way to prevent a '*Maffezini*-like' interpretation of the MFN clauses contained in its agreements without leading to an unwanted watering-down of the provision.[105]

Furthermore, on 30 May 2006, the European Commission (DG Trade) presented an Issue Paper for the attention of the EC's so-called 133 Committee in view of its future competence to negotiate investment treaties on behalf of the European Community and thus taking over this competence from the Member States, as envisaged in the most recent proposals for treaty amendments. In this Chapter the Commission suggested with regard to the inclusion of an appropriate MFN clause in future agreements:

The scope of application of the MFN clause is focused and limited to establishment, thus clearly signalling that it could not extend to BIT provisions on expropriation and dispute settlement.

It appears necessary to exclude from the benefit of this clause the most deep-integration agreements the EU concludes (i.e. to exclude granting to third countries the advantages resulting from—for instance—the EU/Balkans Stabilisation and Association Agreements that could lead at a later stage to EU accession). To that aim, the classical

---

[104] The text is available at http://www.ftaa-alca.org/FTAADraft03/ChapterXVII_e.asp#note13 (last visited 19 November 2007).

[105] See also L. Peterson, *Investment Law and Policy Weekly News Bulletin* (6 February 2004), available at www.iisd.org/pdf/2004/investment_investsd_feb6_2004.pdf (last visited 19 November 2007); and American Society of International Law, *International Law In Brief* (6 February 2004), available at http://www.asil.org/ilib/ilib0703.htm (last visited 19 November 2007).

E. Specific Issues Addressed in Investor-State Arbitration

regional economic integration organisation (REIO) clause needs to be adjusted to avoid a carve-out from the scope of MFN treatment of any FTA, which would be counter-productive.

Here again, this approach is fully consistent with WTO commitments of the EU under the GATS, since the latter contains an MFN provision of general application. It is also consistent with existing EU agreements with third countries that already contain an MFN provision (ex: Article 30 of the EU-Jordan Association Agreement; Article 48 of the Agreement EU-FYROM).[106]

Finally, Switzerland has very recently partly changed its practice regarding the language related to MFN treatments in its BITs in what seems a clear reaction to the *Maffezini* case law. In the agreement with Colombia signed on 17 May 2006,[107] the parties have included an Annex which reads:

For greater certainty, it is further understood that the most favourable nation treatment [...] does not encompass mechanisms for the settlement of investment disputes provided for in other international agreements concluded by the Party concerned.[108]

Specifically Negotiated Provisions

The use of the MFN clause to invoke the applicability of treaty norms between one party of the treaty at stake and a third State is subject to the condition that the two treaties do create *like circumstances*, ie they must regulate the same subject-matter.[109] In the *Tecmed* arbitral award,[110] the arbitral tribunal held that the MFN clause could not be used to invoke those provisions of a Treaty with a third State that were clearly the result of a particular negotiation situation with this third State and thus constituted part of a specific 'package deal' made up of specific rights and obligations ('[...] core matters that must be deemed to be specifically negotiated by the Contracting Parties [...]').[111]

In the view of the *Tecmed* arbitral tribunal, the very nature of these provisions makes them unfit for being invoked by third States under an MFN clause.[112] The provision providing for retroactive application of a BIT to investments made

---

[106] The text was made available at: www.iisd.org/pdf/2006/tas_upgrading_eu.pdf (last visited 19 November 2007); see also on this issue D. Vis-Dunbar and L.E. Peterson, 'European Commission makes another play for power to negotiate investment pacts', *Investment Treaty News (ITN)* (9 July 2006), para. 6; available at http://www.iisd.org/investment/itn (last visited 19 November 2007).

[107] Swiss Federal Council, Despatch to the Swiss Parliament regarding the Agreements on the Promotion and Protection of Investments with Serbia and Montenegro, Guyana, Azerbaijan, Saudi Arabia and Colombia, 22 September 2006, *Official Gazette* [Bundesblatt] (2006) 8455, 8460, available in German at http://www.admin.ch/ch/d/ff/2006/8455.pdf (last visited 19 November 2007).

[108] Article 4 para. 2 Protocol to the Swiss/Colombia BIT, above n. 107.

[109] See also Herdegen, above n. 12, 221.

[110] *Tecmed S.A. v The United Mexican States*, above n. 51.

[111] Ibid., para. 69.

[112] See also Herdegen, above n. 12, 221.

before the entry into force of the BIT was considered to be such a clause that had only been granted to the respective treaty partner in view of the specific negotiating situation and could thus not be invoked by an investor under another BIT.

Already the *Maffezini* tribunal had held that

[...] the beneficiary of the [MFN] clause should not be able to override *public policy considerations* that the contracting parties might have envisaged as fundamental conditions for their acceptance of the agreement in question.[113]

According to the tribunal this would apply, for instance,

(a) where a State has conditioned its consent to arbitration on the exhaustion of local remedies;
(b) where a BIT contains a 'fork-in-the-road'-clause according to which a choice between domestic or international courts or tribunals becomes irreversible once made;
(c) where a particular forum such as ICSID or NAFTA has been chosen;
(d) if the parties have agreed to a highly institutionalized system of arbitration that incorporates precise rules of procedure such as NAFTA.[114]

However, the *Maffezini* tribunal considered a mere requirement to first resort to domestic courts during a period of 18 months did not reflect a fundamental question of public policy which would have limited the scope of the MFN clause.[115]

Relevance for Procedural Provision

Overall, the main question in the *Maffezini*[116] arbitral Award and later similar decisions remained whether the MFN clause applied only to substantive rules (treatment provisions) or also procedural rules, such as the rules relating to dispute settlement or application *ratione temporis* (retrospective application) or *ratione materiae* (umbrella clauses) under a BIT.[117]

According to Reinisch, the *Maffezini* approach was endorsed in cases like *ADF v USA*[118] and *MTD v Chile*[119] which mainly dealt with the 'import' of substantive standards from other BITs. It was also used in *Tecmed v Mexico*[120] and even expanded in *Siemens v Argentina*.[121] Subsequent cases affirming the *Maffezini*

---

[113] *Maffezini v Spain*, above n. 41, para. 62.
[114] Ibid., para. 63.
[115] See Reinisch, above n. 42.
[116] *Maffezini v Spain*, above n. 41, paras 53 *et seq*.
[117] The question as to whether the MFN treatment obligation applied also to procedural standards besides substantive treatment provisions has also arisen in the framework of trade, more specifically in relation to the GATT (1947) in the case *United States—Section No. 337 of the Tariff Act of 1930*, above n. 87.
[118] *ADF v USA*, above n. 48, paras 193 *et seq*.
[119] *MTD v Chile*, above n. 52, para. 103.
[120] *Tecmed v Mexico*, above n. 51.
[121] *Siemens v Argentina*, above n. 53.

E. Specific Issues Addressed in Investor-State Arbitration

approach are *Gas Natural v Argentina*,[122] *Camuzzi v Argentina*,[123] *National Grid plc v Argentina*,[124] as well as *Suez, Sociedad General de Aguas de Barcelona S.A., and Vivendi Universal S.A. v Argentina*,[125] and *AWG Group Ltd v Argentina*.[126] In *Salini v Jordan*,[127] in *Plama v Bulgaria*[128] and in *Telenor v Hungary*,[129] however, ICSID tribunals came to the conclusion that the applicable MFN clauses did not extend to dispute settlement.[130]

Those authors and arbitrators opposed to applying the MFN clause to procedural guarantees, in particular dispute settlement, mostly consider such an application contrary to the intention of the contracting parties.[131] In the *Plama v Bulgaria* case, the arbitral tribunal stated accordingly:

[A]n MFN provision in a basic treaty does not incorporate by reference dispute settlement provisions in whole or in part set forth in another treaty, unless the MFN provision in the basic treaty leaves no doubt that the Contracting Parties intended to incorporate them.[132]

Also the recent steps by Canada, the United States and the EC to limit the scope of their MFN clauses included in BITs seems to hint into this direction.[133] At the same time, many arbitrators and authors seem to consider such limitation unnecessary, or at least not supported by the treaty language used in the past. The *Maffezini* tribunal openly rejected Spain's argument that 'matters' can only be understood to refer to substantive matters or material aspects of the treatment granted to investors and not to procedural or jurisdictional questions. Relying on international precedents and considering the broad wording of the MFN clause which refers to 'all matters subject to this Agreement', the tribunal emphasized that dispute settlement provisions in BITs were '[...] essential to the protection of the rights envisaged under the pertinent treaties; they are also closely linked to the material aspects of the treatment accorded'.[134] Similarly, Gaillard considers it logical to include dispute settlement provisions among the types of treatment subject to MFN.[135] Also, several other authors seem in favour of including

---

[122] *Gas Natural v Argentina*, above n. 60.
[123] *Camuzzi v Argentina*, above n. 59.
[124] *National Grid plc v Argentina*, above n. 65.
[125] *Suez, Sociedad General de Aguas de Barcelona S.A., and Vivendi Universal S.A. v Argentina*, above n. 67.
[126] *AWG Group Ltd v Argentina*, above n. 67.
[127] *Salini v Jordan*, above n. 54.
[128] *Plama v Bulgaria*, above n. 56.
[129] *Telenor v Hungary*, above n. 66.
[130] See Reinisch, above n. 42.
[131] See Herdegen, above n. 12, 221, with reference to the arbitral awards in *Salini v Jordan*, above n. 54, paras 102 *et seq.*; and *Plama v Bulgaria*, above n. 56, para. 223.
[132] Ibid., para. 223.
[133] See preceding section.
[134] *Maffezini v Spain*, above n. 41, para. 55, as summarized by Reinisch, above n. 42.
[135] See E. Gaillard, 'Chronique des sentences arbitrales', 132 *Journal du Droit International* (2005) 135, 163: 'Lorsque la clause est rédigée en des termes très généraux, tout laisse à penser

procedural rules as long as this seems openly excluded by the wording of a treaty or is evident from the context when interpreting the treaty at stake.[136]

F. Outlook

In recent years, arbitrators and commentators have been focusing on the question whether the MFN treatment clause of BITs applies to all types of treatment or whether it is limited to certain kinds of treatment. For some, the case law of various arbitral tribunals diverges heavily. Others have tried to distinguish the different arbitral awards and to develop a coherent theory taking into account the wording and context of specific MFN clauses. These theories which try to establish under what circumstances MFN treatment should have a broad scope (possibly including consent to arbitration, procedural aspects of dispute settlement), and when MFN does not apply seem, however, not extremely convincing. Therefore, more and more States seem to prefer a clear exclusion of procedural provisions, especially dispute settlement. They do so by stating the exception in an appropriate way in the text or the negotiating history of the newer agreements.

Normally the questions relating to MFN treatment in the WTO context are different from the investment context as we are confronted with a multilateral system which provides for a common standard. At the same time, this system is full of exceptions such as those relating to regional trade agreements (Article XXIV GATT, Article V GATS) and preferences accorded to developing countries. This usually prevents the States from invoking dispute settlement provisions or other procedural or substantive rules from FTAs or agreements on double taxation, etc, in the WTO context.

---

que l'intention des rédacteurs du traité était bien de lui permettre de jouer à l'égard de tous les bénéfices que l'Etat d'accueil serait susceptible d'accorder aux ressortissants d'Etats tiers. Or force est de constater que l'accès à un mécanisme efficace et neutre de règlement des différends [...] est bien l'un des bénéfices les plus importants, sinon le plus important, susceptible de résulter du droit contemporain de la protection des investissements.' See also E. Gaillard, 'Establishing Jurisdiction through a Most-Favoured Nation Clause', above n. 40, 3.

[136] See also P. Bernardini, 'Investment Arbitration under the ICSID Convention and BITs', in G. Aksen *et al.* (eds), *Liber Amicorum in Honour of Robert Briner* (2005) 95; C. Schreuer, *The Dynamic Evolution of the ICSID System* (2006) 9. See also Schmid, above n. 71, 46.

5
Arbitrary and Unreasonable Measures

Veijo Heiskanen

A. Introduction

Arbitrary and unreasonable measures are among the many causes of action often available to investors under bilateral and multilateral investment treaties. Various formulations have been adopted to establish a legal standard providing protection against such measures. However, the relevant treaty provision usually provides protection to investors against either arbitrary or unreasonable measures, but rarely for both. Does this mean that, regardless of the formulation, such provisions are intended to provide protection against identical or at least similar measures? Or is there a legally definable difference between 'arbitrary' and 'unreasonable' measures that is of relevance in the context of arbitral decision-making?

To complicate matters, many investment treaties provide for protection against arbitrary and unreasonable measures in the form of a standard that combines protection against arbitrary or unreasonable measures and/or discrimination ('arbitrary or discriminatory measures'; 'arbitrary and discriminatory measures'; 'unreasonable or discriminatory measures'; 'unreasonable and discriminatory measures'). When confronted with such formulations, arbitral tribunals have generally taken the view that the disjunctive 'or' has a normative function and that, accordingly, in order to establish a breach of the standard, it is sufficient for the claimant to demonstrate that one of the two legs of the standard has been breached, ie that arbitrary or unreasonable measures, as the case may be, have been taken, *or* that the claimant has been discriminated against.[1] Thus, in such instances the relevant provision effectively embodies two different standards—one protecting against arbitrary or unreasonable measures, as the case may be, and the other against discriminatory measures. Based on recent case law, the disjunctive formulation of the standard also appears to be the more common one in practice, although other formulations can also be found.[2]

---

[1] For further discussion see below n. 42 and accompanying text.
[2] See, eg, *Ronald S. Lauder v Czech Republic* (UNCITRAL), Award, 3 September 2001, para. 219, concluding that the wording of Article II(2)(b) US/Czech Republic BIT— arbitrary

This chapter focuses on arbitrary and unreasonable measures and, accordingly, will not address discrimination, except where relevant. In practical terms, this means that the chapter deals primarily with treaty provisions that provide protection against arbitrary or unreasonable measures, as the case may be, *or* discrimination.[3]

As regards protection against *arbitrary* governmental measures, the *locus classicus* is the *ELSI*[4] case, the first case brought before the International Court of Justice (ICJ) dealing with substantive standards of investment protection. There, the relevant provision, Article I of the Supplementary Agreement to the Treaty of Friendship, Commerce and Navigation between the United States and Italy of 1948 (the 'FCN Treaty') provided, in relevant part:

The nationals, corporations and associations of either High Contracting Party shall not be subjected to *arbitrary or discriminatory* measures within the territories of the other Contracting Party resulting particularly in: (a) preventing their effective control and management of enterprises which they have been permitted to establish or acquire therein; or, (b) impairing their other legally acquired rights and interests in such enterprises or in the investments which they have made, whether in the form of funds (loans, shares or otherwise), materials, equipment, services, processes, patents, techniques or otherwise.[5]

This formulation of the standard, which appears to have been common in FCN treaties, has been adapted and reformulated in modern bilateral and multilateral investment treaties. However, despite the more concise formulation, the substance of the standard has remained largely unaltered. In *Noble Ventures* the tribunal was faced with the new formulation, contained in Article II(2)(b) of the US/Romania BIT, which provided protection against arbitrary (or discriminatory) measures in terms that appear to have become standard in modern investment protection treaties:

Neither Party shall in any way impair by arbitrary or discriminatory measures the management, operation, maintenance, use, enjoyment, acquisition, expansion, or disposal of investments.[6]

---

and discriminatory measures'—implied that a breach of the standard required both an arbitrary *and* a discriminatory measure by the State. A recent case involved a bilateral investment treaty where the relevant provision ensured foreign investments 'equitable and reasonable treatment'. See *Parkerings-Compagniet AS v Lithuania*, ICSID Case No. ARB/05/8, Final Award, 11 September 2007. The tribunal found that the 'difference of interpretation between the terms "fair" and "reasonable" is insignificant' and concluded that this standard was in effect identical to the fair and equitable treatment standard. Ibid., paras 271–278.

[3] The prohibition of discrimination is addressed in two separate chapters of this book, dealing with the national treatment and most-favoured-nation treatment standards, respectively. See A. Bjorklund, at Chapter 3 above and A. Ziegler at Chapter 4 above.

[4] *Elettronica Sicula S.p.A. (ELSI) (United States of America v Italy)*, Judgment, 20 July 1989.

[5] Article I US/Italy FCN Treaty (1948) (emphasis added).

[6] *Noble Ventures v Romania*, ICSID Case No. ARB/01/11, Final Award, 12 October 2005, para. 47.

A similar formulation can be found in Article 10(1) of the Energy Charter Treaty (ECT), perhaps the most important multilateral treaty in the field of foreign investment protection. But unlike Article II(2)(b) of the US/Romania BIT, the ECT formulation protects investors against 'unreasonable' rather than 'arbitrary' measures:

Each Contracting Party shall, in accordance with the provisions of this Treaty, encourage and create stable, equitable, favourable and transparent conditions for Investors of other Contracting Parties to make Investments in its Area. Such conditions shall include a commitment to accord at all times to Investments of Investors of other Contracting Parties fair and equitable treatment. Such Investments shall also enjoy the most constant protection and security and *no Contracting Party shall in any way impair by unreasonable or discriminatory measures their management, maintenance, use, enjoyment or disposal*. In no case shall such Investments be accorded treatment less favourable than that required by international law, including treaty obligations.[7]

A similar or identical formulation of the standard is often found in bilateral investment treaties. In *Saluka*, which concerned a formulation identical to the ECT standard, contained in Article 3(1) of the Netherlands/Czech Republic BIT, the tribunal referred to this formulation as the 'non-impairment standard'.[8] This seems an appropriate shorthand, and accordingly it will also be used in this chapter.

B. Non-impairment Standard: Three Perspectives

In arbitral practice, breach of the non-impairment standard is usually asserted alternatively or cumulatively with breaches of other related standards, including expropriation, breach of fair and equitable treatment and failure to provide full security and protection. The relationship between these standards is far from clear, however, in particular if one approaches the issue from the standpoint of a less-known standard such as non-impairment. A number of issues arise, both from the point of view of arbitration strategy as well as of arbitral decision-making. Under what circumstances should the claimant pursue breach of the non-impairment standard as the principal basis of its claim? Should this be done only when an expropriation claim is not available? Or when neither an expropriation claim nor a fair and equitable treatment standard claim is available? What is the scope of application of, and the relationship between, the non-impairment standard and the full security and protection standard? Similarly, from the perspective of

---

[7] Article 10(1) ECT (emphasis added).
[8] *Saluka Investments BV (The Netherlands) v The Czech Republic*, Partial Award, 17 March 2006; Article 3(1) of the Netherlands/Czech Republic BIT provides that, with reference to the investments of investors of the other contracting party, '[e]ach Contracting Party [...] shall not impair, by unreasonable or discriminatory measures, the operation, management, maintenance, use, enjoyment or disposal thereof by those investors'.

the arbitral tribunal, in what circumstances should the tribunal rely on a breach of the non-impairment standard as the *ratio decidendi* of its decision? When an expropriation claim has not been proven? Or when neither an expropriation nor a breach of the fair and equitable treatment standard has been proven? If one or both of these have been established, is it still necessary or appropriate to proceed to deal with the non-impairment claim?

In practice, the non-impairment standard is rarely relied upon by investors as the principal or exclusive basis of their case. It is therefore hardly surprising that arbitral decisions usually do not turn on whether or not this particular standard has in fact been breached. Indeed, there appears to be only one case where the only breach of treaty found by the tribunal was that of the non-impairment standard. In *Lauder*, where the claimant asserted a number of alternative causes of action in addition to impairment, including expropriation, breach of fair and equitable treatment, failure to provide full security and protection, and failure to ensure minimum standard of treatment under international law, the tribunal found, after having examined and dismissed each of these claims, that only the 'arbitrary and discriminatory' measures standard had been breached. However, even if the tribunal found that a breach had occurred, it eventually concluded that no compensation was due because the losses sustained by the claimant were not directly or proximately caused by the measure which the tribunal found to be arbitrary and discriminatory:

The arbitrary and discriminatory breach by the Respondent of its Treaty obligations constituted a violation of the Treaty. The alleged harm was, however, caused in 1999 by the acts of CET 21, controlled by Mr Železný. The 1993 breach of the Treaty was too remote to qualify as a relevant cause for the harm caused. A finding on damages due to the Claimant by the Respondent would therefore not be appropriate.[9]

More generally, despite the growing body of arbitral jurisprudence dealing with the various substantive standards of investment protection, arbitral tribunals have struggled to develop a consistent approach to the relationships between the various standards and to define, even approximately, their scope of application. As noted above, the opacity of arbitral practice becomes particularly striking when one approaches it from the perspective of a less-known standard such as the non-impairment standard, rather than expropriation or fair and equitable treatment. When analysing the existing jurisprudence, one is constantly confronted with the interrelation between this and the other related standards. While this chapter is limited to pointing out these issues as they arise, the proper scope of application of each of the different standards, or the methodology that arbitral tribunals employ in determining the sequence in which the various causes of action should be considered, clearly deserves further discussion among investment arbitration professionals.

[9] *Lauder*, above n. 2, para. 235.

Given the varying approaches adopted by different tribunals, it seems convenient to analyse the recent arbitral jurisprudence from three different perspectives—the perspective of 'judicial economy', a 'methodological' perspective, and a 'substantive' perspective. Each of these perspectives is addressed below in turn.

The Perspective of 'Judicial Economy'

From the point of view of arbitral decision-making, one of the key issues in analysing the relationship between the non-impairment standard and the other related investment protection standards is whether, in cases where the claimant asserts a number of alternative or cumulative claims, there is a pragmatic way of establishing a priority between the various causes of action such that it would allow the tribunal to dispose of the case by dealing with only one of them rather than addressing each of them one by one.

As noted above, one such possible approach could be based on 'judicial economy'. In this approach, the tribunal would look at the possibility of prioritization from the perspective of valuation and quantification of the claims. In other words, the tribunal would ask itself whether one (or more) of the various causes of action asserted by the claimant should be given priority because, from the quantification and valuation perspective, compensation for a breach of such a standard, if established, would necessarily subsume any remedies that might be available as a result of a breach of all the other standards.

From this perspective, *expropriation* clearly appears to be the primary cause of action under multilateral and bilateral investment treaties. Assuming the various causes of action are asserted on the basis of the same set of facts, expropriation seems logically to be the one to be considered first since compensation for expropriation by definition covers a total loss of business and thus compensates the claimant for the loss of business as a whole. Accordingly, if the loss of business is compensated as a whole (or as a going concern), there can be, virtually by definition, no loss or damage left to be compensated separately based on a breach of the other, 'lesser' standards. Such losses are effectively subsumed by compensation for expropriation.

Conversely, compensation for breach of standards other than expropriation arguably should be granted only if the governmental measure in question falls short of a full-blown expropriation. From a valuation perspective, such other standards are designed to deal with business interruption rather than a total loss of business. Thus, for example, arbitrary and unreasonable governmental measures may damage a business and cause financial losses, but they do not usually result in a total loss of business, which continues after the interruption—if they did, they would effectively amount to expropriation. The only exception would appear to be the situation where the business is destroyed as a result of acts or omissions attributable to the government, which however neither seeks nor obtains any economic benefit as a result of such destruction. In such a case, the measure in question can perhaps more appropriately be characterized as failure to provide full security and protection (in case the property is destroyed by third parties whose acts are not attributable to the government) or as an arbitrary or unreasonable measure, depending on whether the government is able to provide any (police powers-based) justification for its action, rather than as an expropriation.[10]

Recent case law lends some support to the relevance of judicial economy as an approach to arbitral decision-making. Thus, in *Saluka*, the claimant asserted a number of causes of action, including failure to ensure fair and equitable treatment, impairment, failure to provide full security and protection, and expropriation, in this particular order. Disregarding the order in which the claims were asserted, the tribunal considered the expropriation claim first, dismissing it.[11] Similarly, in *Lauder* the tribunal addressed the expropriation claim first, even though the claimant put it forward as the last item on its list of causes of action. The tribunal did not provide any explanation or justification for its approach, simply stating that it felt it 'appropriate to address the issues in th[at] order'.[12] In *Nykomb*, an ECT case, the tribunal also followed the same approach, prioritizing the expropriation claim even though it appeared to have been the last claim among the claimant's pleadings.[13] In *Occidental* the tribunal also gave priority to the expropriation claim.[14]

By contrast, in *CME* the tribunal adopted a more complex approach. The tribunal first bifurcated the proceedings between liability and quantum, and when dealing with the liability issue, addressed in turn each of the various causes of action asserted by the claimant, finding a series of breaches of the various treatment standards.[15] In its final award on quantum, however, the tribunal quantified the claimant's losses applying only one methodology, focusing on compensating the claimant for the fair market value of the investment as a whole.[16] Of course, this is a methodology that applies in cases where the investment has not only been damaged but irreversibly lost—in other words, in cases of expropriation.

---

[10] See V. Heiskanen, 'The Doctrine of Indirect Expropriation in Light of the Practice of the Iran-United States Claims Tribunal', 8 *Journal of World Investment and Trade* (2007) 315, 230 and notes 31, 36 and 46. For further discussion see below n. 17 and accompanying text.
[11] *Saluka*, above n. 8 paras 252–265.
[12] *Lauder*, above n. 2, paras 193, 195.
[13] *Nykomb Synergetics Technology Holding AB v Latvia*, Stockholm Rules Energy Charter Treaty Arbitration, Final Award, 16 December 2003.
[14] *Occidental Exploration and Production Company v Republic of Ecuador*, LCIA No. UN 3467, Award, 1 July 2004. For further discussion see below n. 25 and accompanying text.
[15] See *CME Czech Republic B.V. v Czech Republic* (UNCITRAL), Partial Award, 13 September 2001, paras 611–614, finding that the facts that constituted an unlawful expropriation also breached fair and equitable treatment, the prohibition of unreasonable or discriminatory measures, the obligation of full security and protection and the minimum standard of treatment under the Netherlands/Czech Republic BIT.
[16] *CME Czech Republic v Czech Republic* (UNCITRAL), Final Award, 14 March 2003.

While the *CME* tribunal can be criticized for having made, in effect, 'unnecessary' findings of liability, to the extent that it went beyond the finding of expropriation, on quantum it in a sense respected judicial economy by refraining from quantifying each of the breaches separately. The question arises, however, whether arbitral tribunals should be even more aggressive and whether they should, when dealing with liability issues, limit their findings to expropriation alone, assuming it can be established, without proceeding any further. There seems to be no serious argument against such a more economical approach. Even in the context of possible annulment proceedings (in an ICSID context) or judicial review (in the context of an *ad hoc* arbitration), it is unlikely that the party seeking annulment or setting aside of the award—which invariably would be the respondent—would argue that the tribunal has failed to exercise its jurisdiction by failing to deal with the other causes of action asserted by the claimant.

In case the expropriation claim fails, does judicial economy provide any guidance for prioritizing the remaining causes of action? This is a more complicated question. From the perspective of quantification and valuation, none of the remaining standards—fair and equitable treatment, full security and protection and the non-impairment standard—would appear to command any priority. A breach of any of these standards does not generally result in a total loss of the investment—otherwise an expropriation would have been found—and in these circumstances judicial economy appears to provide little guidance. As noted above, the only exception would be the situation where the investment has been destroyed as a result of acts or omissions attributable to the government, with no economic benefit to the government itself. In such situations, the government's failure may be properly characterized as a failure to ensure full security and protection (in case of omission) or an arbitrary or unreasonable measure (in case of a positive act), rather than as an expropriation.[17]

'Methodological' Perspective

Where judicial economy fails to provide guidance, the question arises whether the various investment protection standards could be prioritized on another, more formal, or 'methodological' basis. Can it be argued that there is a formal 'hierarchy' among the various standards in the sense that a breach of one of the standards would *ipso jure* amount to a breach of another, related standard? Or vice versa, is it rather arguable that some of the standards are more specific or concrete than others and that therefore an arbitral tribunal should start its analysis from such more specific standards—*lex specialis derogat legi generali*? While arbitral tribunals appear to have recognized that these are legitimate questions, there seems to be no settled methodological approach.

[17] See above n. 10 and accompanying text.

From the perspective of a legal 'hierarchy', and setting aside expropriation, the argument can be made—and indeed has been made and also accepted—that the fair and equitable treatment standard is broader than the two other standards (full security and protection and non-impairment) and that, accordingly, its breach in itself amounts to a breach of the other two standards, or at least one of them. Thus, in *Saluka* the tribunal, having first dismissed the claimant's expropriation claim, went on to determine whether there had been, nonetheless, a breach of the fair and equitable treatment and non-impairment standards. The tribunal first examined the claimant's fair and equitable treatment claim and concluded that it was well-founded. Turning to the non-impairment standard, the tribunal found that this and the fair and equitable treatment standard were 'associated', and that a violation of the former does not 'differ substantially' from a violation of the latter, but merely identifies 'the more specific effects' of any such violation:

> The standard of 'reasonableness' has no different meaning in this context than in the context of the 'fair and equitable treatment' standard with which it is associated, and the same is true with regard to the standard of 'non-discrimination.' The standard of 'reasonableness' therefore requires, in this context as well, a showing that the State's conduct bears a reasonable relationship to some rational policy, whereas the standard of 'non-discrimination' requires a rational justification of any different treatment of a foreign investor.
>
> Insofar as the standard of conduct is concerned, a violation of the non-impairment requirement does not therefore differ substantially from a violation of the 'fair and equitable treatment' standard. The non-impairment requirement merely identifies more specific effects of any such violation, namely with regard to the operation, management, maintenance, use, enjoyment or disposal of the investment by the investor.[18]

The tribunal eventually concluded that the Czech Government had also breached the non-impairment standard, in part on the same grounds which led the tribunal to find a violation of the fair and equitable treatment standard.[19]

However, in *CMS*[20] the tribunal adopted a somewhat different approach. The tribunal first considered the claim for breach of the fair and equitable treatment standard, finding that it had been breached. The tribunal then proceeded to deal with the claimant's claim for breach of the non-impairment standard (prohibition of arbitrary and discriminatory measures). While one would have expected that the tribunal, like the *Saluka* tribunal, would have raised the question of whether a breach of the fair and equitable treatment standard would also, *ipso jure*, amount to a breach of the prohibition of arbitrary or discriminatory measures, the tribunal, somewhat surprisingly, took the reverse approach and asked

---

[18] *Saluka*, above n. 8, paras 460–461.
[19] Ibid., paras 503–504. See also ibid., para. 465, summarizing its findings and concluding that 'by violating the "fair and equitable treatment" standard, […] [the Czech Republic] at the same time violated its non-impairment standard'.
[20] *CMS Gas Transmission Company v The Argentine Republic*, ICSID Case No. ARB/01/8, Award, 12 May 2005.

B. Non-impairment Standard: Three Perspectives

itself whether a finding of a breach of the prohibition of arbitrary or discriminatory measures in itself would also constitute a breach of the fair and equitable treatment standard:

> The standard of protection against arbitrariness and discrimination is related to that of fair and equitable treatment. Any measure that might involve arbitrariness or discrimination is in itself contrary to fair and equitable treatment.[21]

However, the tribunal did not leave matters there, noting that

> [...] [t]he standard is next related to impairment: the management, operation, maintenance, use, enjoyment, acquisition, expansion, or disposal of the investment must be impaired by the measures adopted.[22]

Based on the requirement of impairment, the tribunal eventually found that, although 'some adverse effects can be noted', there had been no sufficient impairment and dismissed the claim.[23]

Some tribunals appear to have adopted an approach that prioritizes the more specific standards. Thus, in *Noble Ventures* the tribunal decided to disregard, without providing any explanation, the order in which the claimant asserted the various causes of action—which was also the same in which standards were listed in the applicable treaty (the US/Romania BIT)—and chose to deal first with the non-impairment standard rather than the fair and equitable treatment standard or indeed expropriation. Finding neither arbitrariness nor discrimination, the tribunal turned to the fair and equitable treatment standard, making, along the way, some interesting observations about the relationship between the various treaty standards:

> Considering the place of the fair and equitable treatment standard at the very beginning of Art. II(2) [of the US/Romania BIT], one can consider this to be a more general standard which finds its specific application in *inter alia* the duty to provide full protection and security, the prohibition of arbitrary and discriminatory measures and the obligation to observe contractual obligations towards the investor. As demonstrated above, none of those obligations or standards has been breached. While this in itself cannot lead to the conclusion that the more general fair and equitable treatment standard has not been breached, it remains difficult to see how the judicial proceedings can be regarded as a violation of Art. II(2)(a) of the BIT.[24]

Thus, characterizing the fair and equitable treatment standard as the 'more general standard' and setting aside on this basis, provisionally, the consideration of this particular standard, the tribunal appears to have applied what could be termed a *lex specialis* approach to arbitral decision-making. However, as noted above, the tribunal did not provide any explanation or justification as to why it preferred this particular approach.

---

[21] Ibid., para. 290.
[22] Ibid.
[23] Ibid., paras 292, 295.
[24] *Noble Ventures*, above n. 6, para. 182.

The non-impairment standard and its relationship to the other investment protection standards has also been raised in a number of other BIT arbitrations, although in none of them has it been asserted by the claimant as the principal or exclusive cause of action. Apart from *Saluka* and *Noble Ventures*, perhaps the most elaborate analysis of the standard has been conducted in *Occidental*[25] and *MTD*.[26]

In *Occidental* the claimant again raised a number of causes of action, including failure to ensure fair and equitable treatment, breach of the non-impairment standard, and expropriation, in this particular order.[27] The tribunal first considered the expropriation claim, dismissing it as being manifestly without merit and thus inadmissible. It then decided to examine the claimant's remaining claims 'following the reverse order', which led it to consider first the impairment claim (ie prohibition of arbitrary or discriminatory treatment).[28] Stressing that 'the claim that these measures [complained of by the claimant] are also discriminatory has a meaning under this Article only to the extent that impairment has occurred', the tribunal was eventually persuaded that the respondent had acted arbitrarily, 'at least to an extent'.[29] The tribunal then went on to consider the claim that the respondent had failed to honour its obligation to accord fair and equitable treatment. The tribunal found a breach and concluded that

> [...] [i]n the context of this finding the question of whether in addition there has been a breach of full protection and security under this Article becomes moot as a treatment that is not fair and equitable automatically entails an absence of full security and protection.[30]

Thus, the tribunal effectively subsumed the full security and protection standard under the fair and equitable treatment standard, while treating the non-impairment standard as a stand-alone cause of action. This approach may well have been adopted by the tribunal because it reflected the structure of the US/Ecuador BIT itself, since the BIT in question was somewhat unusual in that the non-impairment standard was contained in a separate provision of the BIT (Article II (3)(b)), whereas the fair and equitable treatment and the full security and protection standards were included in the same provision (Article II (3)(a)).

In *MTD* the claimant alleged a series of breaches of the Chile/Malaysia BIT and certain other BITs, based on a most-favoured-nation clause, including failure to ensure fair and equitable treatment, breach of foreign investment contracts, breach of the non-impairment standard (prohibition of unreasonable or

---

[25] *Occidental*, above n. 14.
[26] *MTD Equity Sdn. Bhd. and MTD Chile S.A. v Republic of Chile*, ICSID Case No. ARB/01/7, Award, 25 May 2004.
[27] *Occidental*, above n. 14, para. 36.
[28] Ibid., para. 158.
[29] Ibid., paras 162, 165.
[30] Ibid., para. 187. See also *Azurix v Argentine Republic*, ICSID Case No. ARB/01/12, Award, 14 July 2006, paras 406–408.

B. Non-impairment Standard: Three Perspectives

discriminatory measures) and expropriation. In this case, however, the tribunal decided to follow religiously the order in which the claimant had asserted its claims. When reaching the non-impairment claim, the tribunal recognized the potential overlap between the various treatment standards, including that between fair and equitable treatment and the non-impairment standard. Observing that '[t]o a certain extent, this claim [ie the non-impairment claim] has been considered by the tribunal as part of the fair and equitable treatment', the tribunal noted that the approval of an investment against the Government urban policy—the measure that formed the basis of the claimant's claims—'can be equally considered unreasonable'.[31] However, the tribunal found no discrimination, and although the reasoning is not entirely clear, eventually appears to have concluded that there had been no breach of the BIT on this account.[32]

Instead of seeking to establish an order of priority among the many causes of action, one possible methodological approach that indeed could be adopted is that the arbitral tribunal simply respects the manner in which the claimant has chosen to argue its case and examines the causes of action in the same order in which they have been asserted by the claimant. This approach would have the advantage of avoiding any surprises to the parties, even though it might often be considered rather inefficient from the perspective of judicial economy, nor particularly creative from the point of view of legal methodology. Indeed, in practice, instead of following the pleadings of the claimant, certain arbitral tribunals have preferred the opposite approach where they not only disregard the order in which the claimant has chosen to assert the causes of action it relies upon, but simply select one of them as a basis of their decision and disregard, without discussion, all others. This approach, which could be characterized as a *jura novit curia* approach, in effect equates arbitral tribunals with courts—according to this approach, arbitral tribunals, like courts, are not bound by the parties' pleadings and remain free to choose the basis of their decision.[33]

---

[31] *MTD*, above n. 26, para. 196.

[32] See the dispositif of the award, *MTD*, above n. 26, para. 253, referring only to a breach of Article 3(1) of the Malaysia/Chile BIT, which contains the fair and equitable treatment standard, but not mentioning Article 3(3) of the Croatia/Chile BIT, which contains the impairment standard. For a discrimination claim see also *Champion Trading Co v Egypt*, ICSID Case No. ARB/02/09, Final Award, 27 October 2006, paras 125–156, finding no discrimination since the relevant parties were not in 'like situations'.

[33] The *jura novit curia* has been explicitly endorsed by the ICJ and its predecessor, the Permanent Court of International Justice (PCIJ), in a number of decisions. Perhaps the most opportune in this context is the formulation adopted by the ICJ in *The Application of the Convention of 1902 Governing the Guardianship of Infant* (*Netherlands v Sweden*), Judgment, 28 November 1958: '[The Court] retains its freedom to select the ground upon which it will base its judgment, and is under no obligation to examine all the considerations advanced by the Parties if other considerations appear to it to be sufficient for its purpose.'

This approach has recently been adopted by two ECT tribunals—*Nykomb*[34] and *Petrobart*.[35] In both cases the claimants relied, in part, on the non-impairment standard as a legal basis of their claims.

Nykomb arose out of a contract entered into between Windau, a company controlled by Nykomb, a Swedish company, and Latvenergo, the Latvian electricity utility, which obligated Latvenergo to pay Windau a preferential double tariff for the first eight years of production at the Bauska co-generation plant built by Windau pursuant to the contract. As Latvenergo failed to pay the agreed tariff, Nykomb brought a claim before the Arbitration Institute of the Stockholm Chamber of Commerce under Article 26 of the ECT, arguing that Latvenergo's failure constituted a breach of Article 10(1) of the ECT and was attributable to the State. Nykomb asserted a number of alternative causes of action, including breach of fair and equitable treatment, breach of the minimum standard of treatment under international law, impairment by unreasonable or discriminatory measures, and expropriation.[36]

As noted above, the tribunal considered first Nykomb's expropriation claim, dismissing it on the basis that, in the circumstances, '[...] there [was] no possession taking of Windau or its assets, no interference with the shareholders' rights or with the management's control over and running of the enterprise'.[37]

As to the other causes of action, the tribunal noted that the State's failure to ensure that Latvenergo pay Windau the contractually agreed double tariff was capable of constituting a breach of 'various Treaty provisions'.[38] However, since the damage or loss caused by the non-payment to the claimant was in all instances the same, the tribunal concluded that, '[...] in order to establish liability for the Republic it is strictly speaking sufficient to find that one of the relevant provisions has been violated'.[39] The tribunal then proceeded to consider Nykomb's claim that the Republic had failed to comply with its obligation to ensure that Nykomb's investment was not impaired by unreasonable or discriminatory measures. The tribunal concluded that the Republic had indeed acted in a discriminatory manner since it was established, and the Republic did not deny, that Latvenergo was paying double tariff for electricity produced by two other companies which the tribunal considered were comparable to Windau and operated under the same laws and regulations. The Republic failed to prove that the different treatment was justified. This was the crux of the tribunal's reasoning:

The Arbitral Tribunal accepts that in evaluating whether there is discrimination in the sense of the Treaty one should only 'compare like with like'. However, little if anything

---

[34] *Nykomb*, above n. 13.
[35] *Petrobart Limited v Kyrgyz Republic*, SCC No. 126/2003, Energy Charter Treaty Arbitration, Final Award, 29 March 2005.
[36] *Nykomb*, above n. 13. Nykomb did not assert a breach of contract claim under the umbrella clause since it was not party to the contract out of which the dispute arose.
[37] Ibid., 33.   [38] Ibid.
[39] Ibid., 34.

has been documented by the Respondent to show the criteria or methodology used in fixing the multiplier, or to what extent Latvenergo is authorized to apply multipliers other than those documented in this arbitration. On the other hand, all of the information available to the Tribunal suggests that the three companies are comparable, and subject to the same laws and regulations. In particular, this appears to be the situation with respect to Latelektro-Gulbene and Windau. In such a situation, and in accordance with established international law, the burden of proof lies with the Respondent to prove that no discrimination has taken or is taking place. The Arbitral Tribunal finds that such burden of proof has not been satisfied, and therefore concludes that Windau has been subject to a discriminatory measure in violation of Article 10(1).[40]

Having found a breach of the prohibition of unreasonable and discriminatory measures, and apparently recognizing that a finding of any additional breaches would not have affected the quantification of the claim, the tribunal concluded that there was no need to proceed any further in order to examine whether such additional breaches of the ECT had in fact occurred.[41]

The tribunal did not explain why it chose to examine the alleged breach of one particular treaty standard—failure to refrain from unreasonable or discriminatory measures—rather than the other breaches alleged by the claimant. The methodology adopted by the tribunal cannot be explained by reference to the manner in which the claimant pleaded its case, since it appears that the order in which the tribunal chose to examine the claimant's causes of action was not the one in which the claimant asserted them. The most likely explanation for the chosen order appears to be that, based on the evidence, a finding of breach of the reasonable and non-discriminatory measures standard was relatively easy to establish and thus was the obvious standard to be considered first. In any event, as a result of the chosen approach, the award sheds little light on the relationship between the various standards enumerated in Article 10(1) or, more generally, in Part III of the ECT—apart from the position, in effect endorsed by the tribunal, that expropriation is the principal cause of action in terms of judicial economy in that compensation for expropriation subsumes remedies available under all of the other causes of action listed in Article 10(1). Indeed, the tribunal's finding was limited to only one of the two legs of the standard it chose to apply—it found the respondent's action 'discriminatory' but did not say anything about its 'reasonableness'. This suggests, as noted above—and as is indeed indicated by the very formulation of the standard ('unreasonable *or* discriminatory measures')—that the two components of the standard are independent of each other and that, accordingly, it is sufficient, for the purposes of establishing a breach of the standard, that one of the two elements of the standard has been breached.[42]

---

[40] Ibid. (emphasis omitted).
[41] Ibid., concluding that it did 'not find it necessary to adjudge the other Treaty violations asserted in this arbitration'.
[42] A similar approach was adopted by an ICSID tribunal operating under the US/Romania BIT. See *Noble Ventures*, above n. 6, paras 175–183, examining separately a possible breach of the

A claim relating to the breach of the non-impairment standard was also raised, among a number of other causes of action, in *Petrobart*, another ECT arbitration.[43] This case involved a contract between Petrobart, a company based in Gibraltar, and Kyrgyzgazmunaizat ('KGM'), a petroleum supply and distribution company owned by the Kyrgyz Republic, for the sale of gas condensate. Since KGM failed to comply with its payment obligations, Petrobart brought court proceedings against KGM. Petrobart alleged that the State interfered in these proceedings and stripped KGM of its assets by transferring them to two newly established companies, thus preventing Petrobart from satisfying its legal claims, and causing damage. The tribunal held that the respondent had failed to respect Petrobart's rights under the investment agreement, in breach of Article 10(1) of the ECT. However, the tribunal declined to enter into a detailed analysis of all of the claimant's causes of action and instead opted for a more comprehensive approach:

The Arbitral Tribunal does not find it necessary to analyze the Kyrgyz Republic's action in relation to the various specific elements in Article 10(1) of the Treaty but notes that this paragraph in its entirety is intended to ensure a fair and equitable treatment of investments. In the Arbitral Tribunal's opinion, it is sufficient to conclude that the measures for which the Kyrgyz Republic is responsible failed to accord Petrobart a fair and equitable treatment of its investments to which it was entitled under Article 10(1) of the Treaty.[44]

Like the *Nykomb* tribunal, the *Petrobart* tribunal took the view that it was not required to follow the order in which the claimant asserted its causes of action, or indeed even to examine them one by one, but instead was entitled to freely select the legal basis of its decision. Moreover, like the *Nykomb* tribunal, the *Petrobart* tribunal did not provide any explanations or reasons as to why it chose to base its decision on one particular standard—in this case breach of the fair and equitable treatment standard—rather than one of the various other standards asserted by the claimant.

---

two elements of the arbitrary and discriminatory measures standard. See also *Azurix*, above n. 30, para. 391, finding that a measure needs 'only to be arbitrary to constitute a breach' of the standard. Cf. *Lauder*, above n. 2, para. 219, concluding that the wording of Article II(2)(b) of the US/Czech Republic BIT—'arbitrary *and* discriminatory measures'—implied that a breach of the standard required both an arbitrary and a discriminatory measure by the State.

[43] *Petrobart*, above n. 35.

[44] Ibid., 76. The claimant had claimed that the State had breached the following standards of treatment: (1) failure to create stable, equitable, favourable and transparent conditions for investment; (2) failure to accord fair and equitable treatment; (3) breach of prohibition of unreasonable and discriminatory measures; (4) breach of observance of obligations clause; (5) breach of the minimum treatment standard; (6) failure to ensure that domestic law provides effective means for assertion of claims and enforcement of rights with respect to investments; (7) expropriation; and (8) failure to ensure that a State enterprise conducts its activities in accordance with the State's obligations under Part III of the ECT.

'Substantive' Perspective

From a 'substantive' point of view, the key issue is the meaning to be given to terms such as 'arbitrary' and 'unreasonable'. What kind of measures can be characterized as 'arbitrary' or 'unreasonable'? What is required, in terms of law and fact, to establish that these standards have been breached? Is there a difference between the levels of protection provided by the two standards? In the affirmative, which one provides a 'higher' level of protection? And finally, is the level of protection provided by these standards higher than that available under customary international law?

These questions are all the more relevant since the terms 'arbitrary' and 'unreasonable' are rarely, if ever, defined in bilateral or multilateral investment treaties, as noted by arbitral tribunals as a matter of routine. Thus, it is perhaps not surprising that arbitral tribunals have struggled with the interpretation of the two terms, often searching for their meaning in legal dictionaries—as well as in decisions of other tribunals. However, this has not led to a uniform approach. Based on recent jurisprudence, one can distinguish between two competing approaches to determining the substance of the two standards. These may be called, for lack of a better term, the 'I know it when I see it' approach and the 'due process' approach.

'I know it when I see it'

This is an approach where the meaning of standards such as 'arbitrary' or 'unreasonable' is effectively defined as a function of the effect that the evidence and legal argument presented by the parties has on the arbitral tribunal. In other words, in order to be able to convince the arbitrators that the governmental measure in question is indeed 'arbitrary' or 'unreasonable', the claimant must demonstrate it to be 'shocking', or at least 'surprising', without the respondent being able to rebut this effect.

The most prominent example of this approach is the *ELSI* case, where the ICJ defined its understanding of what counts as 'arbitrary' in the following terms:

Arbitrariness is not so much something opposed to a rule of law, as something opposed to the rule of law [...]. It is wilful disregard of due process of law, an act which *shocks*, or at least *surprises* a sense of judicial propriety.[45]

The '*ELSI* standard' is often cited in international investment arbitration as an appropriate way of describing what counts as arbitrary. Thus, in *Noble Ventures* the tribunal referred to the *ELSI* standard (having first noted that the relevant treaty did not define the notions of 'arbitrary' or 'discriminatory') and found that, based on the facts before it, the measures in question could not be considered as

---

[45] *ELSI* case, above n. 4, para. 128 (emphasis added).

being 'opposed to the rule of law'.[46] In *Lauder* the tribunal, again noting that the relevant treaty did not define an arbitrary measure, sought comfort from *Black's Law Dictionary* and concluded that the measure in question was arbitrary 'because it was not founded on reason or fact, nor on the law, [...] but on a mere fear reflecting national preference'.[47] The *Azurix* tribunal also resorted to dictionaries, both legal and others, and concluded that 'the definition in *ELSI* is close to the ordinary meaning of arbitrary since it emphasizes the element of wilful disregard of the law'.[48]

In *Alex Genin* the tribunal was somewhat more elaborate:

The Tribunal has further considered whether the Bank of Estonia's actions constituted an 'arbitrary' treatment of investment as that term is used in Article II(3)(b) of the BIT. In this regard, it is relevant that the Tribunal has found no evidence of discriminatory action. [...] It is also relevant that the Tribunal, having regard to the totality of the evidence, regards the decision of the Bank of Estonia to withdraw the license as justified. In light of this conclusion, in order to amount to a violation of the BIT, any procedural irregularity that may have been present would have to amount to bad faith, a willful disregard of due process of law or an extreme insufficiency of action. None of these are present in the case at hand. In sum, the Tribunal does not regard the license withdrawal as an arbitrary act that violates the Tribunal's 'sense of judicial propriety.'[49]

The *Siemens* tribunal also agreed that 'the definition in *ELSI* is the most authoritative interpretation of international law and it is close to the ordinary meaning of the term emphasizing the willful disregard of the law'.[50] However, it distanced itself from *Alex Genin,* noting that '[t]he element of bad faith added by *Genin* does not seem to find support either in the ordinary concept of arbitrariness or in the definition of the ICJ in *ELSI*'.[51]

Other, perhaps less than helpful formulations, have also been proposed. Thus, in *MCI Power* the tribunal defined arbitrary treatment 'as an act contrary to law' and concluded that, while the governmental measures in question might 'betray an unfriendly attitude', they did not constitute '[...] unfair or inequitable, discriminatory or arbitrary treatment in violation of the parameters established by international law as reflected in the BIT'.[52] This seems, frankly, somewhat circular: if arbitrariness is defined by reference to unlawfulness, then all 'acts

---

[46] *Noble Ventures*, above n. 6, paras 177–178.
[47] *Lauder*, above n. 2, para. 232; according to the dictionary, below n. 54, arbitrary means 'depending on individual discretion; [...] founded on prejudice or preference rather than on reason or fact'.
[48] *Azurix*, above n. 30, para. 392.
[49] *Genin et al. v Estonia*, ICSID Case No. ARB/99/2, Final Award, 25 June 2001, paras 370–371 (footnotes omitted).
[50] *Siemens A.G. v Argentina*, ICSID Case No. ARB/02/08, Award, 6 February 2007, para. 318.
[51] Ibid.; see also *Enron Corporation and Ponderosa Assets, L.P. v Argentine Republic*, ICSID Case No. ARB/01/3, Award, 22 May 2007, para. 281.
[52] *MCI Power Group L.C. and New Turbine, Inc v Ecuador*, ICSID Case No. ARB/03/6, Award, 31 July 2007, paras 369–371.

B. Non-impairment Standard: Three Perspectives

contrary to law' must also be considered arbitrary, which is hardly a tenable position.

The strengths and weaknesses of the 'I know it when I see it' approach are obvious. Its strength is that it provides the arbitral tribunal with ample flexibility in determining the substance of opaque standards such as 'arbitrary' and 'unreasonable'. The only thing that the tribunal is expected and indeed required to do is simply to sit and wait and let the evidence and argument speak for itself (albeit through the counsel). While tribunals following this approach may, and often do, refer to a legal dictionary to get a better sense of the substance of the standard in question, such referrals are not necessarily determinative. What is arbitrary or unreasonable can perhaps be described in a dictionary, but in order to understand what it really *means*, in a concrete context, one must look at the legal argument and evidence produced in the course of the arbitration. In other words, what counts as arbitrary or unreasonable is often a matter of rhetorical *effect* rather than a matter of semantic definition.

The weakness of the 'I know it when I see it' approach is that it tends to lead to an extreme case-by-case approach where the decision taken by one tribunal provides little guidance for another one facing a similar situation; it is for each tribunal to consider and determine, based on the evidence and argument before it, whether the measure in question is indeed 'shocking' or at least 'surprising'. As a result, the approach leaves the outcome of the case largely dependent on legal argument and evidence presented in the particular case at hand—in other words, on the professional skills of the lawyers handling the case and their ability to create the rhetorical effect of shock or surprise. Such effect is not something that can be found in a dictionary or in a textbook; it must be re-created in the concrete context.

The 'I know it when I see it' approach also effectively leaves open the relationship between the two standards—arbitrariness and unreasonableness. What these terms mean, concretely, can, again, only be assessed in the context of each case. Or, paraphrasing Justice Porter Stewart:

I shall not today attempt further to define the kinds of [governmental measures] I understand to be embraced within that shorthand description [arbitrary or unreasonable]; and perhaps I could never succeed in intelligibly doing so. But I know it when I see it [...].[53]

Due process approach

Unlike the 'I know it when I see it' approach, the due process approach seeks to proceduralize the determination of whether a particular governmental measure should be classified as arbitrary or unreasonable. In so doing, it not only enables a more technical approach to the determination of the content of these standards;

---

[53] *Jacobellis v Ohio*, 378 US 184, Mr Justice Stewart, concurring (discussing the definition of unprotected, or 'obscene' speech under the First Amendment).

it also allows the arbitrator to get a better handle on the relationship, or indeed the 'definition' of the two standards.

Under the due process approach, the decision-maker assesses the international legality of the governmental measure in question by focusing on the relationship between the measure and its underlying policy justification. Has any rationale or justification been put forward in support of the measure in the first place? In the affirmative, is such a rationale or justification related to a legitimate governmental policy?

If the answer to the first question is in the negative, and if there is no conceivable rationale that could justify it, the measure can be classified as 'arbitrary'. This 'definition' of arbitrary is also largely in line with the standard definition of arbitrary in legal dictionaries—an arbitrary measure can indeed be defined as a measure taken without any justification, actual or conceivable.[54] If the answer to the first question is yes—if a rationale or justification has in fact been put forward for the measure—then the relevant question is whether there is a reasonable relationship between such a purported justification and a legitimate governmental policy. If there is no such relationship (eg if the measure discriminates between investors based on their eye colour), then the measure in question can be considered 'unreasonable'.[55]

Thus, under the due process approach the distinction between arbitrary and unreasonable governmental conduct boils down to this: a governmental measure can be considered 'arbitrary' if no justification or rationale at all has been provided for the measure (ie if there is no relationship at all, let alone a rational relationship, between the measure and a legitimate governmental policy); and it can be considered 'unreasonable' if a justification or a rationale has in fact been provided for the measure, but there is no reasonable (or rational) relationship between the purported justification and a legitimate governmental policy.

The due process approach seems less popular among arbitral tribunals than the 'I know it when I see it' approach. However, certain arbitral tribunals appear to have applied a sort of due process approach, as outlined above. In *Saluka* the tribunal first appeared to veer towards the 'I know it when I see it' approach, noting that, regardless of their generality, '[t]he standards formulated in Article 3 of the Treaty [including fair and equitable treatment and the prohibition of unreasonable or discriminatory measures], vague as they may be, are susceptible of specification through judicial practice and do in fact have sufficient legal content

---

[54] See, eg, *Black's Law Dictionary* (6th edn, 1990): 'Arbitrary. In an unreasonable manner, as fixed or done capriciously, or at pleasure. Without adequate determining principle; not founded in the nature of things; nonrational; not done or acting according to reason or judgment; depending on the will alone; absolutely in power; capriciously; tyrannical; despotic; [...].'

[55] This implies that there is a close relationship between unreasonable measures, on the one hand, and discrimination, on the other, which probably justifies why they are often coupled in the same standard. This also suggests that the 'discrimination' against which investors are protected by way if a non-impairment standard is broader than that included in the national treatment and most-favoured-nation treatment standards.

B. Non-impairment Standard: Three Perspectives

to allow the case to be decided on the basis of law'.[56] However, when dealing with the non-impairment standard, it seemed to switch to a different approach. While observing that '"impairment" means, according to its ordinary meaning, [...] any negative impact or effect caused by measures' taken by the respondent, the tribunal went on to consider the meaning of the term 'reasonableness' in the following terms:

> The standard of 'reasonableness' has no different meaning in this context than in the context of the 'fair and equitable treatment' standard with which it is associated; and the same is true with regard to the standard of 'non-discrimination'. *The standard of 'reasonableness' therefore requires, in this context as well, a showing that the State's conduct bears a reasonable relationship to some rational policy, whereas the standard of 'non-discrimination' requires a rational justification of any differential treatment of a foreign investor.*[57]

By requiring that 'the State's conduct [must] bear [...] a reasonable relationship to some rational policy', the tribunal appears to have applied a procedural standard to assess the legality of the measure, thus adopting, effectively, the 'due process' approach. As noted above, the tribunal eventually found that the conduct of the respondent had indeed been 'unjustifiable and unreasonable' and thus in breach of the non-impairment standard.[58]

In *LG&E Energy* the tribunal followed a similar approach. While citing first both the *ELSI* standard and *Lauder*, the tribunal went on to consider what 'arbitrariness' would mean in the context of the case before it:

> It is apparent from the Bilateral Treaty that Argentina and the United States wanted to prohibit themselves from implementing measures that affect the investments of nationals of the other Party *without engaging in a rational decision-making process*. Such process would include a consideration of the effect of a measure on foreign investments and a balance of the interests of the State with any burden imposed on such investments.[59]

The tribunal concluded that the acts of Argentina, 'though unfair and inequitable, were the result of reasoned judgment rather than simple disregard of the rule of law', and thus not arbitrary.[60]

Unlike the 'I know it when I see it' approach, the due process approach provides the decision-maker with a technique that allows it to review the international legality of governmental measures in a more objective and generalizable manner. This is its clear strength. However, the approach is not unproblematic. It is a powerful tool in the hands of arbitral tribunals, and in applying the standard,

---

[56] *Saluka*, above n. 8, para. 284.
[57] Ibid., paras 460–461 (emphasis added).
[58] Ibid., para. 481.
[59] *LG&E Energy Corp, LG&E Capital Corp and LG&E International Inc. v Argentine Republic*, ICSID Case No. ARB/02/1, Decision on Liability, 3 October 2006, paras 156–158 (emphasis added).
[60] Ibid., paras 161–163.

arbitral tribunals must tread a fine line between a mere procedural control (Has any justification been provided for the governmental measure? In the affirmative, does the justification rationally relate to any legitimate governmental policy?) and what may be termed a 'strict scrutiny' of governmental measures. In the latter approach, the decision-maker does not stop at 'determining whether there is any *prima facie* reasonable relationship between the purported justification and a legitimate governmental policy, but takes a step further, effectively shifting the burden of proving that there is indeed such a relationship to the government and requiring it to demonstrate that the measure in question not only serves a legitimate governmental purpose but is also necessary in the sense that there are no other, less restrictive alternative measures available.[61]

Were such a 'strict' standard of review adopted, this would effectively result in classifying all governmental regulations adversely affecting foreign investors as inherently suspect and create the assumption that the underlying policy purpose, or the governing legal principle, of multilateral and bilateral investment treaties is, in effect, the protection of foreign investment as a 'fundamental' right. This is a step that would likely have far-reaching consequences from a systemic point of view, converting as it would international investment arbitration from what is in substance a bilateral exercise into a quasi-multilateral regime. While there presently seems to be no evidence that arbitral tribunals have in fact taken such a step, this may be simply a matter of time. Since how else, except by assuming such a broad legal right or principle, can one conceptualize the distinction between permissible and impermissible discrimination between foreign and domestic investors, or as between foreign investors?

The non-impairment standard and customary international law

The question of the relationship between the non-impairment standard and customary international law is equally complicated. Indeed, the question can be raised as to whether customary international law provides *any* protection against arbitrary or unreasonable measures, or whether these must be considered 'purely' treaty standards, ie standards that would not exist but for treaty law.

Most bilateral investment treaties remain silent on the issue. However, as noted above, Article 10(1) of the ECT does touch upon the relationship between treaty standards and customary international law:

Each Contracting Party shall, in accordance with the provisions of this Treaty, encourage and create stable, equitable, favorable and transparent conditions for Investors of other Contracting Parties to make Investments in its Area. Such conditions shall include a commitment to accord at all times to Investments of Investors of other Contracting

---

[61] This is roughly the standard of review applied by WTO panels and the Appellate Body to discriminatory trade measures pursuant to Article XX ('General Exceptions') General Agreement on Tariffs and Trade (GATT). For further discussion see, eg, V. Heiskanen, 'Regulatory Philosophy of International Trade Law', 38 *Journal of World Trade* (2004) 1.

Parties a fair and equitable treatment. Such Investments shall also enjoy the most constant protection and security and no Contracting Party shall in any way impair by unreasonable or discriminatory measures their management, maintenance, use, enjoyment or disposal. *In no case shall such Investments be accorded treatment less favorable than that required by international law, including treaty obligations.*[62]

Thus, the ECT appears to say that, whatever the level of investment protection provided by the various standards incorporated in Article 10(1), 'in no case' shall it be less than the floor required by international law. This is a rather non-committal formulation and leaves open the question of the level of protection actually provided by customary international law. However, it is arguable that in particular the fair and equitable treatment standard is closely related to the customary international law standard and may be considered an emanation of the latter, which is traditionally considered to embody, inter alia, protection against denial of justice.[63] In other words, the minimum treatment standard may be considered as providing, in itself, protection against failure to provide fair and equitable treatment, at least to the extent that the alleged breaches relate to the function of administration of justice.[64] Thus, the sole effect of specifically incorporating the fair and equitable treatment standard in the ECT is, arguably, that Article 10(1) extends the applicability of this standard to governmental functions other than administration of justice (ie the exercise of legislative and executive powers).

However, this position is not uncontroversial, and arbitral tribunals have been hesitant to jump to conclusions. In *ADF*, where the claimant's claims were

---

[62] Article 10(1) ECT (emphasis added).

[63] Cf. Article 1105(1) NAFTA ('Minimum Standard of Treatment'), which provides that '[e]ach party shall accord to investments of investors of another party treatment in accordance with international law, including fair and equitable treatment and full security and protection', and the interpretation of this provision adopted by the NAFTA Free Trade Commission, 'Notes of Interpretation of Certain Chapter 11 Provisions' (31 July 2001) (available at http://www.dfait-maeci.gc.ca/tna-nac/NAFTA-Interpr-en.asp). The Commission took the view that 'Article 1105(1) prescribes the customary international law minimum standard of treatment of aliens as the minimum standard of treatment to be afforded to investments of investors of another Party', and that '[t]he concepts of "fair and equitable treatment" and "full security and protection" do not require treatment in addition to or beyond that which is required by the customary international law minimum standard of treatment of aliens'. For discussion see *The Loewen Group, Inc and Raymond L. Loewen v United States*, Final Award, 26 June 2003, paras 35–39.

See also J. Paulsson, *Denial of Justice in International Law* (2005) 6: 'Although the expression [denial of justice] does not appear in [human rights conventions] and similar texts, it will continue to influence the way in which international treaties are applied. In turn, the application of treaty provisions will contribute to a modern understanding of the old doctrine. The reason for this inevitable cross-pollination is that the elements of the delict of denial of justice tend to reappear as treaty provisions, for example, when they proscribe "discrimination" or when they require "fair and equitable treatment."'

[64] At least one arbitral tribunal has also drawn the reverse conclusion, ie, that the fair and equitable treatment standard in the relevant BIT incorporated the international minimum standard. See *Alex Genin v Estonia*, above n. 49, para. 367: 'While the exact content of th[e] [fair and equitable treatment] standard is not clear, the Tribunal understands it to require an "international minimum standard" that is separate from domestic law, but that is, indeed, a *minimum standard*' (emphasis in original; footnote omitted).

based, inter alia, on Article 1105 of the North Atlantic Free Trade Agreement (NAFTA), the tribunal first appeared to take the view (taking into account the Free Trade Commission's Interpretation of 31 July 2001) that the fair and equitable treatment and full security and protection standards were not part of customary international law 'as a general and autonomous requirement', although it did find that there was, in customary international law, 'a general customary international law standard' requiring such treatment:

> We are not convinced that the Investor has shown the existence, in current customary international law, of a general and autonomous requirement (autonomous, that is, from specific rules addressing particular, limited, contexts) to accord fair and equitable treatment and full protection and security to foreign investments. The Investor, for instance, has not shown that such a requirement has been brought into the corpus of present day customary international law by the many hundreds of bilateral investment treaties now extant. [...] [A]ny general requirement to accord 'fair and equitable treatment' and 'full protection and security' must be disciplined by being based upon State practice and judicial or arbitral caselaw or other sources of customary or *general* international law. [...] Without expressing a view on the Investor's thesis, we ask: are the US measures here involved inconsistent with a general customary international law standard of treatment requiring a host State to accord 'fair and equitable treatment' and 'full protection and security' to foreign investments in its territory.[65]

Similarly, the *Azurix* tribunal, which operated under the US/Argentina BIT, reached the conclusion that the fair and equitable treatment and full security and protection standards, which according to the relevant provision of the BIT were not to fall below that 'required by international law', were no higher than required by international law. This was because:

> [...] the minimum requirement to satisfy this standard has evolved and the Tribunal considers that its content is substantially similar whether the terms are interpreted in their ordinary meaning, as required by the Vienna Convention, or in accordance with customary international law.[66]

If the relationship between the fair and equitable and full protection security standards, on the one hand, and customary international law, on the other, is not entirely clear, this applies *a fortiori* to the non-impairment standard.[67] It is arguable that the non-impairment standard does impose a standard of conduct higher than that required by customary international law, in particular to the extent that it requires governments to conduct their business in a 'reasonable' (and not only in a non-arbitrary) manner, or in a wholly non-discriminatory manner. This

---

[65] *ADF Group Inc. v United States* (NAFTA Arbitration), ICSID Case No. ARB (AF)/00/1, Final Award, 9 January 2003, paras 183–186 (emphasis in original).

[66] *Azurix*, above n. 30, para. 361.

[67] Although it is arguable that the full protection and security standard, at least to the extent it coincides with the customary international law standard of due diligence, is indeed part of customary international law. See above nn. 10, 17 and accompanying text.

was the position adopted by the *Alex Genin* tribunal, at least with respect to the requirement of non-discrimination:

> Article II(3)(b) of the BIT further requires that the signatory governments not impair investment by acting in an arbitrary or discriminatory way. In this regard, the Tribunal notes that international law generally requires that a state should refrain from 'discriminatory' treatment of aliens and alien property. Customary international law does not, however, require that a state treat all aliens (and alien property) equally, or that it treat aliens as favourably as nationals. Indeed, 'even unjustifiable differentiation may not be actionable'.[68]

Indeed, for many governments the requirement that they always conduct their business in a 'reasonable' manner may be a tall order. Politics is not necessarily, and perhaps never, purely a matter of reason and, accordingly, of reasonableness. To the extent that governments have agreed in bilateral and multilateral treaties to have the 'reasonableness' of their regulations and other governmental measures reviewed by international arbitral tribunals, they have agreed to a system of control that is based on a standard that appears to be substantially higher than that required by customary international law. The implications of such heightened level of control have perhaps not been fully appreciated by governmental officials responsible for negotiation and implementation of investment protection treaties.

C. Conclusion

The case law reviewed in this chapter shows that the non-impairment standard rarely plays a dispositive role in international arbitral awards. While a breach of the non-impairment standard is often raised in international investment arbitration, it is not usually, if ever, relied upon by claimants as their primary or exclusive cause of action. Equally infrequently is it relied upon by arbitral tribunals as the *ratio decidendi* of their decisions.

However, even though the non-impairment standard may not be the leading cause of action, it does provide an interesting perspective to the relationship between the various substantive standards of investment protection and the methodology that arbitral tribunals have applied in determining the order in which the causes of action asserted by claimants should be examined and disposed of. Various approaches have been adopted, however, none of them appears to have become preponderant. Some tribunals have preferred to examine the causes of action in the order in which they have been asserted by the claimant, or in the order in which they are listed in the relevant treaty, sometimes tweaking the order for reasons of judicial economy (frequently giving priority to an

---

[68] *Genin*, above n. 49, para. 368 (footnote omitted).

expropriation claim, if asserted) or legal methodology (applying, apparently, concepts of legal 'hierarchy' or doctrines such as *lex specialis*).

By contrast, some tribunals, in particular those operating under the ECT, appear to have concluded that they have full freedom to select the legal basis of their decision and to disregard the order in which the claimant has chosen to argue its case, without having to provide any explanation or justification for the choice made. Such an approach, which may be consistent with and justified under the *jura novit curia* doctrine, is not necessarily inappropriate. However, those who prefer the arbitration paradigm (as opposed to the adjudication paradigm) might justifiably argue that the *jura novit curia* doctrine must be applied with particular care in an arbitration context, if at all. As the jurisdiction of BIT tribunals is based on the parties' consent (even if not on one expressed in a contract), it is not necessarily appropriate to 'arbitrate by ambush', that is, make findings that take the parties by surprise. This, however, is undoubtedly an area where reasonable persons may reasonably disagree, which of course is unlikely to make the issue go away.

From a substantive perspective, the non-impairment standard imposes a standard of conduct on governments that is arguably substantially higher than that required by customary international law. As the body of international arbitral jurisprudence grows, and as governments become more aware of the standard of conduct that is expected from them under the various multilateral and bilateral investment protection treaties—and, consequently, as they become more sophisticated in their treatment of foreign investors—the non-impairment standard is likely to gain in importance. Whether this will lead to systemic changes in the field of foreign investment protection, remains to be seen.

6
Fair and Equitable Treatment Standard: Recent Developments

Katia Yannaca-Small[*]

A. Introduction

The fair and equitable treatment standard is still, to some, a mystifying legal term. Although it has been thoroughly examined, particularly in the last few years, it has not yet been entirely clarified. What is certain is that it is an 'absolute', 'non-contingent' standard of treatment, ie a standard that states the treatment to be accorded in terms which have their own normative content, though their exact meaning has to be determined by reference to specific circumstances of application, as opposed to the 'relative' standards embodied in 'national treatment' and 'most-favoured-nation' principles which define the required treatment by reference to the treatment accorded to other investment in similar circumstances.[1] An absolute standard is one that has its own meaning, and is not necessarily satisfied by treating the investor as well as the host State treats its own nationals or other foreigners. Fair and equitable is a flexible, elastic standard, whose normative content is being constantly expanded to include new elements. Because of this flexibility, it is the most often invoked treaty standard in investor-State arbitration, present in almost every single claim brought by foreign investors against host States.

It has also been increasingly used as an alternative and more flexible way to provide protection to investors in cases where the test for indirect expropriation is too difficult to achieve since the threshold is quite high. It has therefore become a preferred way for tribunals to provide a remedy. As the tribunal in *Sempra v Argentina* said:

It would be wrong to believe that fair and equitable treatment is a kind of peripheral requirement. To the contrary, it ensures that even where there is no clear justification

---

[*] The views expressed in this chapter are those of the author and cannot be construed as reflecting the views of the OECD or of this organization's member governments.
[1] A.A. Fatouros, *Government Guarantees to Foreign Investors* (1962) 135–141, 214–215; UNCTAD, *Bilateral Investment Treaties in the Mid 1990s* (1998).

for making a finding of expropriation, as in the present case, there is still a standard which serves the purpose of justice and can of itself redress damage that is unlawful and that would otherwise pass unattended. [...] It must also be kept in mind that on occasion the line separating the breach of the fair and equitable treatment standard from an indirect expropriation can be very thin, particularly if the breach of the former standard is massive and long-lasting.[2]

Some even call it 'expropriation light'. This 'invasive' character of fair and equitable treatment sometimes also takes over other investment protection standards such as full protection and security[3] and the obligation for non-arbitrariness and non-discrimination[4] (see below in Part C).

In the governmental context, negotiators of bilateral investment treaties have been inserting this standard in almost every single agreement they concluded since the 1960s and, before them, FCN negotiators had done the same as well.[5] The first time the concerned governments attempted to clarify the standard was in 1967, when they were negotiating the text of the draft OECD Convention on the Protection of Foreign Property[6]—they then linked it to the minimum standard of customary international law in an official commentary.[7] Later, in 1984, the same governments linked it to the general principles of international law without, however, giving further clarifications.[8] Discussions were revived in 2001,[9] in the aftermath of the *Metalclad* award.[10]

---

[2] *Sempra Energy v The Argentine Republic*, ICSID Case No. ARB/02/16, 28 September 2007, paras 300, 301.

[3] See G. Cordero Moss at Chapter 7 below.

[4] See Veijo Heiskanen at Chapter 5 above.

[5] K. Vandevelde 'The Bilateral Treaty Program of the United States', 21 *Cornell International Law Journal* (1988) 201–276; S. Vasciannie, 'The Fair and Equitable Treatment Standard in International Investment Law and Practice', 70 *British Yearbook of International Law* (2000) 99–164.

[6] Draft Convention on the Protection of Foreign Property and Resolution of the Council of the OECD on the Draft Convention (1967), 13–15.

[7] 'The phrase "fair and equitable treatment", customary in relevant bilateral agreements, indicates the standard set by international law for the treatment due by each State with regard to the property of foreign nationals. The standard requires that—subject to essential security interests—protection afforded under the Convention shall be that generally accorded by the Party concerned to its own nationals, but, being set by international law, the standard may be more exacting where rules of national law or national administrative practices fall short of the requirements of international law. The standard required conforms in effect to the "minimum standard" which forms part of customary international law', OECD Notes and Comments to Article 1, 2 *ILM* (1963) 241.

[8] Intergovernmental Agreements Relating to Investment in Developing Countries (OECD 1984).

[9] The discussions demonstrated that not all 'investor-home' governments in their negotiations had entirely grasped the real nature of the standard. Some had rarely given a second thought to its potential breadth, perhaps because they saw themselves as essentially capital exporters and not importers and wished the standard to be as protective as possible. As it was the case with the majority of BIT provisions, second thoughts only began to arise when arbitral tribunals began to shed light on these provisions.

[10] *Metalclad Corporation v Mexico*, ICSID Case No. ARB(AF)/97/1, Award, 30 August 2000.

This chapter will tackle the fair and equitable treatment standard from two angles: its position in the international law context; and the elements identified by arbitral tribunals as forming part of this standard.[11]

B. Does the Standard belong to a Specific Legal Order or is it an Autonomous Standard?

The fair and equitable treatment standard is included in almost all investment agreements and free trade agreements with investment chapters. A standard formulation without any reference to international law is:

> Investors and investments of each contracting party shall at all times be accorded fair and equitable treatment in the territory of the other contracting party.[12]

Sometimes there is reference to international law.[13] In the case of NAFTA,[14] the recent US[15] and Canada[16] Model BITs as well as the recent FTAs concluded by the three NAFTA countries,[17] the reference is, more specifically, to the minimum standard of customary international law:

> Each party shall accord at all times to covered investments fair and equitable treatment, in accordance with customary international law, including fair and equitable treatment and full protection and security.

Consequently, when tribunals are called upon to interpret the normative content of the fair and equitable standard in treaties which include explicit language linking or, in some cases limiting, fair and equitable treatment to the minimum standard of international customary law,[18] they have more limited options than

---

[11] C. Schreuer, 'Fair and Equitable Treatment', 2(5) *Transnational Dispute Management* (2005); C. Schreuer, 'Fair and Equitable Treatment (FET): Interaction with Other Standards', 4(5) *Transnational Dispute Management* (2007); S. Schill, 'Fair and Equitable Treatment under Investment Treaties as an Embodiment of the Rule of Law', 3(5) *Transnational Dispute Management* (2006); R. Dolzer, 'Fair and Equitable Treatment: A Key Standard in Investment Treaties', 39 *The International Lawyer* (2005) 87; K. Yannaca-Small, 'Fair and Equitable Treatment in International Investment Law', in OECD, *International Investment Law: A Changing Landscape* (2005); UNCTAD, above n. 1.

[12] Treaties concluded by the Netherlands, Sweden, Switzerland, and Germany. For example, the German Model BIT states: 'Each Contracting Party [...] shall in any case accord such investments fair and equitable treatment' and the Swiss Model BIT states: 'Investments and returns of investors of each Contracting Party shall at all times be accorded fair and equitable treatment [...]'; see UNCTAD, above n. 1.

[13] See France Model BIT (2006).

[14] Article 1105(1) NAFTA (2004).

[15] US Model BIT (2004).

[16] Canada Model FIPA (2004).

[17] US/Chile FTA; US/Australia FTA; US/CAFTA-DR FTA; US/Morocco FTA; US/Singapore FTA; US/Peru FTA; Mexico/Japan FTA (2004).

[18] The international minimum standard is a norm of customary international law which governs the treatment of aliens, by providing for a minimum set of principles which States, regardless of

tribunals which are interpreting the standard found in treaties which either link the standard to international law without specifying custom, or lack any reference to international law. The latter have given a broader scope to the standard than the minimum standard of treatment required by customary international law.

In the context of NAFTA, early arbitral tribunals, such as in the cases of *Metalclad v Mexico*[19] and *S.D. Myers v Canada*,[20] gave different interpretations of the 'fair and equitable' provision of Article 1105(1), establishing a breach of fair and equitable treatment standard based on the transparency[21] and national treatment provisions of the NAFTA, respectively. In order to clarify the interpretation of this provision, the NAFTA Free Trade Commission (FTC) issued a binding interpretation on 31 July 2001, according to which:

Article 1105 (1) prescribes the customary international law minimum standard of treatment of aliens as the minimum standard of treatment to be afforded to investments of investors of another Party. The concepts of 'fair and equitable treatment' and 'full protection and security' do not require treatment in addition to or beyond that which is required by the customary international law minimum standard of treatment of aliens. A determination that there has been a breach of another provision of the NAFTA, or of a separate international agreement, does not establish that there has been a breach of Article 1105 (1).

Since then, all NAFTA tribunals have accepted this binding interpretation. However, some of them have gone further and stipulated that this acceptance goes with the understanding that the provision on the customary international law minimum standard of treatment refers to an evolving customary international law and not one frozen in time. In *Mondev v USA*,[22] the tribunal for instance in its famous holding stated that:

[...] the term 'customary international law' refers to customary international law as it stood no earlier than the time at which NAFTA came into force. It is not limited to

---

their domestic legislation and practices, must respect when dealing with foreign nationals and their property. While the principle of national treatment foresees that aliens can only expect equality of treatment with nationals, the international minimum standard sets a number of basic rights established by international law that States must grant to aliens, independent of the treatment accorded to their own citizens. Violation of this norm engenders the international responsibility of the host State and may open the way for international action on behalf of the injured alien provided that the alien has exhausted local remedies. The classical monograph on the principle is A.H. Roth, *The Minimum Standard of International Law Applied to Aliens* (1949) 127, where it is defined as follows: '[...] the international standard is nothing else than a set of rules, correlated to each other and deriving from one particular norm of general international law, namely that the treatment of alien is regulated by the law of nations.' See Yannaca-Small, above n. 11.

[19] *Metalclad Corporation v Mexico*, above n. 10.
[20] *SD Myers, Inc v Canada*, UNCITRAL (NAFTA), Award (Merits), 13 November 2000.
[21] Mexico, in its defence, supported that transparency is a conventional law concept which has been developed in international trade law (Article X GATT), not the body of international investment-protection law from which the concept of minimum standard of treatment expressed in Article 1105 NAFTA has been derived.
[22] *Mondev International Ltd v United States of America*, ICSID Case No. ARB(AF)/99/2, Award, 11 October 2002.

B. Does the Standard belong to a Specific Legal Order?

the international law of the 19th century or even of the first half of the 20th century, although decisions from that period remain relevant. In holding that Article 1105(1) refers to customary international law, the FTC interpretations incorporate current international law, whose content is shaped by the conclusion of more than two thousand bilateral investment treaties and many treaties of friendship and commerce. Those treaties largely and concordantly provide for 'fair and equitable' treatment of, and for 'full protection and security' for, the foreign investor and his investments.[23]

The tribunal in *ADF v USA*[24] expressed the view that:

[...] what customary international law projects is not a static photograph of the minimum standard of treatment of aliens as it stood in 1927 when the Award in the *Neer* case[25] was rendered. For both customary international law and the minimum standard of treatment of aliens it incorporates, are constantly in a process of development.[26]

This was also the understanding of the OECD governments, which independently of the way they interpret the 'fair and equitable treatment' standard, accept that the minimum standard refers to an evolving customary international law which is not 'frozen' in time, but may evolve depending on the general and consistent practice of states and *opinio juris*, as may be reflected in jurisprudence related to the interpretation and application of these treaties.[27]

Other tribunals, outside NAFTA, faced with investment agreements with no reference to international law, have most often interpreted the relevant provisions of the underlying agreement autonomously, relying on the treaty interpretation rules and international law more broadly.

The *Tecmed v Mexico*[28] tribunal for instance said that:

[...] the scope of the undertaking of fair and equitable treatment under Article 4(1) of the Agreement [...] is that resulting from an autonomous interpretation, taking into account the text of Article 4(1) of the Agreement according to its ordinary meaning (Article 31(1) of the Vienna Convention), or from international law and the good faith

---

[23] Ibid., para. 125.
[24] *ADF Group Inc. v United States* (NAFTA Arbitration), ICSID Case No. ARB (AF)/00/1, Final Award, 9 January 2003.
[25] This decision on the *Neer Claim* became the landmark case for the international minimum standard. This claim was presented to the US–Mexico Claims Commission by the United States on behalf of the family of Paul Neer, who had been killed in Mexico in obscure circumstances. In what has become a classical *dictum*, the Commission expressed the concept as follows: '[...] the propriety of governmental acts should be put to the test of international standards... the treatment of an alien, in order to constitute an international delinquency should amount to an outrage, to bad faith, to wilful neglect of duty, or to an insufficiency of governmental action so far short of international standards that every reasonable and impartial man would readily recognize its insufficiency. Whether the insufficiency proceeds from the deficient execution of a reasonable law or from the fact that the laws of the country do not empower the authorities to measure up to international standards is immaterial', *Neer v Mexico*, 15 October 1926, 4 *UNRIAA* 60.
[26] *ADF Group Inc v United States*, above n. 24, para. 179.
[27] See Yannaca-Small, above n. 11, including conclusions of the discussions.
[28] *Técnicas Medioambientales Tecmed, S.A. v United Mexican States*, ICSID Case No. ARB(AF)/00/2, Award, 29 May 2003.

principle, on the basis of which the scope of the obligation assumed under the Agreement and the actions related to compliance therewith are to be assessed.[29]

In *Siemens v Argentina*,[30] despite the fact that there was no reference to international law or to a minimum standard in the relevant treaty, the tribunal, in applying the treaty, considered itself:

[...] bound to find the meaning of these terms under international law bearing in mind their ordinary meaning, the evolution of international law and the specific context in which they are used.[31]

The *Enron v Argentina*[32] tribunal positioned the fair and equitable standard in the evolutionary context of international law:

The evolution that has taken place is for the most part the outcome of a case by case determination by courts and tribunals, [partly hinging] on the gradual formulation of 'general principles of law'[33] [...] in some circumstances, where the international minimum standard is sufficiently elaborate and clear, fair and equitable treatment might be equated with it. But in other vague circumstances, fair and equitable treatment may be more precise than its customary international law forefathers.[34]

It concluded that, in the specific context, it required a treatment additional to or beyond that of the customary international law.

The second tribunal in *Vivendi v Argentina*,[35] in its recent decision, saw no basis for limiting fair and equitable treatment to the customary international law minimum standard. According to the tribunal, the reference to the principles of international law in the France/Argentina BIT supports 'a broad reading that invites consideration of a wider range of international law principles'. It echoed the *Azurix* tribunal's holding that the requirement of conformity of the fair and equitable treatment standard to the principles of international law 'sets a floor not a ceiling on this standard'[36] in order to avoid a possible interpretation of the standard below what is required by international law. It also considers that contemporary principles of international law apply and not those of a century ago.[37]

The tribunal in *Sempra v Argentina* stated:

It might well be that in some circumstances in which the international minimum standard is sufficiently elaborate and clear, the standard of fair and equitable treatment might

---

[29] Ibid., para. 155.
[30] *Siemens A.G. v Argentina*, ICSID Case No. ARB/02/08, Award, 6 February 2007.
[31] Ibid., para. 291.
[32] *Enron Corporation and Ponderosa Assets, L.P. v Argentine Republic*, ICSID Case No. ARB/01/3, Award, 22 May 2007.
[33] Ibid., para. 257.
[34] Ibid., para. 258 (footnote added).
[35] *Compañiá de Aguas del Aconquija S.A. and Vivendi Universal v Argentine Republic*, ICSID Case No. ARB/97/3, Award, 20 August 2007.
[36] *Azurix v Argentine Republic*, ICSID Case No. ARB/01/12, Award, 14 July 2006, para. 361.
[37] *Vivendi v Argentine Republic*, above n. 35, para. 7.4.7.

be equated with it. But in other cases, it might as well be the opposite, so that the fair and equitable treatment standard will be more precise than its customary international law forefathers. On many occasions, the issue will not even be whether the fair and equitable treatment standard is different or more demanding than the customary standard, but only whether it is more specific, less generic and spelled out in a contemporary fashion so that its application is more appropriate to the case under consideration. This does not exclude the possibility that the fair and equitable treatment standard imposed under a treaty can also eventually require a treatment additional to or beyond that of customary law.[38]

One of the few BIT tribunals which retained that the international law mentioned in the treaty is customary international law, is the tribunal in *M.C.I. Power Group L.C. v Ecuador*,[39] which held that:

[...] the international law mentioned in Article II of the BIT refers to customary international law, i.e. the repeated, general, and constant practice of States, which they observe because they are aware that it is obligatory.[40]

In real terms, what difference does it make if the fair and equitable treatment standard does or does not refer to the minimum standard? Some tribunals have questioned whether substantial differences result from this characterization.

In *Azurix v Argentina*[41] for instance, the tribunal did not consider it to be of material significance for its application of the standard of fair and equitable treatment to the facts of the case and held that:

[...] the question whether or not F&E treatment is or is not additional to the minimum treatment requirement under international law is a question about the substantive content of fair and equitable treatment and whichever side of the argument one takes, the answer to the question may in substance be the same.[42]

Similarly, the tribunal in *Saluka v The Czech Republic*,[43] referring to the controversy between the claimant and the respondent over this question, was of the view that:

[...] whatever the merits of the controversy between the parties may be, it appears that the difference between the treaty standard and the customary minimum standard, when applied to the specific facts of the case, may be more apparent than real.[44]

The acceptance of the evolutionary character of the minimum standard to include new elements as shaped by the over 2500 concluded BITs, as indicated

---

[38] *Sempra Energy v The Argentine Republic*, above n. 2, para. 302.
[39] *MCI Power Group L.C. and New Turbine, Inc. v Ecuador*, ICSID Case No. ARB/03/6, Award, 31 July 2007.
[40] Ibid., para. 369.
[41] *Azurix v Argentine Republic*, above n. 36.
[42] Ibid., para. 364.
[43] *Saluka Investments BV (The Netherlands) v The Czech Republic*, Partial Award, 17 March 2006.
[44] Ibid., para. 291.

by the *Mondev* and other tribunals, may be a path of convergence between the traditional expression of fair and equitable treatment as the minimum standard and new elements brought in a recurrent fashion by arbitral tribunals. Also, as the *Sempra* tribunal stated:

> [...] international law is itself not too clear or precise as concerns the treatment due to foreign citizens, traders and investors. This is the case because the pertinent standards have gradually evolved over the centuries. Customary international law, treaties of friendship, commerce and navigation, and more recently bilateral investment treaties, have all contributed to this development.[45]

C. What is the Normative Content of the Fair and Equitable Treatment Standard as it has been Formulated by Arbitral Tribunals?

The vagueness of the term, which some say is intentional to give tribunals the possibility to articulate the range of principles necessary to achieve the treaty's purpose in particular disputes, had raised some concern among governments that, the less guidance is provided for arbitrators, the more discretion is involved and the more closely the process resembles decisions *ex aequo et bono*, ie, based on the arbitrators' notions of 'fairness' and 'equity'.[46]

Experience has proven these concerns not to be entirely well founded. Tribunals have refrained from reasoning *ex aequo et bono* and have identified a certain number of recurrent elements which they consider as constituting the normative content of the fair and equitable treatment standard, according to the specific facts of each case. These elements can be analysed in four categories; (a) vigilance and protection; (b) due process including non-denial of justice; (c) lack of arbitrariness and non-discrimination; and (d) transparency and stability, including the respect of the investors' reasonable expectations.

Obligation of Vigilance and Protection

In a number of early decisions, the tribunals made reference to the obligation of vigilance, also phrased as an obligation to exercise due diligence in protecting foreign investment, in order to define an act or omission of the State as being contrary to fair and equitable treatment and full protection and security.[47] In these cases, the standards of 'fair and equitable treatment' and 'full protection and security' have been interlocking and examined together by tribunals. The latter standard, full protection and security, is often included in treaties as a separate

---

[45] *Sempra Energy v The Argentine Republic*, above n. 2, para. 296.
[46] Yannaca-Small, above n. 11.
[47] For a comprehensive discussion on this standard, see Cordero Moss at Chapter 7 below.

C. Normative Content of the Fair and Equitable Treatment

obligation and was applied in the past essentially when the foreign investment had been affected by civil strife and physical violence.

The obligation of vigilance has been considered a standard deriving from customary international law. Among the cases which equated the standards of fair and equitable treatment and full protection and security were: *Asian Agricultural Products Ltd (AAPL) v Sri Lanka*,[48] *American Manufacturing & Trading (AMT), Inc v Republic of Zaire*,[49] *Wena Hotels v Egypt*,[50] *Occidental v Ecuador*.[51] The latter tribunal held that 'a treatment that it is not fair and equitable automatically entails an absence of full protection and security' and considered a separate examination moot.[52]

The *Azurix* tribunal, however, found that the two standards were separate and also that the full protection and security standard went beyond physical violence and covered the obligation to create a secure investment environment.[53]

In *PSEG v Turkey*,[54] the tribunal held that the standard applied only exceptionally to legal security—and in this case was very similar to the fair and equitable treatment standard.[55]

Denial of Justice, Due Process

The only investment agreements which explicitly state the scope of application of the fair and equitable standard are the new US Model BIT and a number of US FTAs which stipulate that the obligation to provide fair and equitable treatment '[...] includes the obligation not to deny justice in criminal, civil, or administrative adjudicatory proceedings in accordance with the principle of due process embodied in the principal legal systems of the world [...]'.[56]

A number of cases arise out of denial of justice[57] in the matter of procedure, some deficiency in the vindication, and enforcement of the investor's rights. The principle of 'denial of justice' has been considered as being part of customary international law. Most of the cases examined approach fair and equitable treatment in connection with the improper administration of civil and criminal

---

[48] *Asian Agricultural Products Ltd (AAPL) v Republic of Sri Lanka*, ICSID Case No. ARB/87/3, Award, 27 June 1990.
[49] *American Manufacturing & Trading, Inc. (AMT) v Republic of Zaire*, ICSID Case No. ARB/93/1, Award, 21 February 1997.
[50] *Wena Hotels Limited v Arab Republic of Egypt*, ICSID Case No. ARB/98/4, Award, 8 December 2000.
[51] *Occidental Exploration and Production Company v Republic of Ecuador*, LCIA No. UN 3467, Award, 1 July 2004.
[52] Ibid., para. 187.
[53] *Azurix v Argentine Republic*, above n. 36, para. 408.
[54] *PSEG Global et al. v Republic of Turkey*, ICSID Case No. ARB/02/5, Award, 19 January 2007.
[55] Ibid., para. 259.
[56] See Article 5(2)a US Model BIT (2004).
[57] For a comprehensive analysis see J. Paulsson, *Denial of Justice in International Law* (2005).

justice as regards an alien, including denial of access to courts, inadequate and unjust procedures.

The tribunal in *Waste Management v Mexico*[58] defined a violation of fair and equitable treatment as '[...] involving a lack of due process leading to an outcome which offends judicial propriety—as might be the case with a manifest failure of natural justice in judicial proceedings [...]'.[59]

In *Mondev v USA*,[60] the tribunal went on to apply the standard of denial of justice to the violation of the fair and equitable standard. In connection with whether the investor had the right to submit the claim to NAFTA tribunals, it stated:

The Tribunal is thus concerned only with that aspect of the Article 1105(1) which concerns what is commonly called denial of justice, that is to say, with the standard of treatment of aliens applicable to decisions of the host State's courts or tribunals.[61]

In *Loewen v USA*,[62] the tribunal considered 'manifest injustice in the sense of a lack of due process leading to an outcome which offends a sense of judicial propriety is enough'[63] to identify a breach of fair and equitable treatment.

In *Genin v Estonia*,[64] the tribunal took the position that, in order to amount to a violation of the BIT, any procedural irregularity that may have been present would have to amount to bad faith, a wilful disregard of due process of law or an extreme insufficiency of action.[65]

In *Thunderbird v Mexico*,[66] the tribunal viewed acts that would give rise to a breach of the minimum standard of treatment prescribed by NAFTA 'and customary international law as those that [...] amount to a gross denial of justice or manifest arbitrariness falling below acceptable international standards'.[67]

Lack of Arbitrariness and Non-discrimination

Although most BITs include a separate provision on protection against arbitrary and discriminatory behaviour, some tribunals have interpreted lack of arbitrariness and non-discrimination as elements of the fair and equitable treatment standard.[68]

---

[58] *Waste Management, Inc. v United Mexican States*, ICSID Case No. ARB(AF)/00/3, Award, 30 April 2004.
[59] Ibid., para. 98.
[60] *Mondev International Ltd v United States of America*, above n. 22.
[61] Ibid., para. 96.
[62] *The Loewen Group, Inc. and Raymond L. Loewen v United States*, Final Award, 26 June 2003.
[63] Ibid., para. 132.
[64] *Alex Genin et al. v Estonia*, ICSID Case No. ARB/99/2, Final Award, 25 June 2001.
[65] Ibid., para. 371.
[66] *International Thunderbird Gaming Corporation v Mexico*, UNCITRAL (NAFTA), Award, 26 January 2006.
[67] Ibid., para. 194.
[68] See Veijo Heiskanen at Chapter 5 above. See also C. Schreuer, 'Fair and Equitable Treatment (FET): Interaction with Other Standards', 4(5) *Transnational Dispute Management* (2007).

C. Normative Content of the Fair and Equitable Treatment 121

In *CMS v Argentina*,[69] the tribunal linked the standard of protection against arbitrariness and discrimination to the fair and equitable treatment standard. According to its view, '[...] any measure that might involve arbitrariness or discrimination is in itself contrary to the fair and equitable treatment'.[70]

The *MTD v Chile*,[71] *PSEG v Turkey*,[72] and *Saluka v Czech Republic*[73] tribunals also declined to distinguish the two standards.

One tribunal which examined the two standards separately was the one in *LG&E v Argentina*,[74] which found that it was possible to violate one standard without violating the other: '[...] characterizing the measures as non-arbitrary does not mean that such measures are characterized as fair and equitable [...]'.[75]

NAFTA does not include separate provisions on these elements and NAFTA tribunals have included them in their interpretation of fair and equitable standard.

In *S.D. Myers Inc. v Canada*,[76] the tribunal considered that a breach of Article 1105 occurs only when it is shown that an investor has been treated in such an unjust or arbitrary manner that the treatment rises to the level that is unacceptable from the international perspective.[77]

In *Waste Management v Mexico*,[78] the tribunal stated that: 'the minimum standard of treatment of fair and equitable treatment is infringed by conduct attributable to the State and harmful to the claimant if the conduct is arbitrary, grossly unfair, unjust or idiosyncratic, discriminatory' but it also added conduct that '[...] involves a lack of due process leading to an outcome which offends judicial property [...]'.[79]

Transparency and Stability

The first reference to the principle of transparency, in particular with respect to administrative proceedings, as an element of the fair and equitable treatment was made by the *Metalclad* tribunal, while the tribunal in *Tecmed* substantiated

---

[69] *CMS Gas Transmission Company v The Argentine Republic*, ICSID Case No. ARB/01/8, Award, 12 May 2005.
[70] Ibid., para. 290.
[71] *MTD Equity Sdn. Bhd. and MTD Chile S.A. v Republic of Chile*, ICSID Case No. ARB/01/7, Award, 25 May 2004.
[72] *PSEG v Turkey*, above n. 54.
[73] *Saluka v The Czech Republic*, above n. 43. The tribunal agreed with *SD Myers, Inc. v Canada*, above n. 20, that 'an infringement of the fair and equitable standard requires treatment in such an unjust or arbitrary manner that the treatment rises to the level that is unacceptable from the international perspective'.
[74] *LG&E Energy Corp, LG&E Capital Corp and LG&E International Inc. v Argentine Republic*, ICSID Case No. ARB/02/1, Decision on Liability, 3 October 2006.
[75] Ibid., para. 162.
[76] *S.D. Myers Inc. v Canada* (UNCITRAL), First Partial Award, 13 November 2000.
[77] Ibid., para. 263.
[78] *Waste Management, Inc. v United Mexican States*, above n. 58.
[79] Ibid., para. 98.

this interpretation by putting it in the context of more concrete procedural principles and rights and expanding it to include the investor's legitimate expectations. This set a trend for subsequent tribunals to include the element of the investor's legitimate expectations as one of the main components of fair and equitable treatment. Its application tends to cover the regulatory experience as a whole, where stability and transparency are governmental promises upon which the investor relies for his investment. The principles of transparency, clarity, and stability[80] guide the process of both the definitions of the conditions of the 'legitimate expectations' principle and its application to the particular facts of a specific situation. Good faith, as the underlying principle, is guiding all of these obligations and as it has been commented, '[...] it is relied on as the common guiding beacon that will orient the understanding and interpretation of obligations [...]'.[81]

Except for the *Genin* tribunal interpretation,[82] there is a common thread in the recent awards under NAFTA and BITs which do not require bad faith or malicious intention of the recipient State as a necessary element in the failure to treat investment fairly and equitably.

In *Metalclad v Mexico*,[83] the tribunal defined the concept of 'transparency' (stated in NAFTA Article 1802) as the idea that '[...] all relevant legal requirements for the purpose of investing should be capable of being readily known to all investors'.[84]

In *Tecmed v Mexico*,[85] the tribunal considered that:

[...] [this] provision of the Agreement, in light of the good faith principle established by international law, requires the Contracting Parties to provide to international investments treatment that does not affect the basic expectations that were taken into account by the foreign investor to make the investment. The foreign investor expects the host State to act in a consistent manner, free from ambiguity and totally transparent in its

---

[80] It is worth noting that transparency is favoured and advocated by an increasing number of governments. In the context of international organizations, such as the OECD for instance, these governments acknowledge through soft law the importance of transparency and a stable investment environment for national and foreign investors alike. In the OECD Policy Framework for Investment, developed by both developed and developing country governments and put into application by a number of developing countries, governments stipulate that: 'Transparency, property protection and non-discrimination are investment policy principles that underpin efforts to create a sound investment environment for all. Transparent information on the way governments implement and change rules and regulations dealing with investment is a critical determinant in the investment decision. Transparency and predictability is important for foreign investors who may have to function with very different regulatory systems, cultures and administrative frameworks from their own. Transparency and predictability help to improve the investment environment, because they reduce the risk of inconsistent application of laws and regulations and lower uncertainty faced by investors and others.'
[81] See Dolzer, above n. 11.
[82] *Genin. v Estonia*, above nn. 64, 66.
[83] *Metalclad Corporation v Mexico*, above n. 10.
[84] Ibid., para. 76.
[85] *Tecmed v United Mexican States*, above n. 28.

C. Normative Content of the Fair and Equitable Treatment 123

relations with the foreign investor, so that it may know beforehand any and all rules and regulations that will govern its investments, as well as the goals of the relevant policies and administrative practices or directives, to be able to plan its investment and comply with such regulations.[86]

The stability of the host State's legal order with the existence of predictable and transparent rules and regulations and their consistent application enhance and promote legal security. This is in conformity with the object and purpose of international investment treaties, as stability, predictability, and consistency are necessary for investors in order to plan their investment according to the legal framework of the host country.

In *Occidental (OEPC) v Ecuador*,[87] the tribunal referred to the preamble of the US/Ecuador BIT and concluded that 'the stability of the legal and business framework is thus an essential element of fair and equitable treatment'[88] and that fair and equitable is an objective requirement that does not depend on whether the respondent has proceeded in good faith or not.[89]

In *CMS Gas Transmission Company v Argentina*,[90] the tribunal upheld CMS's claim for violations of fair and equitable treatment under Article II(2) of the US/Argentina BIT, noting that fair and equitable treatment is inseparable from stability and predictability and that there was no need to prove bad faith on the part of Argentina. Rather, an objective assessment of whether the legitimate expectations of the investor were met could be made.[91]

In *LG&E v Argentina*,[92] citing previous awards that have adjudicated on the same fair and equitable standard according to this treaty or identical wording in other treaties, the tribunal acknowledged as well that 'the stability of the legal and business framework is an essential element on the standard of what is fair and equitable treatment'[93] and considered this interpretation to be an emerging standard of fair and equitable treatment in international law.

In *Enron v Argentina*,[94] the tribunal also concluded that a key element of fair and equitable treatment is the requirement of a 'stable framework for the investment' and in *Sempra* the tribunal affirmed that 'what counts is that in the end the stability of the law and the observance of legal obligations are assured, thereby safeguarding the very object and purpose of the protection sought by the treaty'.[95]

---

[86] Ibid., para. 154.
[87] *Occidental v Republic of Ecuador*, above n. 51.
[88] Ibid., para. 183.
[89] Ibid., para. 186.
[90] *CMS Gas Transmission Company v The Argentine Republic*, above n. 69.
[91] Ibid., para. 274.
[92] *LG&E v Argentine Republic*, above n. 74.
[93] Ibid., para. 124.
[94] *Enron Corporation v Argentine Republic*, above n. 32.
[95] *Sempra Energy v The Argentine Republic*, above n. 2, para. 300.

Legitimate Expectations

Legal rules and regulations are only able to create the basis of an environment beneficial to long-term investment when they are applied according to how a reasonable investor would expect them to be applied. The investors' perceptions and their expectations towards the government activity becomes an essential element of their perception of the host country's ordering function of law. As mentioned above, the legitimate expectation principle became a recurrent, independent basis for a claim under the fair and equitable treatment standard. As Professor Wälde argued in his Separate Opinion in the *Thunderbird* case, such growth in scope and role '[...] is possibly related to the fact that it provides a more supple way of providing a remedy appropriate to the particular situation as compared to the more drastic determination and remedy inherent in the concept of regulatory expropriation'.[96] The statement confirms the findings of the *CMS* tribunal[97] which first examined the claim for expropriation and then turned to the legitimate expectation principle to provide protection to the investor. This approach suggests that obligations entailed in the expropriation clause and those of fair and equitable treatment do not necessarily differ in quality, but just in intensity.

In its concluding remarks on the standard, the *CMS* tribunal went so far as to state that the connection between fair and equitable treatment and stability, ie respect of investors' legitimate expectations, 'is not different from the international law minimum standard' and it can thus be said to have acquired customary nature.[98]

In *Saluka v Czech Republic*,[99] the tribunal considered that the standard of 'fair and equitable treatment' is closely tied to the notion of legitimate expectations which, in its view, is the dominant element of that standard.

[...] An investor's decision to make an investment is based on an assessment of the state of the law and the totality of the business environment at the time of the investment as well as on the investor's expectation that the conduct of the host State subsequent to the investment will be fair and equitable.

The standard of 'fair and equitable treatment' is therefore closely tied to the notion of legitimate expectations which is the dominant element of that standard. By virtue of the 'fair and equitable treatment' standard included in Article 3.1 the Czech Republic must therefore be regarded as having assumed an obligation to treat foreign investors so as to avoid the frustration of investors' legitimate and reasonable expectations.[100]

---

[96] *International Thunderbird Gaming Corporation v Mexico*, Separate Opinion (Dissent in Part) by Professor Thomas Wälde, 26 January 2006, para. 37.
[97] *CMS Gas Transmission Company v The Argentine Republic*, above n. 69.
[98] Ibid., para. 284.
[99] *Saluka v The Czech Republic*, above n. 43.
[100] Ibid., paras 301–302.

In *Siemens v Argentina*,[101] the tribunal also understood that the current standard includes the frustration of expectations that the investor may have legitimately taken into account when it made the investment.

> The purpose of the Treaty is to promote and protect investments. It would be inconsistent with such commitments and purpose and the expectations created by such a document to consider that a party to the Treaty has breached its obligation only when it has acted in bad faith [...].[102]

In *ADF v USA*,[103] the tribunal discussed the claimant's expectation allegedly created by existing case law but it denied the existence of a 'legitimate expectation' in the particular case because the expectation was not created by 'any misleading representations made by authorised officials of the US federal government but rather, by legal advice received from private counsel'. The tribunal suggested, *a contrario*, that it is representations from authorized officials that provide the foundation for legitimate expectations if these representations reasonably become the basis for the investor's commitment of capital.[104]

The *Thunderbird* tribunal attempted to clarify the role to be played by the principle of legitimate expectations in the context of investment arbitration, particularly under the NAFTA. It is especially useful in providing a relatively concise description of the circumstances in which the principle will apply:

> [...] the concept of 'legitimate expectations' relates, within the context of the NAFTA framework, to a situation where a Contracting Party's conduct creates reasonable and justifiable expectations on the part of an investor (or investment) to act in reliance on said conduct, such that a failure by the NAFTA Party to honour those expectations could cause the investor (or investment) to suffer damages.[105]

However, the tribunal did not elaborate on the precise role of the legitimate expectations principle in the context of investor-state arbitration.[106] In this respect, Professor Thomas Wälde in his separate opinion, was more precise by approaching the principle of legitimate expectations as forming a central part of the fair and equitable test under NAFTA Article 1105:

> One can observe over the last years a significant growth in the role and scope of the legitimate expectation principle, from an earlier function as a subsidiary interpretative principle to reinforce a particular interpretative approach chosen, to its current role as a

---

[101] *Siemens A.G. v Argentina*, above n. 30.
[102] Ibid., para. 300.
[103] *ADF Group Inc v United States*, above n. 24.
[104] Ibid., para. 189.
[105] *International Thunderbird Gaming Corporation v Mexico*, above n. 66, para. 147.
[106] For a more detailed analysis and comments on the *Thunderbird* case see S. Fietta, 'International Thunderbird Gaming Corporation v. The United Mexican States: An Indication of the Limits of the "Legitimate Expectation" Basis of Claim under Article 1105 of NAFTA?', 3(2) *Transnational Dispute Management* (2006).

self-standing subcategory and independent basis for a claim under the 'fair and equitable standard' as under Art. 1105 of the NAFTA.[107]

But the threshold for such informal and general representations might be quite high. A legitimate expectation is assumed more readily if an individual investor receives specific formal assurances that visibly display an official character and if the official(s) perceive or should perceive that the investor intends, reasonably, to rely on such representation. The more specific the assurances that are given, the more likely they are to give rise to some basis for a legitimate expectation claim. As the *CMS* tribunal stated:

It is not a question of whether the legal framework might need to be frozen as it can always evolve and be adapted to changing circumstances but neither is it a question of whether the framework can be dispensed with altogether when specific commitments to the contrary have been made. The law of foreign investment and its protection has been developed with the specific objective of avoiding such adverse legal effects.[108]

In *Parkerings-Compagniet AS v Republic of Lithuania*,[109] the tribunal reaffirmed that the principal basis for a legitimate expectation is an explicit promise or guaranty from the State:

[...] the expectation is legitimate if the investor received an explicit promise or guaranty from the host-State, or if implicitly, the host-State made assurances or representation that the investor took into account in making the investment. Finally, in the situation where the host-State made no assurance or representation, the circumstances surrounding the conclusion of the agreement are decisive to determine if the expectation of the investor was legitimate. In order to determine the legitimate expectation of an investor, it is also necessary to analyse the conduct of the State at the time of the investment.[110]

It concluded that, due to lack of specific demonstrations by the claimant that the modifications of laws were made specifically to prejudice its investment, the claim that the State acted unfairly, unreasonably, or inequitably in the exercise of its legislative power, could not be sustained.

Proportionality

For those who are concerned about possible abusive claims by investors of violation of their legitimate expectations and, consequently, the potential for abusive interpretation by tribunals—which might have a chilling effect on the governments' exercise of regulatory power—it is worth looking at the balanced,

---

[107] *International Thunderbird Gaming Corporation v Mexico*, Separate Opinion, above n. 96, para. 37.
[108] *CMS Gas Transmission Company v The Argentine Republic*, above n. 69, para. 277.
[109] *Parkerings-Compagniet AS v Lithuania*, ICSID Case No. ARB/05/8, Final Award, 11 September 2007.
[110] Ibid., para. 331.

C. Normative Content of the Fair and Equitable Treatment

proportionate positions taken by some recent tribunals which accompanied their interpretation with a proportionate clarification.

A number of tribunals have followed the *S.D. Myers* reasoning that the determination of a breach of the obligation of 'fair and equitable treatment' by the host State must be made in the light of the high measure of deference that international law generally extends to the right of domestic authorities to regulate matters within their own borders. Therefore, it should not be handled as an inflexible yardstick.

The tribunal in *Saluka* warned against the literal interpretation of the terms 'stability' and 'predictability' in the regulatory environment and noted that:

[...] if their terms were to be taken too literally, they would impose upon host States obligations which would be inappropriate and unrealistic. Moreover, the scope of the Treaty's protection of foreign investment against unfair and inequitable treatment cannot exclusively be determined by foreign investors' subjective motivations and considerations. Their expectations, in order for them to be protected, must rise to the level of legitimacy and reasonableness in light of the circumstances.[111]

It concluded that the determination of a breach of the fair and equitable treatment standard requires a weighing of the claimant's legitimate and reasonable expectations on the one hand and the respondent's legitimate regulatory interests on the other.[112]

The *LG&E* tribunal also followed the same line which includes a balancing approach that the host State's specific investment and regulatory environment must be taken into account when determining the fair and equitable treatment standard.

In *Enron*, the tribunal noted also that the stabilization requirement does not mean the freezing of the legal system or the disappearance of the regulatory power of the State.[113]

The tribunal in *MCI v Ecuador* considered as well that the investor's expectations of fair and equitable treatment and good faith, in accordance with the BIT, must be paired with a legitimate objective. The legitimacy of the expectations for proper treatment entertained by a foreign investor protected by the BIT does not depend solely on the intent of the parties, but on certainty about the contents of the enforceable obligations.[114]

In addition, there is a related trend recognizing that inherent business risks of an investment are to be borne by the investor and cannot be adjudicated under a treaty, which in the case of an investment in developing States, include acceptance of potentially less stable socio-economic and political environments.

---

[111] *Saluka v The Czech Republic*, above n. 43, para. 304.
[112] Ibid., para. 306.
[113] *Enron Corporation v Argentine Republic*, above n. 32, para. 261.
[114] *MCI Power Group v Ecuador*, above n. 39, para. 278.

In *MTD v Chile,* the tribunal reduced by 50 per cent the damages awarded to MTD on account of business risk. It noted: '[...] BITs are not an insurance against business risk and the claimants should bear the consequences of their own actions as experienced businessmen'.[115]

The tribunal in *Parkerings v Lithuania* insisted on the shared responsibility between a State's actions and regulations and an investor's expectations. It recognized the State's 'undeniable right and privilege to exercise its sovereign legislative power' and 'to enact, modify or cancel a law at its own discretion'. It also stated that any businessman or investor knows that laws will evolve over time.[116] On the other hand, it recognized the right of the investor to a certain stability and predictability of the legal environment of the investment and the right of protection of its legitimate expectations provided it exercised due diligence and that its legitimate expectations were reasonable in light of the circumstances. However, an investor must anticipate that the circumstances could change, and thus structure its investment in order to adapt it to the potential changes of legal environment. What is prohibited is for a State to act unfairly, unreasonably, or inequitably in the exercise of its legislative power.[117]

In the case at hand, the tribunal noted that the investor, by deciding to invest notwithstanding a possible instability, took the *business risk* to be faced with changes of laws possibly or even likely to be detrimental to its investment although

[...] he could (and with hindsight should) have sought to protect its legitimate expectations by introducing into the investment agreement a stabilisation clause or some other provision protecting it against unexpected and unwelcome changes.

It then drew a line between contractual expectations and expectations under international law and concluded:

It is evident that not every hope amounts to an expectation under international law. The expectation a party to an agreement may have of the regular fulfilment of the obligation by the other party is not necessarily an expectation protected by international law. In other words, contracts involve intrinsic expectations from each party that do not amount to expectations as understood in international law. Indeed, the party whose *contractual expectations* are frustrated should, under specific conditions, seek redress before a national tribunal.[118]

Professor Wälde, in his partial dissent in the *Thunderbird* case, also expressed the view that the disappointment of legitimate expectations must be sufficiently serious and material. Otherwise, any minor misconduct by a public official could

---

[115] *MTD Equity Sdn. Bhd and MTD Chile S.A. v Republic of Chile,* above n. 71, para. 178.
[116] *Parkerings-Compagniet AS v Lithuania,* above n. 109, para. 332.
[117] Ibid., para. 333.
[118] Ibid., para. 344.

go to the jurisdiction of a treaty tribunal, whose function is not to act as a general-recourse administrative law tribunal.[119]

D. Conclusion

To use the words of the *PSEG* tribunal, the standard of fair and equitable treatment has acquired prominence in investment arbitration as a consequence of the fact that other standards traditionally provided by international law might not in the circumstances of each case be entirely appropriate.[120] This is particularly the case when the facts of the dispute do not clearly support the claim for direct expropriation, but when there are, nevertheless, events that appear to call for redress for the investor and need to be assessed under a different standard. Because the role of fair and equitable treatment changes from case to case, it is sometimes not as precise as would be desirable. Yet, it clearly does allow for justice to be done in the absence of the more traditional breaches of international law standards.

There is diversity in the way the 'fair and equitable treatment' standard is formulated in investment agreements. Because of the differences in its formulation, the proper interpretation of the 'fair and equitable treatment' standard depends on the specific wording of the particular treaty, its context, the object and purpose of the treaty, as well as on negotiating history or other indications of the parties' intent.

There is a debate about whether the fair and equitable treatment standard is part of the minimum standard of customary international law or is an autonomous standard. Because of NAFTA's language linking the fair and equitable treatment standard to the minimum standard and NAFTA Free Trade Commission's binding interpretation linking the minimum standard to customary international law, NAFTA tribunals follow this interpretation with the understanding, however, that the customary international law minimum standard of treatment refers to an evolving customary international law and not one frozen in time. On the other hand, BIT tribunals lean towards interpreting it more broadly as an autonomous standard going beyond the minimum standard. Some tribunals have questioned whether substantial differences result from this characterization.

An analysis of the opinions of the arbitral tribunals which have attempted to interpret and apply the 'fair and equitable treatment' standard identified a number of elements which, singly or in combination, have been treated as encompassed in the standard of treatment: (a) the obligation of vigilance and

---

[119] *International Thunderbird Gaming Corporation v Mexico*, Separate Opinion, above n. 96, para. 14.
[120] *PSEG v Turkey*, above n. 54, para. 238.

security which usually interacts with the standard of full protection and security; (b) denial of justice and due diligence; (c) protection against arbitrariness and discrimination, which often tends to override specific treaty provisions on arbitrariness and non-discrimination; and (d) transparency, stability, and the investor's legitimate expectations.

The investor's legitimate expectations has emerged as a recurrent essential element of the fair and equitable treatment standard. The principle, traditionally related to transparency, can also be considered a further development of the concepts of stability and predictability. It has often been applied as a more supple way of providing a remedy appropriate to a particular situation as compared to the more drastic determination and remedy inherent in the concept of regulatory expropriation. It relates in particular to specific assurances of an official character given to the investor—either through laws and regulations or other administrative acts—and the host State's officials' perception that the investor intends, reasonably, to rely on such representation. Most tribunals have adopted a proportionate approach and agree that the disappointment of legitimate expectations must be sufficiently serious and material and that the investor should bear the inherent business risks of his investment.

Transparency, stability, and legitimate expectations are, among the interpretative elements of fair and equitable treatment, the only ones not 'well grounded' in customary international law but which emerge from general principles and the recurrent opinion of arbitral tribunals in the last few years. It is too early to say whether we are witnessing a sign of evolution of the international custom as it is also too early to establish a definitive list of elements for the interpretation of the 'fair and equitable treatment' standard since the jurisprudence is still constantly evolving.

7

Full Protection and Security

Giuditta Cordero Moss

A. Introduction

This chapter will analyse recent investment arbitration practice in respect of the standard of investment protection known as full protection and security, in the attempt of identifying a possible emerging consensus on its scope of application and interpretation.

The standard of full protection and security is less frequently applied than other standards, hence arbitration practice is not common and the legal literature is rather scarce.[1]

Traditionally, it enjoys an undisputed scope of application in the field of physical protection of the assets and individuals connected with an investment, as will be seen in section D. The protection that the legal system affords in order to prevent or prosecute actions that threaten or impair the physical safety of the investment can be considered as an extension of the just mentioned physical security: both the police forces and the judicial or administrative systems of the host State can be engaged in securing the physical safety of a foreign investment, as will be seen in section E.

More recently, the standard has been invoked in connection with a broader scope that goes beyond the physical protection granted by police or similar forces as well as the availability of the judicial systems, and expands to a more abstract kind of security.

When the security of an investment is not intended as physical safety, but as legal security, the application of the full protection and security standard exceeds its traditional scope of application. Thus, legal security has at times been invoked to sanction regulatory actions or other behaviour that has violated the legal terms

---

[1] Among the most significant recent analyses devoted specifically to this standard see H.E. Zeitler, 'The Guarantee of "Full Protection and Security" in Investment Treaties Regarding Harm Caused by Private Actors', in *Stockholm International Arbitration Review* (2005) 1, 3. See also UNCTAD, *Investor-State Disputes Arising from Investment Treaties: A Review*, UNCTAD Series on International Investment Policies for Development, UNCTAD/ITE/IIT/2005/4.

under which the investment was undertaken or has affected the stability of the legal framework for the investment, as will be analysed in section E.

Expanding the scope of full protection and security to this kind of legal protection renders the standard strikingly similar to another well-known and more widespread standard of protection, that of fair and equitable treatment. Recent arbitration practice has recognized this aspect and it has at times considered the full protection and security as absorbed by the fair and equitable treatment, as seen in section E. Thus, it remains questionable to what extent the standard of full protection and security has a meaning that goes beyond the traditional physical protection and yet is not overlapping with other standards of protection.

Another matter that is sometimes debated in arbitral practice, although not as often as in respect of fair and equitable treatment, is whether the standard is an independent standard of customary international law or rather has to be interpreted under the circumstances and the applicable treaty. Section C will attempt to identify any emerging tendencies in arbitration practice as to the consequences, if any, of considering full protection and security as a standard of customary international law or as a standard based on the applicable treaty.

This question has repercussions on the kind of obligations that the standard entails: section D will examine arbitration practice's position as to whether it is an obligation with strict liability or an obligation based on the exercise of diligence, and, in the latter case, whether the diligence expected is a subjective standard under the circumstances or, rather, an objective standard. This latter distinction has a borderline to the scope of appreciation that a State has in the exercise of its sovereign prerogatives, as will be seen in section D.

B. The Sources

The most important awards that have dealt with the question of full protection and security were based on a few investment treaties, listed below and grouped according to the wording with which the protection standard is expressed. As the overview shows, the wording in which the standard of full protection and security is expressed may vary, both in respect of the formulation itself and in respect of the context.

Thus, while the most common formulation is 'full protection and security', it is possible to see 'the most constant protection', or simply 'protection and security' and 'full legal protection and full legal security'.

In respect of the context there are several possibilities: the standard may be free standing, alternatively it may be an addition to the obligation of according fair and equitable treatment or to the obligation of abstaining from arbitrary or discriminatory measures, or it may appear as specification of the latter obligations. Another variation is that the standard is sometimes mentioned alone,

Overview of the Different Formulations

The precise formulations of full protection and security clauses in bilateral investment treaties (BITs) differ markedly. This chapter will provide a brief overview of different kinds of full protection and security clauses together with an indication of investment cases in which they have been invoked.

A number of BITs provide that investments shall be accorded fair and equitable treatment and shall enjoy full protection and security. Such a formulation can be found in Article 2(2)(i) Czech Republic/Slovak Republic BIT,[2] Article 2(2) United Kingdom/Egypt BIT,[3] and Article II 2(a) United Kingdom/Sri Lanka BIT.[4]

A few BITs provide that investments shall enjoy full legal protection and full legal security like Article 4(1) Germany/Argentina BIT.[5]

BIT provisions that investments shall be accorded fair and equitable treatment and shall not be impaired by unreasonable or discriminatory measures and, more particularly, that they shall be accorded full protection and security can be found in Article 3.1 and Article 3.2 of the Netherlands/Czech and Slovak Republic BIT[6] as well as Article 3.1 and Article 3.2 Netherlands/Poland BIT.[7]

An example of a BIT providing that investments shall be accorded full protection and security in accordance with the principle of fair and equitable treatment can be seen in Article 5.1 France/Argentina BIT.[8]

BITs providing that investments shall be accorded full protection and security in accordance with international law are found in US practice such as Article 3(1) United States/Mexico BIT.[9]

---

[2] The treaty between the Czech and the Slovak Republic never came into force. However, in *Ceskoslovenska obchodni banka a.s (CSOB) v Slovak Republic*, ICSID Case No. ARB/97/4, Award, 29 December 2004, the tribunal found that the parties had incorporated it into their agreement. Therefore, in respect of the application of the standard of full protection and security, the award refers to the wording of the treaty, paras 62 *et seq*. and 161 *et seq*. The wording referred to herein is taken from the Award, para. 63.

[3] *Wena Hotels Limited v Arab Republic of Egypt*, ICSID Case No. ARB/98/4, Award, 8 December 2000.

[4] *Asian Agricultural Products Ltd (AAPL) v Republic of Sri Lanka*, ICSID Case No. ARB/87/3, Award, 27 June 1990.

[5] *Siemens A.G. v The Argentine Republic*, ICSID Case No. ARB/02/8, Award, 6 February 2007.

[6] *CME Czech Republic B.V. (The Netherlands) v The Czech Republic*, Partial Award, 13 September 2001; and *Saluka Investments BV (The Netherlands) v The Czech Republic*, Partial Award, 17 March 2006.

[7] *Eureko B.V. v Republic of Poland*, Partial Award, 19 August 2005.

[8] *Compania de Aguas del Aconquija S.A. and Vivendi Universal S.A. v Argentine Republic II*, ICSID Case No. ARB/97/3, Award, 20 August 2007.

[9] *Tecnicas Medioambientales Tecmed S.A. (Tecmed) v The United Mexican States*, ICSID Case No. ARB(AF)/00/2, Award, 29 May 2003.

134   *Full Protection and Security*

BITs providing that investments shall be accorded fair and equitable treatment, shall enjoy full protection and security and shall in no case be accorded treatment less than that required by international law are, for instance, Article II 2(a) United States/Czech Republic BIT,[10] Article II.2(a) United States/Argentina BIT,[11] Article II (3)(a) United States/Ecuador BIT,[12] Article II (2)(a) United States/Romania BIT,[13] Article II (3) United States/Turkey BIT,[14] or Article II (4) United States/Zaire BIT.[15]

An example of Treaties of Friendship, Commerce and Navigation providing that investments shall receive the most constant protection and security for their persons and property, and shall enjoy in this respect the full protection and security required by international law is Article V(1) of the treaty between the United States and Italy.[16]

Importance of the Formulations

As seen, the standard of full protection and security is expressed in a variety of formulations in the different investment treaties. Thus, it would be reasonable to expect that the differing wording of the treaties leads to different interpretations of the standard, particularly as to the relationship between full protection and security on the one hand, and fair and equitable treatment on the other hand, as well as the relationship between the treaty-based obligation and the standard of international law. However, arbitration practice does not seem to attach a significant importance to the wording of the applicable treaty in the interpretation of the obligation of granting full protection and security. The wording of the treaty is often the starting point for the tribunal's reasoning, but it does not seem to play a decisive role in the result.

In *Siemens v Argentina* the wording of the treaty seems to have played an important role, but only to a certain extent. The applicable treaty deviates from the other treaties examined in arbitration practice in that it speaks of 'legal security'. Hence, the wording of the treaty seems to provide a clear basis for assuming that the protection and security that is meant in the treaty goes beyond the traditional police protection and covers the investment environment and the legal framework. Based on this wording, the award even questions that the

---

[10] *Ronald S. Lauder v The Czech Republic*, Award, 3 September 2001.
[11] *Azurix Corp v The Argentine Republic*, ICSID Case No. ARB/01/12, Award, 14 July 2006.
[12] *Occidental Exploration and Production Company v The Republic of Ecuador*, LCIA Case No. UN 3467, Award, 1 July 2004.
[13] *Noble Ventures, Inc. v Romania*, ICSID Case No. ARB/01/11, Award, 12 October 2005.
[14] *PSEG Global Inc. and Konya Elektrik Üretim Ve Ticaret Limited Sirketi v Republic of Turkey*, ICSID Case No. ARB/02/5, Award, 19 January 2007.
[15] *American Manufacturing & Trading, Inc (AMT) v Republic of Zaire*, ICSID Case No. ARB/93/1, Award, 21 February 1997.
[16] *Case concerning Elettronica Sicula S.p.A. (ELSI) (United States of America v Italy)*, Decision, 20 July 1989.

B. The Sources

traditional physical security is covered.[17] However, the tribunal does not consider the formulation of the standard as determinant and comes to the conclusion that the very definition of investment made in the treaty, as including also intangibles, speaks for a legal protection rather than for a physical protection.[18] So far the *Siemens* tribunal seems to have remained alone in considering that the definition of investment determines the scope of application of the obligation of full protection and security, even if most treaties examined herein have a definition of investment that directly or indirectly includes intangibles.

The *Siemens* tribunal, further, does not attach particular importance to the wording of the treaty when it considers the standards of legal protection and legal security and of fair and equitable treatment, respectively, as one single standard, despite the fact that the treaty lists them as two separate standards.[19]

Also, the *Azurix*[20] and the *Occidental*[21] awards consider jointly the obligations relating to fair and equitable treatment and to full protection and security, in spite of the circumstance that the respective treaties list them as two separate obligations. The *Azurix* award openly recognizes that the two standards appear in the treaty as separate obligations, but proceeds nevertheless to apply them as if they were a unity.

Another example of an award that does not seem to attach specific importance to the wording of the treaty is the decision recently rendered in *Vivendi v Argentina II*. The tribunal holds that the standard of full protection and security extends beyond the protection from physical interference. The starting point for this reasoning is the wording of the treaty, which does not mention the words 'physical interference' and thus does not restrict the scope of the obligation to protection from physical interference.[22] The tribunal then refers extensively to arbitral jurisprudence in support of its opinion on the extended scope of the protection, without commenting on the fact that the jurisprudence referred to in this connection is based on treaties that present a variety of formulations: full protection as a specification of fair and equitable treatment,[23] full protection as a separate standard,[24] and full protection as a separate standard and reference to public international law.[25]

It may thus be concluded that arbitral practice does not deem the wording of the treaty as decisive for the scope of application of the standard of full

---

[17] *Siemens v Argentina*, above n. 5, para. 303.
[18] Ibid.
[19] Ibid., paras. 304, 309.
[20] *Azurix v Argentina*, above n. 11, para. 408.
[21] *Occidental v Ecuador*, above n. 12, para. 187.
[22] *Vivendi v Argentina*, above n. 8, para. 7.4.15.
[23] Netherlands/Czech Republic BIT and Netherlands/Poland BIT.
[24] Czech Republic/Slovak Republic BIT and United Kingdom/Egypt BIT.
[25] United States of America/Argentina BIT; United States of America/Ecuador BIT; and United States of America/Italy BIT.

protection and security—not even when the analysis of the question starts from the formulation of the treaty.

C. International Standard

Arbitral awards sometimes discuss whether the standard of full protection is an independent standard to be judged on the basis of the applicable treaty and of the circumstances of the case, or whether customary international law plays a role in determining its content.

As seen above, the applied treaties have a variety of formulations regarding the relationship between the protection accorded by the treaty and the standard of protection existing under general international law. It does not seem that these formulations are given a decisive role in arbitration practice. In any case, in arbitration practice the variety of approaches taken does not seem to have substantial consequences in respect of the concrete application of the standard.

There are three theoretical approaches to the question: that the standard of customary international law represents the ceiling for the obligations contained in the treaty, that it represents the floor, or that it is equivalent.

International Law as a Ceiling

The standard of international law is seen as a ceiling in the interpretative note issued to Article 1105(1) of the NAFTA by the Free Trade Commission in 2001: the note states that the obligation to provide full security and protection in the NAFTA does not require a treatment in addition to or beyond that which is required by the customary international law minimum standard of treatment of aliens.[26] This interpretation has been deemed to be binding by tribunals applying the NAFTA,[27] but it is not necessarily relevant in other disputes.[28]

International Law as a Floor

The tribunal in *Azurix v Argentina*, applying a treaty that requires a treatment no less favourable than that required by international law, affirms that the standard of international law is to be understood as a floor for the treaty-based

---

[26] NAFTA Free Trade Commission on 31 July 2001 (available at http://www.dfait-maeci.gc.ca/tna-nac/NAFTA-Interpr-en.asp).
[27] *Mondev International Ltd v United States*, Award, 11 October 2002, para. 120.
[28] *Siemens v Argentina*, above n. 5, affirms in para. 291 that the interpretation of the NAFTA standard cannot be extended to the interpretation of the standard under other treaties. See also *Occidental v Ecuador*, above n. 12, para. 192.

protection.[29] The tribunal continues noticing, however, that it is not of material significance whether international law is a floor or a ceiling, because the standard of international law evolves, and the content of the obligations is substantially similar whether interpreted according to the ordinary meaning of the treaty's wording or according to the standard under international law.[30]

International Law as Equivalent

The tribunal of *AAPL v Sri Lanka*, applying a treaty that does not mention the relationship between the standard of international law and treaty protection, affirmed that the treaty-based protection is the same protection afforded under international law, and would be applicable even in the absence of a specific clause in the treaty. The tribunal analyses the wording of the treaty and affirms that the wording 'full protection' possibly suggests a higher degree of responsibility than the customary standard.[31] Nevertheless, the tribunal ends up applying the minimum standard of customary international law.[32]

The tribunal in *AMT v Zaire*, applying a treaty that considers international law as a floor for the treaty protection, assumes that the treaty obligation has to be consistent with the minimum required by international law.[33]

Also, the tribunal in *Noble Ventures v Romania*, applying a treaty that provides for treatment no less favourable than required by international law, affirms that it is doubtful whether the treaty obligation is larger than the general duty to provide for full protection and security in customary international law.[34] The arbitral tribunal rendered its decision in respect of the violation of the full protection and security standard exclusively by reference to the ICJ's decision in *ELSI* and comparing the set of facts in the two cases, although the wording in the applicable BITs was quite different—respectively, 'full protection and security and no less than international law' in the treaty between the United States and Romania, and 'the most constant protection and security and the full protection and security required by international law' in the treaty between the United States and Italy.

Even if not in the context of a treaty on investment protection, the *Eurotunnel* tribunal recently confirmed the general attitude taken by arbitration practice, according to which the application of the standard under international law would not add much to the protection accorded by the applicable treaty.[35]

---

[29] *Azurix v Argentina*, above n. 11, para. 361.
[30] Ibid., paras 364 *et seq*.
[31] *AAPL v Sri Lanka*, above n. 4, paras 46–53.
[32] Ibid., paras 67–69.
[33] *AMT v Zaire*, above n. 15, paras 6.06, 6.07.
[34] *Noble Ventures v Romania*, above n. 13, para. 164.
[35] *The Channel Tunnel Group Limited, France-Manche S.A. v United Kingdom and the Republic of France (Eurotunnel)*, Partial Award, 30 January 2007, para. 275.

D. Physical Safety

The obligation to ensure full protection and security has an undisputed scope of application in the context of physical safety of persons and installations connected with protected investments, as expressed in the award rendered in *PSEG v Turkey*.[36] It is described as creating an obligation to preserve the public order and normal security by use of police and public powers, as repeatedly underlined in the *Eurotunnel* Award.[37] The undisputed scope of application thus refers, essentially, to civil strife and physical violence, as affirmed in the *Saluka* award.[38]

Causality

The physical damage against which the protection is directed may be caused by the State, State organs or otherwise be attributable to the State, or may be caused by third parties.

When the physical damage is due to third parties, it does not seem that arbitration practice requires a particular connection of causality to consider the State liable. Thus, the *Eurotunnel* tribunal affirms, without further ado, that disorder is attributable to the State.[39] The tribunal in *Wena v Egypt* simply notices that the State was aware of the harmful actions taken against the investor.[40]

Only the tribunal in *Tecmed v Mexico* seems to assume a certain connection of causality between the harmful events and the State's behaviour, in that it lists the fact that the authorities did not encourage or support the adverse movements as one of the reasons for not considering the State liable in that connection.[41] However, the tribunal might have mentioned the absence of this circumstance as a response to the claimant's allegation that the State had played that role. Hence, this reference in the award is not necessarily an argument for affirming the converse, ie that the authorities' encouragement is a prerequisite for the State's liability.

The irrelevance of a direct causality is to be explained in light of the obligation arising out of the standard of full protection and security: the obligation is not to refrain from causing damage, but to exercise due diligence, or take the necessary measures of vigilance, in order to prevent damage. Thus, the obligation may be violated irrespective of the origin of the damage. Whenever it falls within the public powers to prevent an interference, failure to do so is a breach of the obligation to grant full protection and security.

---

[36] *PSEG v Turkey*, above n. 14, para. 258.
[37] *Eurotunnel*, above n. 35, paras 305, 310, 315.
[38] *Saluka v Czech Republic*, above n. 6, para. 483.
[39] *Eurotunnel*, above n. 35, para. 305.
[40] *Wena v Egypt*, above n. 3, para. 85.
[41] *Tecmed v Mexico*, above n. 9, para. 171.

Forms of Behaviour

The threshold for considering the standard as violated is rather high, since, as will be seen below, the obligation to provide full protection and security is discharged if the State has taken some measures of vigilance that do not seem unreasonable, and the room for sovereign appreciation is quite wide.

Thus, tribunals tend to accept the measures taken by the States as sufficient to meet the obligation. As will be seen below, it is the lack of measures to prevent harmful events, the lack of measures to restore the situation prior to the harmful event, or the lack of imposition of sanctions that lead to a violation of the standard, as in the *Wena* award. If measures have been taken, the threshold for questioning them seems to be quite high. The *Eurotunnel* award, as will be seen below, assumes that the measures taken may be questioned only if they have caused intolerable consequences.

A notable exception to the tribunals' general inclination not to question the quality of the measures taken is the majority in *AAPL v Sri Lanka*. As will be seen, however, this part of the award was criticized by the minority of the tribunal.

Due diligence

Arbitral tribunals often discuss the question of the nature of the obligations arising out of the standard of full protection and security. The clearly prevailing attitude, as will be seen below, is that the standard requires a State to exercise the diligence due to ensure the safety of the investments. This is often referred to as being an obligation of means, or obligation of conduct, as opposed to an obligation of result, also referred to as strict liability. This means that the State is deemed to have discharged its obligation even if the measures taken to protect the investment have not achieved the desired protection, as long as it has acted diligently.

While the quality of the obligation as one of conduct and not of result is explicitly affirmed in most awards, much remains to be specified before the concrete content of the obligation is identifiable. As the award in the *Eurotunnel* case puts it, the general classification of obligations into obligations of result and obligations of conduct, useful as it may be for various purposes, is no substitute for their application in the concrete circumstances of a given case.[42]

What seems to be established is that a State is under an obligation of vigilance, and does not grant an insurance against damage that may affect the investment,[43] or a warranty that property shall never in any circumstances be occupied or disturbed.[44] The State is not under a strict liability.[45]

---

[42] *Eurotunnel*, above n. 35, para. 314.
[43] *Wena v Egypt*, above n. 3, para. 84.
[44] *ELSI*, above n. 16, para. 108.
[45] See on this point *AAPL v Sri Lanka*, above n. 4, paras 46–53; *Saluka v Czech Republic*, above n. 6, para. 484; *Tecmed v Mexico*, above n. 9, para. 171; and *Noble Ventures v Romania*, above n. 13, para. 164.

Only in the case of *AMT v Zaire* does an award seem to have assumed a strict liability. Although the tribunal confirmed the general view that the State is under an obligation of vigilance,[46] it found that this obligation was violated 'by mere recognition of the existing reality of the damage caused'. This line of reasoning seems to support a strict liability. The tribunal affirmed that it did not intend to engage in debate on whether the State is under an obligation of result or of conduct,[47] but it found that the State was responsible for its inability to prevent disastrous consequences of events. If the tribunal had assumed that the obligation of the State is a due diligence obligation, it would have been more correct to argue that the State was responsible for not having taken sufficient measures for the protection of the investment, rather than for not having been able to prevent damage. In view of the circumstances of the case, however, it is difficult to consider these statements as unequivocally supporting the view of a strict liability; this is because the State had recognized the existence of the damage and had apparently not argued that it had taken any measures to prevent it.

Having established that the standard of full protection and security is not an obligation to compensate any damage that may affect an investment, but an obligation to exercise due diligence in preventing any such damage, it remains to be seen what this entails specifically.

Subjective or objective standard?

Awards contain few guidelines as to the content of the due diligence obligation, often referred to as the obligation to take all measures necessary to ensure the safety of the investment. In particular, there is no clearly prevailing view as to the nature of the standard, whether it is objective or subjective. The latter view seems to be taken by the tribunal in *Lauder v Czech Republic* that stated that the measures to be taken were those reasonable under the circumstances.[48]

It is, however, not relevant whether the State has acted in good faith or not.[49]

The tribunal in *AAPL v Sri Lanka* affirms the existence of a sliding scale relating to the standard of due diligence, from an old subjective criterion to an objective standard of vigilance.[50] Due diligence is said to consist of the reasonable measures of prevention which a well-administered government could be expected to exercise under similar circumstances. The majority of the tribunal applied this criterion in a not uncontroversial way, questioning the procedure followed by the government of Sri Lanka in an armed action undertaken to regain control of an area occupied by insurgents. All top managers of AAPL's farm, which was located in the area of which the government had lost control,

---

[46] *AMT v Zaire*, above n. 15, para. 6.05.
[47] Ibid., para. 6.08.
[48] *Lauder v Czech Republic*, above n. 10, para. 308.
[49] See *Occidental v Ecuador*, above n. 12, para. 186; and *AAPL v Sri Lanka*, above n. 4, para. 77.
[50] Ibid., paras 76 *et seq*.

were suspected of participating in the insurrection. The farm was destroyed during the armed action; the tribunal found that there was no conclusive evidence as to what effectively caused the destruction. However, the tribunal considered that the government should have tried peaceful communication to get the suspect elements excluded from the investor's staff before undertaking a military counter-insurgency. Further, the tribunal found that the government should have instituted judicial investigations against the suspected persons, or should have undertaken necessary measures to get them off the farm. On the basis of this reasoning, the State's responsibility is deemed established.[51]

A considered dissenting opinion points out that the disputed action was a strategic and highly sensitive security operation to regain control of the area of insurgency, taking place in a situation of national emergency. According to the dissenting opinion, the government was under a compelling sovereign duty to undertake a military operation to regain control of the area. The timing and modalities of the operation, thus the minority of the tribunal, must fall within the government's exclusive discretion, and the award should not question the exercise by the state of its own sovereign prerogatives.

Sovereign appreciation

If the exercise of due diligence is a question of verifying the ability of the measures taken to reach the aim, as the majority in the *AAPL* case does, there is the risk of interference with sovereign appreciation, as pointed out in the dissenting opinion.

The prevailing approach in arbitration practice seems to be more inclined to examine whether the measures taken by the State obviously deviate from a reasonable standard, rather than suggesting alternative, more effective measures.

The International Court of Justice (ICJ) confirms that the State enjoys a measure of sovereign appreciation in its decision in *ELSI*. Even if the authorities were found to have tolerated the occupation of the plant by workers,[52] the protection accorded to the investment was not found to be below the standard.[53] Furthermore, even if the legal system had reacted after an undoubtedly too long time, the protection was not deemed to be below the standard, because there was a mechanism in place.[54]

The tribunal in *Saluka v Czech Republic* found that the obligation was not breached if the State's behaviour was not totally unreasonable and unjustifiable by some rational legal policy; that measures taken did not transcend the limits of a legislator's discretion if they were not totally devoid of legal concerns;[55] and

[51] Ibid., para. 83.
[52] *ELSI*, above n. 16, para. 106.
[53] Ibid., para. 108.
[54] Ibid., para. 111.
[55] *Saluka v Czech Republic*, above n. 6, para. 490, relating to suspension by the authorities of trading in the investor's shares as well as amendment of legislation on right to appeal. The tribunal

that a breach of the international obligations on justice assumed a manifest lack of due process.[56]

Also the *Eurotunnel* tribunal found that the limits of sovereign appreciation are exceeded only when the State's failure to maintain the public order becomes intolerable.[57]

The tribunal in *Tecmed v Mexico* found that, even if the authorities had encouraged the community's adverse movements against the investment and their reaction was not as quick, efficient, and thorough as it should have been,[58] there was no evidence that they did not react reasonably in accordance with parameters inherent in a democratic state.[59]

Similarly, the tribunal in *Noble Ventures v Romania* found that, even if officials refused to exercise adequate measures to protect the investment from unlawful activities, there was no specific failure to exercise due diligence.[60] In this case, the State had failed to properly react to repeated occupations by the employees, beating of management, theft, and acts of intimidation.

E. Application beyond Physical Safety

Some awards explicitly exclude the standard of full protection and security from application beyond the physical safety of the investment, whereas others openly affirm the opposite. Yet other awards do not take an express position on the question, but indirectly extend the scope of application of the standard. The question remains rather controversial, particularly if considered together with the relationship between this standard and the principle of fair and equitable treatment.

---

is not certain that these measures actually fall within the scope of application of the standard, but sees no need to analyse the question since there would be no breach anyway.

[56] *Saluka v Czech Republic*, above n. 6, para. 493, on the absence of further appeals. Also in this connection the tribunal is uncertain about the applicability of the standard of full protection and security.

[57] *Eurotunnel*, above n. 35, paras 306, 310. As mentioned, this award is not based on an investment treaty, but says that application of the international standard would not have added anything to the reasoning and is therefore relevant to the assessment of the scope of the protection in international law. The tribunal considers that it was within the room for sovereign appreciation of the State when the French government requisitioned part of the premises of the investment for the purpose of locating a hostel for immigrants close to the tunnel between France and England. This is even if, seen in retrospect, such decision represented a threat to the safety of the investment, ibid., para. 307. The State liability arose when the incursions rose to startling proportions and it was sufficiently clear that the hostel was being used as a base for criminal activity, and it was due to the State's failure to use its public powers to maintain conditions of normal security and public order, ibid., paras 309–319.

[58] *Tecmed v Mexico*, above n. 9, para. 175.

[59] Ibid., para. 171.

[60] *Noble Ventures v Romania*, above n. 13, para. 166.

Scope of Application Restricted to Physical Safety

In some awards, such as in *Saluka v Czech Republic*,[61] the tribunals emphasize that the standard does not refer to protection against any kind of impairment, but only to the impairment against the physical integrity of an investment and against interference by use of force. The undisputed scope of application thus refers, essentially, to civil strife and physical violence.[62]

Thus, in *Tecmed v Mexico* the tribunal found that the revocation of administrative permits as a consequence of adverse movements against the investor's activity was a violation by the State of its obligation to accord fair and equitable treatment, and not a violation of the standard of full protection and security.[63]

Similarly, the tribunal in *PSEG v Turkey* discussed measures that led to the failure to ensure stable and predictable business environment, notably normative changes, arbitrary modification of regulatory framework violating legitimate expectations, inconsistent administrative acts, continuing legislative changes under the obligation of according fair and equitable treatment, and not in connection with the standard of full protection and security.[64]

Also the tribunal in *Eureko v Poland* found that a stable investment climate is part of the obligation of fair and equitable treatment, not full protection and security.[65] The tribunal found that the investor's rights had been violated, that it was abundantly clear that the treatment accorded to it was unfair and inequitable, that its contractual rights were breached arbitrarily and for political/nationalistic reasons, that the investor had been exposed to an outrageous and shocking conduct;[66] but none of this was considered to be a breach of full protection and security. The only reference made to this standard in the award relates to allegations of harassment that the tribunal, however, found not to be substantiated. If the alleged harassment had been repeated, then there could possibly have been liability under the standard of full protection and security for failure to prevent it.[67]

As already seen in respect of the relationship between the treaty protection and international law, also in connection with the scope of application of the protection, the wording of the treaty does not seem to play a central role. Thus, while the majority of the treaties applied in the cases mentioned above contain the obligation to ensure full protection and security as a separate obligation, the treaty applied in the last mentioned case considers the standard of full protection as a specification of the obligation to accord fair and equitable treatment.

---

[61] *Saluka v Czech Republic*, above n. 6, para. 484.
[62] Ibid., para. 483.
[63] *Tecmed v Mexico*, above n. 9, paras 154, 163, 164.
[64] *PSEG v Turkey*, above n. 14, para. 259.
[65] *Eureko v Poland*, above n. 7, paras 240, 248, 250, 251, 253.
[66] Ibid., paras 226, 231–234.
[67] Ibid., para. 237.

Scope of Application beyond Physical Safety

Some awards deem the standard of full protection and security to extend beyond the mere physical safety of the investment. Various degrees may be detected in this extension of the scope of application

Availability of the legal system

The traditional scope of application has some ramifications that go beyond the mere exercise of police powers. This concerns, particularly, the availability of the judicial and administrative system to protect the interests of the investor.

Thus, the tribunal in *Wena v Egypt* found that one of the violations of the obligations connected with full protection and security was the circumstance that the State had not imposed any sanctions against those who had unlawfully seized the investment.[68]

Also in *Tecmed v Mexico* the tribunal affirmed that the availability of the judicial system was an element of the full protection and security to be enjoyed by the investor. In this specific case, however, in relation to the investor's attempt to reverse the administrative measures that affected the investment, the tribunal found that the legal system was sufficiently available and the standard had therefore not been violated.[69]

Similarly, from the argumentation of the decision in *ELSI* it seems that the International Court of Justice considered the availability of a legal mechanism to verify the lawfulness of the requisition of the plant as an element of the full protection and security to be enjoyed by the investor. However, in the specific circumstances the Court found that the legal mechanism was present and that, even if the time taken to obtain a decision—16 months—was undoubtedly too long, it could not be deemed as a denial of justice and the obligation was not breached.[70]

Also, the tribunal in *Lauder v Czech Republic* affirmed that the State has a duty to keep the judicial system available and to properly examine claims and decide according to domestic and international law.[71] The tribunal found that that duty had not been violated in this specific case.

Similarly, the tribunal in *Saluka v Czech Republic* affirmed the obligation to make available appeal mechanisms against police searches, and administrative decisions affecting the investment. It also found that the obligation had not been violated in this specific case.[72]

Legal security as an independent standard

Some awards go beyond the requirement that the State makes available its judicial and administrative system so that the investor can protect its interests, and

---

[68] *Wena v Egypt*, above n. 3, paras 82, 84, 94, 95.
[69] *Tecmed v Mexico*, above n. 9, para. 171.
[70] *ELSI*, above n. 16, para. 111.
[71] *Lauder v Czech Republic*, above n. 10, para. 314.
[72] *Saluka v Czech Republic*, above n. 6, paras 496, 493.

E. Application beyond Physical Safety

expressly affirm that the standard of full protection and security extends to the stability of the investment climate and the legal framework.

As already seen above, the award in *Siemens v Argentina* has a special basis for affirming that the standard of protection extends to the legal security of the investment and means, substantially, the certainty of the legal system. In particular, the wording of the applicable treaty explicitly refers to *legal* security, as opposed to the other treaties applied in the jurisprudence that is examined here.[73]

Another award that affirms this large understanding of the standard is *CME v Czech Republic*. The majority of the tribunal affirmed that the State is under the obligation to ensure that neither by amendment of its laws nor by actions of its administrative bodies is the agreed and approved security and protection of the investment withdrawn or devalued.[74] It must be remembered, however, that this award is accompanied by a dissenting opinion. Also, it must be noticed that the *CME* tribunal comes to a decision opposite to the decision taken, on the same facts and substantially between the same parties, by the tribunal in the *Lauder v Czech Republic* case. For the sake of completeness, however, it must be pointed out that the *Lauder* award is decided on the facts, and that it cannot be taken as a position in principle of the tribunal against the extension of the standard of full protection and security to the legal security. The tribunal found in *Lauder* that the amendments made to the media legislation were not a threat to the investment.[75] It remains open whether, had the amendments been deemed actually to affect the investment, the tribunal would have considered the standard of full protection and security breached.

Also, in *CSOB v Slovak Republic* the tribunal found that the State's conduct in the interpretation of the terms of the contract deprived the investor of any meaningful protection for its loan and thus breached the commitment to grant full protection and security.[76]

Recently, the tribunal in *Vivendi v Argentina II* rendered an award that extensively examines the scope of application of the full protection and security standard. As already mentioned in section B above, the tribunal referred to previous arbitral practice and made an antithetic interpretation of the treaty based on its wording to support its opinion that the standard apply to any act or measure which deprive an investor's investment of protection and full security. Such actions or measures need not threaten physical possession or the legally protected terms of operation of the investment.[77] According to the tribunal, the standard can apply to more than physical security of an investor or its property, because either could be subject to harassment without being physically harmed or seized.[78] The Award does not identify any further the specific content of this standard. In

---

[73] *Siemens v Argentina*, above n. 5, para. 303.
[74] *CME v Czech Republic*, above n. 6, para. 613.
[75] *Lauder v Czech Republic*, above n. 10, para. 311.
[76] *CSOB v Slovak Republic*, above n. 2, para. 170.
[77] *Vivendi v Argentina*, above n. 8, para. 7.4.15.
[78] Ibid., para. 7.4.17.

the evaluation of the facts, the tribunal did not make mention of violation of the full protection and security standard, and deemed all the actions and omissions attributable to the State as a violation of the principle of fair and equitable treatment.[79] The enlarged scope of the obligation relating to full protection and security, thus, was affirmed by the tribunal but not applied to the facts of the case, and the tribunal's observations in this connection may be broadly defined as an *obiter dictum*.

Further awards *de facto* applied the standard of full protection and security as extensively as those mentioned above, even though they make no express argument in that connection. These awards applied the standard as if it was equivalent to the standard of fair and equitable treatment. They will be examined below.

As already observed in section B above, the wording of the treaties applied by each tribunal does not seem to have played a significant role in the definition of the scope of application of the standard. The award rendered in *Siemens v Argentina* is the only award that gives particular consideration to the wording of the treaty, since the BIT between Germany and Argentina provides, as mentioned, for legal security. The wording of the other treaties upon which the awards mentioned here are based are not comparable. While the treaties applied in the *CSOB* and in the *Siemens* awards consider the two obligations as separate, the treaties applied in the *CME* and in the *Vivendi II* awards consider the obligation of full protection as a specification of the obligation to accord fair and equitable treatment.

Overlap with other Standards

The obligation to grant full protection and security has an uncertain borderline to other provisions usually contained in investment treaties. By far the most important principle that requires a careful coordination is that of fair and equitable treatment. Also, the provisions on reimbursement of damages due to actions in combat have occasionally been considered as overlapping with the obligation of full protection and security.

Fair and equitable treatment

It has been explicitly affirmed in arbitration practice, for example by the tribunal in *Azurix v Argentina*, that the obligation of full protection and security may be breached even if no physical violence or damage occurred and goes beyond police protection and is meant to secure the investment environment.[80] Simultaneously, the award recognized and even emphasized that there is an inter-relationship with the obligation to grant fair and equitable treatment, and found that the State failed

---

[79] Ibid., paras 7.4.18–7.4.46 and 7.5.23.
[80] *Azurix v Argentina*, above n. 11, paras 406, 408.

to provide fair and equitable treatment and therefore, with the same actions, also breached the obligation of full protection and security. The tribunal noticed that the two standards are closely interrelated, and referred to earlier tribunals that had found that the obligation of full protection and security was breached *because* the investment was subject to unfair and inequitable treatment, as in the *Occidental v Ecuador* case, or, conversely, found that a breach of full protection and security causes a breach of the fair and equitable treatment standard, as in *Wena v Egypt*. The tribunal in *Azurix* further pointed out that in the applicable treaty between the United States and Argentina the two obligations of full protection and security and fair and equitable treatment are separate, as they were in the treaty applied in the aforementioned *Occidental* award. The tribunal noticed that, nevertheless, the violation of the full protection and security standard was considered absorbed in the unfair and inequitable treatment in the *Occidental* award. The *Azurix* award also does so, again in spite of the wording of the treaty, which considers the two standards as separate.[81]

The line of thought of the aforementioned *Occidental* award is that the stability of the legal and business framework is an essential element of the obligation to accord to the investments fair and equitable treatment.[82] The tribunal established that there had been a violation of the fair and equitable treatment obligation, and affirmed that it becomes moot to enquire whether in addition there was a breach of full protection and security, as a treatment that is not fair and equitable automatically entails an absence of full protection and security of the investment.[83]

According to the tribunal in *Occidental v Ecuador*, alteration of the legal and business environment in which the investment was made is a violation of the protection standards, as both fair and equitable treatment and full protection and security require that the State provides stability and predictability.[84]

In *Wena v Egypt*,[85] the two standards of protection had already been dealt with concurrently and found violated, without specifying which actions violated which obligations. The description of the facts in that case contains behaviour relating to physical security,[86] to availability of the legal system in relation to prevention or prosecution of physical damage,[87] as well as regulatory abuse.[88] While the former two forms of behaviour relate to the traditional scope of application of full protection and security, the latter falls within the area of the above-mentioned expanded scope that in turn overlaps with the obligation of fair and equitable treatment. Also, the treaty between the United States and Egypt, as the treaties applied in *Azurix* and *Occidental*, provides for the obligation to ensure full

---

[81] Ibid., para. 407.
[82] *Occidental v Ecuador*, above n. 12, para. 183.
[83] Ibid., para. 187.
[84] Ibid., para. 191.
[85] *Wena v Egypt*, above n. 3, paras 84, 95.
[86] Ibid., paras 85, 89.
[87] Ibid., paras 90, 93.
[88] Ibid., para. 92.

protection and security and to accord fair and equitable treatment as two separate standards.

The close relationship between the extended standard of full protection and security and the obligation to accord fair and equitable treatment is pointed out also in the *PSEG v Turkey* award, that finds that only exceptionally will the standard be related to a broader ambit than the physical security as the aforementioned *CME* partial award had postulated; and, in such case, there would be a very close relation to the fair and equitable treatment obligation.[89] The award affirmed this in general terms and did not seem to attach particular importance to the difference in wording between the treaty applied in the *CME* award (where full protection and security is a specification of fair and equitable treatment) and the treaty applicable in the *PSEG* case (where the two standards are separate obligations).

The difficulty to distinguish between the two standards is evident also in the already mentioned award in *Siemens v Argentina* that, also based on the wording of the treaty, explicitly applies the standard of protection to the legal security rather than to the physical security of the investment. Renegotiation of the contracts for the sole purpose of reducing the price and without any declaration of public interest, delayed payment without any basis on the contract or the applicable regulation, or denial of access to administrative files for filing an appeal—all these forms of behaviour are deemed to violate both the standard of fair and equitable treatment and that of full protection and security.[90] The treaty, however, provides for fair and equitable treatment and full protection and legal security as two separate standards; the tribunal fails to elaborate on the distinction in the treaty between the two standards.

Also, the *CSOB* award made reference to fair and equitable treatment and full protection and security together,[91] in spite of the applicable treaty that provides for two separate obligations.

The partial award issued in *CME v Czech Republic* failed to distinguish the full protection and security from other standards, and saw the same actions and inactions targeted to remove the security and legal protection of the investment as a basis for the claim for expropriation,[92] fair and equitable treatment,[93] discriminatory measures,[94] and full protection and security.[95] The overlap between the standards is possibly explained in view of the applicable BIT that considers the obligation to ensure full protection and security as a specification of the standard of fair and equitable treatment.

[89] *PSEG v Turkey*, above n. 14, para. 258.
[90] *Siemens v Argentina*, above n. 5, paras 308, 309.
[91] *CSOB v Slovak Republic*, above n. 2, para. 161.
[92] *CME v Czech Republic*, above n. 6, para. 609.
[93] Ibid., paras 611, 610.
[94] Ibid., para. 612, probably erroneously entitled fair and equitable treatment.
[95] Ibid., para. 613.

The *Vivendi v Argentina II* award, finally, subordinated the standard of full protection and security to the principle of fair and equitable treatment. The standard is said to apply to any act or measure which deprives an investor's investment of protection and security, provided it constitutes also unfair and inequitable treatment.[96] This is explicitly based on the specific wording of the treaty, which subjects the obligation to provide full protection and security to the principle of fair and equitable treatment. After having assessed this interrelationship between the two standards, the award ignored the standard of full protection and security and measured the State's behaviour exclusively against the principle of fair and equitable treatment.[97]

The overlap of the two standards, in conclusion, finds a justification in the wording of the treaty only in the *CME* and in the *Vivendi II* case. The other awards have simply disregarded that the respective treaties listed the two standards as two separate obligations and have treated them as equivalent.[98]

As already seen, some awards openly affirm that, if the principle of fair and equitable treatment has been violated, there is no need to establish in addition a violation of the provision on full protection and security. Other awards do not state this expressly but act *de facto* in accordance with this approach. Failing a specific elaboration on what exactly distinguishes one standard from the other makes the standard of full protection and security redundant, as it is not possible to identify which actions or omissions may constitute violation thereof on an independent basis.

Action in combat

Another situation where occasionally awards have shown uncertainty in the choice of which treaty provision to apply, is when the physical damage to the investor is due to armed action. In these cases, there may be a link to the provisions that the treaties may contain on damages due to action in combat.

Thus, the majority in *AMT v Zaire* affirmed that the liability of the State had a basis either in the provision of full protection and security, or in the provision on riot and combat, or in both.[99] These alternative bases were criticized in the separate opinion by Arbitrator Golsong, who considered the provision on riot and combat as a *lex specialis* that as such absorbs the rule on full protection and security.

---

[96] *Vivendi v Argentina*, above n. 8, para. 7.4.15.
[97] Ibid., paras. 7.4.18–7.4.46 and 7.5.23.
[98] Also UNCTAD, above n. 1, 37 *et seq.*, deals with the standard of full protection and security under the same heading as the fair and equitable treatment principle. The paper defines the particular scope of the standard in relation to periods of insurrections, civil unrest, or other public disturbance, but notices also the emerging trend to extend its scope to legal protection and security, ibid., nn. 40 *et seq*. The paper fails to elaborate on the relationship between the full protection and security and the fair and equitable treatment.
[99] *AMT v Zaire*, above n. 15, para. 6.14.

Similarly, the dissenting opinion in *AAPL* affirmed that the provision on full protection and security must yield to the special provision on loss due to war or armed conflict and is not attributable to the State.

F. Conclusion

An analysis of the arbitration practice on the obligation to provide full protection and security shows that the standard is interpreted substantially in the same way under the treaties and under general international law, and that the wording of the treaty is not decisive for its interpretation.

It seems also to be established that the protection standard creates a due diligence obligation to take measures that prevent the investment from being harmed. The State enjoys a rather wide discretion to discharge this obligation in accordance with its own sovereign appreciation.

The protection refers uncontroversially to physical harm to the investment, to be prevented by employing police powers.

The protection standard requires, further, the availability of the judicial and administrative system for claims relating to the protection of the investment.

Stability of the legal framework, certainty of the business environment, and lack of arbitrary measures are not specific to the full protection and security standard and overlap with the obligation to accord fair and equitable treatment. It becomes, therefore, questionable to what extent it is useful to interpret a standard of protection in such a way that it doubles another standard of protection—particularly if the applicable treaty lists the two standards as two separate bases for liability, as is often the case.

8
Indirect Expropriation

Anne K. Hoffmann

A. Introduction

The issue of what constitutes an expropriation has been one of constant debate and evolvement over the last decades. Developments such as a rapidly changing, ever more globalized world which is increasingly based upon private property and the proliferation of bilateral investment treaties (BITs) as well as arbitrations conducted on their basis have brought about new developments and focused even more attention on the difficult questions surrounding the doctrine of expropriation. Thereby, it is undisputed that international law allows that property of nationals as well as foreign investors may be expropriated, provided that certain requirements are met. For an expropriation to be legal, it must not be discriminatory against the investor, it must be for a public purpose, in accordance with due process of law and it must be accompanied by full compensation which is prompt, adequate, and effective.[1] The classic or traditional case of an expropriation is that of a 'direct' expropriation, ie the outright and overt taking of property, often achieved by means of transfer of title. Such direct expropriations have, however, become less frequent. States have recognized the importance of attracting foreign direct investment and thus do not want to be perceived as threatening those investments by means of expropriation. Hence, the typical form in which they occur today is that of an 'indirect expropriation'. As has been widely acknowledged,

[...] it is not the physical invasion of the property that characterizes nationalizations or expropriations that has assumed importance, but the erosion of rights associated with ownership by State interferences.[2]

This is reflected in modern bilateral and multilateral investment treaties which mostly protect the investor from expropriation as well as 'measures having an

---

[1] See for a detailed discussion A. Reinisch, 'Legality of Expropriations' at Chapter 9 below.
[2] UNCTAD, *Taking of Property*, Series on Issues in International Investment Agreements (2000) 20.

effect equivalent or tantamount to expropriation'.[3] This approach indicates a reluctance to give up a paradigm of law that was developed in the context of direct expropriations, despite the fact that their legal form has meanwhile undergone a change. At the same time, this phrase captures a broad spectrum of intentional and obvious indirect expropriations as much as a variety of inappropriate regulatory acts, omissions, and other conduct that undermines the framework created to protect foreign investments. Indirect expropriations appear in a great multiplicity and although the general concept is not new, the unanswered questions surrounding them are manifold. Of particular importance in this regard is the distinction between simple regulatory measures and those which amount to indirect expropriations. Attempts to define where the demarcation line between these two concepts is to be drawn have frequently been made. This chapter will attempt to show the current state of the law of foreign investment with regard to indirect expropriations, in particular the criteria used to determine when such an expropriation occurred, as well as address recent jurisprudence. Moreover, it will, on the basis of the aforesaid, discuss whether the current practice of tribunals faced with expropriation claims is satisfactory and look at possible solutions for the problems presently occurring in this constantly evolving area of law.

B. The Current State of Affairs Regarding the Doctrine of Indirect Expropriation

It has been pointed out that in the modern world of the law of expropriation, the question is not so much whether the requirements of a legal expropriation have been met, but whether it has occurred in the first place.[4] Thus, a lot of emphasis has been placed upon defining what constitutes an expropriation, and especially—in light of most States' general acceptance of foreign direct investment which led to a diminished frequency of direct expropriations—what measures shall be considered 'indirect expropriations'. The concept of indirect expropriation is not new, but although decisions of international tribunals[5] as well as the analyses of

---

[3] See, eg, Article 13 Energy Charter Treaty: '(1) Investments of Investors of a Contracting Party in the Area of any other Contracting Party shall not be nationalized, expropriated or subjected to a measure or measures having effect equivalent to nationalization or expropriation [...].'; or Article 4(2) Germany/China BIT (2003): 'Investments by investors of either Contracting Party shall not directly or indirectly be expropriated, nationalized or be subjected to any other measure the effects of which would be tantamount to expropriation or nationalization in the territory of the other Contracting Party (hereinafter referred to as expropriation) except for the public benefit and against compensation.'

[4] See C. Schreuer, 'The Concept of Expropriation under the ECT and other Investment Protection Treaties', in C. Ribeiro (ed.), *Investment Arbitration and the Energy Charter Treaty* (2006) 108, 111.

[5] See, eg, *Goetz and Others v Republic of Burundi*, Award, 2 September 1998; *Metalclad Corp. v United Mexican States*, Award, 30 August 2000; *S.D. Myers Inc. v Government of Canada*, Partial Award, 13 September 2001; *Middle East Cement Shipping and Handling Co. S.A. v Arab Republic of*

B. Current State of Affairs Regarding Indirect Expropriation 153

commentators[6] have shed some light on the problems involved, the picture shaping is far from clear yet and one can barely speak of a comprehensive doctrine on this issue.

At this point it seems appropriate to add an observation with regard to terminology. The term 'expropriation' used in this chapter is frequently, most often by American scholars, replaced by the term 'taking'. In the author's view, both are interchangeable. More importantly, as much as the concept of 'indirect expropriation' is well established in international law, there exists a great variety of terms used to describe the various forms in which these expropriations appear. These terms include for example '*de facto*', 'disguised', 'consequential', 'regulatory', or 'creeping' expropriations. BITs frequently refer to 'measures tantamount to' or 'equivalent to' expropriation. The boundaries between these different forms of indirect expropriations are blurred and—apart from the creeping expropriation[7] which has somewhat clearer contours due to the emphasis on the sequence of steps—often used interchangeably.[8] It is suggested that the following

---

Egypt, Award, 12 April 2002; *Técnicas Medioambientales Tecmed S.A. v The United Mexican States*, Award, 29 May 2003; *Waste Management, Inc. v United Mexican States*, Award, 30 April 2004; *Compania de Aguas del Aconquija S.A. and Vivendi Universal v Argentine Republic (Vivendi II)*, Award, 20 August 2007.

[6] See, eg, G.C. Christie, 'What Constitutes a Taking of Property under International Law?', 38 *British Yearbook of International Law* (1962) 305; B.H. Weston, '"Constructive Takings" under International Law: A Modest Foray into the Problem of "Creeping Expropriation"', 16 *Virginia Journal of International Law* (1975) 103; R. Higgins, 'The Taking of Property by the State: Recent Developments in International Law', III *Recueil des Cours* (1983) 259; R. Dolzer, 'Indirect Expropriation of Alien Property', 1 *ICSID Review—Foreign Investment Law Journal* (1986) 48; R. Dolzer, 'Indirect Expropriations: New Developments?', 11 *NYU Environmental Law Journal* (2002) 64; W.M. Reisman and R.D. Sloane, 'Indirect Expropriation and its Valuation in the BIT Generation', 74 *British Yearbook of International Law* (2003) 115; J. Paulsson and Z. Douglas, 'Indirect Expropriation in Investment Treaty Arbitrations', in N. Horn and S. Kröll (eds), *Arbitrating Foreign Investment Disputes* (2004) 145; Y.L. Fortier and S. L. Drymer, 'Indirect Expropriation in the Law of International Investment: I know it when I see it, or Caveat Investor', 19 *ICSID Review—Foreign Investment Law Journal* (2002) 293; N. Rubins and S. Kinsella, *International Investment, Political Risk and Dispute Resolution* (2005) 182; Schreuer, above n. 4; V. Heiskanen, 'The Doctrine of Indirect Expropriation in Light of the Practice of the Iran-United States Claims Tribunals', 8 *Journal of World Investment and Trade* (2007) 215; K. Hobér, *Investment Arbitration in Eastern Europe: In Search of a Definition of Expropriation* (2007); C. McLachlan, L. Shore, and M. Weiniger, *International Investment Arbitration. Substantive Principles* (2007), paras 8.71 *et seq.*; A. Reinisch, 'Expropriation', in P. Muchlinski, F. Ortino, and C. Schreuer (eds), *The Oxford Handbook of International Investment Law* (forthcoming 2008).

[7] See for a persuasive definition the dissenting opinion of Keith Highet in *Waste Management, Inc. v United Mexican States*, Award, 2 June 2000: 'a "creeping" expropriation is comprised of a number of elements, none of which can—separately—constitute the international wrong [ie the creeping expropriation]. These constituent elements [may] include non-payment, non-reimbursement, cancellation, denial of judicial access, actual practice to exclude, non-conforming treatment, inconsistent legal blocks, and so forth. The "measure" at issue is the [creeping] expropriation itself, it is not merely a subcomponent part of expropriation', 40 *ILM* (2001) 56, 73.

[8] An interesting analysis of the issue is contained in the *Tecmed* decision: 'Generally, it is understood that the term "equivalent to expropriation [...]" or "tantamount to expropriation" [...] refers to the so-called "indirect expropriation" or "creeping expropriation", as well as to the above-mentioned de facto expropriation. Although these forms of expropriations do not have a clear

considerations apply to all of these forms of 'indirect' expropriations. Thus, this is the term which will be used throughout this chapter.

Although provisions on indirect expropriation are a common feature of treaties[9] and other instruments[10] dealing with the protection of foreign investments, most of them do not offer more than a general reference to indirect expropriation. As Professor Dolzer phrased it:

> The current version of investment treaties do not in any way illuminate the issue of indirect expropriations; they rather state the problem, and presumably the rules of general international law are meant to provide the solution.[11]

There is a visible reluctance to include a definition of 'expropriation' in those instruments. As Dolzer and Stevens point out:

> Such apparent reluctance to attempt a definition of 'expropriation' in the BITs may be explained by the fact that a host state, as is well known, can take a number of measures which have a similar effect to expropriation or nationalization, although they do not de jure constitute an act of expropriation, such measures are generally termed 'indirect', 'creeping' or 'de facto' expropriation.[12]

Certain steps in that direction have, however, been taken in some codification attempts by individuals or institutions. Thus, for example, the so-called Harvard Draft Convention on the International Responsibility of States for Injuries to Aliens by Professors Sohn and Baxter states in Article 10:

> 3(a) A 'taking of property' includes not only an outright taking of property but also any such unreasonable interference with the use, enjoyment, or disposal of property as to

---

unequivocal definition, it is generally understood that they materialize through actions or conduct, which do not explicitly express the purpose of depriving one of rights or assets, but actually have the effect. This type of expropriation does not necessarily take place gradually or stealthily—the term "creeping" refers only to a type of indirect expropriation—and may be carried out through a single action, through a series of actions in a short period of time or through simultaneous actions. Therefore, a difference should be made between creeping expropriation and de facto expropriation, although they are usually included within a broader concept of "indirect expropriation" and although both expropriation methods may take place by means of a broad number of actions that have to be examined on a case-by-case basis to conclude if one of such expropriation methods has taken place'. *Tecmed v Mexico*, above n. 5, para. 114.

[9] R. Dolzer, 'Indirect Expropriation of Alien Property', 1 *ICSID Review—Foreign Investment Law Journal* (1986), 48, 56.

[10] See eg Article III Abs-Shawcross Draft Convention on Investment Abroad (1959), in UNCTAD, *International Investment Instruments: A Compendium* (2001), Volume V, 396; Article 3 OECD Draft Convention on the Protection of Foreign Property (1967), in UNCTAD, *International Investment Instruments: A Compendium* (1996), Volume II, 114; United Nations, *Code of Conduct on Transnational Corporations* (1983), in UNCTAD, *International Investment Instruments: A Compendium* (1996), Volume I, 161, 174; *The Guidelines on the Treatment of Foreign Direct Investment*, adopted by the Development Committee of the Board of Governors of the IMF and the World Bank (1992), Section IV, in UNCTAD, *International Investment Instruments: A Compendium* (1996), Volume I, 247, 252.

[11] Dolzer, above n. 9, 56.

[12] R. Dolzer and M. Stevens, *Bilateral Investment Treaties* (1995) 99 (footnote omitted).

B. Current State of Affairs Regarding Indirect Expropriation

justify an interference that the owner thereof will not be able to use, enjoy, or dispose of the property within a reasonable period of time after the inception of such interference. (b) A 'taking of the use of property' includes not only an outright taking of use but also any unreasonable interference with the use or enjoyment of property for a limited period of time.[13]

In the 1967 OECD Draft Convention, expropriation was defined as a measure which led to

[...] deprive ultimately the alien of the enjoyment or value of his property, without any specific act being identifiable as outright deprivation. As instances may be quoted excessive or arbitrary taxation; prohibition of dividend distribution coupled with compulsory loans; imposition of administrators; prohibition of dismissal of staff; refusal of access to raw materials or of essential export or import licences.[14]

Similar language partly relying upon the notions of unreasonable interference, undue delay and the effective enjoyment of property is contained in the Restatement (Third) of the Foreign Relations Law of the United States.[15]

However, the greatest contribution to the attempts to define which prerequisites need to be met in order to qualify certain State measures as an indirect expropriation has undoubtedly been made by the various tribunals seized with this issue. Even before the advent of modern treaty arbitration, international courts and tribunals had to deal with cases involving claims concerning indirect expropriations, starting with the *Norwegian Shipowners'* case in 1922.[16] This decision was followed by others of the Permanent Court of International Justice (PCIJ) and the International Court of Justice (ICJ), the Iran-US Claims Tribunal, tribunals of the International Centre for Settlement of Investment Disputes (ICSID), courts applying the European and American Conventions on Human Rights and a number of ad hoc tribunals.

---

[13] L.B. Sohn and R.R. Baxter, 'Responsibility of States for Injuries to the Economic Interests of Aliens', 55 *American Journal of International Law* (1961) 545, 553.

[14] OECD Draft Convention on the Protection of Foreign Property of 1967, above n. 10.

[15] 'A State is responsible under international law for injury resulting from: (1) a taking by the state of the property of a national of another state [...] Comment (g.) on this provision explains: Subsection (1) applies not only to avowed expropriations in which the government formally takes title to property, but also to other actions of the government that have the effect of "taking" the property, in whole or in large part, outright or in stages ("creeping expropriation") [...] A state is responsible [...] when it subjects alien property to taxation, regulation, or other action that is confiscatory, or that prevents, unreasonably interferes with, or unduly delays, effective enjoyment of an alien's property or its removal from the state's territory. Depriving an alien of control of his property, as by an order freezing his assets, might become a taking if it's long extended'. American Law Institute, *Restatement (Third) of the Foreign Relations Law of the United States* (1986), Volume II, § 712, at 196, 200.

[16] *Norwegian Shipowners' Claims (Norway v US)*, Permanent Court of Arbitration, 1922.

The Criteria Used to Define Indirect Expropriations

In the following, this body of case law shall be the basis of the analysis as to which criteria have played a significant role when tribunals decided whether or not certain measures of the host State amounted to an indirect expropriation.[17]

The substantiality of the interference: the 'sole effect doctrine'

There is a general consensus that the most significant criterion in the case law concerning measures potentially amounting to indirect expropriation is the severity or significance of the impact the measure had on the owner's ability to use and enjoy his property.[18] The effect incurred through the measures taken is the most important criterion in current jurisprudence, in some cases the only one. Following Prof. Dolzer, this approach will hereinafter be referred to as the 'sole effect doctrine'.[19]

A vivid expression of that approach is contained in *Biloune v Ghana* in which the tribunal noted that:

[t]he motivations for the actions and omissions of Ghanaian governmental authorities are not clear. But the Tribunal need not establish those motivations to come to a conclusion in the case. What is clear is that the conjunction of the stop work order, the demolition, the summons, the arrest, the detention, the requirement of filing assets declaration forms, and the deportation of Mr Biloune without possibility of re-entry had the effect of causing the irreparable cessation of work on the project. Given the central role of Mr Biloune in promoting, financing and managing MDCL, his expulsion from the country effectively prevented MDCL from further pursuing the project. In the view of the tribunal, such prevention of MDCL from pursuing its approved project would constitute constructive expropriation of MDCL's contractual rights in the project and, accordingly, the expropriation of the value of Mr Biloune's interest in MDCL, unless Respondents can establish by persuasive evidence sufficient justification for these events.[20]

---

[17] It shall just be briefly noted here that it is common ground today that protection from expropriation relates not only to tangible property or physical assets but to all rights and interests that have an economic content, including immaterial and contractual rights. Instead of extensive arbitral case law or commentators, the author refers representatively to UNCTAD which observed: 'In the past, the concern was only with the physical property of a foreign investor. In modern times, the concern is not so much with the physical property but with the antecedent rights that are necessary for the enjoyment of these property rights as well as with incorporeal property. [...] Most recent BITs include intellectual property within the definition of investment so that, if there are infringements of intellectual property rights by State interference, there would be a taking. So too, contractual rights and regulatory rights associated with the making of an investment are included within the definition of foreign investment in treaties.' See UNCTAD, *Taking of Property*, Series on Issues in International Investment Agreements (2000) 36.

[18] C. Schreuer, 'The Concept of Expropriation under the ECT and other Investment Protection Treaties', in C. Ribeiro (ed.), *Investment Arbitration and the Energy Charter Treaty* (2006) 108, 145.

[19] R. Dolzer, 'Indirect Expropriations: New Developments?' 11 *NYU Environmental Law Journal* (2002) 79.

[20] *Biloune and Marine Drive Complex Ltd v Ghana Investments Centre and the Government of Ghana*, Award on Jurisdiction and Liability, 27 October 1989, 95 *ILR* (1989) 183, 209.

B. Current State of Affairs Regarding Indirect Expropriation 157

Further, the Iran-US Claims Tribunal referred to the severity of the deprivation in order to determine whether an indirect expropriation had occurred. In *Starrett Housing v Iran*, the crucial question was whether the State did '[...] interfere with property rights to such an extent that these rights are rendered so useless that they must be deemed to have been expropriated'.[21]

Similarly, in the *Tippetts* case, the tribunal held that:

While assumption of control over property by a government does not automatically and immediately justify a conclusion that the property has been taken by the government [...] such a conclusion is warranted whenever events demonstrate that the owner was deprived of fundamental rights of ownership and it appears that this deprivation is not merely ephemeral.[22]

Additionally, substantial case law based upon BITs as well as NAFTA and the ECT has evolved which also focuses upon the requirement of substantial and significant deprivation of the owner's rights in order to regard a certain measure as an expropriation.

One of the early decisions introducing the requirement of 'substantial deprivation' in order for an expropriation to be affirmed is the one in *Pope & Talbot v Canada* in which the claimant asserted that the export control regime reduced its ability to export a product. Thereby denying the occurrence of an expropriation,[23] the tribunal stated:

Even accepting (for the purpose of this analysis) the allegations of the Investor concerning diminished profits, the Tribunal concludes that the degree of interference with the Investment's operations due to the Export Control regime does not rise to an expropriation (creeping or otherwise) within the meaning of Article 1110. While it may sometimes be uncertain whether a particular interference with business activities amounts to an expropriation, the test is whether that interference is sufficiently restrictive to support a conclusion that the property has been 'taken' from the owner. [...] under international law, expropriation requires a 'substantial deprivation'.[24]

Of particular importance in this regard is also the *Metalclad* award where with regard to the refusal of a construction permit by the municipality the tribunal found that an

[...] expropriation under NAFTA includes not only open, deliberate and acknowledged takings of property, such as outright seizure or formal obligatory transfer of title in favour of the host State, but also covert or incidental interference with the use of

---

[21] *Starrett Housing Corp v Iran*, Iran-US Claims Tribunal, 19 December 1983, 4 *Iran-US CTR* 122, 154.
[22] *Tippetts, Abbett, McCarthy, Stratton v TAMS-AFFA Consulting Engineers of Iran*, Iran-US Claims Tribunal, 22 June 1984, 6 *Iran-US CTR* 219, 225.
[23] *Pope & Talbot Inc v The Government of Canada* (UNCITRAL, NAFTA), Interim Award, 26 June 2000, para. 96.
[24] Ibid., para. 102 (footnote omitted).

property which has the effect of depriving the owner, in whole or in significant part, of the use or reasonably-to-be expected economic benefit of property [...].[25]

The tribunal in *CME v Czech Republic*, citing this reasoning, adopted the same approach.[26]

Similarly, in *S.D. Myers v Canada*, the investors proceeded against an export ban which lasted for 18 months and affected their ability to export hazardous waste for disposal. The tribunal stated:

> An expropriation usually amounts to a lasting removal of the ability of an owner to make use of its economic rights although it may be that, in some contexts and circumstances, it would be appropriate to view a deprivation as amounting to an expropriation, even if it were partial or temporary.[27]

Of particular interest in this regard is also the reasoning of the tribunal in *Tecmed v Mexico* as it explains its considerations concerning the determination of the issue at hand in some detail:

> To establish whether the Resolution is a measure equivalent to an expropriation under the terms of section 5(1) of the Agreement, it must be first determined if the Claimant, due to the Resolution, was radically deprived of the economical use and enjoyment of its investments, as if the rights related thereto—such as the income or benefits related to the Landfill or to its exploitation—had ceased to exist. In other words, if due to the actions of the Respondent, the assets involved have lost their value or economic use for their holder and the extent of the loss. This determination is important because it is one of the main elements to distinguish, from the point of an international tribunal, between a regulatory measure, which is an ordinary expression of the exercise of the state's police power that entails a decrease in assets or rights, and a de facto expropriation that deprives those assets and rights of any real substance.[28]

Lastly, the decision in *Generation Ukraine v Ukraine* shall be mentioned here which concerned a dispute regarding the failure of the Kyiv City State Administration to provide lease agreements and where the tribunal held:

> The Tribunal finds that the conduct of the Kyiv City State Administration...does not come close to creating a persistent or irreparable obstacle to the Claimant's use, enjoyment or disposal of its investment.[29]

Hence, the existing case law shows that the main criterion in order to determine whether or not certain measures taken by a government amount to an indirect expropriation is the degree of the interference. It must lead to a 'substantial'

---

[25] *Metalclad Corp v United Mexican States*, Award, 30 August 2000, para. 103.
[26] *CME v Czech Republic*, Partial Award, 13 September 2001, para. 606: '[...] covert or incidental interference with use of property which has the effect of depriving the owner, in whole or in significant part, of the use or reasonably to be expected economic benefit of property [...]'.
[27] *S.D. Myers Inc. v Government of Canada*, Partial Award, 13 November 2000, para. 283.
[28] *Técnicas Medioambientales Tecmed S.A. v United Mexican States*, above n. 5, para. 115.
[29] *Generation Ukraine Inc. v Ukraine*, Award, 16 September 2003, para. 20.32.

B. Current State of Affairs Regarding Indirect Expropriation

or 'radical' deprivation of the owner's right, and not be merely 'ephemeral'. It is necessary that a 'persistent or irreparable obstacle' to the enjoyment of the investment has been created.[30] At the same time, it has been recognized that this substantial deprivation can be of a 'partial' nature.[31]

The Durational Aspect

Within the recent investment arbitration jurisprudence, the issue arose as to whether only temporary interference could constitute an expropriation. Some tribunals have held that in order for the deprivation to be substantial and significant, it must be 'permanent' and 'irreversible'.[32] However, this approach is not universal. Thus, in *S.D. Myers v Canada*, although the tribunal agreed, that generally an expropriation

[...] usually amounts to a lasting removal of the ability of an owner to make use of its economic rights, [...] it may be that in some contexts and circumstances, it would be appropriate to view a deprivation as amounting to an expropriation, even it were partial or temporary.[33]

In that very case, the tribunal did not find that the temporary interference at issue, lasting for about 18 months, amounted to an expropriation. In *Wena Hotels v Egypt*, on the other hand, the tribunal found that the seizure of two hotels for about one year was not merely 'ephemeral', but sufficient to constitute an expropriation.[34] Similarly, in *Middle East Cement*, the tribunal considered the suspension of an export licence for four months as not merely 'ephemeral'.[35] Therefore, the case law with regard to this specific aspect remains incoherent. Even if one could argue that merely temporary measures can amount to an

---

[30] The tribunal in *PSEG Global, Inc, The North American Coal Corporation, and Konya Ingin Electrik Uretim ve Ticaret Limited Sirketi v Turkey*, Award, 19 January 2007, paras 272 *et seq.*, came on the basis of this approach to the conclusion that no expropriation occurred. Similarly, in *Enron Corporation and Ponderosa Assets, L.P. v Argentine Republic*, Award, 22 May 2007, paras 234 *et seq.*, the tribunal decided on the basis of the intensity of the interference that no expropriation had occurred. In *Vivendi II*, above n. 5, paras 7.5.1 *et seq.*, on the other hand, the tribunal decided that the respondent State had expropriated the investor by finding that a substantial deprivation had occurred.

[31] See *S.D. Myers v Canada*, above n. 27; *Metalclad v Mexico*, above n. 25; *Iurii Bogdanov, Agurdino-Invest Ltd and Agurdino-Chimia JSC v Republic of Moldova*, Award, 22 September 2005, at 17, which states: 'the concept of indirect expropriation applies only to measures having the effect of expropriation that affect the totality or a substantial part of the investment'.

[32] See, eg, *Tecmed*, above n. 5, para. 116: 'It is understood that the measures adopted by a State, whether regulatory or not, are an indirect de facto expropriation if they are irreversible and permanent', citing the decisions in *Tippetts* and *Phelps Dodge* of the Iran-US Claims Tribunal.

[33] *S.D. Myers v Canada*, above n. 27, para. 283.

[34] *Wena Hotels Ltd v Arab Republic of Egypt*, Award, 8 December 2000, para. 9. In *Consortium RFCC v Kingdom of Morocco*, Award, 22 December 2003, para. 68, the tribunal also found that measures of only temporary character can constitute an expropriation.

[35] *Middle East Cement Shipping and Handling Co. S.A. v Arab Republic of Egypt*, Award, 12 April 2002, para. 107.

indirect expropriation, the boundary of when an interference becomes such an expropriation remains unclear since in one case 18 months were held not be sufficient whereas in another case one year sufficed. Each decision will depend upon the specific circumstances of the case and the evaluation by those called upon to make it.

Interference by Actions and Omissions

Especially with regard to indirect expropriation which can entail a variety of State interferences, the issue whether governmental liability can arise because of omissions is of particular importance. In principle, the doctrine of State responsibility acknowledges that a failure to act can lead to a State's liability as much as can certain actions.

Nevertheless, certain investment arbitration awards[36] and commentators[37] suggest that only actions will be sufficient to hold a State responsible with regard to potentially expropriatory measures. Thus, the tribunal in *Olguin v Republic of Paraguay* held that:

For an expropriation to occur, there must be actions that can be considered reasonably appropriate for producing the effect of depriving the affected party of the property it owns, in such a way that whoever performs those actions will acquire, directly or indirectly, control, or at least the fruits of the expropriated property. Expropriation therefore requires a teleologically driven action for it to occur; omissions, however egregious they may be, are not sufficient for it to take place.[38]

However, the majority of investment decisions indicate a different approach. They acknowledge that a failure to act is often central to the dispute in question, although few cases rely merely on those failures. Typically, case law relies on a combination of actions and omissions.[39] This approach appears sensible in light of the fact that it should not make a difference whether a State does not issue a necessary licence in the first place or whether it issues it in order to withdraw it shortly thereafter.

The Enrichment of the Host State

The idea that an expropriation requires the enrichment of the host State has been widely abandoned in the relevant case law, in particular because it negates the

---

[36] *Olguin v Republic of Paraguay*, Award, 26 July 2001; *Sea-Land Service Inc v Iran*, Iran-US CTR, 1984.
[37] C. McLachlan, L. Shore, and M. Weiniger, *International Investment Arbitration. Substantive Principles*, (2007), para. 8.73.
[38] *Olguin v Republic of Paraguay*, above n. 36, para. 84.
[39] See eg *Metalclad v Mexico*, above n. 25, paras 106–107; *CME Czech Republic B.V. v Czech Republic*, Partial Award, 13 September 2001, paras 591 *et seq.*

B. Current State of Affairs Regarding Indirect Expropriation 161

protection against indirect expropriation.[40] Nevertheless, not all decisions follow this line. Thus, for example, the tribunal in *Olguin v Paraguay* expressed the view that '[...] whoever performs those actions will acquire, directly or indirectly, control, or at least the fruits of the expropriated property'.[41]

Similarly, the tribunal in *Lauder v Czech Republic* stated:

In addition, even assuming that the actions taken by the Media Council in the period from 1996 through 1999 had the effect of depriving the Claimant of his property rights, such actions would not amount to an appropriation—or the equivalent—by the State, since it did not benefit the Czech Republic or any person or entity related thereto [...].[42]

The intentions of the State

Although, as shown above, the criterion of the effect of the measure upon the investment is thus far most crucial and, in accordance with the sole effect doctrine, in many cases the only one considered, other awards reflect further aspects which were taken into account by tribunals faced with claims for indirect expropriation. Some of them looked at the intentions of a government to expropriate or even if denying that the intentions of the host government played a role, still referred to this element.

Thus, the tribunal in *Biloune v Ghana Investment Centre*, although ultimately emphasizing the importance of the effect of the measures, stated:

The motivations for the actions and omissions of Ghanaian governmental authorities are not clear. But the Tribunal need not establish those motivations to come to a conclusion in the case.[43]

In *Tecmed v Mexico*, the tribunal stated:

The government's intention is less important than the effects of the measures on the owner of the assets or on the benefits arising from such assets affected by the measures; and the form of the deprivation measures is less important than its actual effects.[44]

Similarly, the tribunal in *Vivendi II* found:

There is extensive authority for the proposition that the state's intent, or its subjective motives are at most a secondary consideration. While intent will weigh in favour of showing a measure to be expropriatory, it is not a requirement, because the *effect* of the measure on the investor, not the state's intent, is the critical factor.[45]

---

[40] Y.L. Fortier and S.L. Drymer, 'Indirect Expropriation in the Law of International Investment: I know it when I see it, or Caveat Investor', 19 *ICSID Review—Foreign Investment Law Journal* (2002) 293, 314 with further references; *Tecmed v Mexico*, above n. 5, para. 113.
[41] *Olguin v Republic of Paraguay*, above n. 36, para. 84.
[42] *Lauder v Czech Republic*, Award, 3 September 2001, para. 203.
[43] *Biloune v Ghana*, above n. 20.
[44] *Tecmed v Mexico*, above n. 5, para. 116, citing decisions of the Iran-US Claims Tribunal in *Tippetts* and *Phelps Dodge*.
[45] *Vivendi II*, above n. 5, para. 7.5.20 (footnote omitted, emphasis in original).

A rare instance in which a tribunal relied exclusively upon the intention of the government is the case of *CCL v Kazakhstan*. There, the tribunal rejected an expropriation claim on the basis that the claimant had not shown that any motivation to expropriate lay behind any of the government's actions in connection with the concession agreement at issue.[46]

Investment-backed expectations of the investor

A further relevant factor is the one which is—pursuant to the ruling of the tribunal in *Metalclad*[47]—frequently termed as the 'investment-backed expectations of the investor'.[48] One might also refer to it as the reliance of the investor upon certain given circumstances which he, at least in part, bases his decision upon to make an investment in the host State or, in short, 'legitimate expectations'. All these expressions are essentially based upon the same principle, that of 'stability', ie the reliance on a regulatory and business environment which does not fundamentally change during the course of the investment with the ultimate effect of jeopardizing the reasonable expectations of the investor. This issue is usually considered by tribunals when discussing the standard of either expropriation or Fair and Equitable Treatment (FET).[49] Concerning the latter, it has been suggested that the principle of legitimate expectations has evolved 'from an earlier function as a subsidiary interpretative principle' to become 'a self-standing subcategory and independent basis for a claim under the "fair and equitable standard"'.[50]

Various awards made reference to this principle.[51] Suffice it here to cite the award in *Thunderbird v Mexico* in which the tribunal held:

Having considered recent investment case law and the good faith principle of international customary law, the concept of 'legitimate expectations' relates, within the context of the NAFTA framework, to a situation where a Contracting Party's conduct creates reasonable and justifiable expectations on the part of an investor (or investment) to act in reliance on said conduct, such that a failure by the NAFTA Party to honour those expectations could cause the investor (or investment) to suffer damages. The threshold

---

[46] *CCL v Republic of Kazakhstan*, Final Award, 2004, 1 *SIAR* (2005) 123, 173.
[47] *Metalclad v Mexico*, above n. 25, paras 103, 107.
[48] See, eg, J. Coe and N. Rubins, 'Regulatory Expropriation and the Tecmed Case: Context and Contributions', in T. Weiler (ed.), *International Investment Law and Arbitration: Leading Cases from the ICSID, NAFTA, Bilateral Treaties and Customary International Law* (2005) 597, 624.
[49] See also C. Yannaca-Small at Chapter 6 above.
[50] See *International Thunderbird Gaming v The United Mexican States*, Separate Opinion of Prof. T. Wälde of 26 January 2006, para. 37.
[51] See, eg, *Kuwait v Aminoil*, Final Award, 24 March 1982, 21 ILM 976, 1034; *Revere Copper and Brass Inc v Overseas Private Investment Corporation*, Award, 24 August 1978, 56 ILR 258, 271; *Antoine Goetz and Others v Republic of Burundi*, Award, 10 February 1999, para. 124; *Consortium RFCC v Kingdom of Morocco*, above n. 34, para. 69; *Methanex Corporation v United States of America*, (NAFTA), Award, 3 August 2005, 44 ILM (2005) 1345, Part IV, Chapter D, paras 7, 9, 10; *Eureko B.V. v Republic of Poland*, Partial Award, 19 August 2005, paras 242, 243; *Azurix v Argentine Republic*, ICSID Case No. ARB/01/12, Award, 14 July 2006, paras 316–322.

B. Current State of Affairs Regarding Indirect Expropriation

for legitimate expectations may vary depending on the nature of the violation alleged under the NAFTA and the circumstances of the case.[52]

This standard applies equally to any other investment treaty. It shows that increasingly the expectation of economic benefit becomes one variable in the considerations that need to be taken into account when determining whether an expropriation has actually occurred.

The requirement of proportionality

An issue related to those of stability and the legitimate expectations of the investor is that of the distribution of burden between the investor and the host government. Both concepts allow shifting the focus from the investor and the question whether he had been substantially deprived of his investment to the business situation in the host State. Until recently, these considerations mostly played a role in the jurisprudence of the European Court of Human Rights.[53] The notion of proportionality recognizes that when the property owner carries too big a burden in comparison to the aim which the State tries to achieve, the measure at issue must be deemed to be disproportionate. It will therefore more likely be a deprivation of property which entitles its owner to compensation in accordance with the Convention's First Protocol. The proportionality doctrine which the Court developed openly favours non-nationals who 'will generally have played no part in the election or designation of the [measures'] authors nor have been consulted in its adoption'.[54] It follows that 'there may well be a legitimate reason for requiring nationals to bear a greater burden in the public interest than non-nationals'.[55]

These very considerations featured for the first time in modern investment treaty arbitration in *Tecmed v Mexico* which was based upon the Spain/Mexico BIT.[56] In this case, the tribunal ruled that the measures taken by the host State amounted to an indirect expropriation. But its analysis did not end there. It continued and shifted the burden thereafter to Mexico in order to evaluate whether the expropriation was justified as falling within the State's police powers.

The tribunal explained its approach as follows:

After establishing that regulatory actions and measures will not be initially excluded from the definition of expropriatory acts, in addition to the negative financial impact of such actions or measures, the Arbitral Tribunal will consider, in order to determine if they are to be characterized as expropriatory, whether such actions or measures are proportional to the public interest presumably protected thereby and to the protection legally granted

---

[52] *International Thunderbird Gaming Corporation v Mexico*, Award, 26 January 2006, para. 147.
[53] See, eg, *James & Others v United Kingdom*, 3 EHRR (1986) 19, 20.
[54] Ibid., para. 64.
[55] Ibid.
[56] *Tecmed v Mexico*, above n. 5.

to investments, taking into account that the significance of such impact has a key role upon deciding the proportionality.[57]

It furthermore described the application of its proportionality test more concretely by suggesting that 'a serious urgent situation, crisis, need or social emergency' could be 'weighed against the deprivation or neutralisation of the economic or commercial value of the Claimant's investment' to lead to the conclusion that an otherwise expropriatory regulation '[does] not amount to an expropriation under the Agreement and international law'.[58] Hence, the availability of measures which cause less of a burden for the investor and the urgency of the public need are factors considered in the proportionality analysis.

This approach was endorsed subsequently by the arbitral decisions in *Azurix*[59] and *LG&E*.[60]

Notably, the proportionality doctrine bears some similarity to the controversial necessity defence to State liability. Article 25 of the ILC text allows governments to invoke necessity to avoid liability for an otherwise unlawful act when the measure

[...] is the only means for a State to safeguard an essential interest against a grave and imminent peril [and] does not seriously impair an essential interest of the State or States towards which the obligation exists, or of the international community as a whole.[61]

Thus, in this scenario too, the focus will shift from the investor and his investment to the situation in the host state which under certain circumstances, to be interpreted by the Arbitral tribunal, will allow the State to take measures which would otherwise be regarded as a breach of the relevant provision of the investment treaty.[62]

---

[57] Ibid., para. 122.
[58] Ibid., para. 139.
[59] In *Azurix* the tribunal stated 'that these additional elements provide useful guidance for purposes of determining whether regulatory actions would be expropriatory and give rise to compensation'. *Azurix Corp v Argentine Republic*, above n. 51, para. 312.
[60] In *LG&E v Argentina*, the Tribunal held: 'With respect to the power of the State to adopt its policies, it can generally be said that the State has the right to adopt measures having a social or general welfare purpose. In such a case, the measure must be accepted without any imposition of liability, except in cases where the State's action is obviously disproportionate to the need being addressed.' *LG&E Capital Corp, LG&E International Inc v Argentine Republic*, Decision on Liability, 3 October 2006, para. 195. Notably, the tribunal thus turned the reasoning around in comparison to the *Tecmed* Award, above n. 5, where the tribunal explained that initially the measure will not be excluded from any liability, but that the respondent State, once an initial liability was found, will be entitled to show that, under the given circumstances, the measures taken were justified and proportionate. This will then lead to an exclusion of liability for the measures will not be deemed expropriatory.
[61] Report of the International Law Commission, *ILC Articles on Responsibilty of States for Internationally Wrongful Acts*, 56th Session., Supp. No. 10, UN Doc. A/56/10 (Nov. 2001), Article 25.
[62] For a discussion of the necessity defence under international law, see eg *CMS Gas Transmission Company v The Argentine Republic*, Award, 12 May 2005, paras 304 *et seq.*; *LG&E Energy Corp, LG&E Capital Corp, LG&E International Inc. v Argentine Republic*, above n. 60, paras 201 *et seq.*

C. Indirect Expropriation and the State's Right to Regulate

The doctrine of indirect expropriation came into particular spotlight with the increase of cases involving States taking measures in connection with their right to regulate and exercise the public order function, their sovereign powers.[63] These cases have occasionally been referred to as suggesting that a measure taken in exercise of the State's sovereign powers automatically means that the measure at issue is not an expropriation and thus requires no compensation. Statements in that regard have been made by arbitral tribunals. Thus, in *Methanex*, the arbitrators ruled that

[...] as a matter of general international law, a non-discriminatory regulation for a public purpose, which is enacted in accordance with due process and, which affects, inter alios, a foreign investor or investment is not deemed expropriatory and compensable unless specific commitments had been given by the regulating government to the then putative foreign investor contemplating investment that the government would refrain from such regulation.[64]

Equally, in the majority award in *S.D. Myers*, two arbitrators observed in a somewhat general statement:

The general body of precedent usually does not treat regulatory action as expropriation. Regulatory conduct by public authorities is unlikely to be the subject of legitimate complaint under Article 1110 of the NAFTA, although the tribunal does not rule out that possibility.[65]

However, contrary to some suggestions, it is submitted that in modern investment arbitration there exists no general exception to the rule that investors have to be compensated for regulatory measures which have an expropriatory effect. This was confirmed in the award in *Santa Elena* which stated:

Expropriatory environmental measures—no matter how laudable and beneficial to society as a whole—are, in this respect, similar to any other expropriatory measures that a state may take in order to implement its policies: where property is expropriated, even for environmental purposes—whether domestic or international—the state's obligation to pay compensation remains.[66]

---

[63] For analyses of the issues involved see, eg, T. Wälde and A. Kolo, 'Environmental Regulation, Investment Protection and "Regulatory Taking" in International Law', 50 *International and Comparative Law Quarterly* (2001) 811; Coe and Rubins, above n. 48; A. Newcombe, 'The Boundaries of Regulatory Expropriation in International Law', 20 *ICSID Review—Foreign Investment Law Journal* (2005) 1; U. Kriebaum, 'Regulatory Takings: Balancing the Interests of the Investor and the State', 8 *Journal of World Investment and Trade* (2007) 717.

[64] *Methanex v USA*, above n. 51, Part IV-Chapter D, para. 7.

[65] *S.D. Myers v Canada*, above n. 27, para. 281.

[66] *Compania del Desarollo de Santa Elena, S.A. v Republic of Costa Rica*, Final Award, 17 February 2000, para. 171.

And the tribunal in *Feldman v Mexico* stated similarly that '[n]o one can seriously doubt that in some circumstances governmental regulatory activity can be a violation of Article 1110'.[67]

The majority of investment treaty claims today would be exempted as they are based upon regulatory measures concerning, for example, health and safety, environmental, or taxation issues. Consequently, the tribunal in *Pope & Talbot* observed that:

> Regulations can indeed be characterised in a way that would constitute creeping expropriation. [. . .] Indeed much creeping expropriation could be conducted by regulation, and a blanket exception for regulatory measures would create a gaping loophole in international protection against expropriation.[68]

Furthermore, considerable conceptual difficulty arose if one accepted that the purpose of a measure may lead to this measure not being defined as an expropriatory measure for the purposes of compensation. As set out above, expropriations are not *a priori* prohibited under international law. Rather, expropriations are lawful, provided that certain requirements are met. One of these requirements is that the investment was expropriated for a public purpose. Hence, the traditional notion of defining a legal expropriation is based upon two consequent steps: (i) the determination whether a measure amounted to an expropriation (using one or more of the criteria set out above), and (ii) defining whether the expropriation was lawful according to certain standards, one of which is the 'public purpose' requirement. If, as some arbitrators and commentators appear to suggest, the criterion of 'public purpose' is used to define whether an expropriation occurred, ie for step (i), it is no longer useful regarding step (ii), namely the determination of the question whether the possible expropriation was lawful—step (ii) was used to make step (i) which entails considerable difficulty for the classic concept of expropriation and its distinction of 'lawful' and 'unlawful' for the purpose of compensation.[69] Only if we reconsider this dichotomy at the same time, we will be able to use, if desired, the criterion of the purpose of a measure taken by a government in order to define whether this measure amounted to an expropriation.

D. Recent Developments

The lack of express guidelines as to what exactly constitutes an indirect expropriation in combination with an evolving case law which is not always coherent have caused concerns as to both the predictability and fairness of investment

---

[67] *Feldman v Mexico*, ICSID Case No. ARB(AF)/99/1, Award, 16 December 2002, para. 110.
[68] *Pope & Talbot v Canada*, above n. 23, para. 99.
[69] For a discussion of the issue, see A. Reinisch, 'Legality of Expropriations', at Chapter 9.

arbitration especially towards host States. These concerns are recently reflected in more detailed specifications in treaty provisions concerning expropriations.

Thus, for example, since 2003 the explicit reference to whether a measure is designed to protect 'legitimate public welfare objectives' has been incorporated into five free trade agreements concluded by the United States[70] and one bilateral investment treaty concluded between the United States and Uruguay. The terms of these agreements with regard to indirect expropriation are identical to those in the updated Draft US Model BIT released in 2004. Accordingly, the criteria for the determination of indirect expropriation are the following:

The determination of whether an action or series of actions by a Party, in a specific fact situation, constitutes an indirect expropriation, requires a case-by-case, fact-based inquiry that considers, among other factors:
– the economic impact of the government action, although the fact that an action or series of actions by a Party has an adverse effect on the economic value of an investment, standing alone, does not establish that an indirect expropriation has occurred;
– the extent to which the government action interferes with distinct, reasonable, investment-backed expectations; and
– the character of the government action.[71]

With regard to the significance of the character of the measure, the same provision goes on to establish the important presumption that:

Except in rare circumstances, non-discriminatory regulatory actions by a Party that are designed and applied to protect legitimate public welfare objectives, such as public health, safety, and the environment, do not constitute indirect expropriations.[72]

E. Concluding Considerations

Findings on indirect expropriations are relatively rare. Tribunals having the choice to establish liability by means of other substantive treaty standards, such as that of 'fair and equitable treatment', often avoid having to make distinct findings on this issue. Nevertheless, over the last decades a body of case law has emerged and slowly continues to fill the gaps which arise due to the 'laconic wording'[73] of the characterizations of indirect expropriations in investment treaties.

---

[70] US/Singapore FTA; US/Chile FTA; US/Central America and the Dominican Republic FTA; US/Morocco FTA; and US/Australia FTA.
[71] See Annex B, Article 4(a) Draft US Model BIT (2004). In particular, the factor of 'the extent to which the government action interferes with distinct, reasonable, investment-backed expectations' (Article 4(a)(iii)) is the same as that identified in the landmark case of *Penn Central Transport Co v New York City*, United States Supreme Court, 1978, 438 US 104.
[72] See Annex A, Article 4(b) Draft US Model BIT (2004).
[73] R. Dolzer, 'Indirect Expropriation of Alien Property', 1 *ICSID Review—Foreign Investment Law Journal* (1986) 48, 55.

This case law shows that the majority of decisions as to whether an indirect expropriation occurred base their reasoning on the sole effect doctrine. Some take additional considerations like the intention of the State, the legitimate expectations of the investor, the purpose and, recently, the proportionality of the State measures into account. The sole effect doctrine undoubtedly has its advantages, one of them being the fact that it is a rather objective measuring device. However, using this approach results in a rather one-sided focus upon the interests of and the harm done to the investor. In the author's view, the decision as to whether a compensable expropriation occurred should include the 'application [...] of general principles of fairness, equality and balancing of interest [sic] that are neither immutable nor universal'.[74] These principles are reflected in the criteria of intentions and purpose of the State measures, the investment-backed expectations of the investor and the proportionality test, all of which have also been considered in some of the recent decisions and treaties and have led to a somewhat softer application of the sole effect doctrine. Undoubtedly, there will be difficulty in determining the intentions of the host State or the true expectations of the investor, simply because they contain a certain degree of subjectivism. The conceptual difficulty with the use of the purpose criteria has been mentioned above. However, the proportionality requirement recently introduced into investment treaty arbitration appears to be a convincing and methodologically clear approach when attempting to balance the interests of both the State and the investor fairly. This overall shift of focus is useful as 'it allows us to focus on the legal situation in the host country at the time of the investment' thereby emphasizing the fact that in principle 'each state has the right to set its own rules of property which the foreigner accepts when investing'.[75] At the same time, it acknowledges 'the notion that expectations deserve more protection as they are increasingly backed by an investment'.[76] Certain voices might raise the argument that a more differentiated standard in that regard is incompatible with the declared aim of investment treaties to promote and foster foreign investment. It appears doubtful that the application of a differentiated standard would necessarily have led to a different, less investor-friendly, outcome of those cases already decided or will do so in the future. But even if that should be the case at all, it might be a short-term argument as it can only be investment-friendly to visibly consider the interests of all parties to the treaty so that they will continue to be bound by them.[77]

---

[74] G. Sacerdoti, 'The Admission and Treatment of Foreign Investment under Recent Bilateral and Regional Treaties', 1 *Journal of World Investment and Trade* (2000) 59, 121.
[75] R. Dolzer, 'Indirect Expropriations: New Developments?', 11 *NYU Environmental Law Journal* (2002) 64, 78.
[76] Ibid.
[77] With regard to the debate of the right approach concerning the creation of a balance between the interests, it has recently been suggested that this might be achieved by using the criterion of proportionality in order to regulate the amount of damages. By doing so, it is suggested that the existing 'all or nothing' approach could be made more flexible by deciding whether an

E. Concluding Considerations

In addition to the considerations regarding a fair balance of interests, the need for legal certainty also plays an important role in the jurisprudence on indirect expropriation. Complaints of an incoherent case law from all sides, investors and States, are frequent and understandable. But with the predominant case-by-case approach '[...] it is evident that the question of what kind of interference short of outright expropriation constitutes a "taking" under international law presents a situation where the common law method of case by case development is pre-eminently the best method, in fact probably the only method, of legal development'.[78] Even attempts to define legal notions like the one of indirect expropriation, for example in letters and protocols attached to treaties, are of limited use. They will give limited certainty as they will always contain terms and phrases, such as legitimate expectations, which in turn will again require interpretation. Hence, ultimately it will be those three arbitrators who, based upon the facts and the circumstances of each case and individual considerations, which will always be influenced by their experience, views and legal training, will come to a decision. We should lose the fear of the apparent uncertainty which naturally goes hand in hand with the development of a jurisprudence in a relatively new area of law—this is not a feature unique to modern investment arbitration. Nevertheless, it will be crucial to make clear what the basic criteria are upon which the decisions are based, for example with regard to indirect expropriation, the sole effect doctrine, police power exceptions, legitimate expectations, or a standard based upon all of them. This will not fully eliminate inconsistent awards, ie awards which though based on the same or similar treaty clauses and similar facts will come to different conclusions. This is to be accepted as long as this is a conscious deviation and the arbitrators explain why they came to a different conclusion. Another phenomenon, however, is that of incoherent decisions, ie those where the tribunal deviates from previous decisions although facts or legal concepts are similar without explaining why, or maybe without even mentioning the decision which was previously decided differently. The first phenomenon makes life for all who seek

---

exceptional public interest should entitle the State to reduce the full compensation paid otherwise. See U. Kriebaum, 'Regulatory Takings: Balancing the Interests of the Investor and the State', 8 *Journal of World Investment and Trade* (2007) 717. Adopting this approach would go beyond the one endorsed by Judge Higgins who also proposed to reflect the State's right to regulate on the damage side. She stated that '[...] governments may indeed need to be able to act qua government and in the public interest. That fact will prevent specific performance (including restitution) from being granted against them. But that is not to liberate them from the obligation to compensate those with whom it has entered into specific arrangements. That is the reasonable place to strike the balance between the expectations of foreign investors and the bona fide needs of the governments to act in the public interest.' Thereby she opposed the view set out above whereby measures undertaken for regulatory purposes and in the public interest should not be considered expropriatory. See Higgins, above n. 6, 338, 339.

[78] G.C. Christie, 'What Constitutes a Taking of Property under International Law?', 38 *British Yearbook of International Law* (1962) 307, 338.

legal certainty less comfortable. However, it has to be accepted in an evolving field of law. The second phenomenon is highly unsatisfactory and rightly causes frustration. We will always have to accept that different individuals weigh certain facts differently and give them different importance. This should not deter the legal community from attempting to create a jurisprudence as predictable as possible under these circumstances.

9
Legality of Expropriations

August Reinisch

A. Introduction

Over the last decades, the focus of expropriation law has shifted from direct to indirect expropriations and to ascertaining at what stage a governmental measure constitutes an indirect, *de facto*, or creeping expropriation.[1] Declining figures of outright takings of property inversely correspond to an increase of various legislative and regulatory measures that *de facto* or indirectly deprive investors of their property. Thus, most recent investment arbitrations address the issue of indirect expropriation at length.[2] The question of the legality of an expropriation,

---

[1] See A. Hoffmann at Chapter 8 above. R. Doak Bishop, J. Crawford, and W. M. Reisman, *Foreign Investment Disputes* (2005) 837 *et seq.*; R. Dolzer, 'Indirect Expropriation of Alien Property', 1 *ICSID Review—Foreign Investment Law Journal* (1986) 41; R. Dolzer, 'Indirect Expropriations: New Developments?', 11 *NYU Environmental Law Journal* (2002) 64; Y.L. Fortier and S.L. Drymer, 'Indirect Expropriation in the Law of International Investment: I Know It When I See It, or *Caveat Investor*', 19 *ICSID Review—Foreign Investment Law Journal* (2004) 293; R. Higgins, 'The Taking of Foreign Property by the State', 176 *Recueil des Cours* (1982-III) 259; U. Kriebaum and A. Reinisch, 'Property, Right to, International Protection', in *Encyclopedia of Public International Law* (forthcoming); V. Lowe, 'Regulation or Expropriation?', 55 *Current Legal Problems* (2002) 447; A. Lowenfeld, *International Economic Law* (2002) 392 *et seq.*; P. Muchlinski, *Multinational Enterprises and the Law* (2nd edn, 2007) 588 *et seq.*; A. Newcombe, 'The Boundaries of Regulatory Expropriation in International Law', 20 *ICSID Review—Foreign Investment Law Journal* (2005) 1; Y. Nouvel, 'Les mesures équivalent à une expropriation dans la pratique récente des tribunaux arbitraux', 106 *RGDIP* (2002) 79; A. Reinisch, 'Expropriation', in P. Muchlinski, F. Ortino, and C. Schreuer (eds), *The Oxford Handbook of International Investment Law* (forthcoming 2008); N. Rubins and N.S. Kinsella, *International Investment, Political Risk and Dispute Resolution. A Practitioner's Guide* (2005) 155 *et seq.*; T. Wälde and A. Kolo, 'Environmental Regulation, Investment Protection and "Regulatory Taking" in International Law', 50 *International and Comparative Law Quarterly* (2001) 811; C. Yannaca-Small, '"Indirect Expropriation" and the "Right to Regulate" in International Investment Law', in OECD (ed.), *International Investment Law. A Changing Landscape* (2005) 43; UNCTAD, *Taking of Property* (2000) 11 *et seq.*

[2] See *Azurix v Argentine Republic*, ICSID Case No. ARB/01/12, Award, 14 July 2006; *CME Czech Republic B.V. v Czech Republic*, UNCITRAL, Partial Award, 13 September 2001; *CMS Gas Transmission Company v The Argentine Republic*, ICSID Case No. ARB/01/8, Award, 12 May 2005; *Compañiá de Aguas del Aconquija S.A. and Vivendi Universal v Argentine Republic*, ICSID Case No. ARB/97/3, Award, 20 August 2007; *EnCana Corporation v Republic of Ecuador*, LCIA Case No. UN 3481, UNCITRAL, Award, 3

however, which had figured prominently in traditional international law,[3] seems to have become less important.[4]

In spite of these developments, there is a considerable tradition of investment cases which deal with the aspects of the lawfulness of expropriations both under customary international law[5] and according to applicable treaty standards.[6]

February 2006; *Enron Corporation and Ponderosa Assets, L.P. v Argentine Republic*, ICSID Case No. ARB/01/3, Award, 22 May 2007; *Eureko B.V. v Republic of Poland,* Partial Award, 19 August, 2005; *Feldman v Mexico*, ICSID Case No. ARB(AF)/99/1, Award, 16 December 2002; *GAMI Investments, Inc. v United Mexican States*, Award, 15 November 2004; *Ronald S. Lauder v Czech Republic,* UNCITRAL, Award, 3 September 2001; *LG&E Energy Corp, LG&E Capital Corp and LG&E International Inc v Argentine Republic*, ICSID Case No. ARB/02/1, Decision on Liability, 3 October 2006; *MCI Power Group L.C. and New Turbine, Inc v Ecuador*, ICSID Case No. ARB/03/6, Award, 31 July 2007; *Metalclad Corporation v Mexico*, ICSID Case No. ARB(AF)/97/1, Award, 30 August 2000; *Methanex Corporation v United States of America*, NAFTA, Award, 3 August 2005; *Middle East Cement Shipping and Handling Co S.A. v Arab Republic of Egypt*, ICSID Case No. ARB/99/6, Award, 12 April 2002; *MTD Equity Sdn Bhd and MTD Chile S.A. v Republic of Chile*, ICSID Case No. ARB/01/7, Award, 25 May 2004; *Occidental Exploration and Production Company v Republic of Ecuador*, LCIA No. UN 3467, Award, 1 July 2004; *Pope & Talbot Inc v The Government of Canada*, UNCITRAL (NAFTA), Interim Award, 26 June 2000; *PSEG Global et al. v Republic of Turkey*, ICSID Case No. ARB/02/5, Award, 19 January 2007; *Saluka Investments BV (The Netherlands) v The Czech Republic*, Partial Award, 17 March 2006; *S.D. Myers, Inc v Canada*, UNCITRAL (NAFTA), Award (Merits), 13 November 2000; *Siemens A.G. v Argentina*, ICSID Case No. ARB/02/08, Award, 6 February 2007; *Técnicas Medioambientales Tecmed, S.A. v United Mexican States*, ICSID Case No. ARB (AF)/00/2, Award, 29 May 2003; *Telenor Mobile Communications A.S. v Republic of Hungary*, ICSID Case No. ARB/04/15, Award, 13 September 2006; *International Thunderbird Gaming Corporation v Mexico*, UNCITRAL (NAFTA), Award, 26 January 2006; *Waste Management, Inc v United Mexican States*, ICSID Case No. ARB(AF)/00/3, Award, 30 April 2004.

[3] According to Muchlinski, '[t]he legality of expropriation has been one of the most contentious problems in international law'. Muchlinski, *Multinational Enterprises*, above n. 1, 597.

[4] This may also explain why some recent treatises on international investment law deal almost exclusively with different forms of expropriations, but hardly address the issue of their legality. Cf. C. McLachlan, L. Shore, and M. Weiniger, *International Investment Arbitration. Substantive Principles* (2007) 265 *et seq*.

[5] A number of ad hoc arbitrations such as the *Libyan Oil Concession* cases, *British Petroleum v Libya*, Award, 10 October 1973 and 1 August 1974; *Texaco Overseas Petroleum Company (Topco)/California Asiatic (Calasiatic) Oil Company v Libya*, Award, 19 January 1977; *Libyan American Oil Company (Liamco) v Libya*, 12 April 1977, which were based on agreements containing internationalization clauses, were decided on the basis of international law rules on expropriation. In a similar way, many of the early ICSID awards in cases which were brought on the basis of direct contracts between investors and host States decided expropriation issues on the basis of international law. See, eg, *Amco Asia Corporation v Republic of Indonesia*, ICSID Case No. ARB/81/1, Award, 20 November 1984; *Benvenuti & Bonfant v People's Republic of the Congo*, Award, 15 August 1980; *Adriano Gardella v Ivory Coast*, Award, 29 August 1977; *Kaiser Bauxite v Jamaica*, Award, 6 July 1975; *AGIP v Congo*, Award, 30 November 1979; *Klöckner v Cameroon*, Award, 21 October 1983; *SOABI v Senegal*, Award, 25 February 1988; *LETCO v Liberia*, Award, 31 March 1986; *Atlantic Triton v Guinea*, Award, 21 April 1986; *Vacuum Salt v Ghana*, Award, 16 February 1994; *Mobil Oil v New Zealand*, Findings on Liability, Interpretation and Allied Issues, 4 May 1989.

[6] Many recent expropriation claims based on international investment agreements, so-called treaty claims, are decided on the basis of the specifically applicable BIT or other IIA. Cf. Article 1131(1) NAFTA: 'A Tribunal established under this Section shall decide the issues in dispute in accordance with this Agreement and applicable rules of international law.'

Moreover, recent ICSID cases like *ADC v Hungary*[7] have demonstrated that the question of an expropriation's legality is alive and well. This chapter will briefly discuss the general international law on the legality of expropriation; it will then portray the situation under international investment agreements (IIAs);[8] but in the main it will analyse the relevant case law of investment tribunals in detail, trying to ascertain the relevant criteria for assessing the legality of expropriations. Particular emphasis will be put on the judicial and arbitral practice with regard to the determination of a 'public purpose', of 'non-discrimination', 'due process', and the level of 'compensation'.

Legality Requirements under General International Law

The protection of private property has been a traditional part of international law, in particular, of the law on the treatment of aliens. Thus, statements like the one uttered by the US-Panama Claims Commission in the *de Sabla* case that 'acts of a government in depriving an alien of his property without compensation impose international responsibility'[9] reflected the prevailing view of the 1930s. For a long time the protection of the property of foreigners against expropriation has played such a dominant role that the initial attempt of the International Law Commission (ILC) to codify the law of State responsibility was largely dominated by the issue of State responsibility for injury to the person or property of aliens.[10] It is thus not surprising that in the course of his reports, the first Special Rapporteur of the ILC on State Responsibility concluded that the expropriation of foreigners may lead to international responsibility of the expropriating State unless carried out in conformity with certain internationally required preconditions, such as 'public utility' or 'public interest', non-discrimination, and 'lack of arbitrariness'.[11] These considerations clearly reflect the traditional legality requirements which can also be found in some of the United Nations General Assembly (UNGA) resolutions confirming the

---

[7] *ADC Affiliate Limited and ADC & ADMC Management Limited v Republic of Hungary*, ICSID Case No. ARB/03/16, Award, 2 October 2006.
[8] The term 'IIAs' refers to bi- and multilateral investment agreements between States; it encompasses the more than 2500 bilateral investment treaties (BITs), free trade agreements with investment chapters as well as multilateral investment relevant treaties such as the North American Free Trade Agreement between the Government of Canada, the Government of the United Mexican States, and the Government of the United States of America (NAFTA), or the Energy Charter Treaty, Annex 1 to the Final Act of the European Energy Charter Treaty Conference.
[9] *de Sabla Claim (US v Panama)*, Award, 29 June 1933, 6 *UNRIAA* 358, 366.
[10] See, in particular, the Special Rapporteur's Fourth Report on State Responsibility, F.V. García Amador, 'Responsibility of the State for injuries caused in its territory to the person or property of aliens—measures affecting acquired rights', UN Doc. A/CN.4/119, *Yearbook of the International Law Commission* (1959-II). See also L.B. Sohn and R.R. Baxter, 'Responsibility of States for Injuries to the Economic Interests of Aliens', 55 *American Journal of International Law* (1961) 545; F.V. García Amador, L.B. Sohn, and R.R. Baxter, *Recent Codification of the Law of State Responsibility for Injuries to Aliens* (1974).
[11] García Amador, Fourth Report on State Responsibility, above n. 10, paras 42 *et seq.*

right to expropriate as an expression of the permanent sovereignty over natural resources. For instance, paragraph 4 of the well-known 1962 UNGA Resolution on Permanent Sovereignty over Natural Resources 1803 provided:

> Nationalization, expropriation or requisitioning shall be based on grounds or reasons of public utility, security or the national interest which are recognized as overriding purely individual or private interests, both domestic and foreign. In such cases the owner shall be paid appropriate compensation, in accordance with the rules in force in the State taking such measures in the exercise of its sovereignty and in accordance with international law.[12]

While this text was, of course, the result of intense negotiations and remained partly ambiguous,[13] it clearly expressed a consensus that expropriation had to be (1) in the public interest, and (2) accompanied by compensation. Subsequent UNGA resolutions attempting to establish a New International Economic Order,[14] of course, retracted from that position and merely affirmed the right to expropriate without any firm (international) obligation to compensate foreign owners or to respect the requirement of 'public utility' or the like. Thus, the 1973 UNGA Resolution on Permanent Sovereignty over Natural Resources 3171 affirmed

> [...] that the application of the principle of nationalization carried out by States, as an expression of their sovereignty in order to safeguard their natural resources, implies that each State is entitled to determine the amount of possible compensation and the mode of payment, and that any disputes which might arise should be settled in accordance with the national legislation of each State carrying out such measures.[15]

Similarly, Article 2(2) of the 1974 Charter of Economic Rights and Duties of States stated:

> Each State has the right [...] (c) To nationalize, expropriate or transfer ownership of foreign property, in which case appropriate compensation should be paid by the State adopting such measures, taking into account its relevant laws and regulations and all circumstances that the State considers pertinent. In any case where the question of compensation gives rise to a controversy, it shall be settled under the domestic law of the

---

[12] UNGA Res. 1803 (XVII), UN GAOR, 17th Session, Agenda Item 39 para. 4, UN Doc. A/RES/1803 (XVII) (1962).
[13] See, Lowenfeld, above n. 1, 407 *et seq*. See also N. Schrijver, *Sovereignty Over Natural Resources* (1997) 37 *et seq*.
[14] See G. Varges, *The New International Economic Order Legal Debate* (1983); Th. Oppermann and E.U. Petersmann (eds), *Reforming the International Economic Order* (1987); J. Bhagwati (ed.), *The New International Economic Order: The North-South Debate* (1977); R. Rothstein, *Global Bargaining: UNCTAD and the Quest for a New International Economic Order* (1979); C. Murphy, *Emergence of the NIEO Ideology* (1984); K. Sauvant and H. Hasenpflug (eds), *The New International Economic Order: Confrontation or Cooperation between North and South* (1977); R.-J. Dupuy (ed.), *Le nouvel ordre économique international: aspects commerciaux, technologiques et culturels* (1981).
[15] UNGA Res. 3171 (XXVIII), UN GAOR, 287th Session, para. 3, UN Doc. A/RES/3171 (XXVIII) (1973).

nationalizing State and by its tribunals, unless it is freely and mutually agreed by all States concerned that other peaceful means be sought on the basis of the sovereign equality of States and in accordance with the principle of free choice of means.[16]

The political controversy surrounding the adoption of the latter two resolutions is well known as is the doctrinal controversy about the legal relevance of these texts.[17] Suffice it to re-state the majority view which acknowledges that the resolutions may have cast doubt on the traditional expropriation standard, while they have not created new customary international law.

Nevertheless, the traditional legality requirements are still upheld by many commentators[18] and in a number of textbooks. For instance, the Restatement (Third) of the Foreign Relations Law of the United States provides as follows:

A state is responsible under international law for injury resulting from:
(1) a taking by the state of the property of a national of another state that
    (a) is not for a public purpose, or
    (b) is discriminatory, or
    (c) not accompanied by provisions for just compensation.[19]

More cautiously, UNCTAD has summarized the state of the law by saying that

[i]n customary international law, there is authority for a number of limitations or conditions that relate to:

the requirement of a public purpose for the taking;
the requirement that there should be no discrimination;
the requirement that the taking should be accompanied by payment of compensation; and,
the requirement of due process.[20]

In a 2004 UNCTAD publication, however, it is asserted more broadly that

[u]nder customary international law and typical international investment agreements, three principal requirements need to be satisfied before a taking can be considered to be lawful: it should be for a public purpose; it should not be discriminatory; and compensation should be paid.[21]

While it characterized the first two requirements as 'generally accepted', it noted that, though the third was also 'widely accepted in principle', there was no universal agreement relating to the manner of assessment of the compensation

---

[16] UNGA Res. 3281 (XXIX), UN GAOR, 29th Session, UN Doc. A/9631 (1974).
[17] See Lowenfeld, above n. 1, 410 *et seq.*; Rubins and Kinsella, above n. 1, 162 *et seq.*
[18] See C. Schreuer, 'The Concept of Expropriation under the ECT and other Investment Protection Treaties', in C. Ribeiro (ed.), *Investment Arbitration and the Energy Charter Treaty* (2006) 108, 109; A. Sheppard, 'The Distinction between Lawful and Unlawful Expropriation', in C. Ribeiro (ed.), *Investment Arbitration and the Energy Charter Treaty* (2006) 169. More cautiously Muchlinski, *Multinational Enterprises*, above n. 1, 598 *et seq.*
[19] American Law Institute (ed.), *Restatement (Third) of the Foreign Relations Law of the United States*, § 712 (1987).
[20] UNCTAD, above n. 1, 12.
[21] UNCTAD, *International Investment Agreements: Key Issues* (2004) 235.

due.[22] In a similar fashion, a critic of the traditional 'Western' approach to the law of expropriation like Sornarajah maintains that '[w]ithin the context of the rules on expropriation, the issue of whether full compensation represents international law had remained a contested proposition'.[23] He does acknowledge, however, that '[t]here is general agreement that a taking which lacks a public purpose and a discriminatory taking are illegal in international law'.[24]

Legality Requirements in International Investment Agreements

As opposed to the uncertain state of the customary international law on the conditions under which a State may lawfully expropriate the property of foreigners, treaty-based investment law contains fairly clear rules on the legality requirements for expropriation. These largely correspond to the traditional 'Western' views demanding a public purpose, non-discrimination as well as compensation often among the lines of the *Hull* formula demanding 'prompt, adequate and effective'[25] compensation.[26] Thus, numerous BITs and other IIAs[27] contain provisions that are based on the assumption that expropriations of the property of nationals of the other contracting party or parties are, in principle, permissible. This permissibility is regularly made conditional upon the requirement that such takings are made for a public purpose, non-discriminatory, and accompanied by compensation.[28] The precise level of compensation expressly demanded varies from treaty to treaty. Also a fourth requirement, that the taking is made in accordance with due process, is not always included and, if included, may vary.[29]

A straightforward and typical listing of the traditional legality requirements can be found in the 2004 US Model BIT which provides:

1. Neither Party may expropriate or nationalize a covered investment either directly or indirectly through measures equivalent to expropriation or nationalization ("expropriation"), except:

   (a) for a public purpose;
   (b) in a non-discriminatory manner;
   (c) on payment of prompt, adequate, and effective compensation; and
   (d) in accordance with due process of law and Article 5 [Minimum Standard of Treatment] (1) through (3).[30]

---

[22] Ibid.
[23] M. Sornarajah, *The International Law on Foreign Investment* (2nd edn, 2004) 149.
[24] Ibid., 395.
[25] On the so-called *Hull* formula see below text at n. 160.
[26] Cf. UNCTAD, *Bilateral Investment Treaties 1995–2006: Trends in Investment Rule-Making* (2007) 44.
[27] Eg Article 1110 NAFTA; Article 13 ECT.
[28] Cf. Muchlinski, *Multinational Enterprises*, above n. 1, 692; UNCTAD, above n. 1, 24.
[29] See below text at n. 139.
[30] Article 6(1) US Model BIT (2004).

Almost identical language is included in Article 13(1) of the 2004 Canadian Model BIT,[31] in Article 1110(1) NAFTA[32] and in Article 13(1) of the Energy Charter Treaty.[33]

Textual variations can be found in many BITs. For instance, the 1998 China/Poland BIT provides:

> Either Contracting Party may for security reasons or a public purpose, nationalize, expropriate or take similar measures (hereinafter referred to as 'expropriatory measures') against investments investors of the other Contracting Party in its territory. Such expropriatory measures shall be non-discriminatory and shall be taken under due process of national law and against compensation.[34]

The 1991 Czechoslovakia/Netherlands BIT provides:

> Neither Contracting Party shall take any measures depriving, directly or indirectly, investors of the other Contracting Party of their investments unless the following conditions are complied with:
> (a) the measures are taken in the public interest and under due process of law;
> (b) the measures are not discriminatory;
> (c) the measures are accompanied by provision for the payment of just compensation.[35]

Even BITs, where the express language differs markedly from the straightforward listing of the traditional legality requirements, often provide the same standard in substance. Good examples of this are the German BITs. Their expropriation provisions are still strongly influenced by the wording of the first modern BIT, the Germany/Pakistan BIT (1959), which provided:

> Nationals or companies of either party shall not be subjected to expropriation of their investments in the territory of the other party except for public benefit and against compensation, which shall represent the equivalent of the investments affected.[36]

---

[31] Article 13(1) Canadian Model BIT (2004).
[32] Article 1110(1) NAFTA provides: 'No party shall directly or indirectly nationalize or expropriate an investment of an investor of another Party in its territory or take a measure tantamount to nationalization or expropriation of such an investment ("expropriation"), except: for a public purpose; on a non-discriminatory basis; in accordance with due process of law and Article 1105; and on payment of compensation in accordance with paragraphs 2 through 6.'
Article 1105(1) NAFTA requires treatment 'in accordance with international law, including fair and equitable treatment and full protection and security'.
[33] Article 13(1) ECT provides: 'Investments of Investors of a Contracting Party in the Area of any other Contracting Party shall not be nationalized, expropriated or subjected to a measure or measures having effect equivalent to nationalization or expropriation (hereinafter referred to as "Expropriation") except where such Expropriation is: (a) for a purpose which is in the public interest; (b) not discriminatory; (c) carried out under due process of law; and (d) accompanied by the payment of prompt, adequate and effective compensation.'
[34] Article 4(1) China/Poland BIT (1998).
[35] Article 5 Czechoslovakia/Netherlands BIT (1991).
[36] Article 3(2) Germany/Pakistan BIT (1959).

178　　　　　　　　　Legality of Expropriations

The current 2004 German Model BIT provides:

> Investments by investors of either Contracting State shall not directly or indirectly be expropriated, nationalized or subjected to any other measure the effects of which would be tantamount to expropriation or nationalization in the territory of the other Contracting State except for the public benefit and against compensation.[37]

While this language does not list due process and non-discrimination in the usual way, these requirements are included in the German Model BIT by the express provisions that '[t]he legality of any such expropriation, nationalization or comparable measure and the amount of compensation shall be subject to review by due process of law'[38] and that '[i]nvestors of either Contracting State shall enjoy most-favoured-nation treatment in the territory of the other Contracting State in respect of the matters provided for in this Article'.[39]

B. The Interpretation Given to the Legality Requirements in the Practice of Investment Arbitration

Public Purpose

The need of a public purpose or public interest in order to legitimate an expropriation has long been considered part of customary international law.[40] The public purpose requirement was also reaffirmed in Article 4 of the 1962 General Assembly Resolution No. 1803 on Permanent Sovereignty over Natural Resources which referred to 'grounds or reasons of public utility, security or the national interest which are recognized as overriding purely individual or private interests'.[41] In the 1974 Charter of Economic Rights and Duties of States,[42] however, the public purpose criterion no longer appears.

Today the requirement of a 'public purpose' or 'public interest' for an expropriation to be considered lawful can be found in almost all IIAs.[43] Many BITs and other treaties require that measures must be taken in the 'public interest'[44] or for a 'public purpose'[45] or 'public benefit'[46] sometimes for a 'public

---

[37] Article 4(2) German Model BIT (2004).
[38] Article 4(2) last sentence German Model BIT (2004).
[39] Article 4(4) German Model BIT (2004).
[40] P. Malanczuk, *Akehurst's Modern Introduction to International Law* (7th edn, 1997) 235; Garcia Amador, Fourth Report on State Responsibility, above n. 10, para. 58; K. Hobér, *Investment Arbitration in Eastern Europe: In Search of a Definition of Expropriation* (2007) 38.
[41] UNGA Resolution 1803 (XVII), above n. 12.
[42] UNGA Resolution 3281 (XXIX), above n. 16.
[43] Cf. UNCTAD, above n. 1, 24 *et seq*.
[44] Article 5 Czechoslovakia/Netherlands BIT (1991).
[45] Eg Article 6(1)(a) US Model BIT (2004); Article 13(1) Canadian Model BIT (2004).
[46] Article XI Netherlands/Sudan BIT (1970); Article 4(2) German Model BIT (2004).

B. *The Interpretation Given to the Legality Requirements*   179

purpose related to the internal needs'[47] or that the measure must be for 'a purpose which is in the public interest'.[48] Writers largely concur on the need for this legality requirement; though they usually do not seem to regard it as a very high hurdle for States. Thus, legal commentators have stressed that 'the requirement of public purpose for a taking to be lawful is not much of a limitation in modern times'[49] and that '[. . .] it is very easy for an expropriating state to couch any taking in terms of some "public purpose" '.[50] Indeed, investment tribunals in general have been rather reluctant to second-guess the sovereign determination of a public purpose '[. . .] perhaps because the concept of public purpose is broad and not subject to effective re-examination by other states'.[51] Nevertheless, as recent cases have proven, the test is not wholly irrelevant and may be used by tribunals not only in cases of blatant misuse, such as expropriations for the private gain of a ruling elite[52] or expropriations carried out in the context of the commission of serious human rights violations, crimes against humanity, or genocide.[53]

The case law has been rather consistent in acknowledging the existence of a 'public purpose' requirement. Thus, most arbitral and judicial pronouncements addressing the legality requirements for expropriations reaffirm the public purpose requirement—though some of them may have given rise to conflicting interpretation. A good example is the well-known statement by the arbitrator in the *Shufeldt Claim* that '[. . .] it [was] perfectly competent for the Government of Guatemala to enact any decree they like and for any reasons they see fit, and such reasons are no concern of this tribunal'.[54] Some critics take this as evidence of an arbitral award which 'questioned the need for the requirement of public purpose,'[55] while one may also rely on this statement as an affirmation of the public purpose principle which merely indicates that tribunals would be reluctant to question the expropriating State's assessment of a public purpose.

In the 1921 *Norwegian Shipowners' Claims* case,[56] the arbitral tribunal examined whether the taking of foreign property was 'justified by public needs'.[57] Though it expressly tested the legality of the United States taking of contractual rights of Norwegian citizens on the basis of US law, ie the takings clause

---

[47] UK/Costa Rica BIT (1982); Article 5(1) France/Hong Kong BIT (1995).
[48] Article 13(1)(a) ECT.
[49] Sornarajah, above n. 23, 395.
[50] Rubins and Kinsella, above n. 1, 177. See also Muchlinski, *Multinational Enterprises*, above n. 1, 599.
[51] *Restatement (Third) of the Foreign Relations Law of the United States*, above n. 19, Comment (e).
[52] Cf. the Restatement's suggestion that 'a seizure by a dictator or oligarchy for private use could be challenged under this rule'. *Restatement (Third) of the Foreign Relations Law of the United States*, above n. 19, Comment (e).
[53] Muchlinski, *Multinational Enterprises*, above n. 1, 600.
[54] *Shufeldt Claim (US v Guatemala)*, Award, 24 July 1930, 2 *UNRIAA* 1079, 1095.
[55] Sornarajah, above n. 23, 396.
[56] *Norwegian Shipowners' Claims (Norway v US)*, Award, 30 June 1921, 1 *UNRIAA* 307, 332.
[57] Ibid.

enshrined in the Constitution's Fifth Amendment, it emphasized that the public law of the parties was '[...] in complete accord with the international public law of all civilised countries'.[58] Thus, the tribunal's reference to the 'power of a sovereign state to expropriate, take or authorize the taking of any property within its jurisdiction which may be required for the "public good" or for the "general welfare" '[59] may be regarded as a requirement of US constitutional law as well as of international law.

Also, in the *German Interests in Polish Upper Silesia* case[60] before the Permanent Court of International Justice (PCIJ) public purpose was referred to as an expropriation requirement. In this case, the PCIJ primarily addressed the right of Poland to expropriate German property pursuant to the Geneva Convention Concerning Upper Silesia[61] which it characterized as a '[...] derogation from the rules generally applied in regard to the treatment of foreigners and the principle of respect for vested rights'.[62] In passing, the Permanent Court also referred to 'generally accepted international law' and found that 'expropriation for reasons of public utility, judicial liquidation and similar measures' were not prohibited by the Geneva Convention.[63] One may thus conclude that 'public utility' was regarded by the PCIJ to constitute one of the legality requirements for an expropriation.

One of the rare exceptions from the older case law where a tribunal not only examined but actually rejected the assertion that an expropriation served a public purpose is the *Walter Fletcher Smith Claim* case[64] in which the arbitrator found '[...] that the expropriation proceedings were not, in good faith, for the purpose of public utility'.[65] In the arbitrator's view, the violent taking of a piece of land belonging to a US national in order to serve for the enlargement of an urbanization project did not conform to the public purpose test. He held that

[...] the properties seized were turned over immediately to the defendant company, ostensibly for public purposes, but, in fact, to be used by the defendant for purposes of amusement and private profit, without any reference to public utility.[66]

---

[58] Ibid.
[59] Ibid.
[60] *Case concerning certain German Interests in Polish Upper Silesia (Germany v Poland)*, Judgment, 25 May 1926.
[61] Article 6 provided: 'Poland may expropriate in Polish Upper Silesia, in conformity with the provisions of Articles 7 to 23, undertakings belonging to the category of major industries including mineral deposits and rural estates. Except as provided in these clauses, the property, rights and interests of German nationals may not be liquidated in Polish Upper Silesia.' 1922 Geneva Convention concerning Upper Silesia, Martens, XVI *Nouveau Recueil Général de traités* No. 80, 645; English version of Article 6 cited in *Case concerning certain German Interests in Polish Upper Silesia*, above n. 60, at 21.
[62] Ibid., 22.
[63] Ibid.
[64] *Walter Fletcher Smith Claim (US v Cuba)*, Award, 2 May 1929.
[65] 2 *UNRIAA* 913, 915.
[66] Ibid., 917 *et seq.*

B. The Interpretation Given to the Legality Requirements

It should be noted that the award in this case was based on Cuban law and that the arbitrator did not make any explicit statements on international law concerning expropriation. Nevertheless, the ruling seems to reflect the prevailing view on international law as well.

In the 1970s, arbitral tribunals in the *Libyan Oil Concessions* arbitrations have expressed different views with regard to the freedom of host States to determine the public purpose of their measures. At one end of the spectrum, the arbitrator in the *LIAMCO* case expressed the view that States were almost totally free to decide on the public purpose of takings by stating that '[m]otives are indifferent to international law, each State being free to judge for itself what it considers useful or necessary for the public good'.[67] He even concluded that '[...] the public utility principle is not a necessary requisite for the legality of a nationalization'.[68] Nevertheless, the arbitrator found that the language of the nationalization law '[...] was drafted in a general non-discriminatory language, which clearly indicated that Libya's motive for nationalization was its desire to preserve the ownership of its oil'.[69] Though he stressed the non-discrimination obligation[70] to the point of declaring the public purpose requirement irrelevant, this language would clearly also satisfy a public purpose test.

In another *Libyan Oil Concessions* case, in *British Petroleum v Libya*, the *ad hoc* arbitrator explicitly assessed the public purpose requirement and found that the expropriation was unlawful because it was politically motivated as an act of retaliation for a British foreign policy decision. In the words of the tribunal, the measures had been adopted '[...] for purely extraneous political reasons and [...] arbitrary and discriminatory in character'.[71]

More recent cases also reaffirm the relevance of the 'public purpose' test. In the jurisprudence of the Iran-US Claims Tribunal the 'public purpose' requirement figures quite prominently. For instance, in *American International Group*, the tribunal held that a nationalization was not unlawful because there was '[...] not sufficient evidence before the tribunal to show that the nationalization was not carried out for a public purpose'.[72] In the *INA Corp* case, the Iran-US Claims Tribunal even more broadly asserted that '[...] it has long been acknowledged that expropriations for a public purpose [...] are not per se unlawful'.[73] In the *Amoco* case, the same tribunal stated:

A precise definition of the 'public purpose' for which an expropriation may be lawfully decided has neither been agreed upon in international law nor even suggested. It is clear

---

[67] *Libyan American Oil Company (Liamco) v Libya*, 12 April 1977, 62 *ILR* 140, 194.
[68] Ibid.   [69] Ibid., 195.
[70] See below text at n. 119.
[71] *British Petroleum v Libya*, Award, 10 October 1973 and 1 August 1974, 53 *ILR* 297, 329.
[72] *American International Group Inc, et al. v Islamic Republic of Iran, et al*, Award No. 93-2-3, 19 December 1983, 4 *Iran-US CTR* (1983) 96, 105.
[73] *INA Corp v Government of the Islamic Republic of Iran*, Award No. 184-161-1, 13 August 1985, 8 *Iran-US CTR* (1985) 373, 378.

that, as a result of the modern acceptance of the right to nationalize, this term is broadly interpreted, and the States, in practice, are granted extensive discretion. An expropriation, the only purpose of which would have been to avoid contractual obligations of the State or of an entity controlled by it, could not, nevertheless be considered as lawful under international law.[74]

In the specific case, however, the tribunal had no difficulty to find that the expropriatory '[...] act was adopted for a clear public purpose, namely to complete the nationalization of the oil industry in Iran'.[75]

Also the European Court of Human Rights affirmed that, as a general principle, it would not question a State's view that a taking was in the public interest.[76] The concept of a broad discretion of States to determine for themselves what is in their 'public interest' corresponds to the Court's doctrine of a 'margin of appreciation' left to Member States.[77] However, there are also cases where the Strasbourg Court has stated the absence of a 'public interest' demanded by Article 1 of the First Additional Protocol.[78]

Also, ICSID tribunals have generally endorsed the 'public purpose' requirement. For instance, the tribunal in the *AMCO v Indonesia* case considered that, as a matter of general international law,

[...] the right to nationalize supposes that the act by which the State purports to have exercised it, is a true nationalization, namely a taking of property or contractual rights which aims to protect or to promote the public interest.[79]

Similarly, the tribunal in the *Santa Elena* case clearly stated that '[i]nternational law permits the Government of Costa Rica to expropriate foreign-owned property within its territory for a public purpose [...]'.[80]

Also in the so-called *Pyramids* case, an ICSID tribunal endorsed the public purpose requirement, finding that 'as a matter of international law, the Respondent was entitled to cancel a tourist development project situated on its own territory for the purpose of protecting antiquities'.[81] Thus, the cancellation of a contract to build hotels in the vicinity of the ancient pyramids of Gizeh

---

[74] *Amoco International Finance Corp v Iran*, 15 *Iran-US CTR* (1987) 189, 233, para. 145.
[75] Ibid., para. 146.
[76] See *James v United Kingdom*, 8 *EHRR* 123 (1986).
[77] See H.C. Yourow, *The Margin of Appreciation Doctrine in the Dynamics of the European Court of Human Rights Jurisprudence* (1996); E. Benvenisti, 'Margin of Appreciation, Consensus and Universal Standards', 31 *NYU Journal of International Law and Policy* (1999), 843.
[78] See *Brumărescu v Romania*, Appl. No. 28342/95, ECtHR, 28 October 1999, [1999] ECHR 105, para. 79, where the ECtHR held that neither the 'Supreme Court of Justice itself nor the Government have sought to justify the deprivation of property on substantive grounds as being "in the public interest".'
[79] *Amco Asia Corporation v Republic of Indonesia*, ICSID Case No. ARB/81/1, Award, 20 November 1984, 1 *ICSID Reports* 413, 466.
[80] *Compañía del Desarrollo de Santa Elena, S.A. v Republic of Costa Rica*, ICSID Case No. ARB/96/1, Award, 17 February 2000, para. 71.
[81] *Southern Pacific Properties (Middle East) Limited v Arab Republic of Egypt*, ICSID Case No. ARB/84/3, Award, 20 May 1992, para. 158.

B. The Interpretation Given to the Legality Requirements

was considered a 'lawful exercise of the right of eminent domain' because it was '[...] exercised for a public purpose, namely, the preservation and protection of antiquities in the area'.[82]

At the same time, ICSID tribunals have generally shared the reluctance of other international courts and tribunals to question the determination of host States of what they considered to be in their public interest. The tribunal in the *Goetz* case very aptly summarized this approach by stating that

> [...] [i]n the absence of an error of fact or law, of an abuse of power or of a clear misunderstanding of the issue, it is not the Tribunal's role to substitute its own judgement for the discretion of the government of Burundi of what are 'imperatives of public need [...] or of national interest'.[83]

Also in the NAFTA case of *Feldman v Mexico*, an ICSID Additional Facility tribunal referred to the public purpose requirement as one of the 'conditions (other than the requirement for compensation)' as being 'not of major importance'.[84] The tribunal used the public purpose as well as the due process requirements as elements in order to determine whether an expropriation had taken place at all—foreshadowing the *Methanex* and *Saluka* doctrine.[85] Its considerations on public purpose are still relevant because they confirm the willingness, albeit reluctant, to scrutinize a State's decision on measures in the public interest. The tribunal considered that the change in Mexico's tax refund system was a measure for which there were '[...] rational public purposes'.[86]

In spite of the general deference of investment tribunals to governmental policy choices, ICSID as well as Iran-US Claims Tribunal awards have sometimes come to the conclusion that expropriatory acts had been unlawful because they did not serve a public purpose.

For instance, in the *LETCO* case,[87] an ICSID tribunal found that the revocation of a concession '[...] was not for a *bona fide* public purpose, was discriminatory and was not accompanied by an offer of appropriate compensation'.[88] The case concerned the unilateral abrogation of a concession for the exploitation of timber reserves in Liberia. With regard to the public policy requirement, the tribunal stated that

> [t]here was no legislative enactment by the Government of Liberia. There was no evidence of any stated policy on the part of the Liberian Government to take concessions of this kind into public ownership for the public good. On the contrary, evidence was given to

---

[82] Ibid.
[83] *Goetz and Others v Republic of Burundi*, ICSID Case No. ARB/95/3, Decision on Liability, 2 September 1998, para. 126.
[84] *Marvin Feldman v Mexico*, ICSID Case No. ARB(AF)/99/1, 16 December 2002, para. 99.
[85] See A. Hoffmann, 'Indirect Expropriation' at Chapter 8 above.
[86] *Feldman v Mexico*, above n. 84, para. 136.
[87] *Liberian Eastern Timber Corporation (LETCO) v Republic of Liberia*, ICSID Case No. ARB/83/2, Award, 31 March 1986.
[88] *LETCO v Liberia*, above n. 87, 2 *ICSID Reports* 343, 367.

the Tribunal that areas of the concession taken away from LETCO were granted to other foreign-owned companies [...].[89]

Most recently, the legality of an expropriation was a central issue in the ICSID case of *ADC v Hungary*.[90] The case concerned a contract to renovate, to build and to operate terminals at the Budapest Airport entered into in 1995 between ADC and ADCM, two Cypriot companies, and ATAA, a Hungarian State entity responsible for the operation of the airport, after a lengthy tender procedure. In 2001, the Hungarian government transformed the ATAA into two successor entities, one responsible for air traffic control, the other for the operation of the airport. In a letter to the investors it informed them that the restructuring of the airport operations also required the termination of the agreements with claimants as of 1 January 2002 because the applicable governmental decree prohibited the cession or transfer of any airport operations to third parties. As a result of these acts the investor had to leave the airport premises and no longer received any revenues as originally agreed upon.

In 2005, the Hungarian government privatized the airport operations entity through a sale of a 75 per cent majority interest which was awarded to BAA, a British Airways-affiliated airport operator, after a tendering process.

The tribunal found that the government decree and the subsequent take-over of all activities of the investor at the airport by the Hungarian airport operations entity constituted an expropriation of the claimants' investments. Then, the arbitral tribunal addressed at length the question of the legality of the taking and came to the conclusion that the expropriation

[...] was unlawful as: (a) the taking was not in the public interest; (b) it did not comply with due process [...]; (c) the taking was discriminatory and (d) the taking was not accompanied by the payment of just compensation to the expropriated parties.[91]

The traditional legality requirements were assessed on the basis of the applicable Cyprus/Hungary BIT which provided as follows:

Neither Contracting Party shall take any measures depriving, directly or indirectly, investors of the other Contracting Party of their investments unless the following conditions are complied with:

(a) The measures are taken in the public interest and under due process of law;
(b) The measures are not discriminatory;
(c) The measures are accompanied by provision for the payment of just compensation.[92]

With regard to the public purpose requirement, the *ADC* tribunal found that

[...] a treaty requirement for '*public interest*' requires some genuine interest of the public. If mere reference to '*public interest*' can magically put such interest into existence

---

[89] Ibid., 366.   [90] *ADC v Hungary*, above n. 7.
[91] Ibid, para. 476.
[92] Article 4(1) Cyprus/Hungary BIT (1989).

B. The Interpretation Given to the Legality Requirements

and therefore satisfy this requirement, then this requirement would be rendered meaningless since the Tribunal can imagine no situation where this requirement would not have been met.[93]

Thus, the *ADC* tribunal clearly rejected the view, espoused by some arbitral awards, that States are basically free to determine whatever they wish to consider as public purpose or interest. Instead, it demanded a 'genuine interest of the public' and *de facto* reversed the burden of proof by requiring the expropriating State to demonstrate such genuine public interest. With regard to the Hungarian argument that its action was necessary for the harmonization of the Hungarian government's transport strategy, laws and regulations with EU law, the tribunal laconically remarked that Hungary '[…] failed to substantiate such a claim with convincing facts or legal reasoning'.[94] Similarly, the tribunal concluded that with regard to the claimed '[…] *strategic interest of the State* […] Respondent never furnished it with a substantive answer'.[95] As a result, '[w]ith the claimed "*public interest*" unproved and the tribunal's curiosity thereon unsatisfied', the tribunal rejected the arguments made by the Respondent.[96]

However, these final remarks on the unmet burden of proof by an expropriating State should not be overestimated since, in the particular case, it was the specific circumstances of the taking leading to a subsequent privatization which made the lack of a genuine public interest particularly obvious.[97]

Also, the recent award in *Siemens v Argentina*[98] demonstrates that ICSID tribunals are willing to examine the legality of expropriations. The tribunal found that the fulfilment of the public interest requirement contained in the applicable Argentina/Germany BIT[99] was questionable. In its view, the abrogation of the contract

[…] was an exercise of public authority to reduce the costs to Argentina of the Contract recently awarded through public competitive bidding, and as part of a change of policy by a new Administration eager to distance itself from its predecessor.[100]

It was this aspect of the facts that overshadowed the otherwise legitimate public interest of the respondent State to take measures against the fiscal crisis.[101]

---

[93] *ADC v Hungary*, above n. 7, para. 432.
[94] Ibid., para. 430.
[95] Ibid., para. 431.
[96] Ibid., para. 433.
[97] Cf. the tribunal's remarks that 'the subsequent privatization and the agreement with BAA render[ed] this whole debate somewhat unnecessary'. *ADC v Hungary*, above n. 7, para. 433.
[98] *Siemens A.G. v Argentina*, above n. 2.
[99] Article 4(2) Argentina/Germany BIT (1991).
[100] *Siemens A.G. v Argentina*, above n. 2, para. 273.
[101] The tribunal found that the response of the 2000 Emergency Law to the fiscal crisis was 'a legitimate concern of Argentina and the Tribunal defers to Argentina in the determination of its public interest'. Ibid.

However, the tribunal concluded that specific application of the emergency measures through

> Decree 669/01 became a convenient device to continue the process started more than a year earlier long before the onset of the fiscal crisis. From this perspective, while the public purpose of the 2000 Emergency Law is evident, its application through Decree 669/01 to the specific case of Siemens' investment and the public purpose of same are questionable.[102]

The tribunal did not make any final determination on the public purpose requirement since it held that the lack of any compensation had rendered the expropriation unlawful 'in any case'.[103]

On the basis of the existing case law there can be no doubt that 'public purpose' must be considered a legality requirement both under investment treaty and unwritten international law standards. The practice of international courts and tribunals also demonstrates that—in spite of a broad deference to expropriating States—they are willing to assess whether such public purpose has been genuinely pursued.

Non-discrimination

The non-discrimination requirement is a standard element both in customary international law and in most treaty provisions addressing the legality of expropriations.[104] The precise content of this non-discrimination requirement, however, remains unclear. It is said that a '[...] discriminatory taking is one that singles out a particular person or group of people without a reasonable basis'.[105] Thus, an expropriation or programme of expropriations '[...] that singles out aliens generally, or aliens of a particular nationality, or particular aliens, would violate international law'.[106] Since 'discrimination' is regarded as 'unreasonable distinction', expropriations of certain persons may not be unlawful if such distinction is '[...] rationally related to the state's security or economic policies might not be unreasonable'.[107] Sometimes, it is even asserted that 'the non-discrimination requirement demands that governmental measures, procedures and practices be non-discriminatory even in the treatment of members of the same group of aliens'.[108]

Racially motivated expropriations are usually regarded as evident examples of illegal takings.[109] Thus, the Aryanization policy of Nazi Germany involving

---

[102] Ibid.   [103] Ibid.
[104] A.F.M. Maniruzzaman, 'Expropriation of Alien Property and the Principle of Non-Discrimination in International Law of Foreign Investment: An Overview', 8 *Journal of Transnational Law and Policy* (1998) 57.
[105] Rubins and Kinsella, above n. 1, 177.
[106] *Restatement (Third) of the Foreign Relations Law of the United States*, above n. 19, Comment (f).
[107] Ibid.
[108] UNCTAD, above n. 1, 13.
[109] Ibid.; Sornarajah, above n. 23, 399.

B. The Interpretation Given to the Legality Requirements

the systematic taking of Jewish property is regarded as discriminatory expropriation,[110] as is the taking of property belonging to ethnic Indians by the Idi Amin regime in Uganda. These extreme forms of discrimination are usually also regarded as lacking a legitimate public purpose.[111]

In practice, it was often the singling out of particular nationals, often as a result of political retaliation, which was considered to constitute a discriminatory taking. For instance, US courts considered the initial wave of expropriations after the Cuban revolution which was exclusively directed against US nationals to be unlawful under international law.[112]

Many BITs and IIAs provide that expropriations or expropriatory measures must be 'not discriminatory', 'non-discriminatory',[113] taken 'on a non-discriminatory basis',[114] 'in a non-discriminatory manner',[115] or use comparable language. Multilateral IIAs also make non-discrimination a requirement for the expropriation of foreign investors.[116]

The case law of international tribunals has equally affirmed the existence of a non-discrimination requirement for expropriations in general.

In some of the *Libyan Oil Concession* cases, a discriminatory character of the expropriatory acts was found. For instance, in *British Petroleum v Libya*, the sole arbitrator regarded the expropriation as unlawful because it was politically motivated. He found that

[...] the taking of the property by the Respondent of the property [...] clearly violates public international law as it was made for purely extraneous political reasons and was arbitrary and discriminatory in character.[117]

Also, the arbitrator in the *LIAMCO* case[118] reaffirmed the principle that a discriminatory expropriation would be unlawful as such.[119] He held that it was

[...] clear and undisputed that non-discrimination is a requisite for the validity of a lawful nationalization. This is a rule well-established in international legal theory and practice [...]. Therefore, a purely discriminatory nationalization is illegal and wrongful.[120]

---

[110] *Oppenheimer v Inland Revenue Commissioner* [1975] 1 All ER 538.
[111] See above text at n. 53.
[112] *Banco Nacional de Cuba v Sabbatino*, 307 F.2d 845, at 868 (1962), 'Since the Cuban decree of expropriation not only failed to provide adequate compensation but also involved a retaliatory purpose and a discrimination against United States nationals, we hold that the decree was in violation of international law', reversed on Act of State grounds 376 US 398 (1964); *Banco Nacional de Cuba v Farr*, 243 F.Supp. 957 (SDNY 1965), affirmed, 383 F.2d 166 (2d Cir. 1967), cert. denied 390 US 956 (1968). See also *Restatement (Third) of the Foreign Relations Law of the United States*, above n. 19, Reporters' Note 5.
[113] Article 4(1) China/Poland BIT (1998).
[114] Article 5(1) France/Hong Kong BIT (1995).
[115] Article 6(1) US Model BIT (2004); Article 13(1) Canadian Model BIT (2004).
[116] UNCTAD, above n. 1, 13.
[117] *British Petroleum v Libya*, Award, 10 October 1973 and 1 August 1974, 53 *ILR* 297, 329.
[118] *Libyan American Oil Company (Liamco) v Libya*, above n. 5.
[119] Ibid., 62 *ILR* 140, 194.
[120] Ibid.

He concluded, however, that there was no actual discrimination involved. According to the arbitrator's findings

[...] LIAMCO was not the first company to be nationalized, nor was it the only oil company nor the only American company to be nationalized [...]. Other companies were nationalized before it, other American and non-American companies were nationalized with it and after it, and other American companies are still operating in Libya. Thus, it may be concluded from the above that the political motive was not the predominant motive for nationalization, and that such motive *per se* does not constitute a sufficient proof of a purely discriminatory measure.[121]

On the other hand, even the fact that one foreign investor is expropriated while another one is not does not necessarily imply a discriminatory taking if there were 'adequate reasons' for distinguishing. Thus, the tribunal in the *Aminoil* case[122] did not find an unlawful discrimination although the US claimant had been expropriated while a non-US oil company (Arabian Oil) was not. According to the tribunal, the

[...] nationalisation of Aminoil was not thereby tainted with discrimination [...]. First of all, it has never for a single moment been suggested that it was because of the American nationality of the Company that the Decree Law was applied to Aminoil's Concession. Next, and above all, there were adequate reasons for not nationalising Arabian Oil.[123]

This reasoning was also adopted by the Iran-US Claims Tribunal in the *Amoco* case. The tribunal said that

[it] finds it difficult, in the absence of any other evidence, to draw the conclusion that the expropriation of a concern was discriminatory only from the fact that another concern in the same economic branch was not expropriated. Reasons specific to the non-expropriated enterprise, or to the expropriated one, or to both, may justify such a difference in treatment.[124]

On a more general level, however, the tribunal clearly reaffirmed that '[d]iscrimination is widely held as prohibited by customary international law in the field of expropriation'.[125]

A discriminatory expropriation was found in *Eureko* where an UNCITRAL tribunal concluded that the challenged Polish measures were aimed at excluding foreign investors from the Polish insurance business and thus discriminatory. It therefore found a violation of the expropriation provision of the applicable BIT. According to the tribunal, the challenged measures, ie the refusal to conduct a public offering, 'proclaimed by successive Ministers of the State Treasury as being pursued in order to keep [an insurance business] under majority Polish control

---

[121] Ibid., 195.
[122] *Kuwait v American Independent Oil Company (Aminoil)*, Award, 24 March 1982.
[123] Ibid., para. 87.
[124] *Amoco International Finance Corp v Iran*, above n. 74, para. 142.
[125] Ibid., para. 140.

B. *The Interpretation Given to the Legality Requirements* 189

and to exclude foreign control such as Eureko' were 'clearly discriminatory'.[126] What is interesting in this case is the fact that the discrimination was not one between different groups of foreigners but rather one between foreigners and nationals of the host State.

ICSID cases equally confirmed the relevance of the non-discrimination requirement. In *LETCO* the tribunal stressed that '[...] even if the Government had sought to justify its action as an act of nationalization, it would have had to [...] show that its action [...] was non-discriminatory'.[127] Since the tribunal found evidence that '[...] areas of the concession taken away from LETCO were granted to other foreign-owned companies [...] run by people who were "good friends" of the Liberian authorities'[128] it concluded, inter alia, that 'the taking of LETCO's property was [...] discriminatory'.[129]

Also in the recent ICSID case of *ADC v Hungary*, actions taken by the host State against the investor were considered discriminatory.[130] The tribunal found '[...] that in order for a discrimination to exist, particularly in an expropriation scenario, there must be different treatments to different parties'.[131] The investor had argued that the regulatory framework prohibiting the operation of the airport by any third party other than the Hungarian airport operator entity was specifically aimed at it since it was the only operator of the airport. Hungary had argued that the new framework applied to all persons and business entities other than the statutorily appointed operator and was thus not discriminatory.

The tribunal expressly rejected '[...] the Respondent's argument that as the only foreign parties involved in the operation of the Airport, the Claimants [were] not in a position to raise any claims of being treated discriminately'.[132] In a rather short and almost cryptic reasoning the tribunal held that 'the comparison of different treatments is made here between that received by the Respondent-appointed operator and that received by foreign investors as a whole'[133] in order to add that it '[...] therefore reject[ed] the contentions made by the Respondent and conclud[ed] that the actions taken by the Respondent against the Claimants [were] discriminatory'.[134]

Apparently, the *ADC* tribunal was not impressed by the argument that since the foreign investor was the only foreign airport operator affected by a measure which affects all airport operators, whether foreign or domestic, could not be discriminatory. Rather, it compared the treatment 'received by foreign investors as a whole', which probably means by foreign investors in general, with that received by the investor in the specific case. Since the regulatory measure was very

---

[126] *Eureko B.V. v Republic of Poland*, above n. 2, para. 242.
[127] *LETCO v Liberia*, above n. 87, 2 *ICSID Reports* 343, 366.
[128] Ibid., at 366.
[129] Ibid., at 367.
[130] *ADC v Hungary*, above n. 7, para. 443.
[131] Ibid., para. 442.   [132] Ibid., para. 441.
[133] Ibid., para. 442.   [134] Ibid., para. 443.

specific—a general prohibition of airport operations by parties other than certain State entities—it could affect only a very limited number of investors, in the *ADC* case, apparently only the claimant. Thus, it is correct that the Hungarian measures did in fact single out the investment of the claimant.

However, it remains questionable whether this in itself is sufficient to constitute an illegal discriminatory taking. Any expropriation—short of a general nationalization—will target specific groups of property owners or investors, whether airport operators, oil exploring companies, or highway construction entities. The fact that there may be only one affected entity, and that this one entity may be a foreign investor, is usually not enough to constitute a discriminatory taking which singles out particular persons without a reasonable basis.[135] The fact that only foreigners are affected by an expropriatory measure as such may be incidental.[136] Illegal discrimination usually requires the targeting of foreign investors as a result of unreasonable policies or motives such as racism or political retaliation against nationals of certain States. There is no indication in the *ADC* case that the Hungarian government expropriated the foreign airport operator because of its Cypriot nationality—as opposed to any other nationality—nor even that the foreign ownership of the investor was a decisive ground for the expropriation. Whether justified by a public purpose or not, the intention of Hungary obviously was to bring the airport operation again under State control. In that sense one may recognize a similarity to the *Eureko* case.[137] However, the fact that airport operations were subsequently handed over to a privatized company majority-owned by foreigners demonstrates that foreign versus domestic ownership apparently did not play a major role in this context. Rather, the subsequent privatization may indicate that the expropriation was motivated by the expectation of higher profits than under the arrangements with ADC.

In general, the practice of international investment tribunals strongly endorses the non-discrimination requirement as a condition for the legality of an expropriation both under customary international law as well as under the specifically applicable IIA provisions. While tribunals tend to qualify politically motivated or other egregious forms of discrimination as unlawful, they do apply a more nuanced approach to expropriations which affect only some foreigners if such discrimination may be the result of legitimate government policies. A major factor for the assessment of discrimination issues in the course of expropriations is the burden of proof required by tribunals. While most tribunals require the complaining investors to demonstrate that they have been discriminated against, some appear to shift the burden of proof to the expropriating State. In addition, there is case law demonstrating that not only discrimination among foreign investors but also between foreigners and nationals of the expropriating State

---

[135] Rubins and Kinsella, above n. 1, 177.
[136] Cf. I. Brownlie, *Principles of Public International Law* (6th edn, 2003) 515.
[137] See above text at n. 126.

Due Process

The requirement that an expropriation must be made under 'due process of law' is often referred to as a typical legality requirement for an expropriation. Whether it can be seen as a customary international law requirement remains, however, less certain.[138]

In treaty-based investment law, 'due process' is often provided for in BITs and other IIAs. The requirement that any expropriation must be made or accomplished 'under due process of law' or 'in accordance with due process of law'[139] is a provision that can be found in many but not in all investment treaties. However, while many IIAs list 'due process' as one of the legality requirements, they usually do not define its meaning. The due process prerequisite is usually understood as a requirement to provide for a possibility to have the expropriation and, in particular, the determination of the amount of compensation reviewed before an independent body.[140] In some BITs, the due process provision seems to require primarily that the expropriation is accomplished pursuant to domestic law.[141]

While due process is usually just mentioned as a legality requirement, some BITs contain explanatory language with regard to the due process requirement as a possibility to have the expropriation and, in particular, the determination of the amount of compensation reviewed. For instance, the 1991 UK Model BIT provides that

[t]he national or company affected shall have a right, under the law of the Contracting Party making the expropriation, to prompt review, by a judicial or other independent authority of that Party, of his or its case and of the valuation of his or its investment in accordance with the principles set out in this paragraph.[142]

Some Austrian BITs are even more explicit in providing that

[d]ue process of law includes the right of an investor of a Contracting Party which claims to be affected by expropriation by the other Contracting Party to prompt review of its case, including the valuation of its investment and the payment of compensation in accordance with the provisions of this Article by a judicial authority or another competent and independent authority of the latter Contracting Party.[143]

---

[138] It is not included in *Restatement (Third) of the Foreign Relations Law of the United States*, above n. 19.
[139] Article 6(1) US Model BIT (2004); Article 13(1) Canadian Model BIT (2004).
[140] UNCTAD, above n. 1, 31.
[141] Cf. UNCTAD, above n. 26, 47.
[142] Article 5(1) UK Model BIT (1991). Similar language can be found in Article 13(4) Canadian Model BIT (2004).
[143] Article 5(3) Austria/Georgia BIT (2001).

A similar technique is followed in the 2004 Canadian Model BIT[144] as well as in the Energy Charter Treaty. The latter provides:

> The Investor affected shall have a right to prompt review, under the law of the Contracting Party making the Expropriation, by a judicial or other competent and independent authority of that Contracting Party, of its case, of the valuation of its Investment, and of the payment of compensation, in accordance with the principles set out in paragraph (1).[145]

An example of a BIT focusing on the legality of the domestic expropriation procedure can be found in the 2002 Russian Federation/Thailand BIT according to which an expropriation must be made '[...] for public interests in accordance with the procedure established by the laws of the Contracting Party [...]'.[146] Similarly, the 1998 China/Poland BIT provides that '[...] expropriatory measures [...] shall be taken under due process of national law [...]'.[147] At the same time this BIT provides:

> If an investor considers the expropriation mentioned in Paragraph 1 of this article incompatible with the laws of the Contracting Party taking the expropriatory measures, the competent court of the Contracting Parties taking the expropriatory measures may, upon the request of the investor, review the said expropriation.[148]

Some BITs actually set the due process prerequisite somewhat apart from the public purpose, non-discrimination, and compensation requirements. Indeed, since the due process prerequisite is not so much a substantive requirement but rather a procedural obligation in order to guarantee compliance with the substantive requirements it appears sensible to differentiate in this context. This differentiation is clearly expressed in BITs which provide that investments shall not be expropriated 'except for the public benefit and against compensation' and that in case of expropriation '[t]he legality of any such expropriation, nationalization or comparable measure and the amount of compensation shall be subject to review by due process of law'.[149]

Arbitral case law on the due process requirement is limited. One of these rare cases is *Goetz v Burundi*[150] where an ICSID tribunal was faced with the issue whether an expropriatory measure complied with the legality requirements laid down in the applicable BIT. Article 4(1) of the 1989 Belgium/Burundi BIT conditioned the lawfulness of an expropriation on the requirement that 'the measures are taken in a legal manner'.[151] In its examination, the tribunal broadly

---

[144] Article 13(4) Canadian Model BIT (2004).
[145] Article 13(2) ECT.
[146] Article 4(1) Russian Federation/Thailand BIT (2002).
[147] Article 4(1) China/Poland BIT (1998).
[148] Article 4(3) China/Poland BIT (1998).
[149] Article 4(2) Afghanistan/Germany BIT (2005).
[150] *Goetz v Burundi*, above n. 83.
[151] Article 4(1) Belgium/Burundi BIT (1989).

B. The Interpretation Given to the Legality Requirements 193

characterized this condition as follows: '[...] to be internationally lawful, the measure must not only be supported by valid reasons, it must also have been taken in accordance with a lawful procedure'.[152]

In the tribunal's view this requirement was fulfilled.

The recent ICSID case of *ADC v Hungary*[153] also briefly addressed the 'due process' requirement provided for in the applicable BIT.[154] With regard to the more specific content of such a requirement, the *ADC* tribunal held that

> [s]ome basic legal mechanisms, such as reasonable advance notice, a fair hearing and an unbiased and impartial adjudicator to assess the actions in dispute, are expected to be readily available and accessible to the investor to make such legal procedure meaningful. In general, the legal procedure must be of a nature to grant an affected investor a reasonable chance within a reasonable time to claim its legitimate rights and have its claims heard. If no legal procedure of such nature exists at all, the argument that '*the actions are taken under due process of law*' rings hollow.[155]

Since these conditions as well as the two other requirements of a public purpose and non-discrimination were not fulfilled in the specific case, the tribunal held that the expropriation was unlawful.[156] What is interesting in the *ADC* award is the fact that the tribunal had no problem at all to conclude that the unqualified 'due process' requirement of the Cyprus/Hungary BIT should be read in the more expansive fashion of other BITs expressly requiring the possibility of judicial or quasi-judicial review of expropriation decisions.

General conclusions on the 'due process' requirement must remain tentative. As opposed to the public purpose and the non-discrimination prerequisite, the due process requirement seems to be less certainly established in customary international law. It is, however, very widely used in IIAs where it appears in different forms. Sometimes, the due process condition is phrased as a mere legality requirement according to which the expropriation has to be effectuated in conformity with national law and procedure, whereas in a number of IIAs due process expressly requires a right to have the expropriation and, in particular, the compensation decision reviewed. The limited case law suggests that a fair procedure offering the possibility of judicial review is crucial.

---

[152] *Goetz v Burundi*, above n. 83, 43, para. 127.
[153] *ADC v Hungary*, above n. 7.
[154] Article 4(1)(a) Cyprus/Hungary BIT merely requires that 'measures are taken in the public interest and under due process of law'.
[155] *ADC v Hungary*, above n. 7, para. 435.
[156] The tribunal held in a rather casual way: 'As to Respondent's argument that Hungarian law does provide methods for the Claimants to review the expropriation, the Tribunal fails to see how such claim was substantiated and in any event cannot agree in the light of the facts established in this case that there were in place any methods to satisfy the requirement of "*due process of law*" in the context of this case.' *ADC v Hungary*, above n. 7, para. 438.

Compensation

Until the first half of the 20th century, the principle of 'full compensation'[157] for the expropriation of foreign property was fairly well established in international practice.[158] Tribunals like the US-Panama Claims Commission in the *de Sabla* case held that '[...] acts of a government in depriving an alien of his property without compensation impose international responsibility'.[159] Similarly, the succinctly formulated demands contained in a diplomatic note of the US Secretary of State Cordell Hull to his Mexican counterpart, stating that 'no government is entitled to expropriate private property, for whatever purpose, without provision for prompt, adequate and effective payment therefore'[160] have been widely regarded as an expression of customary international law standards.

In the *Norwegian Shipowners' Claims* case,[161] the tribunal referred not only to the 'right of the claimants to receive immediate and full compensation';[162] it also affirmed unequivocally that

[i]nternational law and justice are based upon the principle of equality between States. No State can exercise towards the citizens of another civilised State the 'power of eminent domain' without respecting the property of such foreign citizens or without paying just compensation as determined by an impartial tribunal, if necessary.[163]

Today, however, the traditional consensus as found in the *Hull* formula is no longer generally accepted as an expression of customary international law. The Communist expropriations in Eastern Europe and large-scale nationalizations in many developing countries throughout the 20th century coupled with the attempts to establish a New International Economic Order[164] through a series of resolutions in the UNGA have eroded this consensus, though they may have been unsuccessful in replacing it with new rules which would legitimate uncompensated expropriations.[165] Nevertheless, the opinion seems to prevail that there is

---

[157] *Delagoa Bay and East African Railway Co (US and Great Britain v Portugal)*, in Whiteman (ed.), 3 *Damages in International Law* (1943) 1694, 1648, stating that 'if the present case should be regarded as one of legal expropriation [...] the State, which is the author of the dispossession, is bound to make full reparation for the injuries done by it'.
[158] Cf. P.M. Norton, 'A Law of the Future or a Law of the Past? Modern Tribunals and the International Law of Expropriation', 85 *American Journal of International Law* (1991) 474, 477, stating that out of 60 claims tribunals dealing with injury to aliens between 1840 and 1940 none of the arbitral panels 'held that the appropriate measure of compensation was less than the full value of the property taken, and many specifically affirmed the need for full compensation'.
[159] *de Sabla Claim*, US-Panama Claims Commission, 29 June 1933, 6 *UNRIAA* 358, 366.
[160] Hackworth, 3 *Digest of International Law* (1942) 658–659, § 288.
[161] *Norwegian Shipowners' Claims*, above n. 56.
[162] Ibid., 1 *UNRIAA* 307, 340.
[163] Ibid., 338.
[164] See above text at n. 14.
[165] See *Lowenfeld*, above n. 1, 414.

B. The Interpretation Given to the Legality Requirements

still a customary international law requirement to make at least some compensation in case of expropriation.[166]

Most likely as a result of the uncertain (customary) international law on the question of compensation, most international investment agreements contain fairly detailed rules on the obligation to pay compensation in case of expropriation. The precise level of compensation required varies from treaty to treaty. Many BITs and other IIAs incorporate the *Hull* formula requiring the expropriating State to pay 'prompt, adequate and effective compensation'.[167] Sometimes, they merely demand 'compensation'[168] or the payment of 'just compensation'.[169] In some cases, BIT language reminiscent of the UNGA resolutions uses the term 'appropriate compensation'.[170]

It appears, however, that the qualifying adjective of the type of compensation to be paid has lost much of its importance in view of the fact that most IIAs contain fairly uniform additional language specifying what should be understood by the required compensation. IIAs often contain provisions which clarify that 'fair market value' would be regarded as 'adequate' or 'just' compensation,[171] or that the 'real value' should be regarded as 'appropriate compensation'.[172] A typical example for the former can be found in Article 13(1) ECT which provides:

Such compensation shall amount to the fair market value of the Investment expropriated at the time immediately before the Expropriation or impending Expropriation became known in such a way as to affect the value of the Investment [...].[173]

An example of a similarly high compensation standard reminiscent of the *Hull* formula even where the treaty speaks of 'appropriate compensation' can be found in the France/Hong Kong BIT. It states:

Compensation shall amount to the real value of the investment immediately before the deprivation or before the impending deprivation became public knowledge whichever is the earlier, shall include interest at a normal commercial rate until the date of payment, shall be made without delay, be effectively realizable and be freely convertible.[174]

In addition, many IIAs contain similar detailed rules on the precise method of valuation[175] which usually clarifies that the precepts of the *Hull* formula are to be

---
[166] M. Shaw, *International Law* (4th edn, 1997) 574; Hobér, *Investment Arbitration in Eastern Europe*, above n. 40, 38, arguing that '[...] the standard of compensation under international law is full compensation'.
[167] Article 13(1)(c) ECT; Article 6(1)(c) US Model BIT (2004); Article 13(1) Canadian Model BIT (2004). See also Muchlinski, *Multinational Enterprises*, above n. 1, 692; UNCTAD, above n. 26, 48.
[168] Article 4(2) German Model BIT (2004).
[169] Article 4(1)(c) Cyprus/Hungary BIT (1989).
[170] Article 5(1) France/Hong Kong BIT (1995). See also UNCTAD, above n. 1, 27.
[171] Eg Article 13(1) ECT.
[172] Eg Article 5(1) France/Hong Kong BIT (1995).
[173] Article 13(1) ECT.
[174] Article 5(1) France/Hong Kong BIT (1995).
[175] See also Doak Bishop, Crawford, and Reisman, above n. 1, 1331 *et seq*.

followed. Thus, in addition to the determination of the 'adequacy' of the compensation, 'prompt' means within a reasonable time and with interest and 'effective' requires compensation in a convertible currency.[176]

Compared to the rather intensive political and legal debate about the requirement and appropriate level of compensation, the actual arbitral practice appears rather modest. In general, tribunals have affirmed that States are obliged to pay compensation in case of expropriation—both as a matter of treaty law, enshrined in BITs or other IIAs, and of general international law.

In the *Aminoil* award the tribunal considered that, on the basis of international law, for a lawful expropriation 'appropriate compensation' as demanded in the UNGA Resolution on Permanent Sovereignty over Natural Resources 1803[177] was due.[178] It acknowledged, however, that it was difficult to find a precise meaning of this very imprecise term. Thus, it considered that

[...] the determination of the amount of an 'appropriate' compensation is better carried out by means of an enquiry into all the circumstances relevant to the particular concrete case, than through abstract theoretical discussion.[179]

In the specific case, the tribunal had recourse to the concept of 'legitimate expectations' invoked by both parties in order to decide on compensation. In the words of the tribunal,

[t]hat formula [was] well-advised, and justifiably brings to mind the fact that, with reference to every long-term contract, especially such as involve an important investment, there must necessarily be economic calculations, and the weighing-up of rights and obligations, of chances and risks, constituting the contractual equilibrium.[180]

Also, the practice of the Iran-US Claims Tribunal is rather uniform in requiring full or adequate compensation. In *American International Group v Iran*, one of the early cases before the tribunal, it held that

[...] it is a general principle of public international law that even in a case of a lawful nationalization the former owner of the nationalized property is normally entitled to compensation for the value of the property taken.[181]

Nevertheless, the fierce political debate about the *Hull* formula and the various UNGA resolutions on the subject resonated in some of its judgments. For instance, in the *Ebrahimi* case[182] the tribunal stated:

---

[176] Eg Article 1110(2)–(6) NAFTA; similarly, Article 6(2)–(4) US Model BIT (2004); Article 13(2)–(3) Canadian Model BIT (2004). See also 1992 World Bank Guidelines on the Treatment of Foreign Direct Investment, IV (3)–(8).
[177] See above text at n. 12.
[178] *Kuwait v American Independent Oil Company (Aminoil)*, Award, 24 March 1982, 21 ILR (1982) 976, 1032.
[179] Ibid., 1030, para. 144.   [180] Ibid., 1034, para. 148.
[181] *American International Group Inc, et al. v Islamic Republic of Iran, et al.*, 4 Iran-US CTR 96, 105.
[182] *Shahin Shaine Ebrahimi v Government of the Islamic Republic of Iran*, Award No. 569-44/ 46/47-3, 12 October 1994, 30 *Iran-US CTR* (1994) 170.

B. The Interpretation Given to the Legality Requirements

The Tribunal believes that, while international law undoubtedly sets forth an obligation to provide compensation for property taken, international law theory and practice do not support the conclusion that the 'prompt adequate and effective' standard represents the prevailing standard of compensation [...]. Rather, customary international law favors an 'appropriate' compensation standard [...]. The prevalence of the 'appropriate' compensation standard does not imply, however, that the compensation *quantum* should be always 'less than full' or always 'partial'.[183]

According to a separate opinion in the same case, however,

[...] there is virtual total uniformity in the Tribunal's rulings on the standard of compensation under international law. Every decision rendered by this Tribunal, whether based upon the Treaty of Amity or customary international law, or both of them, has concluded that compensation must equal the full value of the expropriated property as it stood on the date of taking.[184]

In fact, Article 4 of the applicable 1955 Treaty of Amity provided that property '[...] shall not be taken except for a public purpose, nor shall it be taken without the prompt payment of just compensation. Such compensation shall be in an effectively realizable form and shall represent the full equivalent of the property taken'.[185]

The principle that also lawful expropriations require compensation was equally endorsed by ICSID tribunals. For instance, the tribunal in *Benvenuti & Bonfant*, which—in the absence of an explicit choice of law—had to decide pursuant to Article 42(1) ICSID Convention, held that

[the] principle of compensation in case of nationalization is in accordance with the Congolese constitution and constitutes one of the generally recognized principles of international law [...].[186]

In a similar situation, the tribunal in the *AMCO* case was initially more cautious: it merely referred to 'an expropriation which according to Indonesian law and to international law can give rise to a claim for compensation'.[187] Subsequently, however, it found that it was

[...] clearly admitted in international law, as well as in Indonesian law, that the State which nationalizes has to provide compensation for the property and/or contractual rights thus taken from their owner or holder.[188]

---

[183] *Ebrahimi v Iran*, above n. 182, para. 88.
[184] Ibid., Separate Opinion by Allision, para. 36.
[185] Article 4 Treaty of Amity, Economic Relations, and Consular Rights between the Unites States of America and Iran.
[186] *Benvenuti & Bonfant v Congo*, ICSID Case No. ARB/77/2, Award, 8 August 1980, 1 *ICSID Reports* (1993) 330, 357.
[187] *Amco Asia Corporation v Republic of Indonesia*, ICSID Case No. ARB/81/1, Award, 20 November 1984, 1 *ICSID Reports* (1993) 413, 455.
[188] Ibid., 467.

Also, the award in the *Santa Elena* case[189] was based on the application of general international law.[190] The tribunal was of the opinion that '[i]nternational law permits the Government of Costa Rica to expropriate foreign-owned property within its territory for a public purpose and against the prompt payment of adequate and effective compensation'.[191] With regard to the required level of the 'adequate' compensation the tribunal merely noted that there was no dispute between the parties as to the applicability of the '[...] principle of *full compensation for the fair market value of the Property*, i.e., what a willing buyer would pay to a willing seller'.[192]

A number of investment tribunals have dealt with the question whether the compensation requirement demands that compensation has actually been paid. In this context, tribunals have consistently held that an offer of compensation or other provision for compensation, in particular where the exact amount may still be in controversy, is enough to satisfy this legality requirement.

This is already implicit in the finding of the arbitrator in the *BP v Libya* case. In addition to finding that the expropriation of the oil concession was illegal because it was not made for a public purpose and in a discriminatory fashion, he further concluded that 'the fact that no offer of compensation [had] been made indicate[d] that the taking was also confiscatory'.[193]

Apparently, there need not be a specific offer as long as a possibility to obtain compensation exists. This approach was confirmed by the Iran-US Claims Tribunal which held in the *Amoco* case that the fact that there was an administrative procedure according to which former owners could claim compensation was sufficient to render an expropriation lawful even though no compensation had actually been paid. The tribunal stated:

In practice the Special Commission instituted negotiations with the companies party to the nullified contracts, in order to arrive at settlement agreements. Furthermore, in case of failure of the negotiations, the interested companies were entitled to have recourse to the procedures of settlement provided for on the contracts, usually by international arbitration. A number of settlement agreements were in fact executed and, in a few cases, arbitration procedures took place. In view of these facts, the Tribunal deems that the provisions of the Single Article Act for compensation were neither in violation of the Treaty [of Amity between Iran and the US] nor, indeed, in violation of rules of customary international law.[194]

Similar views were uttered by ICSID tribunals. For instance in the *LETCO* case, the tribunal held that the expropriating government would have to show that its action was 'accompanied by payment (or at least the offer of payment) of

---

[189] *Santa Elena v Costa Rica*, above n. 80.
[190] The tribunal decided that in the absence of a choice of law by the parties, '[...] under the second sentence of Article 42(1), the arbitration [was] governed by international law'. *Santa Elena v Costa Rica*, above n. 80, para. 65.
[191] Ibid., para. 71.
[192] Ibid., para. 73 (emphasis in original).
[193] *British Petroleum v Libya*, Award, 10 October 1973 and 1 August 1974; 53 *ILR* 297, 329.
[194] *Amoco International Finance Corp v Iran*, above n. 74, para. 138.

appropriate compensation'.[195] Since the taking of LETCO's property was in fact 'not accompanied by an offer of appropriate compensation'[196] it was not justified.

Thus, the mere fact that compensation has not yet been paid does not render an expropriation illegal. This was endorsed by the tribunal in the *Goetz* case which held that the applicable '[t]reaty require[d] an adequate and effective indemnity; unlike certain domestic rights as regards expropriation, it does not require prior compensation'.[197]

Most recent ICSID tribunals dealing with so-called treaty claims have to decide the issue of compensation on the basis of a specific BIT. Here it is the language of the applicable IIA that will determine the assessment. For instance, in the *ADC v Hungary* case '[i]t [was] abundantly obvious to the tribunal that no just compensation was provided by the Respondent to the Claimants and [it felt] no need to expand its discussion here'.[198]

Rather, the tribunal proceeded to address the question of damages for an unlawful expropriation.[199]

A similar conclusion was reached by the ICSID tribunal in the *Siemens v Argentina* case. It found that

> [...] compensation has never been paid on grounds that, as already stated, the Tribunal finds that are lacking in justification. For these reasons, the expropriation did not meet the requirements of Article 4(2) and therefore was unlawful.[200]

While the precise amount of compensation due in case of expropriation may remain controversial as a matter of customary international law, the general obligation to provide for some compensation is clearly upheld by the jurisprudence of investment tribunals—both as a matter of investment treaty law and of general international law. Since treaties usually contain rather detailed rules on the appropriate level of compensation, also often as well as on the valuation methods concerning expropriated property, the issue of the amount of compensation plays a less prominent role than the highly politicized debate may suggest.

Implications of the Legality/Illegality of an Expropriation for Remedies

The principle is fairly generally accepted: compensation is due in cases of expropriation. This is widely regarded as a rule of general international law and it is usually laid down in IIAs. Where compensation is not paid, or at least offered, and/or other legality requirements are not fulfilled, an expropriation becomes

---

[195] *LETCO v Liberia*, above n. 87, 2 *ICSID Reports* 343, at 366.
[196] Ibid., 367.
[197] *Goetz v Burundi*, above n. 83, 44, para. 130.
[198] *ADC v Hungary*, above n. 7, para. 444.
[199] See below text at n. 221.
[200] *Siemens A.G. v Argentina*, above n. 2, para. 273.

illegal and State responsibility is triggered. The State committing an international wrong has to pay damages in order to put the victim of the unlawful act in a position he or she would have been had the act not been committed.[201] In the case of an illegal taking of property, the primary remedy would thus be restitution in kind. Only where restitution is impossible are monetary alternatives in the form of payments for 'financially assessable damage' considered.[202] Nevertheless, it is sometimes asserted that both lawful and unlawful expropriations trigger the same obligation to compensate.[203] Actual case law, however, largely adheres to the distinction between the two forms of takings.

The pre-eminence of restitution as a consequence of an unlawful expropriation was already expressed by the arbitrator in the *Walter Fletcher Smith Claim* case,[204] who—after having found that the expropriation had been unlawful—considered '[...] that, according to law, the property should be restored to the claimant'.[205]

The best-known formulation of this customary international law is still the so-called *Chorzów Factory* standard of the PCIJ according to which:

[...] reparation must, as far as possible, wipe out all the consequences of the illegal act and re-establish the situation which would, in all probability, have existed if that act had not been committed.[206]

As a consequence, the Court found that:

Restitution in kind, or, if this is not possible, payment of a sum corresponding to the value which a restitution in kind would bear; the award, if need be, of damages for loss sustained which would not be covered by restitution in kind or payment in place of it.[207]

Since the PCIJ had to state the consequences of an illegal expropriation—one prohibited by the 1922 German–Polish Convention Concerning Upper

---

[201] The primacy of restitution is also expressed in the 2001 ILC Articles on State Responsibility, see *Commentaries to the draft articles on Responsibility of States for internationally wrongful acts*, adopted by the International Law Commission at its 53rd session (2001), Report of the International Law Commission on the work of its 53rd session, *Official Records of the General Assembly, Fifty-sixth session, Supplement No. 10* (A/56/10). Article 35 provides: 'A State responsible for an internationally wrongful act is under an obligation to make restitution, that is, to re-establish the situation which existed before the wrongful act was committed, provided and to the extent that restitution: (a) Is not materially impossible; (b) Does not involve a burden out of all proportion to the benefit deriving from restitution instead of compensation.' Article 36 provides: '1. The State responsible for an internationally wrongful act is under an obligation to compensate for the damage caused thereby, insofar as such damage is not made good by restitution. 2. The compensation shall cover any financially assessable damage including loss of profits insofar as it is established.'
[202] See I. Marboe, 'Compensation and Damages in International Law, The Limits of "Fair Market Value"', 7 *The Journal of World Investment and Trade* (2006) 723, 725 *et seq*.
[203] See Sheppard, above n. 18, 196 *et seq*.
[204] *Walter Fletcher Smith Claim*, above n. 64.
[205] Ibid., 2 *UNRIAA* 913, 918.
[206] *Factory at Chorzów (Claim for Indemnity) (Germany v Poland)*, Judgment (Merits), 13 September 1928, *PCIJ* Series A, No. 17 (1928), 40.
[207] Ibid.

B. The Interpretation Given to the Legality Requirements

Silesia[208]—the issue of the consequences of a lawful expropriation was not directly addressed. However, the Court remarked in a dictum that lawful expropriation does not require restitution but only payment of 'the just price of what was appropriated' based on the 'value of the undertaking at the moment of dispossession, plus interest to the day of payment'.[209]

The distinction between damages for illegal acts and compensation for legal expropriations has not always been clearly adhered to.[210] Nevertheless, a number of investment arbitration tribunals have upheld the *Chorzów Factory* standard.

The most extreme follower of the restitution approach certainly was the arbitrator in the *Texaco* case who found that '*restitutio in integrum* is, both under the principles of Libyan law and under the principles of international law, the normal sanction for non-performance of contractual obligations [...]'.[211]

Also in the jurisprudence of the Iran-US Claims Tribunal the 'clear distinction [...] between lawful and unlawful expropriations' found in the *Chorzów Factory* case was mostly endorsed.[212] In the *Amoco* case, the tribunal expressly distinguished between the Iran/US Treaty of Amity which determined the conditions that an expropriation should meet in order to be in conformity with its terms and therefore defined 'the standard of compensation only in case of a lawful expropriation' and a nationalization in breach of the treaty '[...] which would render applicable the rules relating to State responsibility'.[213] However, it must be acknowledged that some Iran-US Claims Tribunal decisions appear to disregard that distinction. According to the *Phillips* decision, 'Article IV, paragraph 2 [of the Iran-US Treaty of Amity],[214] provides a single standard, "just compensation" representing the "full equivalent of the property taken", which applies to all property taken, regardless of whether that taking was lawful or unlawful'.[215] Relying on the *Amoco* decision, the *Phillips* tribunal stated that this Treaty 'standard applies to takings that are "lawful" under the Treaty, but the Treaty does not say that any different standard of compensation would be applicable to an "unlawful" taking'.[216] Whether this *obiter dictum* is correct remains questionable.

ICSID jurisprudence generally adheres to the distinction between lawful and unlawful expropriation and the different consequences stemming from these different acts.

---

[208] For the text of Article 6 see above n. 61.
[209] *Chorzów Factory*, above n. 206, 47.
[210] See already the rather sweeping statement by the tribunal in the *Norwegian Shipowners' Claims* case that '[w]hether the action of the United States was lawful or not, just compensation is due to the claimants under the municipal law of the United States, as well as under the international law'. *Norwegian Shipowners' Claims*, Award, 30 June 1921, 1 *UNRIAA* 307, 334.
[211] *Texaco Overseas Petroleum Company (Topco)/California Asiatic (Calasiatic) Oil Company v Libya*, above n. 5, para. 109.
[212] *Amoco International Finance Corporation v Iran*, above n. 74, para. 192.
[213] Ibid., para. 189.   [214] See above n. 185.
[215] *Phillips Petroleum Co v Iran*, 21 *Iran-US CTR* 79 (1989), para. 109.
[216] Ibid.

In the *SPP v Egypt* case, the tribunal held that

[...] the Claimants are seeking 'compensation' for a lawful expropriation, and not 'reparation' for an injury caused by an illegal act such as a breach of contract. The cardinal point [...] in determining the appropriate compensation is that [...] Claimants are entitled to receive fair compensation for what was expropriated rather than damages for breach of contract.[217]

Similarly, the *Metalclad* tribunal found that

[t]he award to Metalclad of the cost of its investment in the landfill is consistent with the principles set forth in Chorzów [...] namely, that where the state has acted contrary to its obligations, any award to the claimant should, as far as is possible, wipe out all the consequences of the illegal act and re-establish the situation which would in all probability have existed if that act had not been committed (the status quo ante).[218]

Recently, the tribunal in the *CMS v Argentina* case relied again on the *Chorzów Factory* standard by stating the following:

Restitution is the standard used to re-establish the situation which existed before the wrongful act was committed, provided this is not materially impossible and does not result in a burden out of proportion as compared to compensation.[219]

Also the tribunal in *ADC v Hungary* clearly upheld the distinction between lawful and unlawful expropriations and the different legal consequences stemming from that distinction. It refused to apply the BIT provisions which provided that in case of expropriation '[t]he amount of compensation must correspond to the market value of the expropriated investments at the moment of the expropriation' and that '[t]he amount of this compensation may be estimated according to the laws and regulations of the country where the expropriation is made'.[220] In the tribunal's view, these were provisions governing the calculation of compensation in case of lawful expropriations which could not be relied upon in case of unlawful expropriations:

Since the BIT does not contain any *lex specialis* rules that govern the issue of the standard for assessing damages in the case of an unlawful expropriation, the Tribunal is required to apply the default standard contained in customary international law in the present case.[221]

The tribunal then extensively reviewed the use of the *Chorzów Factory* standard in international adjudication and arbitration and concluded that this standard

---

[217] *SPP v Egypt*, above n. 81, para. 183.
[218] *Metalclad Corporation v Mexico*, above n. 2, para. 122.
[219] *CMS Gas Transmission Company v The Argentine Republic*, above n. 2, para. 400.
[220] Article 4(2) and (3) Cyprus/Hungary BIT.
[221] *ADC v Hungary*, above n. 7, para. 483.

B. The Interpretation Given to the Legality Requirements 203

would be applicable to an unlawful expropriation as in the case at hand. The *ADC* tribunal found that:

It is clear that actual restitution cannot take place and so it is, in the words of the *Chorzów Factory* decision, '*payment of a sum corresponding to the value which a restitution in kind would bear*', which is the matter to be decided.[222]

Since the value of the expropriated investment had considerably risen after the expropriation the tribunal found that

[...] it must assess the compensation to be paid by the Respondent to the Claimants in accordance with the *Chorzów Factory* standard, i.e., the Claimants should be compensated the market value of the expropriated investments as at the date of this Award, which the Tribunal takes as of September 30, 2006.[223]

Also the tribunal in *Siemens A.G. v Argentina*[224] upheld the distinction between lawful and unlawful expropriations for the purpose of the legal consequences stemming from that distinction. After having found that the Argentine measures amounted to an illegal expropriation[225] the tribunal stated:

The law applicable to the determination of compensation for a breach of such Treaty obligations is customary international law. The Treaty itself only provides for compensation for expropriation in accordance with the terms of the Treaty.[226]

The *Siemens* tribunal expressly referred to Article 36 of the ILC Articles on State Responsibility[227] and to the *Chorzów Factory* standard[228] and held that under this 'customary international law' standard

Siemens [was] entitled not just to the value of its enterprise as of May 18, 2001, the date of expropriation, but also to any greater value that enterprise [had] gained up to the date of this Award, plus any consequential damages.[229]

The tribunal expressly distinguished this standard from the standard laid down in the applicable BIT providing for compensation '[...] equivalent to the value of the expropriated investment'.[230]

---

[222] Ibid., para. 495 (emphasis in original).
[223] Ibid., para. 499.
[224] *Siemens A.G. v Argentina*, above n. 2.
[225] See above text at n. 100.
[226] *Siemens A.G. v Argentina*, above n. 2, para. 349.
[227] See above n. 201.
[228] 'The key difference between compensation under the Draft Articles and the *Factory at Chorzów* case formula, and Article 4(2) of the Treaty is that under the former, compensation must take into account "all financially assessable damage" or "wipe out all the consequences of the illegal act" as opposed to compensation "equivalent to the value of the expropriated investment" under the Treaty.' *Siemens A.G. v Argentina*, above n. 2, para. 352.
[229] Ibid.
[230] Ibid.

C. Conclusions

The fact that recent investment arbitration has been dominated by issues of indirect expropriation with tribunals focusing on the question whether certain State measures amounted to expropriation, does not mean that the traditional legality requirements for the expropriation of foreign investment have lost their importance. Quite the contrary, the traditional criteria of 'public purpose', 'non-discrimination', 'due process', and 'compensation'—in spite of, or maybe because of, being frequently questioned as customary international law requirements—are often found in investment instruments such as BITs or other IIAs. Having determined that an expropriation took place, investment tribunals regularly scrutinize the lawfulness of an expropriation according to the applicable IIA standards or standards of general international law. In arbitral practice, both standards appear to converge largely with the traditional legality requirements standard.

A close analysis of the relevant arbitration decisions also demonstrates that tribunals are in fact willing to engage in a genuine investigation of whether the legality requirements are fulfilled. Although they may exercise some degree of restraint in adjudicating public policy issues inherent in the determination of 'public purpose', investment tribunals refuse to take 'public purpose' invocations by States at face value. Rather, they will disqualify expropriatory measures lacking a genuine 'public purpose'. Similarly, investment tribunals have demonstrated their resolve to regard as illegal discriminatory expropriations either because they were directed at foreigners as opposed to nationals of the expropriating state or because they singled out particular groups of foreign nationals often motivated by political considerations. Though there is relatively little arbitration practice on the 'due process' requirement, tribunals seem to approximate this legality requirement to a fair trial right, offering affected investors an opportunity to challenge expropriation decisions before an independent and impartial domestic body.

Finally, investment tribunals are fairly consistent in requiring compensation, or at least an offer of compensation, in order to regard an expropriation as lawful. The precise amount of compensation will usually be guided by the express treaty provisions on expropriation. Tribunals have been fairly consistent in permitting the application of these treaty provisions only in cases of lawful expropriations. They largely concur that where an expropriation was carried out either not for a 'public purpose', in a 'discriminatory' fashion, or not in accordance with 'due process', damages for an internationally wrongful act are due.

10
Capital Transfer Restrictions under Modern Investment Treaties

Abba Kolo and Thomas Wälde

A. Introduction

The Asian and Russian financial crises in 1998 and their spiralling effect on other countries and the Argentine economic crisis of 2001 have brought to the fore questions over the power of host States to impose capital controls that are inconsistent with their bilateral and multilateral investment treaty commitments and which adversely affected the rights of foreign investors.[1] Among the questions raised are: to what extent is a host State under a legal duty to comply with the capital repatriation obligations of an investment treaty in the face of economic or financial crisis or threat thereof? Who should bear the risk of such economic turmoil and measures taken by the State to ameliorate the situation; should it be the private investor or the public in whose interest the restrictions were imposed? Should a determination by the national authorities on the appropriateness to

---

[1] Following the Russian financial crisis in 1998 and the government's restructuring of domestic bonds, some non-repatriation claims were raised by foreign investors but it seems the parties were able to reach a settlement and so none could be arbitrated. One of such claims is briefly referred to on the Freshfields' website: http://www.freshfields.com/practice/arbitration/experience/disputes. For more in-depth analysis of the expropriation aspect of the cases see, K. Hober, 'Investment Arbitration in Eastern Europe: Recent Cases on Expropriation', 1 *Transnational Dispute Management* (2004). *Gruslin v Malaysia*, ICSID Case No. ARB/99/3, Award, 27 November 2000, in which the claimants sought to challenge the legal validity of capital restrictions on portfolio investors imposed by Malaysia during the Asian financial crisis. The case was dismissed for lack of jurisdiction under the Belgo-Luxemburg/Malaysia BIT. Some of the claims against Argentina initially sought to challenge, among other things, alleged breach by Argentina of the free capital transfer provisions of the relevant BITs—eg *CMS Gas Transmission Company v The Argentine Republic*, ICSID Case No. ARB/01/8, Decision on Jurisdiction, 17 July 2003, para. 32; ibid., Decision of Merit, 12 May 2005, para. 88; *BP v Argentina*, Decision on Jurisdiction, 27 July 2006, para. 21. Although in none of these cases was a decision made on the merits of the repatriation claim, nonetheless they do suggest the possibility of such claims being raised by foreign investors against host States for alleged breach of the capital transfer provisions of BITs. In the on-going *Duke v Peru* case, the claimant is also seeking compensation for breach of a contractual obligation to permit free transfers. See *Duke Energy Int'l Ltd v Republic of Peru*, ICSID Case No. ARB/03/28, Decision on Jurisdiction, 1 February 2006.

impose restrictions be self-judging or subjected to an international scrutiny under relevant investment treaties and instruments such as the Articles of Agreement of the IMF, GATT, and GATS rules? What margin of appreciation ('deference') should be afforded a host State in an analysis of the rights of the foreign investor to repatriate capital on the one hand, and the regulatory autonomy of the host State on the other? In this chapter, we will explore these questions in the context of investor-State relationship under modern investment treaties and in light of State practice and judicial and arbitral jurisprudence.

Section B briefly discusses the development of international law on capital controls from the 1930s to the unsuccessful attempt by the OECD to negotiate a multilateral agreement on investment. Section C highlights some of the approaches used in bilateral and multilateral investment treaties (BITs/MITs) to balance the conflicting interests involved in capital transfers. It notes that most investment treaties recognize the right of host States to impose exchange restrictions subject to numerous conditions including the necessity for the restrictions, compliance with the Articles of Agreement of the IMF, and that the restrictions must be temporary and applied in a non-discriminatory manner. Although no case has yet been decided based on the repatriation provisions of an investment treaty, we suggest that in interpreting the treaty provisions, international arbitral tribunals should scrutinize the disputed host State measures to find out whether or not they are really necessary, non-discriminatory, proportionate, and least restrictive of investor rights in order to prevent possible abuse of the regulatory autonomy. In such a balancing exercise, the jurisprudence of GATT/WTO, the European Court of Justice and the European Court of Human Rights on national security exceptions might provide useful analogy as do several recent investment awards.[2] Section E discusses whether and under what circumstances exchange restrictions amount to indirect expropriation of a foreign investor's property rights. Here too, although the threshold of the interference with investor rights is a very high one to qualify as expropriatory, nonetheless a breach of the arguably often lower level requirement of fair and equitable treatment standard can be invoked by the foreign investor to obtain damages for losses suffered if the capital transfer restrictions were adjudged to be 'unfair' or 'inequitable' in the circumstances of the case.

B. The Development of International Law on Foreign Exchange Regulation

Capital mobility is said to go back as far as the 18th century, and which was accelerated during the Franco-Prussian War of 1870 up to World War I when Europe acted as the 'banker of the world', providing loan capital for infrastructural

[2] In particular, *Tecmed v Mexico*, ICSID Case No. ARB(AF)/00/2, Award, 29 May 2003; see also the references in Hober, above n. 1.

projects in other parts of the world. Most governments pursued liberal economic policies and did not deem it necessary to restrict capital movement but instead committed themselves to the gold standard.[3] However, during and following World War I, many countries imposed capital controls in order to conserve foreign exchange and raised taxes as a means of reacting to the Great Depression. Protectionism then set in leading to the closure of major capital markets and reduced capital mobility.[4] Although disputes did arise between private parties as well as between private individuals and governments consequent to such exchange controls, nonetheless, there was no developed public international law principle to deal with such problems.[5] Some of the relevant cases decided under national laws at that time were the three *Gold Clause* cases decided by the US Supreme Court in 1935 which involved a challenge against the US government's power to abrogate gold clauses in private and public contracts which provided for payments in gold. The law was aimed at conserving gold reserves during the economic emergency of the Great Depression. In these cases, bondholders challenged the legislation as a breach of contract and a taking of property without due process, contrary to the US Constitution. By a narrow margin of 5 to 4, the US Supreme Court upheld the validity of the law thereby affirming Congress's power over monetary policy.[6]

However, these decisions are opposite to that of the UK House of Lords issued on 15 December 1933 in the case of *Feist v Société Intercommunale Belge d'Electricité* which also involved an agreement to repay bonds in gold or gold coins. However, a change of the law in 1928 effectively withdrew gold coins as legal tender and rendered the performance of the contract impossible as per its terms. In reversing the decision of the Court of Appeal, the House of Lords held that the gold clause was enforceable since the parties inserted the 'special words for some special purpose', namely, to protect the lenders against currency depreciation.[7] In reaching its decision, the House of Lords relied upon the decisions of the Permanent Court of International Justice in similar cases instituted by

---

[3] OECD, *Forty Years' Experience with the OECD Code of Liberalisation of Capital Movements* (2002) 22, available at http://www.oecd.org. Thus, prior to 1907 market forces determined exchange rates with traders avoiding dealing in weaker currencies. D. Vagts, 'International Economic Law and the American Journal of International Law', 100 *American Journal of International Law* (2006) 769, 771–772. On how the old standard operated and factors that led to its collapse or abandonment by various countries see M. Rothbard, *What has Government done to our Money?* (4th edn, 1990) Ch IV, available at: http://www.mises.org/store/product1.aspx?Product_ID=224.

[4] OECD, above n. 3, 23; B. Meyer, 'Recognition of Exchange Controls after the IMF', 62 *Yale Law Journal* (1953) 867.

[5] Vagts, above n. 3, 776.

[6] *Norman v Baltimore & Ohio Railroad Co*, 294 US 240; *Nortz v United States*, 294 US 317; *Perry v United States*, 294 US 330. See Dawson, 'The Gold Clause Cases', 33 *Michigan Law Review* (1935) 637. Similar legislations were enacted by many other countries to deal with similar economic problems. See A. Nussbaum, *Money in the Law: National and International* (2nd edn, 1950) 280–283; M. Schuster, *The Public International Law of Money* (1973) 26–27.

[7] See 28 *American Journal of International Law* (1934) 374; A. Kuhn, 'The Gold Clauses in International Loans', 28 *American Journal of International Law* (1934) 312.

France (on behalf of its nationals) against Brazil[8] and Serbia, respectively, in which the court expressed the opinion that the purpose of the gold clause was to protect against payment in depreciated French francs. According to the court, to construe the 'gold clause as indicating a mere modality of payment, without reference to a gold standard of value, would be, not to construe but to destroy it'.[9] Hence, the decisions might be interpreted as upholding the sanctity of express contractual provisions between foreigners and governments.[10]

The collapse of the gold exchange standard in the 1920s, devaluation of national currencies, and subsequent creation of the International Bank for Settlement in 1930 to facilitate international payments did not stem the tide of nationalism which culminated in World War II during which exchange controls were imposed by several countries. The aftermath of World War II saw the setting up of the Bretton Woods Institutions (The World Bank and the IMF) aimed at, amongst others, ensuring 'orderly and regulated and well-regulated international monetary relations',[11] by helping members dismantle exchange restrictions.[12] To that end the Fund was mandated to provide temporary loan facilities to Member States facing balance-of-payment difficulties and the Articles of Agreement of the IMF recognized exchange controls as a legitimate and/or necessary instrument of economic policy under certain circumstances.[13] However, the Fund did not,

---

[8] *Case Concerning the Payment in Gold of Brazilian Federal Loans Contracted in France (France v Brazil)*, PCIJ, Judgment, 12 July 1929. The arbitral tribunal in *Himpurna v Indonesia*, 1999, reached a similar conclusion (in a contractual not treaty context). In rejecting the defence of *force majeure*, the tribunal held that by '[. . .] pricing in US dollars rather than in Indonesian rupiah the Parties unambiguously allocated the risk of a depreciation of the local currency to PLN'. 14 *Mealey's International Arbitration Report* (1999) A-26—commented upon by M. Kantor, 'International Project Finance and Arbitration with Public Sector Entities: When is Arbitrability a Fiction?', 24 *Fordham International Law Journal* (2001) 1122.

[9] *Serbian Loans*, Judgment, PCIJ Series A No. 20, at 270. See also the *Brazilian Loans* case, Judgment, PCIJ Series A No. 21, at 20–21.

[10] T. Wälde, 'The Serbian Loans Case—A Precedent for Investment Treaty Protection of Foreign Debt?', in T. Weiler (ed.), *International Investment Law and Arbitration: Leading Cases from the ICSID, NAFTA, BITs and Customary International Law* (2005) 383, also available in 1(4) *Transnational Dispute Management* (2004).

[11] This is reflected in Article 1(iv) of the Articles of Agreement of the IMF which states that one of the purposes of the Fund is 'To assist in the establishment of a multilateral system of payments in respect of current transactions between members of the Fund and in the elimination of exchange restrictions which hamper the growth of world trade.' Whilst the IMF played a regulatory role, the World Bank offered loans to countries to execute projects that would enhance economic development. Vagts, above n. 3, 779.

[12] S. Silard, 'Exchange Controls and External Indebtedness: Are the Bretton Woods Concepts still Workable? A Perspective from the IMF', 7 *Houston Journal of International Law* (1984) 53, 77.

[13] Three provisions in the Articles recognize exchange controls as instruments of economic policy. First, under Article VI section 3 Fund Agreement Member States may 'exercise such controls as are necessary' to regulate international capital movements without seeking the approval of the Fund but not 'in a manner which will restrict payments for current transactions' with a view to control the flow of 'hot money'. But under Article VIII section 2(a) Fund Agreement, a Member State may not impose *restrictions on the making of payments and transfers for current international transactions* without the approval of the IMF. The second is Article XIV Fund Agreement which allows Member States to declare, when joining the Fund, that they intend to maintain restrictions on

B. Development of International Law on Foreign Exchange Regulation

and still does not, have jurisdiction over the use by countries of exchange controls on capital transfers even though attempts were made subsequently to amend the Articles of Agreement to extend the Fund's powers over movements of capital across borders.[14]

In view of the importance of trade and financial liberalization for peace and prosperity, some European countries continued with sectoral integration initiatives leading to the creation of the European Economic Community in 1958 by the Treaty of Rome with freedom of movement of goods, persons, services, and capital as the core elements of achieving integration. In 1961, the then existing Organisation for European Economic Cooperation was renamed the Organisation for Economic Co-operation and Development (OECD) and its membership was broadened to include Canada and the United States. Under Article 2(d) of the OECD Convention, Member States are obligated to '[...] pursue their efforts to reduce or abolish obstacles to exchange of goods and services and current payments and maintain and extend the liberalisation of capital movements'. In order to implement this obligation, the Organisation adopted the Code of Liberalisation of Capital Movements and the Code of Liberalisation of Current Invisible Operations which committed the members to 'progressive liberalisation' or gradual liberalization process, non-discrimination among parties, and transparency. Adherence to the Codes is mandatory upon joining the organization.[15]

Although under the safeguard provisions of the Code, a Member State is permitted temporarily to derogate from Code obligations if it demonstrates that it needs to introduce restrictions because of a seriously deteriorating balance-of-payments situation[16] or take actions it considers necessary, including capital controls, for the protection of its essential security interests.[17] Liberalization has been so successful over the years to the extent that

[...] members no longer consider for themselves recourse to capital controls as a workable tool as part of broader changes in governance approaches and in a context of highly integrated financial markets.[18]

---

current transactions for a transitional period notwithstanding the prohibitions in Article VIII(3). Thirdly, by virtue of Article VI section 1(a) Fund Agreement, the Fund may request Member Sstates to impose capital controls in order to prevent a large or sustained outflow of capital that could make it necessary for them to resort to the Fund for financial assistance. See C. Lichtenstein, 'The Battle for International Bank Accounts: Restrictions on International Payments for Political Ends and Article VIII of the Fund Agreement', 19 *NYU Journal of International Law and Politics* (1987) 982; W. Holder, 'Fund Jurisdiction over Capital Movements—Comments', Panel on Preventing Asian Type Crises: Who if any one should have Jurisdiction over Capital Movement?, 5 *ILSA Journal of International and Comparative Law* (1999) 407.

[14] Ibid.
[15] OECD, above n. 3.
[16] Article 7 Code of Liberalisation of Capital Movements, in ibid.
[17] Ibid.
[18] OECD, above n. 3.

This has been achieved in part, due to the requirement under the Codes for Member States periodically to submit their reservations and derogations for scrutiny by the OECD Committee on Capital Movements and Invisible Transactions which submits its report to the Council which may then recommend to a member that it undertake further liberalization and relax or remove existing reservations, such recommendations usually have strong political weight.[19] For the Member States, the Codes have not only assisted them to achieve liberalization but have enabled

> [...] member countries with less developed economies or those going through temporary economic difficulties to benefit from consultation and understanding by their peers. At the same time, the Codes have served as a useful yardstick by which the liberalisation efforts of member countries can be assessed and compared over time.[20]

For private entrepreneurs, the Codes do not provide direct derivative rights in their favour (as do most modern investment treaties) but create a stable investment climate for long-term businesses in the member countries.[21]

The liberalization on capital movement by the OECD is also reflected in the Draft Multilateral Agreement on Investment (MAI). Article IV(4) of the Draft MAI obligated Member States to ensure free transfers of capital relating to investment. However, it also recognized the right of a Member State to impose restrictions on transfers to protect specified interests, including the rights of creditors or to ensure compliance with laws and regulations (eg tax laws) provided such restrictions are not used as a disguise to avoid the State's commitments under the Agreement (Article IV(4),(6)). Furthermore, under Article VI (Exceptions and Safeguards), a member may impose restrictions on transfers when it is facing or threatened by serious balance-of-payment difficulties, provided such restrictions are consistent with the Articles of Agreement of the IMF, do not exceed what is necessary to deal with the circumstances, and are imposed as temporary measures to be reviewed every six months. A Member State taking such measures is required not only to promptly inform the IMF but also to subject the measure for expert review by the IMF. This suggests recognition by the negotiating parties of the autonomy of Member States to impose restrictions on capital movement during periods of crisis whilst subjecting such restrictions to supranational scrutiny so as to prevent possible abuse or misuse by some Member States.

The most extensive liberalization of capital movement so far has been achieved by the European Union under the Maastricht Treaty. Free movement of capital is

---

[19] J. Alvarez, 'Political Protectionism and United States International Investment Obligations in Conflict: The Hazards of Exon-Florio', 30 *Virginia Journal of International Law* (1989) 1, 48–49; P. Muchlinski, *Mutinational Enterprises and the Law* (2nd edn, 2007) 248–251.
[20] OECD (ed.), *OECD Codes of Liberalisation of Capital Movements and Current Invisible Operations: User's Guide 2007* (2007) 16.
[21] Ibid., 14.

B. Development of International Law on Foreign Exchange Regulation 211

one of the four fundamental freedoms that form the basis of the Union.[22] Thus, Article 56(1) of the Maastricht Treaty (which came into force on 1 January 1994) sets out the basic rule on capital movement and states that '[...] all restrictions on the movement of capital between member states and between member states and third countries shall be prohibited'. Although the rules on movement of capital to third countries are said to be more 'complex than the provisions regarding movement within the EC'[23] nevertheless, unlike other treaties, the EU rules seek to regulate capital movement well beyond Member States to include third countries. Furthermore, the European Court of Justice (ECJ) has defined 'capital movement' very broadly: ranging from liquidation of an investment in real property to investment in real estate on the territory of a non-Member State by a non-resident, receipt of dividends from a foreign country and acquisition of securities, but not the exportation of cash.[24] However, even within the EU, some form of restrictions on capital is recognized. These are set out in Article 58(1) TEC which allows Member States to apply their tax laws which distinguish between taxpayers who are not in the same situation with regard to their place of residence or with regard to the place where their capital is invested, or measures taken to prevent infringement of national law and regulations, or to require

---

[22] The others are: free movement of persons, goods, and services. However, due to the sensitive nature of capital, it was the last to be formally liberalized by the adoption by the Article 1(1) Council of Europe of Directive 88/361 (1988) which provided that 'Member states shall abolish restrictions on movement of capital taking place between persons resident in Member states'. Thus, until the mid-1990s, free movement of capital within the EU only existed in principle rather than in practice as member countries were free to impose restrictions though urged by Article 68 EEC to be 'as liberal as possible' in granting exchange authorizations. See C. Barnard, *The Substantive Law of the EU: The Four Freedoms* (2004) 462–463; European Commission, 'Internal Market, The Free Movement of Capital', available at http://ec.europa.eu/internal_market/capital/index_en.htm.

[23] S. Peers, 'Free Movement of Capital: Learning Lessons or Slipping on Spilt Milk?', in C. Barnard and J. Scott (eds), *The Law of the Single European Market: Unpacking the Premises* (2002) 333, 335. Indeed, the EU Association Agreements with the 12 Mediterranean countries contain provisions on free movement of capital and grounds for limiting same which include balance of payments and national security concerns. However, such restrictions are only allowed for a limited period of time which must not go beyond what is necessary to deal with the problem. See S. Fares, 'Current Payments and Capital Movements in the EU-Mediterranean Association Agreements', 30(1) *Legal Issues of Economic Integration* (2003) 15.

[24] Eg *Manfred Trummer and Peter Mayer*, Case C-222/97 (1999) ECR I-1661 (prohibition on the creation of mortgages to cover a pre-existing foreign currency denominated debt); *Klaus Konle v Republik Oesterreich*, Case C-302/97 (1999) ECR 1-3099 (restriction on right to acquire and dispose of immovable property on the territory of another Member State), commented on in 37 *Common Market Law Review* (2000) 181; *Magarethe Ospelt v Schlössle Weissenberg Familienstiftung*, Case C-452/01, (2003) ECR 1-9473 (refusal of authorization to acquire agricultural land based on failure to meet residency requirements), commented on in 42 *Common Market Law Review* (2005) 1133; *Commission v Portuguese Republic*, Case C-367/98, commented on in 40 *Common Market Law Review* (2003) 493 (requirement of prior approval for the acquisition of substantial shareholdings); *Commission v French Republic*, Case C-483/99, commented on ibid.; *Commission v Belgium* (*Golden Shares* cases), Case-503/99, commented on ibid.; Peers, above n. 23, 336–337; L. Flynn, 'Coming of Age: The Free Movement of Capital Case Law', 39 *Common Market Law Review* (2002) 773, 776–778; A. Landsmeer, 'Movement of Capital and Other Freedoms', 28(1) *Legal Issues of Economic Integration* (2001) 57; idem., 'Capital Movements: On the Interpretation of Article 73b of the EC Treaty', 27(2) *Legal Issues of Economic Integration* (2000) 195.

declaration of capital movements for administrative or statistical purposes, or to take measures which are justified on grounds of public policy or public security; or restrictions justifiable under the right of establishment chapter (Article 58(2)). However, Article 58(3) TEC states that such measures '[...] shall not constitute a means of arbitrary discrimination or a disguised restriction on the free movement of capital and payments'. In deciding whether a measure is an unlawful restriction, the ECJ uses a number of criteria which include: non-discrimination, overriding reasons based on general interest, suitability for securing the objective which they pursue, and proportionality, ie that the measure does not go beyond what is necessary to attain the objective pursued.[25]

Exchange controls and restrictions are also dealt with in the GATT 1994 and GATS in the context of trade restrictions and payments for services, both of which require such restrictions to be in conformity with the Articles of Agreement of the IMF. For example, Article XV GATT permits Member States to use exchange controls and restrictions in accordance with the Fund's Articles, and Article XI of GATS safeguards the rights and obligations of Fund members, including their right to use exchange actions in conformity with the Fund's Articles.[26] By Article XXI(b) GATT, nothing in the Agreement is to prevent a contracting party from taking any action '[...] which it considers necessary for the protection of its essential security interests'. The jurisprudence suggests that 'essential security interests' might include exchange control measures taken by a Member State to protect its economic interests, even though it is unsettled as to whether the article is self-judging or a claim to national security is subject to international scrutiny.[27] To sum up, it could be said that the development of

---

[25] Flynn, above n. 24, 798–802; Landsmeer, above n. 24.
[26] Article XI GATS (Payments and Transfers) provides that:

'1. Except under the circumstances envisaged in Article XII [Restrictions to Safeguard the Balance of Payments], a Member shall not apply restrictions on international transfers and payments for current transactions relating to its specific commitments.
2. Nothing in this Agreement shall affect the rights and obligations of the members of the International Monetary Fund under the Articles of Agreement of the Fund, including the use of exchange actions which are in conformity with the Articles of Agreement, provided that a member shall not impose restrictions on any capital transactions inconsistently with its specific commitments regarding such transactions, except under article XII or at the request of the Fund.'

In the *US—Measures Affecting the Cross-border Supply of Gambling & Betting Services* case, Antigua claimed amongst others that the United States maintained measures that restricted international money transfers and payments relating to the cross-border supply of gambling and betting services in violation of Article XI:I GATS. The United States denied the claim. Although the Dispute Settlement Panel did not rule on the issue due to insufficiency of facts and arguments submitted by the parties, nonetheless, it did emphasize the crucial role played by Article XI in securing the value of specific commitments undertaken by members under the GATS. It then noted that, 'Article XI does not deprive members from regulating the use of financial instruments, such as credit cards, provided that these regulations are consistent with other relevant GATS provisions, in particular Article VI'. See *US—Measures Affecting the Cross-border Supply of Gambling & Betting Services*, WT/DS285/R, paras 6.441–6.442.
[27] In *India—Quantitative Restrictions on Imports of Agricultural, Textile and Industrial Products*, 6 April 1999, WT/DS90/R, as modified by Appellate Body Report, WT/DS90/AB/R, AB-1999-3,

capital control rules has not only been slow but also taken diverse approaches; the more homogeneous market-oriented economies of Europe and the OECD adopting a more liberal attitude to capital movements as compared to the more heterogeneous organizations such as the IMF and GATT. However, one common element found in all the resulting instruments is the recognition of the right of Member States to impose exchange restrictions under certain circumstances.

C. Treatment of Capital Transfer Restrictions under Modern Investment Treaties

One of the main reasons why countries accede to investment treaties is to encourage investment by affording protection and reasonable standard of treatment to foreign investors while at the same time safeguarding the host State's sovereignty to regulate their economy.[28] This is achieved by vesting foreign investors with substantive rights and the procedural means to enforce the rights against inconsistent host State actions.[29] One of the substantive provisions on investor/investment protection in such treaties is the requirement of free repatriation or transfer of funds. From the point of view of the foreign investor, the essence of making an investment is to make profits and distribute the same to its shareholders, who might reside in its home country or in several countries. Repatriation of funds might also be needed by the foreign investor for other purposes such as to service external loans, pay licence fees and royalties, purchase raw materials and machinery for production, and pay for other services. These are critical for the success of an

---

the WTO Dispute Settlement Panel was willing to scrutinize India's quantitative restrictions based on Article XXI GATT. W. Cann Jr, 'Creating Standards and Accountability for the Use of the WTO Security Exception: Reducing the Role of Power-based Relations and Establishing a New Balance between Sovereignty and Multilateralism', 26 *Yale Journal of International Law* (2001) 413; M. Hahn, 'Vital Interests and the Law of GATT: An Analysis of GATT's Security Exception', 12 *Michigan Journal of International Law* (1991) 558; D. Akande and S. Williams, 'International Adjudication on National Security Issues: What Role for the WTO?', 43 *Virginia Journal of International Law* (2003) 365, 402–403; *Sempra Energy International v Argentina*, ICSID Case No. ARB/02/16, Award, 28 September 2007, para. 384.

[28] *Saluka Investments BV (The Netherlands) v The Czech Republic*, Partial Award, 17 March 2006, para. 300; *El Paso Energy v Argentina*, Decision on Jurisdiction, 27 April 2006, para. 70.

[29] S. Franck, 'Foreign Direct Investment, Investment Treaty Arbitration, and the Rule of Law', 19(2) *Pacific McGeorge Global Business and Development Law Journal* (2007) 337, 341–345; R. Dolzer and M. Stevens, *Bilateral Investment Treaties* (1995); G. Sacerdoti, 'Bilateral Investment Treaties and Multilateral Instruments on Investment Protection', 269 *Recueil des Cours—Collected Courses* (1997) 251, 255. To some extent, investment treaties enhance 'good governance' by sanctioning unprincipled and arbitrary actions of the host State institutions. See R. Dolzer, 'The Impact of International Investment Treaties on Domestic Administrative Law', 37 *NYU Journal of International Law and Politics* (2005) 953; G. Harten and M. Loughin, 'Investment Treaty Arbitration as a Species of Global Administrative Law', 17 *European Journal of International Law* (2006) 121; Hague Academy of International Law (ed.), *New Aspects of International Investment Law* (2006).

investment.[30] Hence, the importance of the repatriation provision in investment treaties. On the other hand, a host State might be concerned about the depletion of its foreign reserves through such transfers and the adverse effect it might have on the economy especially during times of economic difficulties. Therefore, it will not want to curtail its discretion to adopt measures, including exchange restrictions, in order to deal with economic difficulties.[31] To balance these competing goals, different approaches have been adopted by different investment treaties, which may broadly be summarized into three or four—each of which may have variations.

The first approach is to provide for free transfer unrestrained by domestic law or economic circumstances of the host State. Typical of this is the Finland/Brazil BIT (1995) which states in Article 7 (1) that '[e]ach [...] party shall with respect to investments in its territory by investors of the other [...] party allow the free transfer into and out of its territory [...]' of funds.[32] In a similar vein, Article 14 of the Energy Charter Treaty (ECT) obligates a Member State to guarantee free transfer of funds in and out of its territory by investors from other State parties subject to measures to protect the right of creditors and satisfaction of judgments obtained '[...] through the equitable, non-discriminatory,

---

[30] B. Land, *Similarities and Differences between Oil and Mining Contracts*, LLM dissertation (1996) 128–130, available at http://www.oilandgas.com/ogel, Volume 5(2) (2007). Not only does repatriation of capital occur in the day-to-day operations of multinational corporations but most of those surveyed indicated that the ability to repatriate funds is a key element in their investment decision-making process. See W. Shan, 'Foreign Investment in China and the Role of Law: Empirical Evidence from European Union Investors', 2(3) *Transnational Dispute Management* (2005) 31–32; C. Wendrich, 'The World Bank Guidelines as a Foundation for a Global Investment Treaty: A Problem-Oriented Approach', 2(5) *Transnational Dispute Management* (2005) 136–138.

[31] The home government of the foreign investor also has an economic interest in seeing that funds are repatriated not only for tax purposes but also to boost its economy. Thus, both the foreign investor and its home government will want an assurance that funds will be repatriated. On the other hand, officials of the host State's Central Bank and finance department might probably view such repatriation provisions as detrimental to the economy, whilst domestic investors might view such clauses as providing foreign investors preferential treatment. T. Wälde and A. Kolo, 'Investor-State Disputes: The Interface between Treaty-based International Investment Protection and Fiscal Sovereignty', 35 *Intertax* (2007) 424, 435–436; Muchlinski, above n. 19, 690–691; T. Wälde, 'International Investment under the 1994 Energy Charter Treaty', in T. Wälde (ed.), *The Energy Charter Treaty* (1996) 251; C. Wallace, *The Multinational Enterprise and Legal Control: Host State Sovereignty in an Era of Economic Globalisation* (2002) 430; UNCTAD, *Transfer of Funds* (2000) 6. A recent challenge of the legality of capital transfer provisions of the revised Colombia/Spain BIT in Colombia's Constitutional Court on the ground that it limits the autonomy of the country's Central Bank to regulate its foreign reserves and to stabilize the balance of trade was dismissed by the court. See, 'Colombian Court upholds Constitutionality of BIT with Spain', *ITN News* (15 October 2007), available at http://www.iisd.org/investment/itn/news.asp.

[32] Finland/Brazil BIT (1995); Article 6 UK/Chile BIT (1996) provides to the same effect. See also Article 6 UK/Ecuador BIT (1994); Article 6 UK/Venezuela BIT (1995); Article 7 Indian Model BIPA (2003); Article 6 UK/Nigeria BIT (1990); Article 6 UK/Azerbaijan BIT (1996); Article 6 UK/Czech Republic BIT (1990); Article 6 UK/South Africa BIT (1998); Article 6 UK/Kazakhstan BIT (1995); Article 6 UK/Pakistan BIT (1994); Article 6–6(2) UK/Zimbabwe BIT permits Zimbabwe to subject investments that were admitted prior to 1 May 1993 to restrictions then in existence.

C. Treatment of Capital Transfer Restrictions

and good faith application of its laws and regulations'.[33] Since these treaties do not contain provisions that allow for imposition of exchange restrictions during balance-of-payment difficulties, the pertinent question is whether the host State can restrict such transfers by law or regulation when faced with economic crisis or otherwise.

The opposite approach is to subject the free transfer to the host State exchange law and regulations which might change at any time unconstrained by economic circumstances or other treaties such as the IMF Agreement. A classic example of such is the China/Kuwait BIT which states that: '[...] [e]ach [...] party shall, subject to its laws and regulations, guarantee to the investors of the other [...] party the transfer of their investments and returns held in its territory'.[34] Here, the question is whether the 'provision protects the [foreign] investor only against restrictions on transfers that violate [the] host country laws'[35] or international law as well.

An intermediate approach is to provide for exceptions to the freedom to transfer through measures taken during periods of balance-of-payment problems provided such measures are necessary, consistent with the IMF (or WTO[36]) Agreement, imposed in a non-discriminatory manner and on a temporary basis. For instance, the proviso to Article 6 of the France/Uganda BIT permits a party to temporarily restrict transfers in case of 'serious balance of payments difficulties [...] or the threat thereof' provided such a restriction is promptly notified to the other party, shall not exceed six months, is consistent with the Articles of Agreement of the IMF, and imposed in an 'equitable, non-discriminatory and in good faith basis'.[37] In this case, the question is how and who decides on whether

---

[33] This limitation on transfer is obtainable in most investment treaties and it is aimed at allowing the enforcement of the host State's bankruptcy or insolvency laws against a foreign investor without violating the host country's transfer obligations. See UNCTAD, above n. 31, 35–36.

[34] Article 6 China/Kuwait BIT (1985); Article 6(1) China/Botswana BIT (2000); Article 7(1) Korea/Malaysia BIT (1988). Indeed, Article 2(b) of the Protocol to the China/Thailand BIT (1985) gives wide discretion to the Chinese authorities in approving or refusing transfer applications. It simply states that in case of balance-of-payment difficulties, '[...] the nationals and companies of the Thai Kingdom who have invested in the People's Republic of China may apply to the competent authorities of the People's Republic of China, who shall accord their "sympathetic consideration" and render favourable assistance'. Presumably, in this case, what amounts to a 'sympathetic consideration' and 'favourable assistance' is entirely left for the Chinese authorities to decide provided the decision is not arbitrary or discriminatory.

[35] UNCTAD, International *Investment Agreements: Trends and Emerging Issues* (2006) 39.

[36] Exchange Restrictions under WTO rules contemplate a restriction on the importation of goods (eg equipment and machinery or other inputs for an investment) into the host State. Article 14(7) Canada Model BIT states that '[...] [n]otwithstanding paragraph 1 [Free Transfers] a party may restrict transfers in kind in circumstances where it could otherwise restrict transfers under the WTO Agreement'. See also Article 14(6) ECT, and Article IV.4.5 Draft MAI which permit a State party to restrict the transfer of a return in kind which is allowable under GATT provided the State party ensures that transfers of returns in kind is effected as authorized in an investment agreement or authorization between itself and the foreign investor.

[37] See also Article 15 ASEAN Framework Agreement (1998); Article 72 Japan/Mexico Economic Partnership Agreement (2004); Article VI Draft MAI; Article 2104 NAFTA states that 'Nothing in the Agreement shall be construed to prevent a party from adopting or maintaining

or not a measure is necessary. Is it the host State, the IMF or an international tribunal? What amounts to a discriminatory exchange restriction?

The fourth approach is closely related to the first one in that it subjects the right to transfer not only to the domestic laws and regulations of the host State imposed during balance-of-payment difficulties, in a non-arbitrary and non-discriminatory manner and consistent with the IMF Agreement, but also insulates such measures from third party scrutiny. This approach is illustrated by the 2005 India/Singapore Comprehensive Economic Cooperation Agreement. While Article 6.6 of the India/Singapore Agreement obligates each party to allow transfer of funds, Article 6.7 permits a party to impose restrictions when faced with/or threatened by balance-of-payment difficulties, provided such restrictions are consistent with the IMF Agreement, are 'necessary to deal with the [economic] circumstances', be 'temporary' and 'applied on a national treatment basis'. Article 6.12 goes further to exempt from the investment disciplines any action taken by a party 'which it considers necessary for the protection of its essential security interests'. By virtue of Article 6.12.4 and Annex 5 such security exception measures '[...] shall be non-justiciable in that it shall not be open to any arbitral tribunal to review the merits of any such decision'.[38] What is the

measures that restrict transfers where the party experiences serious balance-of-payments difficulties, or the threat thereof [...]'. However, the provision goes further to state that the country imposing the restriction '*must* enter into bona fide consultations with the IMF on economic adjustment measures to address the fundamental underlying economic problems causing the difficulties' and 'adopt economic policies in consonance with these consultations' (emphasis added). A. Egea, 'Balance-of-Payments Provisions in the GATT and NAFTA', 30 *Journal of World Trade* (1996) 5. In contrast to NAFTA, the capital transfer provisions of the Chile/US Free Trade Agreement seem to give Chile more powers and leeway by limiting some of the rights of US investors. Article 10.8 [the freedom to transfer] is made subject to Annex 10-C which states among other things that, except in very limited circumstances (such as transfer of proceeds of foreign direct investment and/or payments pursuant to a loan or bond issued in foreign market), an investor may submit a claim against Chile for alleged violation of the transfer guarantee only after one year has elapsed since the event giving rise to the claim. This would allow for a longer cooling-off period and encourage a negotiated settlement of the transfer dispute—the more so as Chile shall not be liable for damages suffered during the one-year period provided such restrictive measures did not substantially impede transfers. Most importantly from Chile's perspective, claims arising from the restrictive measures shall be subject to the applicable domestic law, probably that of Chile. In other words, once the restrictions were found to be in conformity with Chilean law, the claim is unlikely to succeed. If this interpretation is correct then it is improbable that any claim for violation of the capital transfer provisions will succeed because Chile will ensure that all restrictions comply with its law. US/Singapore FTA (2003), Annex 15A, provides for similar rules which also contains an exchange of letters between the US and Singapore governments setting out what the parties described as an 'interpretative guidance' on the said provisions.

[38] The non-justiciability of security measures seems to be an emerging trend in Investment and Free Trade Agreement negotiations of many countries, including the United States, probably as a result of increased security concerns. For example, the proposed US/Peru FTA and US/Panama FTA are likely to contain the new key provisions of US Trade Compromise agreed upon by the US Congress which provide amongst others for no greater substantive rights to foreign investors than US investors in the United States and non-challengeability of measures based on national security concerns. See Office of the United States Trade Representative, Bipartisan Agreement on Trade Policy: Investment (May 2007), available at www.ustr.gov; Mark Kantor, 'US Trade

effect of such apparently self-judging provision and how can it be reconciled with the parties' international obligations under the IMF Agreement and the investment treaty? Does such a provision oust the jurisdiction of international tribunals (perhaps including the ICJ) completely and subject any dispute arising thereof to diplomatic negotiations between the parties? In other words, how should these provisions be interpreted? We shall explore some of these interpretative questions in the next section.

D. Application of the Doctrine of Necessity under International Law to Exchange Restriction Measures

As we have seen above, the right to impose exchange restrictions under most instruments such as the OECD Codes, GATS, IMF Agreement and BITs is available to a Member State only when it faces balance-of-payment problems or economic emergency such as that faced by Argentina in 2001, Malaysia, Indonesia, and Korea, etc, during the Asian financial crises of 1997/1998. However, as noted above in the first category of investment treaties, the free transfer provision seems absolute, ie there is no explicit right of a host State to restrict transfers when faced with balance-of-payment problems or a general exception based on national security or other similar situations. The absence of balance-of-payment provisions in the first category of investment treaties will not prevent a host State from invoking the doctrine of necessity or emergency under customary international law as a basis to derogate from its transfer obligations under such investment treaties. Thus, under customary international law as reflected in Article 25 of the International Law Commission's (ILC) Articles on State Responsibility, necessity might be relied upon by a State as a ground to derogate from its international obligations which otherwise might be wrongful. The act or measure sought to be relied upon by the State must have been occasioned by an 'essential interest' of the State, that interest must have been threatened by a 'grave and imminent peril', the measure must have been the 'only means' of safeguarding that interest, the act must not have 'seriously impaired an essential interest of the State towards which the obligation existed', and the State seeking to rely on the measure must not have 'contributed to the occurrence of the state of necessity' all of which must be cumulatively satisfied.[39] Hence, the threshold for the plea of necessity is very high, otherwise it might be used by States to elude their international obligations which would be contrary

---

Compromise—USTR Summaries of Investment and Port Security Provisions' (14 May 2007). There remains, though, the issue that exceptions defined as self-judging could be examined under the concept of 'abuse of right'.

[39] *Gabcikovo-Nagymaros Project (Hungary v Slovakia)*, ICJ, 25 September 1997, paras 51, 52; *Sempra v Argentina*, above n. 27, para. 355; *CMS v Argentina*, ICSID Case No. ARB/01/8, Decision of the *Ad hoc* Committee on the Application to Annulment, 25 September 2007, paras 129–130.

to the stability and predictability of the law.[40] Accordingly, this calls for a restrictive interpretation of provisions derogating from treaty obligations.

In any case, a situation of necessity might not exonerate the State from compensating those affected by its conduct.[41] This is so because necessity is only a 'ground recognised by customary international law for precluding the wrongfulness of an act not in conformity with an international obligation'[42] which applies on an exceptional basis and '[...] without prejudice to the question of compensation for any material loss caused by the act in question'.[43]

What is an 'essential interest' of the State depends on the facts of each case,[44] but it is acknowledged that it is not limited to matters relating to the very survival of the State such as a military invasion, but also includes threats to its economic, ecological, or other vital interests.[45] Thus, in the *CMS*, *Enron*, *LG&E*, and *Sempra* cases, the tribunals agreed that a severe economic crisis such

---

[40] *Enron v Argentina*, Award, 22 July 2007, para. 304: 'There is no disagreement either about the fact that state of necessity is a most exceptional remedy subject to very strict conditions because otherwise it would open the door to elude any international obligation.'; *CMS Gas Transmission Company v The Argentine Republic*, ICSID Case No. ARB/01/8, Award, 12 May 2005, para. 317; *LG&E Energy Corp, LG&E Capital Corp and LG&E International Inc v Argentine Republic*, ICSID Case No. ARB/02/1, Decision on Liability, 3 October 2006, para. 228; *Gabcikovo-Nagymaros Project*, above n. 39, para. 51; J. Crawford, *The International Law Commission's Articles on State Responsibility* (2002) 178 and fn 398 and accompanying text.

[41] See Article 27 ILC Articles; *Gabcikovo-Nagymaros Project*, above n. 39, para. 48; *CMS v Argentina*, above n. 40, paras 390, 392; *Enron v Argentina*, above n. 40, para. 313; *BG v Argentina*, Final Award, 24 December 2007, para. 412; Crawford, above n. 40.

[42] *Gabcikovo-Nagymaros Project*, above n. 39, para. 51; *Legal Consequences of the Construction of a Wall in the Occupied Palestinian Territory*, ICJ, Advisory Opinion, 9 July 2004, para. 140; *CMS v Argentina*, above n. 40, para. 317; *Enron v Argentina*, above n. 40, para. 303.

[43] Article 27(b) ILC Articles. Although the *CMS*, *Enron* and *LG&E* tribunals all agreed on this principle, nonetheless they differed on whether damages are payable for the duration of the emergency. Whilst the *CMS*, *BG* and *Enron* tribunals held the host State liable, the *LG&E* tribunal exonerated it from any liability during the emergency and shifted the cost on to the foreign investor. See S. Schill, 'International Investment Law and the Host State's Power to Handle Economic Crises: Comment on the ICSID Decision in LG&E v Argentina', 24(3) *Journal of International Arbitration*. (2007) 265, 281, 284; A. Reinisch, 'Necessity in International Investment Arbitration—An Unnecessary Split of Opinions in Recent ICSID Cases? Comments on CMS v. Argentina and LG&E v. Argentina', 3(5) *Transnational Dispute Management* (2006), also in 8(2) *Journal of World Investment and Trade* (2007) 191; R. Luzi, 'Bilateral Investment Treaties and Economic Crises: Do states have carte blanche?', an unpublished paper (2007), on file with the authors; J. Alvarez and K. Khamsi, 'The Argentine Crisis and Foreign Investors: A Glimpse of the Foreign Investment Regime' (unpublished manuscript, March 2008) on file with the authors; contrast with W. Burke-White and A. von Staden, 'Investment Protection in Extraordinary Times: The Interpretation and Application of Non-Precluded Measures Provisions in Bilateral Investment Treaties', *University of Pennsylvania Law School Working paper*, No. 152 (2007) 64–65, available at http://lsr.nellco.org/upenn/wps/papers/152/.

[44] *CMS v Argentina*, above n. 40, para. 252. Although the ICJ accepted, in principle, the plea of necessity in the *Gabcikovo-Nagymaros Project*, above n. 39, it rejected it as a defence based on the facts of the case. See also *Serbian Loans*, above n. 9; *Russian Indemnity Case*, 1912; *Societe Commerciale de Belgique*, PCIJ Series A/B, No. 78 (1939); *Case Concerning Oil Platforms (Iran v US)*, ICJ, 6 November 2003, para. 76; *Military and Paramilitary Activities (Nicaragua v US)*, ICJ, 27 June 1986.

[45] *Gabcikovo-Nagymaros Project*, above n. 39, para. 53; *Sempra v Argentina*, above n. 27, para. 374.

D. Application of the Doctrine of Necessity to Exchange Restrictions

as that faced by Argentina in 2001 could constitute a threat to essential interest to justify reliance on necessity under customary international law and under the emergency clause of the US/Argentina BIT.[46]

Under Article 25(1) of the ILC Articles, the measures adopted by a State invoking necessity have to constitute the 'only way' or 'only means' for that State to protect its essential interest. This position was accepted by the *CMS*, *Enron*, *Sempra* and *LG&E* tribunals respectively which affirmed that, 'the plea of necessity is excluded if there are other (otherwise lawful) means available, even if they may be more costly or less convenient',[47] and that '[...] the act must be the only means available to the State in order to protect an interest'.[48] But whilst the *CMS* tribunal held that the fact that other options such as 'dollarisation of the economy, granting of subsidies to the affected population or industries' were available to Argentina meant that the measures adopted were not the only means available, hence one of the requirements of necessity was not met,[49] the *LG&E* tribunal did not apply such a strict test. Instead, it rejected the claimant's contention that the defence should not be available because the measure adopted by Argentina was not the only means available to respond to the crisis and held that the measure (Emergency Law) was a 'necessary and legitimate' means to respond to the crisis,[50] and that in the circumstance of the case, the '[...] economic recovery package was the only means to respond to the crisis'.[51] These cases suggest that whether or not measures taken by a host State in an emergency situation are justified under customary international law might depend on the margin of appreciation to be accorded the State by an international tribunal.

In applying the concept of 'margin of appreciation' ('deference') to foreign exchange restriction measures, an arbitral tribunal should weigh the host State measure against the investor rights by using criteria such as the economic background to the crisis, ie whether or not it had more to do with domestic policies

---

[46] Article XI US/Argentina BIT (1991) provides: 'This Treaty shall not preclude the application by either party of measures necessary for the maintenance of public order, the fulfilment of its obligations with respect to the maintenance or restoration of international peace and security, or the protection of its own essential security interests.'

[47] *CMS v Argentina*, above n. 40, para. 324; *Enron v Argentina*, above n. 40, para. 309.

[48] *LG&E v Argentina*, above n. 40, para. 250.

[49] *CMS v Argentina*, above n. 40, paras 323–324; *Enron v Argentina*, above n. 40, paras 308–309. In this sense the tribunal's approach is consistent with that of the ICJ and other international tribunals. See *Gabcikovo-Nagymaros Project*, above n. 39, para. 55; *Legal Consequences of the Construction of a Wall in the Occupied Palestinian Territory*, above n. 42, para. 140; *LAFICO v Burundi*, 96 ILR (1996) 279, 319; *The Russian Indemnity* case (1912), above n. 44; *The Neptune* case discussed in Luzi, above n. 43. See generally, Crawford, above n. 40, 178–186.

[50] *LG&E v Argentina*, above n. 40, paras 239–240. It further stated: 'The Tribunal accepts that the provisions of the Emergency Law that abrogated calculation of the tariffs in U.S. dollars and PPI adjustments, as well as freezing tariffs were necessary measures to deal with the extremely serious economic crisis. Indeed, it would be unreasonable to conclude that during this period the Government should have implemented a tariff increase pursuant to an index pegged to an economy experiencing a high inflationary period.' Ibid., para. 242.

[51] Ibid., para. 257.

or the effect of a 'contagion' ('endogenous' or 'exogenous' factors),[52] whether or not there was consultation with the IMF and those to be directly and immediately affected by the proposed measure, whether or not the measure adopted is the least restrictive or burdensome on foreign investors, the declared or expected duration of the measure, and whether there was an element of discrimination. Thus, where the preponderance of evidence suggests that the crisis was foreseeable in the sense that the country was, for instance, treading the same path that led to economic crisis in the past or in other similarly situated countries, or borrowing beyond its means to service debts,[53] or allowed its trade deficits to grow too wide, or failed to undertake structural reforms (eg in the banking and the financial sectors) despite advice by domestic and international experts, these should count against the host State.

Similarly, where it is apparent that the exchange restrictions were imposed excessively, ie substantially longer or more extensively than required and without providing for palliative measures—such as repatriation of limited amounts by foreign investors, to an extent that the foreign investors were made to bear a disproportionate burden of the measures—then the margin of appreciation should go against the host State. This approach is consistent with State practice and international jurisprudence.[54]

Many investment treaties permit the imposition or maintenance of exchange restrictions during balance-of-payment difficulties subject to certain requirements including: that the measures are consistent with the Articles of Agreement of the IMF, shall not be more than necessary to deal with the balance-of-payment difficulties, be temporary and applied in a non-discriminatory manner.[55] Some

---

[52] *CMS v Argentina*, above n. 40, para. 328; *Enron v Argentina*, above n. 40, para. 311. A 'contagion effect' occurs '[...] where a country pursuing sound economic and financial policies is the victim of a panic generated by another country's financial troubles'. F. Gianviti, 'The Prevention and Resolution of International Financial Crises—A Perspective from the International Monetary Fund', in M. Giovanoli (ed.), *International Monetary Law: Issues for the New Millennium* (2000) 103.

[53] For example, the 1982 Mexican economic crisis which necessitated the imposition of exchange controls was caused, to a large extent, by over-borrowing by both the public and private sectors on the assumption that Mexico's oil reserves would generate sufficient revenues to meet its debt service. See *West v Multibanco Comermex*, 807 F.2d 820 (1987); S. Zamora, 'Peso-Dollar Economics and the Imposition of Foreign Exchange Controls in Mexico', 32 *American Journal of Comparative Law* (1984) 99. A similar factor contributed to the 1998 Asian financial crises. See, A. Lowenfeld, *International Economic Law* (2002) 565–616.

[54] *Sempra v Argentina*, above n. 27, paras 249–251.

[55] Article 2104(3) NAFTA; Article VI Draft MAI states that Member States may impose exchange restrictions in the event of serious balance-of-payment difficulties provided such measures are consistent with the Articles of Agreement of the IMF, shall not exceed what is necessary, shall be temporary and be eliminated as soon as conditions permit, shall be promptly notified to the Parties Group and the IMF, shall be subject to review and approval within six months after, and the measures shall be approved by the IMF. Similarly, Article III(6)(d) World Bank Guidelines on the Treatment of Foreign Direct Investment (1992) states that countries should permit free transfer and that such transfers shall be allowed in instalments in the event of imposition of restrictions due to balance of payment problems provided such transfers are allowed to be made 'within a period which will be as short as possible and will not in any case exceed five

D. Application of the Doctrine of Necessity to Exchange Restrictions 221

investment treaties provide for the imposition of reasonable exchange restrictions for temporary periods, not exceeding a certain time frame (eg six months or one year) provided a certain percentage (eg 50 per cent) of such transfers is allowed during such period.[56] These criteria could be said to be similar to those used by international courts and tribunals (such as the ECJ, ECtHR, GATT/WTO dispute settlement panels) in their analysis of the margin of appreciation and proportionality in given cases or the determination of possible breach of the fair and equitable standard of treatment by arbitral tribunals. Such scrutiny enables a tribunal to review the measures adopted by the host State so as to ascertain whether the chosen means sufficiently take into account the interests of the foreign investor. Such a review is necessary because

> [...] completely refraining from reviewing the host state's measures would result in insufficient protection for foreign investors in emergency situations and would allow states broadly to avoid their international obligations.[57]

Thus, in *Saluka v Czech Republic*, the tribunal cited with approval the decision in *S.D. Myers v Canada* to the effect that governments enjoy a margin of appreciation to regulate their domestic matters in the public interest while at the same time taking into account the legitimate expectations of foreign investors.[58] Accordingly,

> [...] the determination of a breach of the [FET by the host state] requires a weighing of the [investor's] legitimate and reasonable expectations on the one hand and the [host state's] legitimate regulatory interests on the other.[59]

---

years from the date of sale' or liquidation of the investment. For an analysis of the World Bank Guidelines see Wendrich, above n. 30.

[56] Article 6(4) China/Kuwait BIT (1985); Article 5 UK/Russia BIT (1989) provide for exchange restrictions to be exercised 'equitably and in good faith' manner as provided for by the State's laws provided such powers shall not be used to impede the transfer of returns of a 'minimum of 20% a year'. See also Article 6(1) UK/Bolivia BIT (1990); Article 6 France/Uganda BIT (undated) which permits temporary restrictions on transfers 'provided that this restriction: (i) shall be promptly notified to the other party, (ii) shall be consistent with the Articles of Agreement with the IMF (iii) shall not exceed in any case six months, (iv) would be imposed in an equitable, non-discriminatory and good faith basis'. Article 6(3) UK/Argentina BIT (1990), providing for restrictions to be exercised equitably and in good faith manner provided such restrictions shall not exceed 18 months in respect to each application to transfer and that the transfer of at least 50 per cent of the capital and of the returns shall be permitted by the end of the first year. However, in no circumstances may such restrictions be imposed on the same investor after a period of three years from the start of such restrictions. Furthermore, it is stated that pending the transfer of his capital and returns, the investor shall have the opportunity to invest them in a manner which will preserve their real value until the transfer occurs.

[57] Schill, above n. 43, 281.

[58] According to the *S.D. Myers* tribunal, the determination of a breach of the obligation of 'fair and equitable treatment' by the host State 'must be made in the light of the high measure of deference that international law generally extends to the right of domestic authorities to regulate matters within their own borders'. *S.D. Myers, Inc v Canada* (UNCITRAL, NAFTA), Award on the Merits, 13 November 2000, para. 263; *Tecmed v Mexico*, above n. 2, para. 122.

[59] *Saluka Investments BV (The Netherlands) v The Czech Republic*, above n. 28, para. 306.

Similarly, in *Tecmed v Mexico*, the tribunal noted the due deference owed to States when assessing issues that affect its public policy or its society as a whole—and the actions taken to protect those values. However, that does not prevent the tribunal from examining the actions of the host State to determine whether such measures are reasonable with respect to their goals and the legitimate expectations of the foreign investor. This approach also finds support in the jurisprudence of the ECtHR, the ECJ and the ICJ on the principle of margin of appreciation.[60]

In the context of exchange restrictions, an international tribunal would defer to the host State authorities to the extent that the measures are legitimate, transparent, non-discriminatory, and least restrictive of investment in achieving the legitimate public purpose.[61] For as the UK House of Lords noted in *In re Helbert Wagg & Co Ltd*,

[a]n international tribunal [...] 'is entitled to be satisfied that the [...] law is a genuine foreign exchange law [...] and is not a law passed ostensibly with that object, but in reality with some object not in accordance with the usage of nations', or, in other words, is not abusive.[62]

An exchange restriction measure which failed to pass such a judicial scrutiny might, at best, amount to a breach of the fair and equitable standard of treatment or the 'national treatment' standard[63] and, at worst, a breach of the expropriation provision of an investment treaty, as discussed below, but before that we will complete our analysis of the *Argentine* cases.

All the tribunals in the four *Argentine* cases referred to above agreed that the emergency clause in the BIT was not self-judging. The tribunal in the *CMS* case held that unlike other US BITs such as those with Russia and Bahrain, and Article XXI GATT which expressly contain self-judging clauses,[64] Article XI of the US/Argentina BIT could not be interpreted as self-judging. The tribunal in the *Enron* case reached the same conclusion. In its opinion,

[w]hile there is nothing that would prevent an interpretation allowing for the inclusion of economic emergency in the context of Article XI, to interpret that such a

---

[60] See generally, Y. Shany, 'Towards a General Margin of Appreciation Doctrine in International Law?', 16(5) *European Journal of International Law* (2006) 907; H. Yourow, 'The Margin of Appreciation Doctrine in the Dynamics of European Human Rights Jurisprudence', 3 *Connecticut Journal of International Law* (1988) 111; Burke-White and von Staden, above n. 43, 46–50; E. Benvenisti, 'Margin of Appreciation, Consensus, and Universal Standards', 31 *NYU Journal of International Law and Politics* (1999) 843.
[61] Wälde, above n. 10; C. Proctor, *Mann on the Legal Aspect of Money* (6th edn, 2005) 520.
[62] *In re Helbert Wagg & Co Ltd*, House of Lords, 1956, Ch. 323, at 352.
[63] Proctor, above n. 61, 514–520.
[64] Whilst the exception provisions of those treaties preclude measures adopted by a party 'which it considers necessary' for the protection of its security interests, the US/Argentina BIT speaks simply of 'necessary' measures, not of those considered by a party to be such. As such, it concluded that Article XI of the Treaty is not a self-judging clause. See *CMS v Argentina*, above n. 40, para. 373; *LG&E v Argentina*, above n. 40, para. 212; *Sempra v Argentina*, above n. 27, para. 388.

D. Application of the Doctrine of Necessity to Exchange Restrictions

determination is self-judging would be definitely inconsistent with the object and purpose [of the treaty]. In fact, the Treaty would be deprived of any substantive meaning.[65]

Accordingly, the tribunal has the jurisdiction to review not only whether or not the measures adopted were taken in good faith but also to examine the substantive measures to determine whether the requirements of necessity under customary law or the treaty have been met.[66]

In order to decide whether or not particular measures are necessary in the investment context, one might draw an analogy from the jurisprudence of other international tribunals such as the ICJ, GATT/WTO, the European Court of Justice and the European Court of Human Rights.[67] For example, in interpreting Article XX(1)(d) of the Iran/US Treaty of Amity, Economic Relations and Consular Rights of 1955 (which provided in similar terms to that between US and Nicaragua that a party could take measures 'necessary' to protect its essential security interests), the ICJ cited with approval its decision in *Military and Paramilitary Activities in and against Nicaragua*,[68] to the effect that 'the measures taken must not merely be such as tend to protect the essential security interests of the party taking them, but must be "necessary" for that purpose' and that 'whether a given measure is "necessary" is not purely a question for the subjective judgment of the party' but has to be 'assessed by the court'.[69] In the *Nicaragua* case, the court noted that measures designed to protect essential security interest must not merely be 'useful' but 'necessary'. In the circumstances

---

[65] *Enron v Argentina*, above n. 40, para. 332; *Sempra v Argentina*, above n. 27, para. 374. According to the tribunals, as a matter of principle, the object and purpose of the treaty is to 'apply in situations of economic difficulties and hardship that require the protection of the internationally guaranteed rights of its beneficiaries', as such, 'any interpretation resulting in an escape route from the obligations defined cannot be easily reconciled with the object and purpose', ibid., para. 379; *Enron v Argentina*, above n. 40, para. 331. Indeed, this interpretation is supported by the negotiation history of the relevant treaties. In his testimony to the US Senate at the time the treaties were being negotiated, Professor Kenneth Vandevelde, then a State Department official involved in the negotiations, explained that a self-judging clause would not only hurt the right of American investors abroad at times when they needed the most protection, such as when they sought to challenge the expropriatory actions of host States before international tribunals, but that a self-judging clause would 'potentially eviscerate the entire agreement. A treaty which permits a party to take any measure necessary to its essential security interests and which permits that party to be the sole judge of what is necessary to such interests arguably imposes merely illusory obligations on the party.' Cited by Luzi, above n. 43, 12.

[66] *Enron v Argentina*, above n. 40, para. 339.

[67] Whilst acknowledging the need for caution in drawing upon the jurisprudence of these institutions because of differences in text and context, nonetheless, cross-referencing amongst international tribunals is now appreciated as a useful technique of developing international law. See A. Bjorklund, 'Reconciling State Sovereignty and Investor Protection in Denial of Justice Claims', 45 *Virginia Journal of International Law* (2005) 809, 865–866.

[68] *Military and Paramilitary Activities (Nicaragua v US)*, *ICJ Reports* (1986) 14.

[69] *Case Concerning Oil Platforms (Iran v US)*, *ICJ Reports*, 1996, para. 43. Accordingly, the provision did not restrict the court's jurisdiction but rather merely affords the parties a possible defence on the merits.

of the case, it held that the mining of Nicaraguan ports, the attack on oil installations, and the embargo by the United States could not be justified. The same conclusion was reached by the court in the *Oil Platform* case. This interpretation is consistent with the approach of the GATT/WTO tribunals in their interpretation of Article XX GATT,[70] the ECJ in its interpretation of the EC Treaty,[71] and the ECtHR in the interpretation of national security as one of the grounds for curtailing any of the human rights guaranteed by the European Convention on Human Rights.[72]

Indeed, even with respect to the apparently self-judging Article XXI(b) GATT (which speaks of nothing in the GATT should be construed as precluding a Member State from 'taking any action *which it considers necessary* for the protection of its essential security interests'[73]), several commentators are of the opinion that the provision does not exclude a good faith judicial scrutiny of the measures taken in order to prevent an abusive use of the right. The GATT Panel in *United States—Trade Measures Affecting Nicaragua*, though limited by the terms of reference from inquiring into whether Article XXI precluded an examination into the merits of the claim, did express its concern by asking: if Article XXI was self-defining, by what means could the contracting parties ensure that it would not be used excessively or for purposes other than those contained in the provision?[74]

---

[70] *US—Restrictions on Imports of Tuna*, GATT Doc. DS29/R, para. 5.35; *US—Sect. 337 of the Tariff Act of 1930*, BISD 36S/345 para. 5.26 (1989); *Thailand—Restrictions on Importation and Internal Taxes on Cigarettes*, BISD 37S/200, para. 75 (20 February 1990); *US—Standards for Reformulated and Conventional Gasoline*, WT/DS2/R, paras 6.25–6.28. See generally, Cann, above n. 27, 452–456; J. Neumann and E. Turk, 'Necessity Revisited: Proportionality in World Trade Organisation Law After Korea-Beef, EC-Asbestos and EC-Sardines', 37(1) *Journal of World Trade* (2003) 199.

Although there are differences between trade and investment in terms of risks and textual (as pointed out in *Methanex v US*, Final Award, para. 6, Part II-Ch. B and para. 37 Part IV-Ch. B), nonetheless there are situations when an analogy could be drawn from the jurisprudence of the WTO, particularly when the text of the treaties are similar such as Article XX GATT and similar national security exception provisions contained in investment treaties.

[71] In interpreting Article 30 Energy Charter Treaty, which permits Member States to take action which would otherwise be contrary to the free movement of goods provisions where such action is necessary for the protection of public security, the ECJ has held that a measure is necessary to protect national security only when it is the measure least restrictive of the freedom being derogated from. See eg the *Richardt* case, [1991] ECR I-4627, at para. 24; *Emergency Stocks of Petroleum Products*, 3 *CMLR* (2001) 62, at 1637; Akande and Williams, above n. 27, 382–383. The ECJ has developed a three-pronged test for determining proportionality of an impugned Member State measure: suitability, indispensability, and proportionality '*sensu stricto*'. See J. Jans, 'Proportionality Revisited', 27 *Legal Issues in Economic Integration* (2000) 239; idem., 'Proportionality Once Again', 33(4) *Legal Issues in Economic Integration* (2006) 347; E. Ellis (ed.), *The Principle of Proportionality in the Laws of Europe* (1999); J. Schwarze, *European Administrative Law* (revised edn, 2006).

[72] *Smith and Grady v UK*, 29 EHR (2000) 493; *Lustig-Prean and Beckett v UK*, 29 EHRR (2000) 548; *Handyside*, EHRR, 7 December 1976; Akande and Williams, above n. 27.

[73] Article XXI(b) GATT (emphasis added).

[74] See Unpublished Panel Report on *United States—Trade Measures Affecting Nicaragua*, 1986 WL 363154, L/6053, para. 5.17 (13 October 1986) (unadopted) cited by Cann, above n. 27, fn. 101; S. Croley and J. Jackson, 'WTO Dispute Procedures, Standards of Review, and Deference

D. Application of the Doctrine of Necessity to Exchange Restrictions 225

This observation in respect of Article XXI GATT is arguably significant in the investment context in general and the right to repatriate capital in particular.[75] This is especially so having regard to, for instance, the national security exceptions of the India/Singapore Comprehensive Economic Cooperation Agreement (2005) and Annex 5 to the Agreement, as well as Article 21.2 of the Central American–Dominican Republic Free Trade Agreement (CAFTA-DR).[76] Article 6.6 of the India/Singapore Agreement guarantees free transfer of capital by each other's investors subject to the equitable, non-discriminatory, and good faith application of each party's bankruptcy, criminal, social security, and other laws. Article 6.7 allows for exchange restrictions to be imposed in the event of serious balance-of-payment difficulties provided the restrictions are consistent with the Articles of Agreement of the IMF, did not exceed those necessary to deal with the difficulties, imposed on a temporary and in a non-discriminatory manner. Whilst the general exceptions clause (Article 6.11) is formulated in a language similar to Article XX GATT, the security exception contained in Article 6.12 is in *pari materia* to Article XXI GATT except that Article 6.12(4) expressly states that the provisions shall be interpreted in accordance with the understanding of the parties on non-justiciability of the security exceptions as set out in Annexes 4 and 5 which form an integral part of the Agreement. Annex 5 states that in either investor-State or State-State arbitral proceedings, if the defendant

[. . .] asserts as a defence that the measure alleged to be a breach is within the scope of a security exception as set out in article 6.12 of the agreement, any decision of the [defendant] on such security considerations shall be non-justiciable in that it shall not be open to any arbitral tribunal to review the merits of any such decision.

In a similar vein, but to a lesser extent, Article 21.2 of CAFTA-DR states that nothing in the agreement shall be construed to preclude a party from applying measures that it considers necessary for the protection of its own security interests.[77]

---

to National Governments', 90 *American Journal of International Law* (1996) 193; J. Jackson, *World Trade Law and the GATT* (1969) 752. Because of the potential for an abusive use of the provision, it has been argued that, '[. . .] allowing WTO members to unilaterally determine when they can invoke the national security clause free from any panel review will undermine not only the rule of law element inherent in the dispute settlement system, but also the international trading system itself. Such a position would leave a big hole in the "rule of law" approach to international trade'. Akande and Williams, above n. 27, 402–403; Croley and Jackson, above n. 74, 209–211. A similar reservation was expressed by the arbitral tribunal in *Sempra v Argentina*, above n. 27, para. 384.

[75] It is quite apparent from the *Argentine, Military and Paramilitary*, and *Oil Platform* cases that the national security/emergency exception clause in investment treaties is a handy means of defence by respondents and that is likely to increase as similar clauses are incorporated into more investment treaties.

[76] It is also important in relation to the recent Joint Proposal by the US Congress to make security exceptions non-justiciable in future US Free Trade Agreements. For the proposal, see http://www.ustr.gov.

[77] See also Article 18 US Model BIT (2004); Article 21.2 US/Morocco FTA (2004) and similar provision in other US FTAs. Having regard to the decisions in the three *Argentine* cases, the

These provisions seem to state in clear terms the absolute right of the parties to decide on security issues and the finality or non-reviewability of such decisions by international tribunals. However, as we suggested earlier in respect of the interpretation of Article XXI GATT, the fact that an international tribunal does not have jurisdiction to scrutinize the merits of security exception claims does not preclude a good faith examination of the claim for the '[...] purpose of determining if they are based upon security concerns and therefore beyond external scrutiny'.[78] To hold otherwise would not only undermine the rule of law-based dispute settlement provisions of the treaty but probably 'vitiate' the entire Agreement or render it meaningless.[79] As Judge Lauterpacht noted in the *Norwegian Loans* case, a self-judging instrument does not manifest the acceptance of any legal obligation at all.[80] This observation is more relevant in the context of investment treaties which are aimed at attracting foreign investment by

[...] reducing the space for unprincipled and arbitrary actions of the host state and thus contribute to good governance, which is necessary condition for the achievement of economic progress in the host state.[81]

Furthermore, it will render both the substantive investor protection and procedural rights crafted by the parties over long and careful negotiations meaningless and a futile exercise. From a policy perspective, it will have the effect of raising the political risk premium for investing in such treaty party States thereby reducing the welfare enhancing objectives of foreign investment.

To sum up, whilst host States should be accorded a margin of appreciation in the determination of what policy measures they should adopt to handle economic crises, such measures must be necessary and proportionate to the public interest sought to be protected having due regard to the interests of foreign investors who are the beneficiaries of such treaties. In the event of disputes, an independent international tribunal should have the jurisdiction to scrutinize the impugned measures in order to prevent possible abuse of the regulatory autonomy.

We cannot solve here generally, without reference to the very specific wording, context, and purpose of an investment treaty, the issue to what extent the principle of 'necessity', derived from customary international law as confirmed by the

concept of national security interest is wide as to cover matters of economic and other vital interests of the State, including exchange restrictions.

[78] Cann, above n. 27, 468.

[79] Akande and Williams, above n. 27, 402–403; Alvarez, above n. 19, fn. 233 and accompanying text.

[80] *Norwegian Loans (France v Norway)*, 6 July 1957, *ICJ Reports* (1957) 9, at 48: 'An instrument in which a party is entitled to determine the existence of its obligation is not a valid and enforceable legal instrument of which a court of law can take cognisance. It is not a legal instrument. It is a declaration of a political principle and purpose.' The *'conditio potestativa'* will as a rule relegate a pretended obligation into the realm of non-binding declarations of intent or 'gentlemen's agreement'.

[81] Dolzer, above n. 29, 953–954.

ILC Articles on State Responsibility, can be read into a specific treaty, such as the Energy Charter Treaty, which sets up a repatriation guarantee without explicit limitation. On the one hand, the argument will be that the treaty drafters must have been familiar with the principle and that their decision to omit any reference to economic emergency meant that an unconditional capital repatriation guarantee was intended. The opposite reasoning suggests that the lack of a reference to an economic emergency (regulated in many, but not all investment treaties) suggests a 'gap' which is to be filled by customary international law as reflected in the ILC Articles. It is also possible to examine the principle of 'necessity' as a peremptory principle of international law the application of which cannot be waived. But any more specific regulation of economic emergency in a treaty should have priority, as *lex specialis*, over the more general and less specific application of the principle as contained in customary international law.[82]

E. Exchange Restrictions and Indirect Expropriation

The expropriation provisions of an investment treaty or customary international law might be invoked by a foreign investor to challenge a host State's exchange restrictions alleged to have substantially impacted on the value of the investment, such as the inability of the investor to repatriate funds to purchase some necessary inputs, equipment, and machinery or to service external loans (thereby increasing the indebtedness of the business) which substantially diminished the value of the investment. The burden of proof is on the foreign investor to demonstrate that the exchange restrictions substantially affected or undermined the value of its investment, and that amounted to expropriation.[83] The factors taken

---

[82] *Sempra v Argentina*, above n. 27, para. 378; *CMS v Argentina* (Annulment decision), above n. 39, 131–133.

[83] Modern investment treaties classify expropriation to include: 'measures having effect equivalent to nationalisation', Article 13(1) ECT; 'direct or indirect nationalisation or [...] measures tantamount to nationalisation', Article 1110 NAFTA; 'nationalise directly or indirectly an investment [...] or measures having equivalent effect', Draft MAI; Article 11 MIGA Convention (1985); Article 3 commentary to the OECD Draft Convention on Protection of Foreign Property (1967) defines creeping nationalisation as measures otherwise lawful 'applied in such a way as to deprive ultimately the alien of the enjoyment or value of his property, without any specific act being identified as outright deprivation'; American Law Institute, *Restatement (Third) of the Foreign Relations Law of the United States* (1986), Volume II, § 712(g). However, distinguishing between regulation and compensable taking has continued to agitate the minds of international tribunals and commentators. See generally, G. Christie, 'What Constitutes a Taking of Property under International Law', 38 *British Yearbook of International Law* (1962) 307; T. Wälde and A. Kolo, 'Environmental Regulation, Investment Protection and "Regulatory Taking" in International Law', 50 *International and Comparative Law Quarterly* (2001) 811; C. Schreuer, 'The Concept of Expropriation under the ECT and other Investment Protection Treaties', in C. Ribeiro (ed.), *Investment Arbitration and the Energy Charter Treaty* (2006) 108; A. Newcombe, 'The Boundaries of Regulatory Expropriation in International Law', 20 *ICSID Review—Foreign Investment Law Journal* (2005); OECD, *Indirect Expropriation* (2005), available at http://www.oecd.org/investment.

into account by international tribunals in deciding whether or not a host State measure amounts to indirect expropriation include: the character or nature of the government action; the economic impact of the government action; and interference with legitimate investment-backed expectations and the nature of the measure.[84]

Although it is within the sovereign right of a country to impose exchange restrictions when confronted with balance-of-payment difficulties, such restrictions must be proportionate to the aims sought to be achieved. Governments enjoy a wide margin of appreciation in deciding how to respond to matters of public interest, but that is subject to judicial scrutiny to ascertain whether the measure adopted strikes a reasonable balance between the public interest on one hand and respect for the right of the individual on the other.[85] Thus, where the exchange restrictions were absolute or total and remained for an indefinite or undue period of time or beyond the permitted period provided for under a relevant investment treaty and/or beyond what is necessary to deal with the balance-of-payment difficulties, it might be regarded as disproportionate and as evidence of indirect expropriation depending on its effect on the investment or proprietary rights[86]—the more so if the restrictions are discriminatory and/or not imposed in good faith but rather as a cloak to deny the foreign investor access to and enjoyment of his funds.[87]

[84] See US Model BIT (2004), Annex B, and similar provision in US FTAs; Canada Model BIT (2004), Annex B 13(1); *Fireman's Fund v Mexico*, Award, 17 July 2006, paras 176j, 176k, and authorities cited therein; M. Muse-Fisher, 'CAFTA-DR and the Iterative Process of Bilateral Investment Treaty Making: Towards a U.S. Taking Framework for Analysing International Expropriation Claims', 19(2) *Pacific McGeorge Global Business and Development Law Journal* (2007) 496; Newcombe, above n. 83; Wälde and Kolo, above n. 31, 440–446.

[85] *Tecmed v Mexico*, above n. 2, para. 122; *LG&E v Argentina*, above n. 40, paras 190–200; *Azurix Corp v Argentina*, Award, 8 December 2003, para. 312; *Jahn & Ors v Germany*, ECHR, Judgment, 30 June 2005, paras 93–95; *Pressos Compania Naviera S.A. v Belgium*, ECHR, Judgment, 20 November 1995, para. 38; *Case of the Former King of Greece v Greece*, 2000-XII ECHR, para. 89; *Chassagnou v France*, ECHR 1999-III, para. 75; Wälde and Kolo, above n. 83, 827–835; E. Freeman, 'Regulatory Expropriation under NAFTA Chapter 11: Some Lessons from the European Court of Human Rights', 42 *Columbia Journal of Transnational Law* (2003) 177.

[86] Under some investment treaties, exchange restrictions should not be in place beyond a stipulated period of time during which the investor must be permitted to transfer a certain minimum percentage of its capital. For instance, under Article 6(4) China/Kuwait BIT (1985), exchange restrictions might only be imposed for a temporary period not exceeding six months to meet balance-of-payment difficulties provided 50% of such transfers are allowed to be repatriated during such period; Article 6(1) UK/Russia BIT (1989) allows for restrictions 'for a limited period' provided transfer of a 'minimum of 20%' of returns a year is 'guaranteed'; see also Article 6(1) UK/Bolivia BIT (1990); protocol to the US/Bangladesh BIT (1986); Article 6(3) UK/Argentina BIT (1990) allows for delay of transfer applications for up to 18 months during which at least 50% of the returns shall be permitted to be transferred in instalments.

[87] In his dissenting opinion in *Schering v Iran*, Richard Mosk observed that: '[...] exchange restriction could constitute a taking subject to compensation under international law. This is dependent upon such factors as whether such restrictions are non-discriminatory, whether such restrictions are justified on bona fide economic grounds and whether such restrictions, in effect, extinguish a foreign national's enjoyment and use of its currency'. *Schering v Iran*, 5 *Iran-US CTR* (1984-I) 361, at 381; *Fireman's Fund v Mexico*, above n. 84, para. 206.

E. *Exchange Restrictions and Indirect Expropriation*

For example, in the *Chobady* claim,[88] the US Foreign Claims Commission rejected the claimant's claim that the devaluation of the Hungarian Krona and exchange restrictions imposed in response to economic crises after World War II amounted to a taking of property because, in the Commission's view, the restrictions were necessary in light of the then prevailing economic circumstances of the country and that, in any event, the plaintiff had limited access to his funds. According to the Commission, '[...] exchange restrictions may limit or reduce the owner's enjoyment and use of his funds, but so long as they do not eliminate or extinguish his ownership thereof, they will not be considered as confiscatory'.[89] A similar conclusion was reached by the Iran-US Claims Tribunal in *Sea-Land Services v Iran* in which it was held that, in view of the revolutionary events in Iran at the time the restrictions were imposed and the margin of discretion enjoyed by the Iranian Central Bank in granting permissions for transfers into foreign currencies, coupled with the fact that the claimants had access to their funds in the local currency, the restrictions did not amount to a compensable taking of property.[90]

---

[88] *Chobady* claim, ILR (1958-II) 292; the *Evanoff* claim, ibid., 301; the *Muresan* claim, ibid., 295, discussed in Schuster, above n. 6, 78–80. In all of these cases, the Commission was probably influenced by the fact that the disputing countries were facing serious economic crises at the time of the restrictions and the restrictions were not total, as the claimants had limited access to their funds in the local currencies.

[89] Cited by Schuster, above n. 6, 79–80.

[90] *Sea-Land Services v Iran*, 6 Iran-US CTR (1984-II) 149. However, the American member of the Tribunal issued a strong dissenting opinion. He noted that '[w]hatever the "discretion" invested in Bank Markazi as the Central Bank of Iran, and whatever discretion Iran might have in controlling its currency, international law limits that discretion when its application results in the confiscation of aliens' funds'. In his opinion, not only did the defendant refuse to convert the claimant's funds into dollars but also denied the claimant access to the local currency in its account by failing to give the necessary authorization and that, in his opinion, amounted to expropriation. Ibid., 212; contrast with *Hood v Iran*, 7 Iran-US CTR (1984-III) 36. See also *Fireman's Fund v Mexico*, above n. 84, in which the tribunal dismissed the claimant's claim seeking to recover $50 million worth of debentures it contributed towards the recapitalization of a Mexican bank. The tribunal held that the claimant 'took a commercial risk that its investment could be adversely affected' having regard to the fact that Mexico was in the process of recovering from a major financial crisis. *Fireman's Fund v Mexico*, above n. 84, paras 179–180. On the other hand, Russia's unilateral restructuring of treasury obligations (officially tagged 'voluntary' restructuring) in 1998/1999 as a result of the country's financial crisis in 1998 which saw the market value of those obligations reduced to approximately 5 per cent of their pre-crisis value probably did not amount to expropriation. However, it could be argued that the freezing of the investment accounts of other foreign investors (for proposed five-year period) who refused to participate in the so-called 'voluntary' restructuring probably amounted to indirect expropriation because, not only did the value of those investments substantially diminish but, more importantly, the owners were deprived of any ability to use, enjoy, or dispose of their investment. Hober, above n. 1, is of the view that the measures taken by the Russian government did not amount to expropriation for two reasons: first, the foreign investors were fully aware of the risks of investing in emerging markets such as Russia at the time they made their investments, more especially during the time leading up to the financial crisis in 1998 when the treasury obligations were trading at a significant discount. It is far from clear why knowledge of the risk that property and contract rights might be affected should obviate investment protection—except possibly under the heading of 'mitigation of risk'. Secondly, the Russian government was prevented from meeting its debt obligations by the financial crisis, something akin to a *force*

The above authorities raise the point of whether a foreign investor that invests in a country susceptible to economic crisis may be deemed to assume the risk of not only business failures arising from events such as fall in prices or inflation, but also that of possible regulatory measures (such as exchange restrictions) which might be imposed by the host State provided such restrictions are bona fide and non-discriminatory.[91] But knowledge of risk cannot, by itself, obviate investment protection, as otherwise there would be no protection in countries with political risk—and it is precisely for such situations that investment treaties have been created.

The blocking of funds from being repatriated for a period longer than necessary to deal with the balance-of-payment problems or beyond the period allowed under the relevant investment treaty, with no prospect of the restrictions being lifted, is prima facie evidence of expropriation.[92] The more so if the foreign investor is also denied access to local use of the funds or is unable to return to

---

majeure and changed circumstances—the more so in view of the fact that the measures were temporary. In *S.D. Myers, Inc v Canada* (UNCITRAL, NAFTA), Award on the Merits, 13 November 2000, paras 283–284, the tribunal took into account the fact that the impugned export ban only lasted for 16 months, an insufficient time for it to amount to expropriation. Aside from the fact that it was uncertain at the time whether or not the restrictions imposed by the Russian government would only last for the proposed five years or longer, the measures were clearly in violation of the BITs between Russia and the UK, France and the Netherlands respectively. Article 6 Russia/UK BIT (1991) permits capital transfer restrictions for only a limited period during which a minimum of 20 per cent of the capital must be allowed to be transferred in a year. Furthermore, the Article states that such transfers shall be effected without delay. Is five years a limited time and did the total restrictions by the Russian authority amount to a violation of the 20 per cent minimum benchmark? Unlike the Russia/UK BIT (1991), the capital transfer provisions of the Russia/Netherlands BIT, Russia/Germany BIT, and Russia/France BIT did not contain stipulations on restrictions during balance-of-payment difficulties, hence one might have to resort to either the Articles of Agreement of the IMF or customary international law as reflected in the ILC Articles on State responsibility to determine legal effect of the impugned measures.

[91] This is also implicit from the decision in the *Methanex* case where the tribunal noted that the claimant had entered into a political economy, 'in which it was widely known, if not notorious, that the governmental environmental and health protection institutions at the federal and state level [...] continuously monitored the use of some of those compounds for environmental and/or health reasons', *Methanex v US*, above n. 70, Part IV, Ch. D, para. 10. In other words, the tribunal seems to suggest that a country that is known to change its laws and regulations as of when it deems necessary in the public interest cannot be held responsible, in the absence of specific commitment to refrain from so doing, for consequent harm suffered by foreign investors who invested aware of such political risk. Such investors are expected to exercise due diligence. See also, *Waste Management, Inc v United Mexican States*, ICSID Case No. ARB(AF)/00/3, Award, 30 April 2004, paras 115–116; *Generation Ukraine v Ukraine*, Award, 16 September 2003, paras 20, 37; *CMS v Argentina*, above n. 40, para. 244; *Olguin v Paraguay*, Award, 26 July 2001, para. 75; P. Muchlinski, '"Caveat Investor?" The Relevance of the Conduct of the Investor under the Fair and Equitable Standard', 55 *International and Comparative Law Quarterly* (2006) 527, 542–552.

[92] According to Joseph Gold, although Article VI, section 3 of the IMF Agreement permits a Member State to impose restrictions on capital transfers, nevertheless, it may not do so in a manner that 'will unduly delay transfers of funds in settlement of commitments' arising from current international transactions. See J. Gold, 'The Iran-US Claims Tribunal and the Articles of Agreement of the IMF', 18 *George Washington Journal of International Law* (1985) 537, 567.

E. Exchange Restrictions and Indirect Expropriation

the host country due to conduct attributable to the host State (eg denial of visa or threat to his safety).[93]

Another important factor to be taken into account in determining indirect expropriation is whether the foreign investor is made to bear a disproportionate burden ('special sacrifice') on behalf of the community. Where the individual or group of investors are singled out and made to give up their property interests for the overall interest of the community, for no fault of theirs, then they should be compensated. Although foreign investors should not expect to be immune from economic crises that befall the host State, it could be argued that if they are made to bear a disproportionate burden which ought to be borne by the community on whose behalf the economic measures were adopted, such foreign investors ought to be compensated. In other words, the minority should not be made to suffer disproportionately for the good or benefit of the community. This is based on the principle of fairness and justice which finds support in the jurisprudence of the ECtHR, ECJ and comparative constitutional law.[94]

Under customary international law and most investment treaties, exchange restrictions must not be discriminatory in the sense that they should not target nationals of a State or the treaty partner.[95] In other words, the differentiation is prohibited if 'it is not justified by economic necessity, and takes on an arbitrary or offensive character',[96] or it is a misuse of discretion or otherwise unfair and inequitable.

---

[93] In his dissenting opinion in *Hood v Iran*, Richard Mosk rejected Iran's assertion that the exchange restrictions were temporary because they had been in place for more than five years during which the claimant was denied the repatriation of its funds and that, being a US national, it could not make use of the local Iranian currency. Accordingly, that amounted to a compensable expropriation of the claimant's funds. *Hood v Iran*, Dissenting Opinion of Richard Mosk, 7 Iran-US CTR (1984-III) 36. Similarly, in *French v Banco Nacional de Cuba*, 23 NY2d.46, 242 NE2d 704, 295 NYS2d 433, at 93, which involved a challenge of the legality of Cuba's exchange restrictions before a US court by a US investor, Judge Keating questioned the majority's finding that the measures did not amount to expropriation. Instead, he was of the opinion that: 'Under the guise of what the majority chooses to call a currency regulation, there has been an expropriation here, and no amount of discussion concerning the currency problems of the post war world can make it otherwise. This is no devaluation or temporary suspension. Eight years of no payments and no substitute arrangements for making adequate compensation is a sufficient period in which to establish an unlawful taking.'

[94] According to the US Supreme Court, one of the principal purposes of the taking clause is to '[...] bar government from forcing some people alone to bear public burdens which, in all fairness and justice, should be borne by the public as a whole'. *Nollan v California Coastal Commission*, 483 US 825 (1987), at 835, note 4; *Dolan v City of Tigard*, 114 S. Ct 2309 (1994); *Eastern Enterprises v EPEL*, US Supreme Court, Judgment, 25 June; *Jahn & Ors v Germany*, above n. 85, para. 94; *The Former King of Greece v Greece*, No. 25701/94, ECHR (2000-XII), para. 89; Wälde and Kolo, above n. 83, 845–846.

[95] As we have seen above, most capital transfer provisions of investment treaties permit restrictions to be imposed on a non-discriminatory basis. That requirement is a restatement of customary international law. In the *Tabar* Claim, *ILR* (1953) 242, the US Foreign Claims Commission ruled that: 'International law and the usual commercial treaties is no bar to foreign exchange restrictions. So long as the control measures are not discriminatory, no principle of international law is violated', referred to by A. Mouri, 'Treatment of the Rules of the International Law of Money by the Iran-US Claims Tribunal', 3 *Asian Yearbook of International Law* (1993) 71, fn. 101.

[96] Nussbaum, above n. 6, 476, quoted by Schuster, above n. 6, 88.

An abusive operation of exchange control occurs when the system is employed for purposes which are extraneous to it, for example, in order to inflict punishment upon an alien to secure tax claims or in an attempt to secure other advantages from the state in which the alien resides.[97]

Thus, a discriminatory exchange control raises a 'red flag' which shifts the burden onto the host State to justify the differences in treatment, failing which a presumption might be made as to the expropriatory character of the measures.

Lastly, the imposition of onerous exchange restrictions in violation of prior contractual commitments contained in either an investment agreement or investment legislations is another element in determining whether or not the measure amounts to expropriation (and breach of, if available, an 'umbrella clause').[98] This is because such commitments create legitimate expectations in favour of the foreign investor worthy of protection under general international law and the umbrella clause of the relevant investment treaty.[99] In other words, a breach of the capital repatriation guarantee of an investment agreement might amount to a breach of both the capital transfers and the umbrella clauses of the investment treaty. Thus, in *CMS v Argentina*, the tribunal held that the claimant had a right to rely on the Gas Decree which specifically provided for the calculation of tariffs in dollars and their conversion into pesos at the time of billing. The guarantee is sufficient to legally give rise to a right of the claimant to this effect.[100] In this case, the tribunal found that although the defendant

---

[97] Proctor, above n. 61, 519; J. Fawcett, 'The International Monetary Fund and International Law', 40 *British Yearbook of International Law* (1964) 32, 58. In the *Case Concerning Rights of Nationals of the United States of America in Morocco*, the French administration in Morocco issued a decree on 30 December 1948 the effect of which was to impose exchange controls on importation of goods from countries other than France and other parts of the French Union. That law was challenged by the United States on several grounds including discrimination contrary to a treaty (the Act of Algeciras) between Morocco and the United States. In rejecting the French argument that the law was not discriminatory as between US nationals and others in the allocation of import licences and currency, the ICJ held that: 'Even assuming the legality of exchange control, the fact nevertheless remains that the measures applied by virtue of the Decree of December 30th 1948, have involved discrimination in favour of imports from France and other parts of the French Union. This discrimination cannot be justified by considerations relating to exchange control.' *Case Concerning Rights of Nationals of the United States of America in Morocco, ICJ Reports* (1952) 176, 186.

[98] *Vivendi v Argentina*, Award, 20 August 2007, para. 7.5.10; F. Vicuna, 'Regulatory Authority and Legitimate Expectations: Balancing the Rights of the State and the Individual under International Law in a Global Society', 5(3) *International Law FORUM* (2003) 188. In *Revere Copper & Brass v OPIC (re Jamaica)*, the tribunal found an expropriation because of the breach of a stabilization promise even though the investor continued to control and operate the project. The case has been (in our view not correctly) quoted in the *Methanex v US* case, above n. 70, for the proposition that a non-discriminatory good-faith regulation cannot be considered as expropriation except in the case of a breach of a specific investment commitment.

[99] T. Wälde, 'The Umbrella Clause in Investment Arbitration', 6 *JWIT* (2005) 183.

[100] *CMS v Argentina*, above n. 40, paras 133, 138. However, this aspect of the award was annulled by the Ad hoc Committee in *CMS v Argentina* (Annulment decision), above n. 39, paras 89–95. In *Fireman's Fund v Mexico*, above n. 84 para. 207, the tribunal held that the inconclusive negotiations between the claimant and the Mexican government officials over recapitalization of financial institutions did not amount to specific undertaking by the government to recapitalize the bank

did breach its obligations, the economic impact was not serious enough to amount to expropriation even though it did amount to a violation of the fair and equitable treatment standard.[101] These decisions suggest that a foreign investor has a legitimate expectation that domestic law is not deployed in a way that is utterly unpredictable and cannot reasonably be foreseen when the investment is undertaken.

To sum up, customary international law and investment treaties limit the right of States to impose exchange restrictions through the requirement of non-discrimination even though how to determine discrimination might at times be difficult. A combination of discriminatory exchange restrictions imposed in breach of commitments made by the host State and which severely impacted on the investment might raise a presumption of indirect expropriation—the more so if the restrictions were also found to be inconsistent with the Articles of Agreement of the IMF.

But even where the foreign investor was unable to prove expropriation, it might be able to obtain damages if it demonstrated that the exchange restrictions violated the possibly, at times, less demanding fair and equitable treatment standard which forms the basis of our analysis in the next section.

F. Other Investment Obligations, in Particular, Fair and Equitable Treatment

The fair and equitable standard is found in almost all investment treaties. It is probably the most important treatment standard in investment disputes.[102] It is

---

in question nor did the recapitalization plan of 1998. As such, there were no reasonable investor-backed expectations created by Mexico, even though Mexico should have pursued the conclusion of an agreement. In *Sempra v Argentina*, above n. 27, paras 312–313, the tribunal held that a breach of commitments contained in a licence falls under the umbrella clause of the BIT.

[101] See also *Thunderbird v Mexico* (NAFTA), Award, Separate Opinion Wälde. *BG v Argentina*, above n. 41, paras 270–271. In the ongoing tax-related dispute *Duke Energy v Peru*, the claimant alleges that the tax authority's (SUNAT) assessment breached Peru's contractual obligation to allow free transfers because the assessment illegitimately or unreasonably reduced the amount of capital available to transfer. On the other hand, Peru argued that it only guaranteed free transfer subject to the company meeting its tax obligations but not before that, nor did it guarantee the repatriation of any minimum level of capital. A lot will depend on the interpretation of the Peruvian tax law and whether or not the assessment did violate the investment agreement and international law. If the assessment was found to be inconsistent with the tax stability guaranteed by the investment agreement, that might also amount to a breach of the repatriation obligation and possibly indirect expropriation depending on its severity on the investment. *Duke Energy Int'l. Ltd v Republic of Peru*, ICSID Case No. ARB/03/28, Decision on Jurisdiction, 1 February 2006.

[102] C. Schreuer, 'Fair and Equitable Treatment (FET): Interactions with other Standards', an unpublished paper (2007) 23, on file with the authors; J.C. Thomas, 'Reflections on Article 1105 of NAFTA: History, State Practice and the Influence of Commentators', 17 *ICSID Review—Foreign Investment Law Journal* (2002) 21; P. Foy and R. Deane, 'Foreign Investment Protection under Investment Treaties: Recent Developments under Chapter 11 of the North

the most relied upon provision by claimants, probably because of its wide scope and imprecise nature in investment law and general international law, and the lighter standard of proving its violation as compared to the standard of proof in expropriation claims.[103] In *MTD v Chile*, the tribunal stated that, 'in their ordinary meaning, the terms "fair" and "equitable" used in Article 3(1) of the BIT mean "just", "even-handed", "unbiased", "legitimate"'.[104]

Recent arbitral decisions have tried to give legal content to the concept of fair and equitable treatment.[105] By way of summary, it could be said that the criteria that have been suggested by arbitral tribunals for determining whether or not a treatment was fair and equitable include:[106]

(a) transparency and the protection of the investor's legitimate expectations;

(b) freedom from coercion and harassment;

(c) procedural propriety and due process;

(d) non-arbitrariness and non-discrimination; and

(e) good faith.[107]

We can only highlight some of the authorities which dealt with these elements and relate how they might be applied to exchange restrictions.

American Free Trade Agreement', 16 *ICSID Review—Foreign Investment Law Journal* (2001) 299; S. Vasciannie, 'The Fair and Equitable Treatment Standard in International Investment Law and Practice', 70 *British Yearbook of International Law* 99 (1999); B. Choudhury, 'Evolution or Devolution? Defining Fair and Equitable Treatment in International Investment Law', 6 *Journal of World Investment and Trade* (2005) 297.

[103] *Sempra v Argentina*, above n. 27, para. 300; Schreuer, above n. 102, at 23; R. Dolzer, 'Fair and Equitable Treatment: A Key Standard in Investment Treaties', 39 *International Lawyer* (2005) 87; UNCTAD, *Fair and Equitable Treatment* (1999) 10; Vasciannie, above n. 102, 163; N. Rubins and N. Kinsella, *International Investment, Political Risk and Dispute Resolution* (2005) 212.

[104] *MTD Equity Sdn Bhd and MTD Chile S.A. v Republic of Chile*, ICSID Case No. ARB/01/7, para. 113; UNCTAD, above n. 103, 40; P. Turner, M. Mangan, and A. Baykitch, 'Investment Treaty Arbitration: An Australian Perspective', 24(2) *Journal of International Arbitration* (2007) 103, 110.

[105] In *Waste Management, Inc v United Mexican States*, Award, 30 April 2004, para. 98, the tribunal formulated a general approach for the determination of fair and equitable treatment when it stated: '[...] the minimum standard of treatment of fair and equitable treatment is infringed by conduct attributable to the state and harmful to the claimant if the conduct is arbitrary, grossly unfair, unjust or idiosyncratic, as discriminatory and exposes the claimant to sectional or racial prejudice, or involves a lack of due process leading to an outcome which offends judicial propriety—as might be the case with a manifest failure of natural justice in judicial proceedings or a complete lack of transparency and candour in an administrative process. In applying this standard it is relevant that the treatment is in breach of representations made by the host state which was reasonably relied on by the claimant'. *Tecmed v Mexico*, above n. 2, para. 154; *Occidental Exploration and Production Company v Republic of Ecuador*, LCIA No. UN 3467, Award, 1 July 2004, para. 183; most recently *Saluka v Czech Republic*, above n. 28.

[106] For a more detailed discussion of these elements, see C. Schreuer, 'Fair and Equitable Treatment in Arbitral Practice', 6 *Journal of World Investment and Trade* (2005) 357; S. Schill, 'Fair and Equitable Treatment under Investment Treaties as an Embodiment of the Rule of Law', *Institute for International Law and Justice Working Paper* (2006/6), available at http://www.iilj.org; Turner, Mangan, and Baykitch, above n. 104.

[107] Schreuer, above n. 106.

Transparency and the Protection of Legitimate Expectations

The principle of transparency entails that laws, judicial and administrative decisions pertaining to foreign investment should be published and made readily available to foreign investors. A foreign investor should be able to know beforehand what rules and regulations would govern its activities so that it conducts its business in accordance with the law.[108] There should be no retroactive legislation,[109] nor surprises sprung onto the foreign investor. The main purpose of transparency is to ensure legal certainty so that the investor will be left in no '[...] doubt about the law applicable at a given time, in a given area and, consequently, as to the lawful or unlawful nature of certain acts or conduct'.[110]

These decisions suggest that under the fair and equitable standard, a host State is under an obligation to deal with the foreign investor in an open and transparent manner and not to hide behind inconsistencies in its own laws or the different interpretations of the laws by government officials. The investor should be in a position to know beforehand the rules of the game and be protected against unfair surprise. This presupposes that the foreign investor's understanding of the tax, foreign exchange, environmental, labour, and other pertinent legislation based on government officials' advice should not subsequently be reinterpreted by government officials to the detriment of the foreign investor—the more so if the foreign investor did rely on such representations in making the investment.[111]

But the principle of legitimate expectations leads to a balancing process between the legitimate expectations of the investor and the government's rights and duties to adapt its regulatory regime to changing circumstances, with standards such as proportionality, discrimination, and the relative weight of the opposing interests to be taken into account.[112] An investor cannot therefore rely on the principle of legitimate expectation as if it were the equivalent of a long-term contractual commitment by the host State. Rather, the host State is under an obligation to take due account of the investor's interest and react to change

---

[108] *Tecmed v Mexico*, above n. 2, para. 154. An extensive survey of both investment awards and related international and national jurisprudence is contained in *Thunderbird v Mexico*, Separate Opinion by Wälde, above n. 101; S. Fietta, 'The Legitimate Expectations Principle', 7 *JWIT* (2006) 423.

[109] UNCTAD, above n. 103, 51; UNCTAD, *Transparency* (2004) 28. In addition to the general provision on fair and equitable treatment, many modern investment treaties contain explicit provisions on transparency. For instance, Article 7 Japan/Korea BIT (2002); Article XVI(2) Canada/Ukraine BIT (1994); Article XVI Canada/South Africa BIT (2002); Article 3(2) Lithuania/Kuwait BIT.

[110] R. Thomas, *Legitimate Expectations and Proportionality in Administrative Law* (2000) 45, citing Advocate-General Mischo's opinion in Case C-331/88 *R v Minister for Agriculture, Fisheries and Food, ex parte Fedesa* (1990) ECR I-4023.

[111] D. Barak-Erez, 'The Doctrine of Legitimate Expectations and the Distinction between the Reliance and Expectation Interests', 11(4) *European Public Law* (2005) 583.

[112] *Thunderbird v Mexico*, above n. 101, Separate Opinion by Wälde; same approach in *Saluka v Czech Republic*, above n. 28; *BG v Argentina*, above n. 41, paras 295–299 and authorities cited therein.

and in particular economic emergencies in a way that reflects that such account has been taken in designing the State's measures to react to the crisis. The principle thus captures situations where the host State, under the pressure of an economic and political crisis, rides roughshod over the interests of foreign investors which have no political voice to influence the host State's conduct.

Freedom from Coercion or Harassment

With respect to freedom from coercion and harassment, the use of unnecessary and/or disproportionate force (eg physical) or pressure (economic) by a host State against a foreign investor can amount to a violation of the fair and equitable standard of treatment. Where the foreign investor is either physically harassed or intimidated by agents of the host State or put under tremendous economic pressure into taking decisions or omitting to take certain actions that might amount to a violation of the fair and equitable treatment standard.[113]

In the context of exchange restrictions, for instance, the announcement by the Russian government (through the Ministry of Finance and the Central Bank) on or about 28 April 1999 directing foreign investors to accept by 1 May 1999 to participate in the government-arranged restructuring or risk having their treasury obligations credited to a special account which would be blocked for five years could have been examined to determine if it was economic coercion contrary to the FET standard. Not only did the government implement the measures against those that refused to participate but 'those foreign holders of treasury obligations that participated in the proposed "voluntary" restructuring scheme saw their investment reduced to a fraction of their market value'.[114] Although the action of the Russian government might not have been arbitrary or discriminatory,

---

[113] D. Vagts, 'Coercion and Foreign Investment Rearrangement', in 72 *American Journal of International Law* (1978); A. Kolo and T. Wälde, 'Renegotiation and Contract Adaptation in International Investment Projects', 1 *Journal of World Investment and Trade* (2000) 1. In *Pope & Talbot*, the tribunal dismissed all the six grounds that were alleged by the claimants as amounting to breach of the fair and equitable treatment but found that the verification and review process used by Canada subjected the investor to 'threats, denied its reasonable requests for pertinent information, required to incur unnecessary expense and disruption in meeting LSD's requests for information, forced to expend legal fees and probably suffer a loss of reputation in government circles'. Accordingly, those actions violated the fair and equitable treatment required by Article 1105 NAFTA. See, *Pope & Talbot Inc v Government of Canada*, Award on Merits Phase 2, 10 April 2001, para. 181. In *Tecmed*, the tribunal found that the operation licence was only designed to force the investor to relocate to another site having to bear additional costs and risk. It noted that '[...] [u]nder such circumstances, such pressure involves forms of coercion that may be considered inconsistent with the fair and equitable treatment to be given to international investment under Article 4(1) of the Agreement and objectionable from the perspective of international law'. *Tecmed v Mexico*, above n. 2, para. 163. The tribunal also identified such coercive government conduct in negotiations with the foreign investor in *Siemens v Argentina*, Merits, Award, 6 February 2007, paras 306 *et seq.*; *BG v Argentina*, above n. 41, para. 349; *Vivendi v Argentina*, above n. 98, paras 7.4.39 *et seq.*

[114] Hober, above n. 1, 21.

it did force many foreign investors to participate in the restructuring scheme against their will and to their detriment.

Procedural Propriety

Another element of fair and equitable treatment is procedural propriety and due process. This requires the observance of the principle of fair hearing and rule of law by a host State's courts and administrative institutions in their dealings with foreign investors and not to deny justice to the foreign investor.[115] Breaches require a minimum materiality and may require recourse to a readily available administrative or judicial appeal.

In *Metalclad*, a failure by the local authority to afford Metalclad an opportunity to appear and present its case before the decision to deny it a construction permit was taken was adjudged to amount to a violation of the fair and equitable principle.[116] Toleration, by a judge, of significant and substantial xenophobic advocacy was part of the *Loewen v US* claim; though the claim was dismissed by the tribunal for other reasons, the tribunal appears to have accepted the basis of the claim.[117]

In the context of exchange restrictions, the cancellation or refusal by the host State authorities to grant an application for foreign exchange permits on alleged violation of, say, the tax or monetary laws of the country without affording the investor a fair hearing might amount to a violation of the fair and equitable standard.[118] Similarly, there can be a violation of fair and equitable treatment if exorbitant conditions were imposed by the host State authorities as requirements for appeal against foreign exchange-related decisions made by State officials which effectively placed the foreign investor in an almost impossible position to meet the conditions, such as the unreasonable security conditions for an appeal imposed on the claimants in the *Loewen v US* NAFTA case. Thus, failure to observe basic principles of natural justice by the courts or administrative

---

[115] Schreuer, above n. 106, 381–383; Choudhury, above n. 102, 305–306; Schill, above n. 106, 18–19; Bjorklund, above n. 67. For an in-depth discussion of the concept see, J. Paulsson, *Denial of Justice in International Law* (2005), reviewed by T. Wälde, 21 *ICSID Review—Foreign Investment Law Journal* (2007) 449–485. In *Azinian v Mexico*, the tribunal gave examples of what might amount to a denial of justice under international law: 'A denial of justice could be pleaded if the relevant courts refuse to entertain a suit, if they subject it to undue delay, or if they administer justice in a seriously inadequate way [...] [A denial of justice could also arise in a situation of] clear and malicious misapplication of the law.'

[116] *Metalclad Corporation v Mexico*, ICSID Case No. ARB(AF)/97/1, Award, 30 August 2000, paras 91–93.

[117] *Loewen Group, Inc. v United States*, Award, 26 June 2003, paras 119, 137.

[118] *Metalclad v Mexico*, above n. 116, paras 91–93; *Middle East Cement Shipping and Handling Co. S.A. v Arab Republic of Egypt*, ICSID Case No. ARB/99/6, Award, 12 April 2002; *Loewen v US*, above n. 117. For criticism of the *Loewen* decision see, D. Wallace Jr, 'Fair and Equitable Treatment and Denial of Justice: Loewen v. US and Chattin v. Mexico', in Weiler, above n. 10, 669; N. Rubins, 'Loewen v. United States: The Burial of an Investor-State Arbitration Claim', 21 *Arbitration International* (2005) 1.

institutions of the host State in relation to foreign exchange matters can amount to a violation of the fair and equitable treatment standard.

Protection against Arbitrariness; Discrimination and 'National Treatment'

Most investment treaties provide that to be permissible exchange restrictions must be imposed and implemented in a non-discriminatory manner. Although it is not explicitly stated that the measures must also be implemented in a non-arbitrary manner,[119] it is implicit that the measures would be arbitrary if they were found to be discriminatory.

Thus, in the context of exchange restrictions, it might be argued that if a particular investor or group of foreign investors from the other State party were targeted in the imposition or implementation of the restrictions that might amount to an arbitrary or discriminatory conduct. Similarly, where the exchange restrictions were imposed in violation of the domestic law of the host State that might also be considered as an arbitrary conduct.

The distinction between 'discriminatory' conduct and conduct that breaches the 'national treatment' is not clear. National treatment involves treatment of foreign investors worse than domestic investors in a 'like' situation without good reason, irrespective of whether the difference in treatment is specifically intended or if it occurs *de facto*. It may be possible to view all breaches of the national treatment standard as discrimination, but discrimination to cover also situations where a national treatment breach cannot be established, for example when a foreign investor is singled out and required to bear a disproportionate burden without a comparison with a better-treated domestic investor being easily available.

Discrimination, and national treatment breaches, will be frequent in a situation of national economic emergency. Emergency measures are here required, but governments will tend to be particularly susceptible to provide privileges and exemptions from otherwise harsh treatment for powerful and favoured domestic interests than for foreign investors. Discrimination can not only constitute a separate claim—of national treatment and/or discriminatory impairment of the investor's investment but a finding of discrimination will also weigh in when government conduct is examined under the heading of 'indirect expropriation' (regulatory taking) or fair and equitable treatment. It constitutes a

---

[119] In the *ELSI* case, the ICJ stated the test of what is an arbitrary conduct as a '[...] wilful disregard of due process of law, an act which shocks, or at least surprises, a sense of judicial propriety'. *Case concerning Elettronica Sicula S.p.A. (ELSI) (United States of America v Italy)*, Decision, 20 July 1989, *ICJ Reports* (1989) 15. In *Waste Management, Inc v United Mexican States*, above n. 91, para. 98, the tribunal observed that the fair and equitable treatment '[...] is infringed by conduct attributable to the state and harmful to the claimant if the conduct is arbitrary, grossly unfair, unjust or idiosyncratic, is discriminatory and exposes the claimant to sectional or racial prejudice'; *Eureko B.V. v Republic of Poland*, Partial Award, 19 August, 2005, para. 233; Vasciannie, above n. 102, 133.

Good Faith

Another subcategory of fair and equitable treatment is the requirement of the host State authorities to act in good faith. This simply means that 'legal instruments must not be used abusively but must be applied in accordance with their intended purpose'.[120] In *Tecmed*, the tribunal noted that the principle of good faith required States, among other things, to use the legal instruments that govern the actions of the investor or the investment in conformity with the function usually assigned to such instruments.[121] Thus, it will be an act of bad faith if government agencies deliberately and without justification, acted to defeat the purpose of an investment agreement as was the case in *Waste Management*,[122] or use the tax, environmental, foreign exchange, or other laws for political or protectionist purposes.

Most investment treaties permit exchange restrictions to be imposed provided they were genuine and not as a cloak to prevent the foreign investor from repatriating its funds.[123] Thus, it will be an act of bad faith for the host State authorities to reinterpret the foreign exchange laws so as to reinvent taxes or place additional hurdles for the foreign investor to overcome before it is allowed to repatriate its funds. A surprise re-interpretation of a host State's tax and foreign exchange laws, contrary to legitimate expectations of the investor in the continuity of settled interpretation and practice, can thus be an instrument to harass foreign investors and undermine their economic viability as a precursor to a governmental take-over (or a private take-over supported by government) without full compensation. Such government action does not need to be executed through formal regulation; re-interpretation of particularly open-ended language in tax and foreign exchange regulation is a less visible but equally or more effective way. Similarly, the presence of discrimination can be camouflaged if the governmental conduct is mainly by selective enforcement, eg if the full force of the law is applied against all or particularly disliked foreign investors while such regulation is as a rule and generally not applied to others. The issue of selective enforcement is much harder to identify and it is not as yet established when

---

[120] Schreuer, above n. 106, 384.
[121] *Teemed v Mexico*, above n. 2, para. 154; *Vivendi v Argentina*, above n. 98, para. 7.4.24.
[122] *Waste Management*, above, n. 91, para. 138.
[123] In *Barcelona Traction, Light and Power Company, Limited (Belgium v Spain)*, foreign exchange permitting requirements were employed by the local competitor in collusion with Spanish authorities to throttle the foreign investment's capacity to repay its debt and thus made it vulnerable to a bankruptcy proceeding contrived to sell it on the cheap to Juan March, see J. Brooks, *Annals of Finance* (republished on OGEL 2005). In the 2004–2006 *Yukos* case, the Russian government employed control over the tax authorities and fiscal procedures in a comparable way.

enforcement only against foreign or particularly disliked investors constitutes discrimination.[124]

To sum up, the underlying concern of the fair and equitable treatment standard is the need for stability and predictability of the legal and business framework under which the foreign investor operates and the protection against unfair surprise contrived by governmental measures. Even though a claimant in a foreign exchange dispute is unable to prove expropriation, it might be entitled to damages if it proved a violation of the less exerting standard of fair and equitable treatment.

G. Remedies and Compensation

If the investment treaty includes a specific obligation ('discipline') and thus a basis for an arbitration-enforceable claim, such as Article 14 of the Energy Charter Treaty, then each separate treaty obligation or claim involves an equally separate determination of compensation. Restitution, ie direct remedial action, is the standard consequence of the breach of any treaty obligation and can be awarded by the competent arbitral tribunal within the limits of the treaty.[125] This means that tribunals (and claimants[126]) must carry out a separate remedy analysis for each claim; if it awards for claimant on the basis of several claims, it must therefore avoid over-recovery, basically by taking into account the remedy or compensation for all other claims when determining the overall remedy. Normally, the highest compensation under one particular claim will include equal or lower compensation amounts based on the other claims. If tribunals (as we suggest) choose the theoretically principal (and often practically most suitable) restitution remedy, financial compensation can then only be awarded if either restitution is refused or if the claimant has suffered damages in excess of what would be cured by restitution, eg interest costs or related costs involved in the time-lag between the breach and the execution of a restitution award.

The first port of call for capital control claims is the foreign exchange repatriation guarantee often found in investment treaties (eg the extensive treatment in

---

[124] S. Hindelang, 'No Equals in Wrong? The Issue of Equality in a State of Illegality', 7 *Journal of World Investment and Trade* (2006) 883.

[125] Article 34 ILC Articles on State Responsibility; Article 26 (8) ECT, for example, limits the remedy for breaches by a subnational entity to monetary damages. Article 1135(1) NAFTA allows, except for property restitution, only monetary damages for the 'final' award (which Wälde has been interpreting as allowing restitutory preliminary awards to be followed, in case of non-compliance, by a monetary award).

[126] It is not yet clear if a tribunal can award restitution if a claimant has asked only for monetary damages. There is an argument that restitution is available to tribunals irrespective of parties' claims, either as implicitly contained as a lesser sanction, in a claim for monetary compensation; alternatively, respondents could ask for restitution as in their view a lesser sanction than monetary damages in case the tribunal decides for the claimant on the merits.

Article 14 ECT or Article 1109 of the NAFTA). If a host State does not permit such guaranteed transfers contrary to a treaty obligation, one remedy combination would be a restitution order (ie to permit transfer) together with an order to pay compensation for damages that remain after the transfer has been permitted, ie interest and other costs involved in the delay of repatriation. Otherwise, eg if the treaty does not permit restitution or both parties and the tribunal consider restitution not practical, a monetary award is required. That monetary award will be based on a comparison between the situation of the claimant had the capital transfer been permitted when required under the treaty as compared with the situation at the time of the award (*Chorzow* rule).[127] The issue is not suitable for an easy resolution. While it would make sense to simply award payment of the not transferred amount plus interest, the tribunal would have to take care of the remaining claimant funds locked-up in the host State. One way is to require the claimant to transfer these local funds to the host State against payment of their full amount, in convertible currency, at the rate when the claimant should have been able to transfer them, plus interest.

If the tribunal determines that a direct expropriation has taken place (which should be rare),[128] then compensation is the full market value. The major issue here would seem to be the selection of the appropriate rate of exchange; normally, that should be the real market rate of exchange at the specific point in time when the claimant was entitled to transfer its capital and would have been likely to do so. That opens up the compensation discussion for debate—the time when the investor was likely to have transferred its local funds; presumably, it is at the time when, after a claimant request, the monetary authorities would have and should have permitted the transaction. In case of an indirect expropriation (the more frequent scenario), the same rule should apply except that the balancing process required for a determination of 'indirect expropriation' (economic deprivation, legitimate expectation, character, and justification for the justificatory measure) allows an argument that compensation should only be the difference between the full value of the funds at a market-based exchange rate on the one hand and, on the other, the value of the funds had the government pursued its monetary regulation in response to an economic emergency situation in a reasonable (non-discriminatory, least-restrictive, not disproportionate) way. That value would normally lie well below full market value.

In case of the other breaches (fair and equitable treatment, unreasonable or discriminatory impairment, national treatment) the methodology required is again

---

[127] T. Wälde and B. Sabahi, 'Compensation, Damages and Valuation in International Investment Disputes', in *2007 Report to ILA Foreign Investment Law Committee* (forthcoming, 2008).

[128] Direct expropriation can consist in the formal 'taking' of local funds covered by the transfer guarantee—similar to the repudiation of a tax refund right that would have been considered in *EnCana Corporation v Republic of Ecuador* (UNCITRAL), LCIA Case No. UN3481, Award, 3 February 2006, para. 183, as expropriation.

a comparison between the situation of the investor-claimant as a result of the unlawful measures and the situation it would have been in had the government acted correctly, ie in compliance with its treaty obligation. Again, restitution has much to recommend here as it would allow the tribunal to order transfer into convertible currency (plus damages in excess of the restitution value) at the time and in the way the tribunal considers warranted by the application of these treaty disciplines. That may include transfer at a time when the respondent government and its economy and financial system are again capable of such transfers, or a combination of gradual or partial transfers with compensation for not justified losses for funds that had to be held in local currency. If the restitution remedy is not chosen, then a monetary compensation award will follow the same principles. A government handling its financial emergency in a non-discriminatory, transparent, and fair way would therefore not come under an obligation to pay compensation; a government that breaches its international investment treaty obligation would, however, have to compensate by payment to the extent its treaty breaches have directly caused a loss. Investor-claimants would not be fully immune from the impacts of a host State's economic and financial crisis.

H. Conclusion

This chapter has addressed capital transfer restrictions as a permissible, albeit limited, means of regulating foreign investment. Although exchange restriction is an aspect of State sovereignty that is usually resorted to when a country is facing balance-of-payment difficulties, nonetheless that power is constrained by general international law and modern investment treaties in order to prevent or minimize abuse of the right and protect the interests of foreign investors. The criteria used to assess the legality of exchange restriction measures include, whether the measures are necessary, proportionate to the legitimate aims sought to be achieved, discriminatory, and the extent of their severity relative to the private investor who should not be made to bear a disproportionate burden on behalf of the community. While governmental measures pursued in good faith, and in accordance with established international guidelines and best practices, will have a wider scope—as opposed to measures which use a legitimate reason as a pretence to disguise a measure that is aimed at singling out the foreign investor—they still can in more special situations amount to a breach, in particular if the burden on foreign investors is disproportionate. Even where the measures are perfectly legal and legitimate, they might amount to indirect expropriation if the investor suffered substantial deprivation of his proprietary rights, plus disappointment of his legitimate expectations and/or is discriminated against. If the usually more demanding threshold for indirect expropriation is not reached, there can still be compensation claims for breach of the other standards—fair and equitable

H. Conclusion

treatment, national treatment, unreasonable and discriminatory impairment, or breach of a repatriation guarantee contained in the investment treaty. We also argued that even an apparently self-judging capital transfer or national security provision of an investment treaty should be interpreted in light of the object and purpose of such a treaty so as not to defeat that very object and purpose. International tribunals are better placed than domestic courts or the State parties to an investment to perform this interpretative function.

It is relatively easy to calculate the compensation due for formal expropriation, but already less so in case of the capital control measure constituting an 'indirect taking'. Here, the 'market value' of the asset taken is the main benchmark. It is difficult, and so far not well understood, how compensation should be determined in cases of the breaches of the other treaty claims, eg fair and equitable and national treatment, unreasonable or discriminatory impairment, or the foreign exchange repatriation guarantee proper. Essentially, we suggest that the financial impact on the investor of the course of conduct that constitutes a treaty obligation breach taken by the government should be compared with the course of conduct it could have taken while being in full compliance with its international obligations; the difference of financial impact as between the actual unlawful conduct and a hypothetical lawful conduct and course of events is the basis for calculating the compensation due to the investor. But restitution as a remedy (if available under the treaty) would consist in ordering the government to allow repatriation of funds plus any financial losses occasioned by the delay.

Bibliography

P. Acconci, 'Most-Favoured-Nation Treatment and International Law on Foreign Investment', in P. Muchlinski, F. Ortino, and C. Schreuer (eds), *The Oxford Handbook of International Investment Law* (forthcoming 2008).

D. Akande and S. Williams, 'International Adjudication on National Security Issues: What Role for the WTO?', 43 *Virginia Journal of International Law* (2003) 365.

J. Alvarez, 'Political Protectionism and United States International Investment Obligations in Conflict: The Hazards of Exon-Florio', 30 *Virginia Journal of International Law* (1989) 1.

American Law Institute (ed.), *Restatement (Third) of the Foreign Relations Law of the United States* (1987).

D. Anzilotti, *Cours de droit international* (1929).

D. Barak-Erez, 'The Doctrine of Legitimate Expectations and the Distinction between the Reliance and Expectation Interests', 11(4) *European Public Law* (2005) 583.

C. Barnard, *The Substantive Law of the EU: The Four Freedoms* (2004).

B. Baron Nolde, 'La clause de la nation la plus favorisée et les tarifs préférentiels' (The Most-Favoured-Nations Clause and Preferential Tariffs), 35 *Recueil des Cours* (1932) 5.

S. Basdevant, *La clause de la nation la plus favorisée* (The Most-Favoured-Nation Clause) (1929).

S. Benson, 'Reviving the Disparate Impact Doctrine to Combat Unconscious Discrimination', 31 *Thurgood Marshall Law Review* (2005) 43.

E. Benvenisti, 'Margin of Appreciation, Consensus, and Universal Standards', 31 *NYU Journal of International Law and Politics* (1999) 843.

P. Bernardini, 'Investment Arbitration under the ICSID Convention and BITs', in G. Aksen *et al.* (eds), *Liber Amicorum in Honour of Robert Briner* (2005) 95.

J. Bhagwati (ed.), *The New International Economic Order: The North-South Debate* (1977).

A. Bjorklund, 'Reconciling State Sovereignty and Investor Protection in Denial of Justice Claims', 45 *Virginia Journal of International Law* (2005) 809.

A. Bjorklund, 'Investment Treaty Arbitral Decisions as Jurisprudence Constante', in C. Picker, I. Bunn, and D. Arner (eds), *International Economic Law: The State and Future of the Discipline* (2008).

J. Boscariol and O. Silva, 'The Widening Application of the MFN Obligation and its Impact on Investor Protection', 11 *International Trade Law and Regulation* (2005) 61.

J. Brooks, *Annals of Finance*, republished in 4 *Oil, Gas and Energy Law Intelligence* (2006).

I. Brownlie, *Principles of Public International Law* (6th edn, 2003).

W. Burke-White and A. von Staden, 'Investment Protection in Extraordinary Times: The Interpretation and Application of Non-Precluded Measures Provisions in Bilateral Investment Treaties', *University of Pennsylvania Law School Working Paper*, No. 152 (2007), available at http://lsr.nellco.org/upenn/wps/papers/152/.

W. Cann Jr, 'Creating Standards and Accountability for the Use of the WTO Security Exception: Reducing the Role of Power-based Relations and Establishing a New Balance between Sovereignty and Multilateralism', 26 *Yale Journal of International Law* (2001) 413.

B. Choudhury, 'Evolution or Devolution? Defining Fair and Equitable Treatment in International Investment Law', 6 *The Journal of World Investment and Trade* (2005) 297.

G.C. Christie, 'What Constitutes a Taking of Property under International Law?', 38 *British Yearbook of International Law* (1962) 305.

O. Chukwumerije, 'Interpreting Most-Favoured-Nations Clauses in Investment Treaty Arbitrations', 8 *The Journal of World Investment and Trade* (2007) 597.

J. Coe and N. Rubins, 'Regulatory Expropriation and the *Tecmed* Case: Context and Contributions', in T. Weiler (ed.), *International Investment Law and Arbitration: Leading Cases from the ICSID, NAFTA, Bilateral Treaties and Customary International Law* (2005) 597.

'Colombian Court upholds Constitutionality of BIT with Spain', *ITN News* (15 October 2007), available at http://www.iisd.org/investment/itn/news.asp.

J. Commission, 'Precedent in Investment Treaty Arbitration: A Citation Analysis of a Developing Jurisprudence', 24 *Journal of International Arbitration* (2007) 129.

S.B. Crandall, 'The American Construction of the Most-Favoured Nation Clause', 7 *American Journal of International Law* (1913) 708.

J. Crawford, *The International Law Commission's Articles on State Responsibility: Introduction, Text and Commentaries* (2002).

S. Croley and J. Jackson, 'WTO Dispute Procedures, Standards of Review, and Deference to National Governments', 90 *American Journal of International Law* (1996) 193.

R. Dattu, 'Essay: A Journey from Havana to Paris: The Fifty-Year Quest for the Elusive Multilateral Agreement on Investment', 24 *Fordham International Law Journal* (2000) 275.

J.P Dawson, 'The Gold Clause Cases', 33 *Michigan Law Review* (1935) 637.

Direction du droit international public, Avis, 11 mars 1994, reprinted in 5 *Revue suisse de droit international et de droit européen* (1995) 25.

R. Doak Bishop, J. Crawford, and W.M. Reisman, *Foreign Investment Disputes* (2005).

R. Dolzer, 'Indirect Expropriation of Alien Property', 1 *ICSID Review—Foreign Investment Law Journal* (1986) 41.

R. Dolzer, 'Indirect Expropriations: New Developments?' 11 *NYU Environmental Law Journal* (2002) 64.

R. Dolzer, 'Fair and Equitable Treatment: A Key Standard in Investment Treaties', 39 *International Lawyer* (2005) 87.

R. Dolzer, 'The Impact of International Investment Treaties on Domestic Administrative Law', 37 *NYU Journal of International Law and Politics* (2005) 953.

R. Dolzer and T. Myers, 'After *Tecmed*: Most-Favored-Nation Clauses in Investment Protection Agreements', 19 *ICSID Review—Foreign Investment Law Journal* (2004) 50.

R. Dolzer and M. Stevens, *Bilateral Investment Treaties* (1995).

R.-J. Dupuy (ed.), *Le nouvel ordre économique international: aspects commerciaux, technologiques et culturels* (1981).

A. Egea, 'Balance-of-Payments Provisions in the GATT and NAFTA', 30 *The Journal of World Trade* (1996) 5.

G. Egli, 'Don't Get Bit: Addressing ICSID's Inconsistent Application of Most-Favored-Nation Clauses to Dispute Resolution Provisions', 34 *Pepperdine Law Review* (2007) 1045.

E. Ellis (ed.), *The Principle of Proportionality in the Laws of Europe* (1999).

European Commission, 'Internal Market, The Free Movement of Capital', available at http://ec.europa.eu/internal_market/capital/index_en.htm.

S. Fares, 'Current Payments and Capital Movements in the EU-Mediterranean Association Agreements', 30(1) *Legal Issues of Economic Integration* (2003) 15.

A.A. Fatouros, *Government Guarantees to Foreign Investors* (1962).

A.A. Fatouros, 'Towards an International Agreement on Foreign Direct Investment?', 10 *ICSID Review—Foreign Investment Law Journal* (1995) 188.

J. Fawcett, 'The International Monetary Fund and International Law', 40 *British Yearbook of International Law* (1964) 32.

S. Fietta, 'Most Favoured Nation Treatment and Dispute Settlement Resolution Under Bilateral Investment Treaties: A Turning Point', 8 *International Arbitration Law Review* (2005) 131.

S. Fietta, 'International Thunderbird Gaming Corporation v. The United Mexican States: An Indication of the Limits of the "Legitimate Expectation" Basis of Claim under Article 1105 of NAFTA?', 3(2) *Transnational Dispute Management* (2006).

S. Fietta, 'The Legitimate Expectations Principle', 7 *The Journal of World Investment and Trade* (2006) 423.

L. Flynn, 'Coming of Age: The Free Movement of Capital Case Law', 39 *Common Market Law Review* (2002) 773.

Y.L. Fortier and S.L. Drymer, 'Indirect Expropriation in the Law of International Investment: I Know It When I See It, or Caveat Investor', 19 *ICSID Review—Foreign Investment Law Journal* (2004) 293.

D. Foster, 'Internationalisation—Contractual Claims in BIT Arbitrations', *Global Arbitration Review*, available at http://www.globalarbitrationreview.com/handbooks/3/sections/5/chapters/32/internationalisation-contractual-claims-bit-arbitrations.

P. Foy and R. Deane, 'Foreign Investment Protection under Investment Treaties: Recent Developments under Chapter 11 of the North American Free Trade Agreement', 16 *ICSID Review—Foreign Investment Law Journal* (2001) 299.

S.D. Franck, 'International Decision: Occidental Exploration & Production Co. v. Republic of Ecuador', 99 *American Journal of International Law* (2005) 675.

S.D. Franck, 'Foreign Direct Investment, Investment Treaty Arbitration, and the Rule of Law', 19(2) *Pacific McGeorge Global Business and Development Law Journal* (2007) 337.

E. Freeman, 'Regulatory Expropriation under NAFTA Chapter 11: Some Lessons from the European Court of Human Rights', 42 *Columbia Journal of Transnational Law* (2003) 177.

D.H. Freyer and D. Herlihy, 'Most-Favored-Nation Treatment and Dispute Settlement in Investment Arbitration: Just How "Favored" is "Most-Favored"?', 20 *ICSID Review—Foreign Investment Law Journal* (2005) 58.

E. Gaillard, 'Chronique des sentences arbitrales', 132 *Journal du Droit International* (2005) 135.

E. Gaillard, 'Establishing Jurisdiction through a Most-Favored-Nation Clause', *New York Law Journal* (2005) 8.

F.V. García Amador, 'Responsibility of the State for Injuries Caused in its Territory to the Person or Property of Aliens—Measures Affecting Acquired Rights', UN Doc. A/CN.4/119, *Yearbook of the International Law Commission* (1959-II).

F.V. García Amador, L.B. Sohn, and R.R. Baxter, *Recent Codification of the Law of State Responsibility for Injuries to Aliens* (1974).

B.A. Garner, *Black's Law Dictionary* (6th edn, 1990).

F. Gianviti, 'The Prevention and Resolution of International Financial Crises—A Perspective from the International Monetary Fund', in M. Giovanoli (ed.), *International Monetary Law: Issues for the New Millennium* (2000) 103.

J. Gold, 'The Iran-US Claims Tribunal and the Articles of Agreement of the IMF', 18 *George Washington Journal of International Law* (1985) 537.

O.R. Goodenough, 'Defending the Imaginary to the Death? Free Trade, National Identity, and Canada's Cultural Preoccupation', 15 *Arizona Journal of International & Comparative Law* (1998) 203.

Hague Academy of International Law (ed.), *New Aspects of International Investment Law* (2006).

M. Hahn, 'Vital Interests and the Law of GATT: An Analysis of GATT's Security Exception', 12 *Michigan Journal of International Law* (1991) 558.

G. Harten and M. Loughin, 'Investment Treaty Arbitration as a Species of Global Administrative Law', 17 *European Journal of International Law* (2006) 121.

V. Heiskanen, 'Regulatory Philosophy of International Trade Law', 38 *Journal of World Trade* (2004) 1.

V. Heiskanen, 'The Doctrine of Indirect Expropriation in Light of the Practice of the Iran-United States Claims Tribunal', 8 *The Journal of World Investment and Trade* (2007) 215.

F. Hepp, *Théorie générale de la clause de la nation la plus favorisée en droit international privé* (A general theory of the MFN clause in private international law) (1914).

M. Herdegen, *Internationales Wirtschaftsrecht* (5th edn, 2005).

R. Higgins, 'The Taking of Foreign Property by the State', 176 *Recueil des Cours* (1982-III) 259.

S. Hindelang, 'No Equals in Wrong? The issue of equality in a state of illegality'', 7 *The Journal of World Investment and Trade* (2006) 883.

K. Hobér, 'Investment Arbitration in Eastern Europe: Recent cases on expropriation', 1 *Transnational Dispute Management* (2004).

K. Hobér, *Investment Arbitration in Eastern Europe: In Search of a Definition of Expropriation* (2007).

W. Holder, 'Fund Jurisdiction over Capital Movements—Comments', Panel on Preventing Asian Type Crises: Who if any one should have Jurisdiction over Capital Movement?, 5 *ILSA Journal of International and Comparative Law* (1999) 407.

F. Horchani, 'Le droit international des investissements à l'heure de la mondialisation', *Journal de droit international* (2004) 368.

S.K. Hornbeck, 'The Most-Favored-Nation Clause', 3 *American Journal of International Law* (1909) 395.

M.-F. Houde and F. Pagani, 'Most Favoured Nation Treatment in International Investment Law', in OECD (ed.), *International Investment Law: A Changing Landscape—A Companion Volume to International Investment Perspectives* (2005).

L. Hsu, 'MFN and Dispute Settlement—When the Twain Meet', 7 *The Journal of World Investment and Trade* (2006) 25.

R.E. Hudec, 'Tiger, tiger in the house: a critical evaluation of the case against discriminatory trade measures', in E.-U. Petersmann and M. Hilf (eds), *The New GATT Round of Multilateral Trade Negotiations: Legal and Economic Problems* (1988) 165.

Ch. Ch. Hyde, 'Concerning the Interpretation of Treaties', 3 *American Journal of International Law* (1909) 46.

International Law Association, *Report of the Committee on International Law on Foreign Investment, presented at the Biennial Meeting 2008* (forthcoming).

International Law Commission, *Report on the Work of its Thirtieth Session* (1978).

International Law Commission, *Most-Favoured-Nation Clause—Report of the Working Group*, UN Doc. A/CN.4/L.719 (2007).

International Law Commission, 'Articles on Responsibility of States for Internationally Wrongful Acts', *Report on the Work of its Fifty-third Session, Official Records of the General Assembly, Fifty-sixth session, Supplement No. 10* (A/56/10).

J. Jackson, *World Trade Law and the GATT* (1969).

J. Jackson, *The World Trading System—Law and Policy of International Economic Relations* (1997).

J. Jans, 'Proportionality Revisited', 27 *Legal Issues in Economic Integration* (2000) 239.

J. Jans, 'Proportionality Once Again', 33(4) *Legal Issues in Economic Integration* (2006) 347.

R. Jennings and A. Watts (eds), *Oppenheim's International Law* (9th edn, 1996).

M. Kantor, 'International Project Finance and Arbitration with Public Sector Entities: When is Arbitrability a Fiction?', 24 *Fordham International Law Journal* (2001) 1122.

M.I. Khalil, 'Treatment of Foreign Investment in Bilateral Investment Treaties', in The World Bank Group (ed.), *Legal Framework for the Treatment of Foreign Investment* (1992), Volume I.

M. Kinnear, A.K. Bjorklund, and J.F.G. Hannaford, *Investment Disputes under NAFTA—An Annotated Guide to NAFTA Chapter 11* (2006).

C. Knahr, 'Investments "in accordance with host state law"', 4(5) *Transnational Dispute Management* (2007).

A. Kolo and T. Wälde, 'Renegotiation and Contract Adaptation in International Investment Projects', 1 *The Journal of World Investment and Trade* (2000) 1.

U. Kriebaum, 'Regulatory Takings, Balancing the Interests of the Investor and the State', 8 *The Journal of World Investment and Trade* (2007) 717.

U. Kriebaum and A. Reinisch, 'Property, Right to, International Protection', in *Encyclopedia of Public International Law* (forthcoming).

A. Kuhn, 'The Gold Clauses in International Loans', 28 *American Journal of International Law* (1934) 312.

J. Kurtz, 'The Delicate Extension of Most-Favoured-Nation Treatment to Foreign Investors: Maffezini v. Kingdom of Spain', in T. Weiler (ed.), *International Investment Law and Arbitration—Leading Cases from the ICSID, NAFTA, Bilateral Treaties and Customary International Law* (2005) 523.

B. Land, *Similarities and Differences between Oil and Mining Contracts*, LL.M. dissertation (1996), available at http://www.oilandgas.com/ogel, Volume 5(2) (2007).

A. Landsmeer, 'Capital Movements: On the Interpretation of Article 73b of the EC Treaty', 27(2) *Legal Issues of Economic Integration* (2000) 195.

A. Landsmeer, 'Movement of Capital and Other Freedoms', 28(1) *Legal Issues of Economic Integration* (2001) 57.
J.-P. Laviec, *Protection et Promotion des Investissements: Etude de Droit International Economique* (1985).
L. Liberti, 'Arbitrato ICSID, clausola della nazione più favorita e problemi di attribuzione', *Rivista dell'arbitrato* (2004) 580.
C. Lichtenstein, 'The Battle for International Bank Accounts: Restrictions on International Payments for Political Ends and Article VII of the Fund Agreement', 19 *NYU Journal of International Law and Politics* (1987) 982.
R.B. Lillich, *The Human Rights of Aliens in Contemporary International Law* (1984).
C. Lo, *The Reciprocity Principle in the International Regulation of Economic Relations*, Thesis Typescript (S.J.D.) Harvard Law School (1989), available at http://de.scientificcommons.org/4449832.
V. Lowe, 'Regulation or Expropriation?', 55 *Current Legal Problems* (2002) 447.
A. Lowenfeld, *International Economic Law* (2002).
R. Luzi, 'Bilateral Investment Treaties and Economic Crises: Do states have carte blanche?', unpublished paper (2007), on file with T. Wälde.
P. Malanczuk, *Akehurst's Modern Introduction to International Law* (7th edn, 1997).
S. Manciaux, *Investissements étrangers et arbitrage entre États et ressortissants d'autres États* (2004).
A.F.M. Maniruzzaman, 'Expropriation of Alien Property and the Principle of Non-Discrimination in International Law of Foreign Investment: An Overview', 8 *Journal of Transnational Law and Policy* (1998) 57.
I. Marboe, 'Compensation and Damages in International Law, The Limits of "Fair Market Value"', 7 *The Journal of World Investment and Trade* (2006) 723.
P. Mavroidis, *The General Agreement on Tariffs and Trade—A Commentary* (2007).
C. McLachlan, L. Shore, and M. Weiniger, *International Investment Arbitration: Substantive Principles* (2007).
A. McNair, *The Law of Treaties* (1961).
B. Meyer, 'Recognition of Exchange Controls after the IMF', 62 *Yale Law Journal* (1953) 867.
A. Mouri, 'Treatment of the Rules of the International Law of Money by the Iran-US Claims Tribunal', 3 *Asian Yearbook of International Law* (1993) 71.
P. Muchlinski, '"Caveat Investor?" The Relevance of the Conduct of the Investor under the Fair and Equitable Standard', 55 *International and Comparative Law Quarterly* (2006) 527.
P. Muchlinski, *Multinational Enterprises and the Law* (2nd edn, 2007).
C. Murphy, *Emergence of the NIEO Ideology* (1984).
M. Muse-Fisher, 'CAFTA-DR and the Iterative Process of Bilateral Investment Treaty Making: Towards a U.S. Taking Framework for Analysing International Expropriation Claims', 19(2) *Pacific McGeorge Global Business and Development Law Journal* (2007) 496.
J. Neumann and E. Turk, 'Necessity Revisited: Proportionality in World Trade Organisation Law After Korea-Beef, EC-Asbestos and EC-Sardines', 37(1) *Journal of World Trade* (2003) 199.
A. Newcombe, 'Canada's New Model Foreign Investment Protection Agreement', 14 *Canadian Council on International Law Bulletin* (2004) 30, available at http://www.ccil-ccdi.ca.

A. Newcombe, 'The Boundaries of Regulatory Expropriation in International Law', 20 *ICSID Review—Foreign Investment Law Journal* (2005) 1.
A. Newcombe, L. Paradell, and D. Krishan, *The Law and Practice of Investment Treaties* (forthcoming 2008).
P.M. Norton, 'A Law of the Future or a Law of the Past? Modern Tribunals and the International Law of Expropriation', 85 *American Journal of International Law* (1991) 474.
Y. Nouvel, 'Les mesures équivalent à une expropriation dans la pratique récente des tribunaux arbitraux' 106 *Revue Générale du Droit international public* (2002) 79.
A. Nussbaum, *Money in the Law: National and International* (2nd edn, 1950).
OECD, *Indirect Expropriation* (2005), available at: http://www.oecd.org/investment.
OECD, *Forty Years' Experience with the OECD Code of Liberalisation of Capital Movements* (2002), available at http://www.oecd.org.
OECD (ed.), *OECD Codes of Liberalisation of Capital Movements and Current Invisible Operations: User's Guide 2007* (2007).
Th. Oppermann and E.U. Petersmann (eds), *Reforming the International Economic Order* (1987).
F. Orrego Vicuña, 'Bilateral Investment Treaties and the Most-Favored-Nation Clause: Implications for Arbitration in the Light of a Recent ICSID Case', in G. Kaufmann-Kohler (ed.), *Investment Treaties and Arbitration: ASA Swiss Arbitration Association Conference in Zurich of January 25 2002* (2002) 133.
F. Orrego Vicuña, 'Regulatory Authority and Legitimate Expectations: Balancing the Rights of the State and the Individual under International Law in a Global Society', 5(3) *International Law FORUM* (2003) 188.
J. Paulsson, *Denial of Justice in International Law* (2005).
J. Paulsson and Z. Douglas, 'Indirect Expropriation in Investment Treaty Arbitrations', in N. Horn and S. Kröll (eds), *Arbitrating Foreign Investment Disputes* (2004) 145.
S. Peers, 'Free Movement of Capital: Learning Lessons or Slipping on Spilt Milk?', in C. Barnard and J. Scott (eds), *The Law of the Single European Market: Unpacking the Premises* (2002) 333.
L. Peterson, 'Malaysian firm wins BIT case against Chile; "wide scope" of MFN clause looms large', International Institute for Sustainable Development (ed.), *INVEST-SD: Investment Law and Policy Weekly News Bulletin* (23 August 2004), available at http://www.iisd.org/investment.
L. Peterson, *Investment Law and Policy Weekly News Bulletin* (6 February 2004), available at http://www.iisd.org/pdf/2004/investment_investsd_feb6_2004.pdf.
L. Peterson, *Investment Treaty News (ITN)* (23 August 2006), available at http://www.iisd.org/pdf/2006/itn_aug23_2006.pdf.
D. Price, 'An Overview of the NAFTA Investment Chapter: Substantive Rules and Investor-State Dispute Settlement', 27 *International Lawyer* (1993) 727.
C. Proctor, *Mann on the Legal Aspect of Money* (6th edn, 2005).
A.H. Qureshi and A.R. Ziegler, *International Economic Law* (2nd edn, 2007).
A. Raphael, 'Discriminatory Jury Selection: Lower Court Implementation of Batson v. Kentucky', 25 *Willamette Law Review* (1989) 293.
A. Reinisch, 'Necessity in International Investment Arbitration—An Unnecessary Split of Opinions in Recent ICSID Cases? Comments on *CMS* v. *Argentina* and *LG&E* v. *Argentina*', 8(2) *The Journal of World Investment and Trade* (2007) 191.

A. Reinisch, 'Maffezini v. Spain Case', in *Encyclopedia of Public International Law* (forthcoming).

A. Reinisch, 'Expropriation', in P. Muchlinski, F. Ortino, and C. Schreuer (eds), *The Oxford Handbook of International Investment Law* (forthcoming 2008).

W.M. Reisman and R.D. Sloane, 'Indirect Expropriation and its Valuation in the BIT Generation', 74 *British Yearbook of International Law* (2003) 115.

E. Root, 'The Basis of Protection to Citizens Residing Abroad', 4 *American Society of International Law Proceedings* (1910) 16.

S. Rosenne, *The Law and Practice of the International Court, 1920–1996* (1997), Volume II, 1083.

A.H. Roth, *The Minimum Standard of International Law Applied to Aliens* (1949).

M. Rothbard, *What has Government done to our Money?* (4th edn, 1990), available at: http://www.mises.org/store/product1.aspx?Product_ID=224.

R. Rothstein, *Global Bargaining: UNCTAD and the Quest for a New International Economic Order* (1979).

N. Rubins, 'Loewen v. United States: The Burial of an Investor-State Arbitration Claim', 21 *Arbitration International* (2005) 1.

N. Rubins and N.S. Kinsella, *International Investment, Political Risk and Dispute Resolution. A Practitioner's Guide* (2005).

G. Sacerdoti, 'Bilateral Investment Treaties and Multilateral Instruments on Investment Protection', 269 *Recueil des Cours* (1997) 251.

G. Sacerdoti, 'The Admission and Treatment of Foreign Investment under Recent Bilateral and Regional Treaties', 1 *The Journal of World Investment and Trade* (2000) 59.

J.W. Salacuse, 'Do BITs Really Work? An Evaluation of Bilateral Investment Treaties and Their Grand Bargain', 46 *Harvard International Law Journal* (2005) 67.

K. Sauvant and H. Hasenpflug (eds), *The New International Economic Order: Confrontation or Cooperation between North and South* (1977).

S. Schill, 'Fair and Equitable Treatment under Investment Treaties as an Embodiment of the Rule of Law', *Institute for International Law and Justice Working Paper* (2006/7), available at: http://www.iilj.org.

S. Schill, 'Fair and Equitable Treatment under Investment Treaties as an Embodiment of the Rule of Law', 3(5) *Transnational Dispute Management* (2006).

S. Schill, 'International Investment Law and the Host State's Power to Handle Economic Crises: Comment on the ICSID Decision in LG&E v. Argentina', 24(3) *Journal of International Arbitration* (2007) 265.

M. Schmid, *Swiss Investment Protection Agreements: Most-Favoured-Nation Treatment and Umbrella Clauses* (2007).

C. Schreuer, 'Fair and Equitable Treatment', 2(5) *Transnational Dispute Management* (2005).

C. Schreuer, 'Fair and Equitable Treatment in Arbitral Practice', 6 *The Journal of World Investment and Trade* (2005) 357.

C. Schreuer, *The Dynamic Evolution of the ICSID System* (2006).

C. Schreuer, 'The Concept of Expropriation under the ECT and other Investment Protection Treaties', in C. Ribeiro (ed.), *Investment Arbitration and the Energy Charter Treaty* (2006) 108.

C. Schreuer, 'Diversity and Harmonization of Treaty Interpretation in Investment Arbitration', 3 *Transnational Dispute Management* (2006).

C. Schreuer, 'Fair and Equitable Treatment (FET): Interaction with Other Standards', 4(5) *Transnational Dispute Management* (2007).
N. Schrijver, *Sovereignty Over Natural Resources* (1997).
M. Schuster, *The Public International Law of Money* (1973).
J. Schwarze, *European Administrative Law* (revised edn, 2006).
G. Schwarzenberger, 'The Principles and Standards of International Economic Law', 117 *Recueil des Cours* (1966) 1.
W. Shan, 'Foreign Investment in China and the Role of Law: Empirical Evidence from European Union Investors', 2(3) *Transnational Dispute Management* (2005).
Y. Shany, 'Towards a General Margin of Appreciation Doctrine in International Law?', 16(5) *European Journal of International Law* (2006) 907.
M. Shaw, *International Law* (4th edn, 1997).
D. Shea, *The Calvo Clause* (1955).
A. Sheppard, 'The Distinction between Lawful and Unlawful Expropriation', in C. Ribeiro (ed.), *Investment Arbitration and the Energy Charter Treaty* (2006) 169.
S. Silard, 'Exchange Controls and External Indebtedness: Are the Bretton Woods Concepts still Workable? A Perspective from the IMF', 7 *Houston Journal of International Law* (1984) 53.
I. Sinclair, *The Vienna Convention on the Law of Treaties* (2nd edn, 1984).
L.B. Sohn and R.R. Baxter, 'Responsibility of States for Injuries to the Economic Interests of Aliens', 55 *American Journal of International Law* (1961) 545.
M. Sornarajah, *The International Law on Foreign Investment* (2nd edn, 2004).
R.C. Snyder, *The Most-Favored-Nation Clause: Analysis with Particular Reference to the Recent Treaty Practice and Tariffs* (1948).
R. Teitelbaum, 'Who's Afraid of Maffezini? Recent Developments in the Interpretation of Most Favored Nation Clauses', 22 *Journal of International Arbitration* (2005) 225.
J.C. Thomas, 'Reflections on Article 1105 of NAFTA: History, State Practice and the Influence of Commentators', 17 *ICSID Review—Foreign Investment Law Journal* (2002) 21.
R. Thomas, *Legitimate Expectations and Proportionality in Administrative Law* (2000).
P. Turner, M. Mangan, and A. Baykitch, 'Investment Treaty Arbitration: An Australian Perspective', 24(2) *Journal of International Arbitration* (2007) 103.
UNCTAD, *International Investment Instruments: A Compendium*, Volume I, UNCTAD/DTCI/30 (Vol.I) (1996).
UNCTAD, *International Investment Instruments: A Compendium*, Volume II, UNCTAD/DTCI/30 (Vol.II) (1996).
UNCTAD, *Bilateral Investment Treaties in the Mid-1990s* (1998).
UNCTAD, *Fair and Equitable Treatment*, UNCTAD Series on issues in international investment agreements, Volume III, UNCTAD/ITE/IIT/11(1999).
UNCTAD, *Most-Favoured Nation Treatment*, Series on Issues in International Investment Agreements, Volume III, UNCTAD/ITE/IIT/10 (1999).
UNCTAD, *National Treatment*, UNCTAD Series on Issues in International Investment Agreements, Volume IV, UNCTAD/ITE/IIT/11 (1999).
UNCTAD, *Taking of Property*, UNCTAD Series on Issues in International Investment Agreements, UNCTAD/ITE/IIT/15 (2000).

UNCTAD, *Transfer of Funds*, UNCTAD Series on Issues in International Investment Agreements, UNCTAD/ITE/IIT/20 (2000).

UNCTAD, *International Investment Instruments: A Compendium*, Volume V, UNCTAD/DITE/2 (Vol.V) (2001).

UNCTAD, *International Investment Agreements: Key Issues*, UNCTAD/ITE/IIT/2004/10 (2004).

UNCTAD, *Key Terms and Concepts in IIAs: A Glossary*, UNCTAD Series on Issues in International Investment Agreements, UNCTAD/ITE/IIT/2004/2 (2004).

UNCTAD, *The REIO Exception in MFN Treatment Clauses*, UNCTAD Series on Issues in International Investment Agreements, UNCTAD/ITE/IIT/2004/7 (2004).

UNCTAD, *Transparency*, UNCTAD Series on Issues in International Investment Agreements, UNCTAD/ITE/IIT/2003/4 (2004).

UNCTAD, *Investor-State Disputes Arising from Investment Treaties: A Review*, UNCTAD Series on International Investment Policies for Development, UNCTAD/ITE/IIT/2005/4 (2005).

UNCTAD, *Recent Developments in International Investment Agreements*, UNCTAD/WEB/ITE/IIT/2005/1 (2005).

UNCTAD, *International Investment Arrangements: Trends and Emerging Issues*, UNCTAD Series on International Investment Policies for Development, UNCTAD/ITE/IIT/2005/11 (2006).

UNCTAD, *International Investment Rule-Setting: Trends, Emerging Issues and Implications*, TD/B/COM.2/68 (2006).

UNCTAD, *Investment Provisions in Economic Integration Agreements*, UNCTAD/ITE/IIT/2005/10 (2006).

UNCTAD, *Bilateral Investment Treaties 1995–2006: Trends in Investment Rulemaking*, UNCTAD/ITE/IIA/2006/5 (2007).

UNCTAD, *World Investment Report*, UNCTAD/WIR/2007 (2007).

E. Ustor, 'Most Favoured Nation Clause', 3 *Encyclopaedia of Public International Law* (1997) 472.

D. Vagts, 'Coercion and Foreign Investment Rearrangement', 72 *American Journal of International Law* (1978) 17.

D. Vagts, 'International Economic Law and the American Journal of International Law', 100 *American Journal of International Law* (2006) 769.

K. Vandevelde, 'The Bilateral Treaty Program of the United States', 21 *Cornell International Law Journal* (1988) 201.

K.J. Vandevelde, 'The Political Economy of a Bilateral Investment Treaty', 92 *American Journal of International Law* (1998) 621.

G. Varges, *The New International Economic Order Legal Debate* (1983).

S. Vasciannie, 'The Fair and Equitable Treatment Standard in International Investment Law and Practice', 70 *British Yearbook of International Law* (2000) 99.

P. Verlooren van Themaat, *The Changing Structure of International Economic Law* (1981).

S. Vesel, 'Clearing a Path Through a Tangled Jurisprudence: Most-Favored-Nation Clauses and Dispute Settlement Provisions in Bilateral Investment Treaties', 32 *Yale Journal of International Law* (2007) 125.

D. Vis-Dunbar and L.E. Peterson, 'European Commission makes another play for power to negotiate investment pacts', *Investment Treaty News (ITN)* (9 July 2006), available at http://www.iisd.org/investment/itn.

T. Wälde, 'International Investment under the 1994 Energy Charter Treaty', in T. Wälde (ed.), *The Energy Charter Treaty* (1996) 251.

T. Wälde, 'The Serbian Loans Case—A Precedent for Investment Treaty Protection of Foreign Debt?', in T. Weiler (ed.), *International Investment Law and Arbitration: Leading Cases from the ICSID, NAFTA, BITs and Customary International Law* (2005) 383.

T. Wälde, 'The Umbrella Clause in Investment Arbitration', 6 *The Journal of World Investment and Trade* (2005) 183.

T. Wälde, Book review of J. Paulsson, Denial of Justice in International Law (2005), 21 *ICSID Review—Foreign Investment Law Journal* (2007) 449.

T. Wälde and A. Kolo, 'Environmental Regulation, Investment Protection and "Regulatory Taking" in International Law', 50 *International and Comparative Law Quarterly* (2001) 811.

T. Wälde and A. Kolo, 'Investor-State Disputes: The Interface between Treaty-based International Investment Protection and Fiscal Sovereignty', 35 *Intertax* (2007) 424.

T. Wälde and B. Sabahi, 'Compensation, Damages and Valuation in International Investment Disputes', in 2007 *Report to ILA Foreign Investment Law Committee* (forthcoming, 2008).

C. Wallace, *The Multinational Enterprise and Legal Control: Host State Sovereignty in an Era of Economic Globalisation* (2002).

D. Wallace Jr, 'Fair and Equitable Treatment and Denial of Justice: Loewen v. US and Chattin v. Mexico', in T. Weiler (ed.), *International Investment Law and Arbitration: Leading Cases from the ICSID, NAFTA, BITs and Customary International Law* (2005) 669.

T. Weiler, 'Prohibitions Against Discrimination in NAFTA Chapter 11', in T. Weiler (ed.), *NAFTA Investment Law and Arbitration: Past Issues, Current Practice, Future Prospects* (2004) 27.

C. Wendrich, 'The World Bank Guidelines as a Foundation for a Global Investment Treaty: A Problem-Oriented Approach', 2(5) *Transnational Dispute Management* (2005).

B.H. Weston, '"Constructive Takings" under International Law: A Modest Foray into the Problem of "Creeping Expropriation"', 16 *Virginia Journal of International Law* (1975) 103.

J. Wolf, 'Vorwort', in L. Glier (ed.), *Die Meistbegünstigungsklausel* (1905).

C. Yannaca-Small, '"Indirect Expropriation" and the "Right to Regulate" in International Investment Law', in OECD (ed.), *International Investment Law. A Changing Landscape* (2005) 43.

C. Yannaca-Small, 'Fair and Equitable Treatment in International Investment Law', in OECD (ed.), *International Investment Law: A Changing Landscape* (2005).

H.C. Yourow, 'The Margin of Appreciation Doctrine in the Dynamics of European Human Rights Jurisprudence', 3 *Connecticut Journal of International Law* (1988) 111.

H.C. Yourow, *The Margin of Appreciation Doctrine in the Dynamics of the European Court of Human Rights Jurisprudence* (1996).

S. Zamora, 'Peso-Dollar Economics and the Imposition of Foreign Exchange Controls in Mexico', 32 *American Journal of Comparative Law* (1984) 99.

E.J.M. Zarazaga, 'Measuring the Benefits of Unilateral Trade Liberalization'; *Economic and Financial Policy Review* (2000) 29.

H.E. Zeitler, 'The Guarantee of "Full Protection and Security" in Investment Treaties Regarding Harm Caused by Private Actors', 3 *Stockholm International Arbitration Review* (2005) 1.

Index

admission of investments
  entry of investors, link with 9–10
  favourable investment, promotion of 11–12
  filter, clause as 27
  future liberalization, provision for 15–16
  grey area, issues in 27
  international investment agreements, approaches in 9
  law and regulations of host state, in accordance with
    actions of State, point of view of 26
    actual violation of 25
    Aguas del Tunari v Bolivia 22–4
    Bayindir v Pakistan 22
    concession contract, termination of 22–4
    definitions article 16–18, 27
    denial of exclusivity 24–5
    Fraport v Philippines 25
    ICSID Convention, jurisdiction under 19, 23
    identification of 18–19
    implications of 26
    Inceysa v El Salvador 24–5
    Ioannis Kardassopoulos v Georgia 26
    jurisprudence 27–8
    legality of investment 22
    meaning 20
    objections to jurisdiction 21
    question of 16
    recent awards 16, 19–28
    Salini v Morocco 20
    scope of 27
    scope of application article 16–18
    Tokios Tokeles v Ukraine 21
  model 10–12
  model treaties, purpose of 28
  most-favoured-nation treatment 12
  other standards, linked with 7
  process of 7
  threshold, as 6
  traditional BIT approach 14
  treaty provisions 9
  unlawful or illegal 27
arbitrary and unreasonable measures
  act contrary to law, as 102
  arbitrariness, law on 88
  breach, establishment of 87
  compliance standards 5
  components, breach of 99
  customary international law, relationship with 106–9
  definition of understanding of 101–2
  discriminatory 87
  due process approach 103–6
  ELSI Standard 101–2
  Energy Charter Treaty 89
  fair and equitable treatment, and 5–6
  formulation of 87–9, 99
  'I know it when I see it' approach 101–3
  legal standard, establishment of 87
  national treatment, and 52–4
  non-impairment standard *see* non-impairment standard
  priority of 95–8
  prohibition 52
  protection from 4, 87, 238
  reasonableness, standard of 105
  strict standard of review 106
  substantive perspective 101–9
  treaty provisions 5
arbitration
  investment, upsurge of 1
ASEAN Investment Area
  Framework Agreement, entry and establishment of investments provisions 15

bilateral investment treaties
  definitions article 16–18, 27
  eligibility for protection under 18
  entry of investment provisions 9 *see also* admission of investments; entry of foreign investment
  law and regulations of host state, identification of 18–19
  national treatment provisions 33–4
  scope of application article 16–18

capital mobility
  history of 206–7
capital movement
  Code of Liberalisation of Capital Movements 209–10
  definition 211
  economic interest, control measures to protect 212
  European Union, in 210–12
  GATT and GATS, exchange controls and restrictions on 212
  restrictions on 211–12

Index

capital repatriation
  blocking, period of 230
  failure, remedy for 241
  GATT provisions 225
  guarantee 240–1
  margin of appreciation 206
  modern investment treaties, treatment of restrictions under 213–17
  obligations
    duty to comply with 205
    questions arising 205–6
  treaty provisions 225
capital transfer
  absolute right of 217
  Draft Multilateral Agreement on Investment 210
  exceptions to freedom of 215
  free, provision for 214
  host state, exchange laws and regulations restricting 215
  modern investment treaties, treatment of restrictions under 213–17
  permissible restrictions 242
  restrictions, application of doctrine of necessity 217–27
  third party scrutiny, measures insulated from 216–17
customary international law
  arbitrary and unreasonable measures, protection against 106–9
  fair and equitable treatment standard 114–17, 129
  full protection and security standard
    ceiling, as 136
    equivalence 137
    floor, as 136–7
    relationship with 132, 135

denial of justice
  fair and equitable treatment standard 119–20
  national treatment 43–4
due process
  expropriation, legality of 191–3
  fair and equitable treatment standard 119–20

Economic Integration Agreements
  entry and establishment of investments, commitments regarding 14
emergency
  economic 238
entry of foreign investment
  admission model see admission of investments
  Economic Integration Agreements, provisions of 14
  full protection, benefiting from 19
  international investment agreements, approaches in 10–11
  Model BITs 11
  pre-establishment model 11, 13–16
European Economic Community
  creation of 209
European Free Trade Association Agreement
  entry and establishment of investments provisions 14–15
European Union
  free movement of capital in 210–12
expropriation
  burden of proof 227
  compensation
    actual payment of 198–9
    adequate 198
    appropriate 195–7
    assessment 175–6, 203
    customary law requirement 194–5
    equality, principle of 194
    full market value 241, 243
    full, principle of 194
    international law rule of 199
    offer of 198–9
    quantum 4
    requirement 204
    requirement of 174
    treaty provisions 195, 199
    valuation method 195–6
  consequential 153
  creeping
    measures being 171
    use of term 153
  current law, crisis in 2
  damages for illegal acts 201
  de facto 153
  direct 151
    rarity of 1
  disguised 153
  due process requirement
    case law 192–3
    treaty provisions 191–3
  fair and equitable treatment, and 3–4
  foreign investor, provisions invoked by 227
  illegal, becoming 199–200
  indirect see indirect expropriation
  judicial economy perspective 91–3
  lawful 166
  lawful and unlawful distinguished 201–2
  legality of
    airport operations, privatization of 184–5, 189–90
    case law 172–3
    compensation requirement 193–9
    due process requirement 191–3

international investment agreements,
    requirements in 176–8
international law, requirements
    under 173–6
interpretation of requirements 178–203
investigation of 204
Model BITs 176–8
non-discrimination requirement 186–91
public purpose or public interest
    requirement 178–86
question of 171–2
remedies, implications for 199–203
specific groups, targeting 190
summary of law 175
traditional requirements 175
matter constituting, debate as to 151
measures having equivalent effect 152–3
measures tantamount to 152–3
most important investment standard, as 1
nationals, property of 151
natural resources, of 174
non-discrimination requirement
    case law 187
    content of 186
    endorsement of 190
    ICSID tribunals, cases before 189
    Libyan Oil Concession arbitrations 187–8
    Polish insurance business, exclusion of
        foreign investors from 188
    racial motivation 186–7
occurrence, question of 152
primary cause of action, as 91
public purpose or public interest
    requirement
    antiquities, protection of 182
    burden of proof 185
    case law 179–80
    definition 181–2
    emergency measures 185–6
    failure of 183
    fiscal crisis, measures against 185–6
    host State, view of 182–4
    ICSID tribunals, endorsement by
        182–3
    Libyan Oil Concession arbitrations 181
    not bona fide 183–5
    rejection of assertion 180–1
    relevance of test 181
    treaty provisions 178–9
public purpose requirement, in customary
    international law 178
racially motivated 186–7
regulatory 153
    awards 1
    persuading tribunal of 1
    tribunals, sympathy of 2
restitution 200–2

shift of focus 171
taking, as 153

fair and equitable treatment standard
absolute nature of 111
arbitrariness, and 5–6
autonomous, whether 113–18
awards 2
bad faith, no need to prove 123
breach of 94–5
    determination of 127
    remedy for 241–3
breadth of 94
business risk 128
coercion or harassment, freedom from 236
compliance standards 5
criteria for determining 234
customary international law, under 114–17,
    129
damages for, quantum 4
denial of justice 119–20
due process 119–20
every treaty, in 112
expropriation light, as 112
flexibility 111
foreign exchange restrictions breaching
    222
formulation, diversity in 129
full protection and security standard
    concurrent violation 147
    joint consideration of 134
    overlap with 146–9
    relationship with 4, 96
    subordination 149
general label, as 6
general nature of 95
good faith requirement 239–40
importance of 233
international law, standard required by 108
interpretation 113–18
invasive character 112
lack of arbitrariness and non-
    discrimination 120–1, 238
lack of clarification 111
legal and business framework, stability
    of 147
legal content 234
legitimate expectations 124–6, 128, 130,
    236
minimum, evolutionary character 117–18
non-impairment standard, and 94
normative content
    denial of justice 119–20
    due process 119–20
    elements of 118, 129–30
    lack of arbitrariness and non-
        discrimination 120–1, 238

fair and equitable treatment standard (*cont.*)
  legitimate expectations 124–6, 128, 130, 235
  proportionality 126–9
  transparency and stability 121–3, 236
  vigilance and protection, obligation of 118–19
  priority of 95–8
  procedural propriety 237
  prominence of 129
  proportionality 126–9
  protection against expropriation, taking over role of 3–4
  protection standard, as 2
  reliance on 234
  scope of application 119
  shared responsibility 128
  specific legal order, whether belonging to 113–18
  stabilization requirements 127
  stable framework for investment, requirement of 123
  standard formulation 113
  transparency and stability 121–3, 235
  treaty references to 3
  underlying concern 240
  vagueness 118
  vigilance and protection, obligation of 118–19
  violation of standard
    burden of proof 2
    findings of 2
foreign exchange
  capital mobility, history of 206–7
  economic interest, control measures to protect 212
  essential security interests 212
  GATT and GATS, controls and restrictions on 212
  gold clauses 207
  gold standard, collapse of 208
  International Bank for Settlements, creation of 208
  International Monetary Fund, role of 208
  regulation, international law development 206–13
  repatriation guarantee 240–1
  restrictions
    abusive 232
    arbitrary, not to be 231
    balance-of-payment difficulties, during 220–1, 228
    discriminatory, not to be 231–2
    doctrine of necessity, application of 217–27
    enjoyment and use of funds, limiting 228–9
    essential interests, state protecting 219
    excessive 220
    fair and equitable treatment standard, breach of 222
    goals and reasonable expectations, compatibility with 222
    good faith requirement 239–40
    indirect expropriation, and 227–33
    judicial scrutiny 222, 224
    legality of 242
    legitimate 222
    limited right to impose 233
    margin of appreciation 219–21, 226
    national treatment standard, breach of 222
    onerous, imposition of 232
    procedural propriety 237
    temporary 221
foreign investment
  country susceptible to economic crisis, in 230
full protection and security standard
  application beyond physical safety
    affirmation 142, 144–6
    combat, action in 149
    de facto 146
    exceptional circumstances, in 148
    exclusion 142–3
    legal security, independent standard 144–6
    legal system, availability of 144
    meaningful protection, deprivation of 145
  borderline 146
  context of 132
  customary international law, whether independent standard of 132
  due diligence 139–40, 150
  fair and equitable treatment standard
    concurrent violation 147
    joint consideration of 134
    overlap with 146–9
    subordination to 149
    subsumed under 96
  forms of behaviour
    due diligence 139–40, 150
    obligation, meeting 139
    sovereign appreciation 141–2
    subjective or objective 140–1
  formulations of
    common 132
    general international law, standard of protection under 135
    importance of 134–6
    legal security 134
    overview 133–4
  general international law, standard of protection under

ceiling, as 136
equivalence 137
floor, as 136–7
relationship with 132, 135
generally 4
international law, standard required by 108
interpretation 150
legal and business environment, alteration of 147
legal security 131
  independent standard, as 144–6
non-impairment standard, and 89
obligations under 132
overlap with other standards
  fair and equitable treatment 146–9
physical interference, protection from 134
physical safety, obligation to ensure
  causality 138
  due diligence 139–40, 150
  forms of behaviour 139–42
  scope of application 138
  sovereign appreciation 141–2
  subjective or objective 140–1
  third parties, caused by 138
scarcity of legal literature 131
scope of application 131–2
sources of 132–6
sovereign appreciation 141–2
strict liability 140
subjective or objective 140–1

indirect expropriation
actions and omissions, interference by 160
balance of interests 168
claims for 1
compensation, calculation of 243
consequential 153
creeping, use of term 153
de facto 153, 171
definition
  criteria 156–9
  Harvard Draft Convention, codification in 154–5
  OECD Draft Convention, in 155
  reluctance to insert in treaties 154
  sole effect doctrine 156–9, 168
  tribunals, by 155
determination, criteria for 167
disguised 153
doctrine, current state of affairs 152–64
duration of 159
environmental measures 165–6
express guidelines, lack of 166–7
findings on 167
foreign exchange restrictions, and 227–33
host state, enrichment of
  case law 160–1

intention of 161–2
investment-backed expectations of investor, relevance of 162
proportionality, requirement of 163–4
incoherent decisions 169–70
inconsistent decisions 169–70
interference short of outright taking 169
investment-backed expectations of investor, relevance of 162
lawful 166
legal certainty, need for 169
legitimate expectations, and 162
legitimate public welfare objectives, protection of 167
measures being 152
partial 158
proportionality, requirement of 163–4
protection from 151
regulatory 153
requirements for 1
shift of focus to 171
simple regulatory measures, and 152
sole effect doctrine 156–9, 168
State's right to regulate, and 165–6
substantiality of 156–9
taking, as 153
temporary 158–9
treaty provisions 154
international investment agreements
entry of investment provisions 9 *see also* admission of investments; entry of foreign
investment
foreign investment, entry of 10–11
law and regulations of host state, identification of 19
international law
private property, protection of 173 *see also* expropriation
international minimum standard
customary international law, in 32
investment standards *see also* **arbitrary and unreasonable measures**
admission *see* admission of investments
breach, compensation for 91
causes of action, prioritizing 93
interrelationship of 1–7
investment arbitration, impact of 1
legal basis of decisions 110
methodological perspective 93–100
substantive, relationship between 109–10

legitimate expectations
explicit promise or guarantee as basis for 126
fair and equitable treatment standard 124–6, 235

262   Index

legitimate expectations (*cont.*)
  indirect expropriation, and 162
  investment arbitration, role in 125

money transfers
  guarantees of 7

most-favoured-nation treatment
  additional standard, inclusion of 77
  clause
    explicit descriptions of scope 75–9
    extension of 76
    extension of favours, prior consent to 65
    general scope 75
    guarantee, general exceptions 79
    international obligations and rights 64
    like situations, application in 76–7
    limited scope of 82–3
    main types 64–6
    purpose of 6
    situations in which operating 74–5
  conditional 66
  contentious issues 6
  continuous nationality, requiring maintenance of 68
  criticism of 66
  dispute settlement 70
    divergence of case law 86
  economic foundation 64–6
  effects, limiting 66
  ejusdem generis principle 74–5
  explicit descriptions of scope 75–9
  first example of 61
  general and explicit exceptions 79–83
  historical development 61–4
  identical treatment, not 65
  investment awards
    ADF v USA 68
    Asian Agricultural Products v Sri Lanka 67
    Bayindir v Pakistan 72
    Berschader v Russia 74
    Camuzzi v Argentina 72
    CMS v Argentina 71
    Continental Casualty v Argentina 73
    Gas Natural v Argentina 72
    Impregilo v Pakistan 71
    Loewen v USA 68
    Lucchetti v Peru 70
    Maffezini v Spain 68
    MTD v Chile 69–70
    National Grid Transco v Argentina 73
    Plama v Bulgaria 71
    Pope and Talbot v Canada 67
    Salini v Jordan 70
    Siemens v Argentina 70
    Suez, Sociedad General de Aguas de Barcelone and Vivendi Universal
      v Argentina and AWG Group v Argentina 73
    Tecmed v Mexico 69
    Telenor v Hungary 73
    Yaung Chi Oo Trading v Myanmar 69
  investor-State arbitration, specific issues in
    ejusdem generis principle 74–5
    explicit descriptions of scope 75–9
    general and explicit exceptions 79–83
    procedural provision 84–6
    specifically negotiated provisions 83–4
  investors, protection of 77
  law of treaties, draft article in 63–4
  material content 65–6
  material scope 64
  meaning 64
  model agreements, issue of scope addressed in 81
  models for 62
  national treatment, combined model 11, 60
  new rights, creation of 65
  non-discrimination obligation 78
  North American Free Trade Agreement 15
  pre-establishment model 11, 13–16
  procedural provision 84–6
  procedural rights, application to 59
  prospective guarantee 81
  questions arising 59
  regional free trade agreements, in 63
  scope of 59
  situations subject to, defining 76
  specific areas, application in 78
  specifically negotiated provisions 83–4
  typical examples 60–1
  WTO context, in 86

national treatment
  analysis, requirements 29–30
  arbitrary and discriminatory treatment, prohibition of 52–4
  background 30–6
  bad treatment of nationals, effect of 31
  bilateral investment treaties, examples of 33–4
  breach, remedy for 241–3
  burden of proof 30, 56–8
  compliance with norm, assessment 50
  conduct breaching 238
  development considerations, addressing 35
  discrimination, protection against 30
  equal treatment, meaning 31
  extent of protection 33
  foreign exchange restrictions breaching 222
  GATS, obligation in 36
  GATT, core obligation in 29, 36
  international minimum standard, and 32
  investment case law 37–58

lack of uniformity in approach to 37
less favourable treatment
  according, determining 50
  appropriate comparator, identification of 48
  investment case law 48–54
  mere differential effect 51–2
  nationality-based discrimination approach 49, 53–4
  nationality considerations, predicated on 49, 51
  practical effect 50
liberalization of investments 14
like circumstances, in
  actual comparator, lack of 38
  comparator and claimant, competitive relationship between 39
  denial of justice case 43–4
  discriminatory effect, question of 42–3
  export of waste, closing border to 39–40
  focus of determination 51–2
  identification of comparator 38–9
  investment case law 38–48
  investments or treatment, as to 39
  lack of competitive relationship, in case of 40
  motivation 52
  NAFTA case 46–8
  outcome-determinative analysis 44
  producers of alternative product, to 45–6
  proof of discrimination 52
  single domestic entity, as 43
  treatment alleged to cause injury, relationship with 41–2
  US-origin products, requirement to purchase 44–5
most-favoured-nation clause, combined model 11, 60
nationality-based discrimination, and
  analysis, starting point for 34
  arbitrariness 34
  criteria 35
no less favourable versus best or most favourable treatment 54–6
North American Free Trade Agreement 15
  decisions 37
  exceptions 35
  government procurement exception 50
  like circumstances, consideration of 46–8
  provisions of 33
obligations
  conventional obligation, as 31
  discrimination, precluding 49
  exceptions 35
  Hanseatic League treaties, obligations in 30–1
  interpretation 36
  investment treaties, in 29
  relative or contingent nature of 29
  reservations 35
  scope of 32
other claims eclipsing 58
pedigree 6
pre-establishment model 11, 13–16
principle of according, basis of 29
protectionist tendency, neutralizing 29
provincial or local government measures, status of 35–6
treaty practice 30–6
UK Model BIT 33
viable or important cause of action, as 58

natural resources
permanent sovereignty over 174

necessity
emergency laws 219
essential interests, state protecting 219
exchange restriction measures, application of doctrine to 217–27
particular measures, judging 223–4
specific treaty, principle read into 226–7
wrongfulness of act, ground for precluding 218

non-impairment standard
breach of
  comprehensive approach to 100
  impairment, requirement of 95
  other breaches, assertion with 89
  ratio decidendi of decision 90
consistency of approach to 90
customary international law, relationship with 106–9
dispositive role in awards, not playing 109
fair and equitable treatment standard, and 94
formulation of 89
full security and protection standard, and 89
judicial economy perspective 91–3
legal basis of claim, reliance on as 98
methodological perspective 93–100
other standards, relationship with 96
reliance on 90
standard of conduct imposed by 110
substantive perspective 101–9

North American Free Trade Agreement
arbitrary treatment, no separate provision on 5
fair and equitable treatment and expropriation, reference to 3
fair and equitable treatment standard, interpretation of 114–15
most-favoured-nation treatment, grant of 15

North American Free Trade Agreement (*cont.*)
  national treatment provision 15, 33
    decisions 37
    exceptions 35
    government procurement exception 50
    like circumstances, consideration of 46–8

Organization of Economic Cooperation and Development (OECD)
  Code of Liberalisation of Capital Movements 209–10
  draft Multilateral Agreement on Investment 210
  role of 209

proportionality
  fair and equitable treatment standard 126–9
  indirect expropriation, as to 163–4

restitution
  breach of treaty obligations, for 240–1
  expropriation, on 200–2

state responsibility
  necessity, derogation from international obligations in 217–27
  injury to person or property of aliens, for 173

taxation
  carve-outs, treaties containing 3

transparency
  definition 122
  fair and equitable treatment standard 121–3, 235

World Trade Organization
  most-favoured-nation treatment in context of 86

Printed in Great Britain
by Amazon.co.uk, Ltd.,
Marston Gate.